THE INTERNATIONAL MONETARY SYSTEM: CHOICES FOR THE FUTURE

THE INTERNATIONAL MONETARY SYSTEM: CHOICES FOR THE FUTURE

edited by
Michael B. Connolly

Praeger Studies in International Monetary Economics and Finance
General Editors: J. Richard Zecher
D. Sykes Wilford

PRAEGER

PRAEGER SPECIAL STUDIES • PRAEGER SCIENTIFIC

Library of Congress Cataloging in Publication Data
Main entry under title:

The Choice of an exchange rate system.

(Praeger studies in international monetary economics
and finance)
Contents: The case for a managed international gold
standard/by Robert A. Mundell—Aspects of the optimal
management of exchange rates/by Jacob A. Frenkel and
Joshua Aizenmann—the mismanaged float: official
intervention by the industrialized countries/by Dean
Taylor—[etc.]
1. Foreign exchange problem—Addresses, essays,
lectures. 2. International finance—Addresses, essays,
lectures. I. Connolly, Michael B. II. Series.
HG3851.C465   332.4′5   82-7483
ISBN 0-03-061794-4   AACR2

Published in 1982 by Praeger Publishers
CBS Educational and Professional Publishing
A division of CBS Inc.
521 Fifth Avenue, New York, New York 10175 U.S.A.

Printed in the United States of America

FOREWORD

by D. Sykes Wilford and J. Richard Zecher

In this book, *The International Monetary System: Choices for the Future*, Michael Connolly has gathered articles in international financial economics that highlight the importance and interdependence of the world's many different financial economic environments. This work is the result of a conference held at the University of South Carolina in May 1981. Expert scholars in the field of international economics met to discuss and grapple with the issues facing the world's policymakers and economic agents. This conference brought together participants from academe, business, and government to explore the increased interdependence among economies and to consider options for the future. It was a total success. The resulting book will take an important place in the international financial economics literature.

As participants in this conference, as well as editors of this series of books, it is our pleasure to write the foreword for this volume. We are extremely excited by what Michael Connolly has done and think that readers will benefit greatly from the work presented. Just as the conference stimulated thought and ideas, this book is designed to further the frontiers of the literature in international financial economics.

In his keynote address Robert Mundell makes, as always, very cogent remarks about how the 1980s is just one moment in the long historical development of international monetary and financial relations. He recognizes that, with the end of the Bretton Woods era in the 1970s, the world entered into a period of financial expansionism and inflation. It certainly is not new that Robert Mundell calls for a more ordered structure of the international financial system. This is a lesson, however, that does not appear to have been well learned.

The contributions by Frenkel and Aizenman, Taylor, and Lapan and Enders provide an insight into the economics of a managed float and highlights of why policy choices are not always easy to make. When factors affecting the correct policy choices and the actual practice of managing a policy are considered, simple choices of an optimal exchange rate regime become clouded. From these papers one is able to observe the complexity of the choice of an exchange rate regime under different conditions. It may be concluded that one compromise choice—managed floating—may yield theoretically more palatable results than experience suggests.

The papers by Klein and Melvin and by Bordo are relevant in the context of present policy debates about the gold standard versus a quantity standard for monetary policy in a world of competing monies. While Bordo's paper on gold provides information about gold standard periods, the Klein and Melvin paper argues against the need to be overly concerned about the evolution of a new dominant money to replace the dollar, even if U.S. monetary policy is somewhat erratic.

The set of papers by Lipschitz and Sundararajan, Worrell, and Connolly and Yousef all deal with exchange rate policies of LDCs. Agreement on the "proper" system is not found in these papers. However, one can conclude that practical choices may not always be optimal choices in today's environment.

John Bilson's contribution on expectation and the gold standard offers an innovative approach to understanding the fixed exchange rate adjustment process. Wallich's paper on the evolution of the international monetary system provides a good summary of where we are and insight as to where we may go. Given the uncertainties associated with the present situation of the new government in France and the European Monetary System, Salin's chapter on the system is of particular interest to policymakers.

Ultimately, the purpose of the conference and this book is to address those issues that must be raised before a meaningful discussion of the proper financial system for the 1980s—and beyond—is defined. Michael Connolly's contribution is to bring together these ideas into one volume. Now, as readers we may draw upon the knowledge of recognized leaders in international financial economics.

We congratulate Michael Connolly on this volume and are confident that it will be an invaluable addition to the literature. As we look forward into the 1980s and see the possible directions for international financial economics, there is no question that this book will be cited in many articles as a valuable resource and an elucidation of the state of the art. We recommend that both the practitioner and the policymaker, as well as the academic investigator, consider and ponder the implications of this excellent book.

ACKNOWLEDGMENTS

The College of Business Administration of the University of South Carolina encouraged and supported the Carolina Currency Conference on the Choice of an Exchange Rate System, May 1–2, 1981, that led to this volume. Special thanks are due to Deans James F. Kane and James Hilton and Professors B. F. Kiker and Stan Fryer. Invaluable logistic support was provided by John Willenborg, Stephen Garris, and Sydney Parrish of the Daniel Management Center.

Bluford Putnam and Sykes Wilford helped greatly in the organization of an international business forum that preceded the conference and contributed support for this volume.

My wife, Annick, and my daughter, Michelle, were partners in the endeavor.

CONTENTS

INTRODUCTION

The 1944 Bretton Woods system of fixed exchange rates partially collapsed in August 1971 with the suspension of dollar convertibility into gold, and less than two years later further collapsed into a worldwide breakdown of currencies into separate currency areas. By mid-1971, foreign central banks could no longer convert dollars into U.S. gold at a fixed rate, and by early 1973 the major currencies were no longer convertible into dollars at fixed rates.

Since then, individual countries have sorted themselves out in one way or another in their exchange rate practices: on the one hand, some have chosen to float independently, albeit typically with intervention, others have chosen to float jointly within small margins of flexibility, a few have experimented with crawling pegs, either preannounced active ones or ex-post passive ones. On the other hand, a good number of countries, frequently small developing ones, have chosen to peg to a major currency, such as the U.S. dollar or the French franc, while others have chosen to peg to a basket of currencies, such as the IMF's Special Drawing Right or individually designed ones.

This volume is concerned with the choice of an exchange rate system. It analyzes theoretical and empirical issues concerning the world monetary system as well as exchange rate systems appropriate for individual countries. This introduction raises the major issues involved, ties together the papers published in this volume, and touches upon some of the existing literature.

In a general sense, the main issue dealt with is the classic debate of fixed versus flexible exchange rates that Milton Friedman (1953) and James Meade (1955) analyze, but within the framework of optimum currency areas suggested by Mundell (1961). Clearly, in a world of flexible rates between some of the major currencies, it is not possible to have a fixed exchange *rate*. Rather, it is possible to have a fixed currency *peg* whereby the value of a currency is fixed in terms of another, but is therefore flexible relative to third currencies. Some of the old arguments still apply, but new considerations have come into play.

Some of the major theoretical considerations in the choice of an exchange rate system are:

1. the relative prevalence of real versus monetary shocks to the economy
2. the source of disturbance, as, for example, whether foreign or domestic
3. the size of country
4. the degree of openness (or relative size of traded versus nontraded sectors)
5. independent versus constrained monetary policy (or money growth versus exchange rate rules)
6. the degree of financial development
7. exchange rate and price stability under different regimes
8. the stability of fixed pegs versus floating rates.

Clearly, the list is not exhaustive.

In dealing with these theoretical issues, the volume addresses broad issues such as the choice of a world system, gold standard versus money growth rules, appropriate exchange rate policies for developed and developing countries, the optimal managed float or currency peg, risk and uncertainty, the evolution of the dollar standard, and international competition between monies.

Robert Mundell's essay proposes a return to the Bretton Woods' system of fixed exchange rates and dollar convertibility into gold. The theoretical framework of his position argues that an exchange rate rule is, in practice, a better rule than a monetary growth rule, which may or may not be adhered to. Fixing the exchange rate to the dollar or gold means abandoning independent monetary policy, and dollar convertibility into gold in a similar way makes U.S. monetary policy dependent upon gold purchases or sales at some official rate. This contrasts diametrically with Friedman's position that monetary growth rules with freely flexible exchange rates are superior, at least for the major currencies. Ultimately, the issue revolves around which rule—a convertibility rule or a money growth rule—will provide a superior performance in terms of price stability, employment, and balance-of-payments adjustment. A further consideration is which system is more stable: that is, less likely to collapse.

Currently, in the United States there is considerable interest in the issue of a return to a gold standard. A Gold Commission has been established to investigate the merits of restoring dollar convertibility into gold, and a formal report was submitted in March 1982 to the Secretary of the Treasury.

Whatever the outcome on this issue, a hard look at the theoretical and empirical underpinnings of the gold standard is warranted. Michael Bordo's essay on the classical gold standard provides evidence on the historical performance of the gold standard in the United States and the United Kingdom between 1880 and 1914, a period in which the gold standard functioned in one of its purest forms. Gold is commodity money, and thus its value in terms of commodities will tend toward its long-run real cost of production via changes in the gold price of commodities. When prices rise, the real value of gold declines, so that, with a lag, gold production declines, thereby slowing the growth in the money supply. Similarly, with falling prices, gold production increases. Thus, long-run price stability should occur, barring gold discoveries or technological innovations lowering the opportunity cost of producing gold. Between two countries whose currencies are pegged to gold, there will exist an automatic "specie-flow" mechanism as suggested by David Hume, whereby gold flows from deficit to surplus countries, triggering an automatic adjustment mechanism. Bordo's paper finds a long-run price cycle consistent with gold as a commodity money, and that the price level itself changed very little from 1821 to 1914 in the United Kingdom. Similar findings hold for the United States between 1834 and 1914, with the exception of the Civil War period until 1878. In both cases, there were long periods of deflation and long periods of inflation, but, on the average, the price level was stable. The record on growth in output and its stability also compares favorably for both countries, and the balance-of-payments mechanism appeared to work smoothly. Bordo falls short, however, of recommending a return to the gold standard, John Bilson's chapter illustrates the importance of expectations to the functioning of the gold standard. In particular, he argues that expectations based upon the gold standard "rules of the game" act as a strong stabilizing force governing price level and capital movements. Thus, the stability of the nineteenth-century gold standard system may be due, he argues, to these expectations. Specifically, he illustrates how both price movements and gold movements will be lessened by individuals knowing the rules of adjustment. Lowered prices, for example, will be followed by gold inflows and inflation according to the rules of the game, and thus individuals will borrow abroad and purchase home goods for sale abroad, so that both price and gold movements will be less than if no expectations were present. This argument may explain in part the smooth functioning of the system without large gold movements.

The essay by Joshua Aizenman and Jacob Frenkel raises the question of the optimal managed float. It draws upon earlier work by Stanley Fischer and Frenkel, where the objective is to smooth variations in consumption relative to the expected income stream. The control variable is an intervention index that varies from zero with a rigidly pegged rate to unity with a freely floating rate. Between these two extremes, the intervention index is the coefficient of an optimal managed float. Broadly speaking, the economy is subject to two types of disturbances: monetary and real. The monetary disturbances are shocks to foreign prices, deviations in exchange rates from purchasing power parity, and shocks to the demand for and supply of money. Real disturbances refer to random shocks to the level of permanent income. A major result confirms Robert Mundell's 1973 argument that when the disturbances are solely of a real origin, the optimal exchange rate regime is that of fixed rates, while if the shocks are solely monetary in origin, a freely floating exchange rate is optimal. When disturbances are both real and monetary, a mixed system of a managed float is optimal. Specifically, Aizenman and Frenkel derive the optimal level of intervention as a function of the variance and covariance of the different types of shocks. Further, they show that access to world capital markets diminishes the need for fixed rates and reserves to cushion from real shocks, since foreign borrowing acts as a buffer to real shocks. Also, they argue that the higher the share of nontraded goods (for example, the less open the economy), the more desirable is fixity in the exchange rate. This result apparently contradicts some of the well-known arguments on openness and the desirability of fixed rates but holds because the relative price changes in the nontraded to traded goods act on the economy in a way similar to the effects of real shocks.

Walter Enders and Harvey Lapan deal with many of the same issues that Aizenman and Frenkel do, but from the perspective of a microeconomic approach of individual optimization. Their chapter challenges some of the traditional conclusions in the literature. In particular, they argue that the choice of the exchange rate regime depends mainly upon attitudes toward risk, and that the sources of disturbances (whether real or monetary or domestic or foreign) is unimportant in the choice of fixed versus flexible exchange rates. They confirm, however, the Aizenman–Frenkel result that the larger the size of the nontraded-goods sector (for instance, the less open the economy), the greater the desirability of fixed exchange rates.

The criterion used to judge desirability has to do with an individual's expected utility and whether it is higher with fixed or flexible rates. In the Aizenman-Frenkel chapter, the criterion is to minimize a quadratic loss function involving the square of the deviation of consumption from expected income. The startling differences in conclusions result in large part from the different criterion for judging the relative desirability of fixed versus flexible rates. Also, Enders and Lapan deal with the two extreme cases, rigidly fixed versus freely floating, while Aizenman and Frenkel deal with an optimal managed float involving a mixed case.

Evidence on the actual practice of intervention in the foreign exchange market is provided by Dean Taylor. He analyzes foreign exchange intervention profits or losses using Milton Friedman's (1953) criterion that stabilizing intervention means, broadly speaking, that a central bank is buying low and selling high and thus making profits. Consequently, if they are making losses, central banks are destabilizing the foreign exchange market. Taylor's evidence on cumulative intervention by nine major central banks shows consistent losses resulting from "leaning against the wind" to resist changes in the equilibrium exchange rate. When the support is dropped, the rate moves to its new level, and the central bank incurs a loss. Taylor's calculations show a loss of over two billion dollars by the U.S. Federal Reserve and Treasury intervention since April 1973 and similarly, for the United Kingdom, a two-billion-dollar loss in foreign exchange intervention since February 1972. Of the nine countries considered, only France made a profit in terms of dollars. Thus, despite the body of literature on the relationship between profitable speculation and stability, Taylor argues that, as an empirical matter, large losses have resulted from the authorities resisting changes in the underlying equilibrium exchange rate. On these grounds, foreign exchange intervention has, in practice, had the effect of being destabilizing.

The essay by Benjamin Klein and Michael Melvin puts the accent on the complex nature of competition in the market for alternative monies in analyzing the role of the dollar in the postwar economic system. Their main hypothesis is that new dominant monies evolve very slowly in the marketplace, and that once established, there is little substitution between them. The theoretical framework is that of Klein's "inflation-uncertainty effect," which stresses that it is the variance or predictability of inflation that is the most important characteristic of alternative monies, whereas the mean or expected rate is a less competitive force, since each money will yield a competitive rate of interest, widely defined. They argue on this basis, for example, that gold is in the process of being demonetized as a result of its higher variability in value, despite its good record in terms of appreciation. By the same token, the role of the dollar as the dominant international money, both as an asset and a medium of exchange, will continue for some time. Consumer confidence in a money—the credibility of the money issuer in fulfilling promises of future supply—is built up slowly with successful performance over time. Consequently, new monies like the Europa and the SDR will always face a hostile reception.

Two chapters deal with foreign exchange policies for developing countries. Both assume that developing countries will, in practice, find it useful to have a currency peg, either fixed or crawling, rather than a freely floating rate. This is so because of optimum currency considerations—size, openness, confidence, currency substitution, financial underdevelopment—and also because a currency peg is a clear signal and discipline regarding money supply performance. The first chapter, by Leslie Lipschitz and V. Sundararajan, assumes that the objective of a currency peg is to stabilize the real terms of trade. The currency weights should take into account uncertainty by incorporating current information about future price and exchange rate movements. In particular, Lipschitz and Sundararajan build in a systematic relationship between bilateral exchange rates and the corresponding bilateral relative price movements in the determination of currency weights. A single currency peg is optimal when purchasing power parity holds continuously, otherwise a basket is preferable. In all instances, the real exchange rate is the appropriate policy variable.

The essay by Michael Connolly and Abdelhadi Yousef takes a different approach to the optimal peg problem. The objective is to choose a peg that imports monetary stability in terms of the rate of inflation and its variability. Each currency peg implies a specific, *endogenous* monetary policy, since the maintaining of the peg is the policy rule. Also, since the exchange rate is a nominal variable, it is aimed at a nominal magnitude: domestic prices. The case for a single currency peg, specifically a dollar one, is quite strong for a number of the Arab countries studied, particularly those that export petroleum, which is priced in dollars. In general, the choice of an optimal peg depends upon three factors: (1) the monetary policy consistent with the peg, (2) trade patterns, and (3) deviations in exchange rates from purchasing power parity. Trade patterns are only important insofar as there are deviations from PPP, since in their absence a single currency peg would be optimal. The empirical application of the theory developed is to a sample of Arab countries. For each country, the various price outcomes are analyzed with single currency pegs, such as the dollar versus the mark, and multiple currency pegs, such as the new five-currency SDR as well as trade basket pegs. DeLisle Worrell's essay examines the impact of exchange rate instability among major reserve currencies on the economies of Barbados and Jamaica. The two economies contrast greatly, with Jamaica pursuing a more independent monetary and exchange rate policy with frequent devaluation relative to the dollar, while Barbados has maintained a relatively fixed peg, initially to the pound but later to the dollar, as in Jamaica. For both countries, the actual practice of a peg to the U.S. dollar is superior to a currency basket in terms of the variance of the exchange rate. Further, Worrell argues that a clearly known exchange rate is convenient for foreign transactions, and that a dollar peg can substitute for developed financial markets. For example, to the extent that the peg is rigidly maintained, individuals need not enter forward contracts for dollars, but effectively have a forward market in home currency, since it is equivalent to the dollar. Thus, a forward sale of, say, British pounds for U.S. dollars is equivalent to a forward sale of pounds for home currency. These gains can be profited from, however, only if the authorities maintain a credible exchange rate and monetary policy. Otherwise, the short-term stability of the exchange rate will be bought at the expense of capital flight and a deteriorating foreign payments position. The concluding essay in the volume by Henry Wallich assesses the evolution of the international monetary system in the 1980s. Governor Wallich discusses the future role of gold, the dollar, the European Monetary System, and the IMF substitution account. His view stresses a continuing important international role being played by the dollar in the world monetary system.

REFERENCES

Friedman, Milton, "The Case for Flexible Exchange Rates." *Essays in Positive Economics.* Chicago: University of Chicago Press, 1953.

Meade, James E., "The Case for Variable Exchange Rates." *Three Banks Review* (September 1955): 3–27.

Mundell, Robert A., "A Theory of Optimum Currency Areas." *American Economic Review* 51 (September 1961): 657–65.

THE INTERNATIONAL MONETARY SYSTEM: CHOICES FOR THE FUTURE

1

THE CASE FOR
A MANAGED
INTERNATIONAL GOLD STANDARD

ROBERT A. MUNDELL

In January 1976, a New International Monetary System was agreed upon at the Jamaica meeting of the Committee of Twenty. The new arrangements accepted the fait accompli of generalized flexible exchange rates that had commenced in June 1973. The new arrangements received critical acclaim in flexible exchange rate monetarist circles in the United States because they meant abandonment of the basic goal of the prewar Bretton Woods monetary order: stable exchange rates. But the acclaim was not unanimous. Others characterized the new arrangements as "organized chaos" or "the agreement to abandon the international monetary order." I was not at all enthusiastic about the new regime and thought that its attempt to demonetize gold and substitute in its place the SDR would prove impractical.

Since actual floating began in 1973, there have been both supporters and critics of the new arrangements. Those who support the new system point to the disappearance of balance-of-payments problems and shortages of reserves; if a country needs reserves, it can purchase them in the exchange market, but at the expense of depreciation. They also say that countries could not have adjusted to the great and violent changes in the world economy that occurred in the 1970s, especially the increase in oil prices, under fixed rates and gold convertibility. They do not link up the exchange rates regime to the disturbances in any causal relation. Supporters of the current system do not link up the inflationary developments of the 1970s with the breakdown of the gold exchange standard.

My view, by contrast, is that there is a deeper causal link between the choice of the global exchange rate regime and the slide into malaise that ruptured unity, saddled the third world with unrepayable debt, lifted interest rates and unemployment, and engulfed the world in inflation. An effective world monetary order should ensure a reasonable stability of the world price level, high employment, and sustainable growth. To each species of monetary arrangements there corresponds a set of mechanisms that have consequences for the working of the system. Each type of *monetary system has a different inflation potential*, based around its mechanism for creating and distributing reserves of the international medium or media and its discipline over national and international money.

1. THE BALANCE–OF–PAYMENTS DISCIPLINE

The popularity of flexible exchange rates is greatest in inflation-happy dictatorships, which think that they are freed from monetary discipline and the need to balance their budgets without recourse to other forms of unpopular or legitimate taxation to finance budget deficits. When governments are left free to print money, they can exact "seigniorage" or an "inflation tax" on the holders of the money, much like the real income a counterfeiter can get by faking paper money. When a government gives up the discipline of a commitment to a fixed exchange rate—or, in the case of the United States, the Bretton Woods discipline of gold convertibility—governments may finance budget deficits by accepting credit from the central banks, leading to an expansion of the reserve base of the national money. This possibility is ruled out or severely restricted under fixed exchange rates, since excess credit to the government or bond purchases in the open market lead to a loss of gold or foreign reserves. There is, therefore, under fixed rates a monetary discipline that forces central banks to expand or contract the money base when they buy or sell foreign exchange or reserves to support the exchange rate parity to which it is committed. When a country fixes its currency to an international currency (or basket of currencies) it cannot inflate or deflate faster than the international rate of inflation of the currencies of which the basket is composed. When fixed exchange rate discipline is absent, the country succumbs to excess monetary expansion. Depreciation of the exchange rate is not as effective a constraint on monetary expansion as reserve losses, and if all countries participate in the excess inflation, neither depreciation nor reserve losses alone will check it.

To prevent all countries from inflating together, there must be an outside medium. There must be a global anchor to provide a reference target to measure worldwide inflation and establish a ceiling on equilibrium prices. Gold (or convertible SDRs) would serve if it were interconvertible into national currencies and kept at a fixed price and limited supply. If the dollar is the principal international medium of exchange, there must be a convertibility requirement on it or some alternative discipline to limit the rate of expansion of the supply of dollars.

2. FOUR PROBLEMS
OF THE INTERNATIONAL MONETARY SYSTEM

To see the magnitude of the current problem correctly, we need to recognize four problems of an International Monetary System. First, there is the need to settle on a commodity, or a reserve asset, or a national currency to play the role of an outside or extranational world currency. The problem of choosing what that asset or assets will be can be called the *anchor problem*. The anchor is the ultimate asset. The ultimate asset might be gold, silver, platinum, or oil; it should be some important and easily standardized commodity; low storage and transport costs per unit of value are important, however, so default-free claims to oil would be preferable to oil itself. The ultimate asset problem was not included among the traditional problems studied by the Bellagio (Princeton, 1964) study group on international monetary reform, but it is nevertheless crucial to an understanding of the problem of international liquidity.

Second, there is an *adjustment problem*: there must be a mechanism for bringing export surpluses into balance with net voluntary lending and outward transfers; what we call adjustment or reequilibration of the balance of payment. This also means that there must be a mechanism for bringing the level of domestic expenditure or absorption into line with national income, to make the difference between the two consistent with the desired rate of international borrowing or lending.

Third, there is a *confidence problem*: there must be confidence in the mechanism by which one kind of reserve asset can be exchanged into another at a predictable price. Under bimetallism this meant confidence in the bimetallic ratio, the number of ounces of silver required to buy an ounce of gold; under the gold/dollar Bretton Woods system, it meant maintaining the equilibrium relation between the quantity of dollars outstanding and the quantity of gold; under a dollar/SDR system it would mean administering the price at which the dollar exchanges for the SDR.

Fourth, there is the liquidity or *inflation problem*, the mechanism of monetary discipline and coordination by which the growth of international reserves and national moneys used as foreign exchange reserves are kept under control. Under the gold standard, and to a certain extent under bimetallism, this control was automatic; national currencies were composed of or convertible into gold, which was the anchor, and the supply of specie was determined by its cost of production and discovery. Under the gold exchange standard, the monetary policy of a reserve currency country was restrained by the requirement of gold convertibility (at a fixed par value), and the monetary policies of the other countries were regulated by the discipline of convertibility into the reserve currency at the established exchange rate parity.

Under flexible exchange rates, by contrast, these *international disciplines* are abandoned, and the outcome is left up to the *self-discipline* of the national monetary and budgetary authorities. Each country solves its inflation problem in its own national way, without international discipline. The international process of mutual reinforcement, tension, and coordinated aspiration falls apart, and every country is left to fend for itself. The decentralized result has always been, and always will be, a mess. It tends to break down when currency policies of countries of different sizes are brought into confrontation with one another, leading to currency areas, mergers, and unions that may destroy political harmonies.

3. HOW THE INTERNATIONAL GOLD STANDARD WORKED

These four problems of an international monetary system give us a framework for analysis of the past systems and point the way to evaluations of the choices to be made in the 1980s. The modern international gold standard emerged from the crisis in bimetallism that followed the U.S. Civil War and the Franco-Prussian War (bimetallism had depended on the pivot role played by the United States and France in fixing the range of the bimetallic ratio). For more than a century, gold became the dominant reserve asset and standard of international value. The gold standard mechanism worked automatically in theory, although it was "managed" in practice with countries obeying the "rules of the game." When gold became scarce, because of rapid population or output growth or a reduction in supply, the world price level would fall or rise at a slower rate, but so would marginal costs of mining and discovery, arresting the decline. Similarly, if new discoveries or inventions increased production, inflationary pressures would raise marginal costs in mining and act as a check on supply, reducing the inflation. Other factors could and did play an important, and sometimes unsettling, part. Of great importance was the fact of countries joining or leaving the gold standard, generating deflationary pressure when they joined and inflationary pressure when they left, noteworthy examples being Germany and Scandinavia in the 1870s, Russia, Austria, and Hungary in the 1890s, and Japan in the 1900s. Nevertheless, variations of the supply and shifts of demand were minor compared to the huge outstanding stock, or else they tended to offset one another, thus lending a stability much superior to that in the twentieth century to the price level as measured by the purchasing power of a given quantity of gold. Of course individual countries would experience inflation or deflation different from the world standard if they changed the gold parities of their currencies. The hyperinflations of many countries during wartime and postwar periods of inflationary finance are solemn reminders of this.

The adjustment mechanism under the gold standard was understood as a consequence of adherence to a practical set of rules, but its theoretical underpinnings have created great controversies among economists, bankers, and officials. Classical economists in the early twentieth century, including, surprisingly, Keynes, put too much emphasis on the need for changes in price levels. They neglected transfers in spending power. On the other hand, after 1936 Keynesians overplayed the role of changes in employment, neglecting *both* spending shifts (separate from those related to changes in employment) and price effects. A complete view of adjustment has to take account of the link between changes in the money supply and shifts of expenditure that do not require price or employment changes, building supplementary changes in the latter as residual adjustment measures. Actual adjustment requires reductions of expenditure from deficit countries, which are losing gold, and increases in expenditure in surplus countries, which are gaining it, leading to increased "absorption" in the former countries, and decreased "absorption" in the latter. These expenditure shifts automatically facilitate the attainment of equilibrium in the balance of payments. Between financial centers where capital is mobile, the timing of adjustment of the balance of payments is cushioned, as long as the countries remain acceptable credit risks, by international capital movements, which serve their appropriate function of optimizing the spreading of the costs of adjustment over time, creating a better intertemporal balance between consumption and production. Provided the central banks did not deliberately intervene to impede the process, lending would occur automatically in the different money centers, spreading out the time available for basic adjustment.

The amount of actual lending historically depended on the degree of *capital market integration.* The level of international integration of capital markets was in practice very high between 1880 and 1914 particularly because of the centralization of financial operations in London. Most centers felt the impulses coming from London, which operated as the information center of the system, particularly after the invention of the telegraph. Today the dollar rates of interest in New York on TBs and CDs play the same role as bank rate in London and as the sterling bill played in the pre–1914 gold standard.

The gold standard even in the 1870–1914 period was not worldwide. There were, first of all, some countries that maintained inconvertible paper currencies (and flexible exchange rates). Countries using these currencies were on the periphery of the metropolitan imperial system. Other countries adhered to a silver standard. Whether the standard in a single country was gold or silver made little practical difference, as long as the worldwide price of gold in terms of silver was fixed, as it was when at least one country was on a bimetallic standard. Throughout the Middle Ages, a double standard had prevailed. The discovery of America led to a great increase in the stock of gold and silver in Europe, contributing to a price revolution in Europe and, according to Earl Hamilton, to the growth of modern capitalism.*

The vast silver supplies from Bolivia had made silver the predominant metal, but gold discoveries in Brazil advanced the use of gold in the eighteenth century. Britain after 1717 edged toward gold as Newton, then Master of the Mint, overvalued gold. In 1792 the United States adopted the double standard at a ratio of 15 to 1, which slightly overvalued silver so the circulating medium—largely

---

*The estimate of the increase is:

	gold	silver
1493	17.7	225.1
1660	48.2	1,005.3

foreign—was silver and, of course, paper notes. In 1834 the ratio was changed to 16 to 1, which overvalued gold and thus drove out silver, whereas in France, which from 1803 had control of the bimetallic ratio at $15\frac{1}{2}$ to 1, silver drove out gold.

The gold discoveries in the middle of the nineteenth century brought about a revolution in the international monetary system. The monetary gold stock doubled in a decade from perhaps 38 million ounces to 88 million ounces, leading to an increase of prices of perhaps 25%; the modesty of the price change was due to the cushioning effect of bimetallism as gold replaced silver in the French Empire of Napoleon III. Meanwhile the U.S. currency became inconvertible during the Civil War, and after the war the confederate currency system collapsed while the Northern greenbacks were at a heavy discount against the prewar gold parity. Instead of devaluing or contracting the issues, the greenbacks were allowed to remain until the demand for them caught up with supply so that convertibility was finally resumed in 1878. The dramatic discovery and opening of the Witswatterrand in 1885 paved the way for a great increase of supply. The only thing that delayed a new confidence problem in the 1890s with the expansion of gold supply was the increase in demand for gold created by the new gold countries. By 1914, the Russian Empire alone had bought up 16% of the world stock of monetary gold.

The effectiveness of the metallic systems in the nineteenth century in adjusting to great disturbances was remarkable when judged by performance of paper currencies of the twentieth century. The fluctuations in the value of gold were nevertheless of great concern to the Victorians. Pain is always felt at the margin! In the late nineteenth century most countries wanted to standardize gold, and several official conferences were convened to promote a common gold or silver unit. Alfred Marshall advocated *Symmetallism* (essentially an alloy of gold and silver, like the elektrum of ancient Lydia) and was thus a pioneer in the development of currency baskets, but he later lost enthusiasm for the plan, which, his contemporaries convinced him (perhaps wrongly), was impractical.

The gold standard survived the great depression of the 1890s and the Knickerbocker panic of 1907, and even the Great War of 1914-18, during which the United States centralized, but still adhered to gold. The U.S. dollar-based gold exchange standard was again made international when Germany (1924), Great Britain (1925), and France (1927) rejoined it, followed by most continental countries.

It collapsed in 1931. But five years later, with the Tripartite Agreement of the United States, France, and Britain, it was reestablished on a new basis of a gold price of $35 an ounce, the price set by President Roosevelt in 1934. That price lasted, as we know, until 1971, when the key currency system based on the dollar broke down. The Bretton Woods system was based on the dollar, with gold as the noncirculating anchor. Gold was not reestablished after the war as a circulating international medium. After 1950, when, as a result of U.S. postwar inflation, gold had again become scarce, gold hoarding, based on the expectation of an ultimate increase in price, began. This was reflected in the rising interest rates on dollar assets during the 1950-69 period.

The Bretton Woods system, relying on the dollar for reserve expansion, resulted in a secular drift upward in the price level of the reserve country, of about 1 to 2% annually in the 1950s and early 1960s, and 3 to 4% annually in the late 1960s. Thus, the "gold exchange standard," as the system was often called, had a slight inflationary basis, that was, however, increasing.

4. THE DEFECT OF THE SYSTEM

The Bretton Woods system had a problem, this problem being not with the system itself, but with the way the principal countries were operating it. Gold pinned the system down, at least theoretically. It was the anchor. However, the United States was unwilling to take the medicine of losing gold reserves when its deficit built up an excessive dollar overhang abroad. The United States was reluctant either to lose gold or to disinflate in the 1960s. It scrapped the 25% gold cover behind high-powered Federal Reserve money. It would not in practice allow other countries to cash in their dollars for U.S. gold upon threat of breaking up the system. Collectively, the world as a whole was thus in a stalemate: the United States would not accept the global discipline of gold on world monetary expansion, nor would it raise the world price of gold chosen to an equilibrium price at which gold could again be convertible. The pressure continued to build up as the excess supply of currencies against gold mounted, and the recession of 1970-71 decreased world demand for dollars. It broke down in August 1971, when European central banks finally exercised their legal right and brought claims for conversion of excess dollars into gold. The United States responded by declaring the dollar inconvertible, for the second time in 200 years. Because the dollar was previously the only link of the international monetary system to gold, this cut the link of paper currencies all over the world to the anchor of gold.

5. THE PROBLEM OF GLOBAL DISCIPLINE UNDER FIXED RATES

There has been too little recognition of the fact that the balance-of-payments discipline of fixed exchange rates is not sufficient by itself to stop world inflation. Fixed exchange rates impose a common discipline on countries adhering to it and make all countries find a common price level. But fixed rates based on paper currencies do not prevent countries collectively from inflating at a common and excessive rate.

It was just this problem that broke up the rates fixed at the Smithsonian in December 1971. The U.S. Central Bank was creating dollar reserves faster than Europe was prepared to absorb them, leading to a second devaluation of the dollar in 1973. The purely nominal price of gold was put up from $38 an ounce (the Smithsonian price) to $42.2 an ounce. Meanwhile, the European countries had experimented with a Europa monetary bloc, which, in March 1973, attempted a joint float against the dollar. This broke up because of uneven inflation in June.

By June 1973 it had become clear that the destruction of the international monetary system had become complete. The Committee of Twenty, which had been appointed by the I.M.F. governors to advance international monetary reform, made the astonishing announcement that *steps toward reform would have to be put off until inflation had been brought under control!*

This was astonishing because it showed that the Committee did not regard reform of the international monetary system as a vehicle for stopping world inflation.

The breakdown of the dollar system coincided with the emergence of a more decentralized multipolar view of the world economy. U.S. production is now about 20% of world production, no longer so dominant. The United States has also appeared to be vulnerable because of its apparent loss of political leadership in different parts of the world. Because of the inflation of dollar prices, which in 1978 and 1979 had risen to more than 15% per annum, speculation pushed the dollar price of gold close to $850 an ounce in January 1980, feeding world inflation. The opposite problem arose after tight money under Reaganomics had reversed the inflation, lowered the price of gold below $350 an ounce, and halved the value of international central bank reserves.

6. CONTINUING PRESENCE OF THE DOLLAR FELT EVERYWHERE

One should never underestimate the ability of the United States to defend the effectiveness and importance of the dollar as a "dominant currency." In comparing its position with its near rivals, the mark, yen, pound, franc, or rouble, one should reflect on the following considerations:

1. The value of the stock of outstanding dollar contracts and claims of one kind or another probably exceed $5 trillion, larger than that of any other currency by a large multiple. This makes the dollar-denominated assets *more marketable*.

2. The dollar fluctuates less than other currencies. This means that the dollar is *more stable*.

3. Over fifty currencies peg, at least for short periods, to the dollar. This extends the scope of the dollar area worldwide and makes its market *more broad* than any other currency area.

4. New York is the largest capital market in the world, and the New York-London Eurodollar money market establishes the norm for ruling world interest rates. This makes the dollar *more convenient*.

5. The dollar is now, and has been for some time, the main invoice currency, replacing the pound sterling, the former leading currency. This makes the dollar *more known* and utilized.

6. The dollar is the numéraire of oil prices and the currency of payment. This makes the dollar *more demanded* for working and even savings balances.

7. The dollar is by far the main reserve asset except for gold. This makes the dollar *more available*, and the asset that is the closest to high-powered reserve money.

8. The dollar is a world money in the sense that it is known and acceptable almost everywhere. This reinforcing phenomenon feeds on itself and makes the dollar *more universal*.

For these reasons, it would be premature to assume that the position of the dollar and the threat of diversification into sterling, marks, gold, yen, or roubles is an indication of the end of the dollar area. The dollar faces great difficulties in achieving stability against commodities, but so do the other currencies.

As we shall see, to anticipate my argument, I do not expect gold to replace the dollar. I do, however, want to unite once again the power of gold with the awesome position of the dollar in the world to achieve a more stable international monetary system.

7. THE RISE OF A DOMINANT MONEY UNDER FLEXIBLE RATES

Floating exchange rates reinforce the power of the dominant currency if it remains stable. The reason lies in the great economics of scale in using a single money rather than many monies in an economic system. This is quickly seen in the historical development of paper currencies, which, provided their convertibility into specie was not in question, could be made completely divisible. Two 5-dollar bills always exchange for one 10-dollar bill. Bank money exchanges for currency at a fixed rate (one for one).

The tendency for one money to dominate has also always been present in the world economy, even though success at achieving the dominance has been affected by the degree of integration of the world monetary economy. By the 1970s, global economic integration had become very high, especially in the North Atlantic and Pacific basins. The floating rate system meant a great new demand for reserves as a means of international payment. Gold was effectively immobilized as a medium of exchange after the 1968 agreement not to stabilize the free market price. Foreign exchange was the primary alternative to gold, and dollars were the most popular and useful form of foreign exchange.

That is why the floating exchange rate system secured use and spread of the dollar throughout the international economy. The dollar flooded the world economy in the 1970s in the period of the greatest unpopularity of that currency.

8. THE INSTABILITY OF PRICES WITHOUT GOLD CONVERTIBILITY

It is this phenomenon, and the international anarchy to which it is conducive, that has left in shambles the concepts of international price level stability. Within one decade, the price of basic commodities, such as gold, silver, oil, have multiplied ten-fold, a rate of inflation that ten years ago would have been inconceivable. "Surprise" arises from this shattering of ignorance, which is informative; it tells us that our failure to predict the future in the past shows our present lack of understanding of the past. The model that most economists were using of the international monetary system was wrong.

The error can be recognized in hindsight. It was in not understanding the anchor control function of gold convertibility. As long as at least one currency is convertible into gold, inflation is circumscribed. Inflationary pressure or even expectations lead to a drain of gold from the central banks under the gold standard, and a reduction in the quantity of money; or at least a brake on its rate of increase. Once gold becomes inconvertible at a fixed price and the currency value of gold is allowed to rise, the system becomes inflation-unstable. An increase in commodity prices leads to an increase in gold prices, and an increase in the price of gold raises the value of gold reserves and leads to overly expansionary monetary policy on the part of central banks. Money becomes completely accommodating.

That has been the problem in the 1970s, and it looks as if it will also be the problem in the 1980s. An increase in the price of oil leads to an increased demand for dollars to pay for it. With a constant stock of money this would create high interest rates, deflationary pressure on commodity prices, and a surplus on the oil markets, forcing renewal of the original oil prices increase in the 1970s. Instead, the United States responded by increasing the monetary reserves of the banking system, feeding monetary reserves to banks both at home and into the Euromarkets and other centers, accommodating the demand for money. The excess of dollar liquidity, which is transferred to oil-producing countries, is redeposited in banks, increasing the circular flows of dollars, or else invested in gold. This bids up the price of gold, which further inflates international reserves and new chains of liquidity expansion. It takes very little time for the inflationary conflagration to spread to other markets, first to the other precious metals and then throughout the global system, until it finally (and anticipations could speed up the recognition lag) bids up U.S. wages and the wages of the other major countries, infecting their GNP deflators and cost-of-living-indexes, which follow the global inflation.

If the Fed does eventually wake up and control the inflation by tight money, the system rides overkill in the deflationary direction: tight money, high interest, collapse of gold, silver, and copper, and so forth result in world recession, deflation, unemployment, and depression.

9. THE ROLE OF MONETARY MANAGEMENT AND THE ONLY SOLUTION

The final part of the monetary saga is the role of monetary management. At the international level this is a joke. There is no international monetary management. The great dangers that lie ahead are compounded by the likelihood that international monetary dithering will continue as in the past.

The problem simply reduces to monetary discipline, the problem of getting control of the international supply of money, preventing excessive inflation or deflation. That could be achieved by each country acting on its own. But the events of the past decade have clearly shown that it will not be achieved in that way. There is widespread disillusion with the attempt to regulate the quantity of money instead of the exchange rate. This is proved by the decision of the United States on November 1, 1978, to defend the value of the dollar, and the inauguration of the European monetary system on March 13, 1979, which established a fixed exchange rate zone in Europe. Obviously, if the Europeans fix intra-European rates and the United States fixes the dollar, the core of the world economy is back to a fixed rate system. But a fixed rate system by itself will not prevent all countries from harmonizing to a hyperinflationary rate of price increase. *It is only asset convertibility of a currency to an anchor that can achieve that.* For this reason, the extra degree of freedom in the system should be devoted to making one or more currencies convertible into a commodity. It is only in this way that the *brake* upon monetary expansion can be achieved. Multilateral surveillance is an exercise that is harmless but has not succeeded.

10. THE STRATEGIC ROLE OF THE QUANTITY OF DOLLARS AND THE PRICE OF GOLD

Only a few commodities could serve as the basis for solving the final asset problem. But only one asset, gold, is now practical. Central banks now hold about a billion ounces of gold, worth hundreds of billions of dollars. Fixing the price of silver or platinum would not solve the inflation problem, which has its heart in the relation between the supply of dollars and the price of gold. Gold is unique because of the central bank hoards. It is only when *both* the *supply of dollars* and the *price of gold* are regulated that the price instability can be ameliorated. The solution therefore is to fix the dollar price of gold, reestablishing dollar convertibility, and allow gold stocks to affect the quantity of dollars issued.

At what price should gold be stabilized? The higher the gold price, the higher the equilibrium price level, so the answer depends both on the date at which stabilization takes place and the distribution of wealth that is desired. It would be useless to suggest a number for the gold price before agreement on the principles and need for the stabilization have been settled. Once the Group of Five or the Committee of Twenty have made that agreement, it should not be difficult to arrive at a number for the optimum price of gold.

There are other problems that need to be considered, such as the mechanism that may need to be brought into play in order to ensure a just distribution of reserves, and many compromises may be necessary to accommodate the needs of countries in very different economic positions with respect to gold holdings, gold production, and consumption. When there are no stable alternatives on hand, the details of the correct solution soon fall into place.

11. CONCLUDING REMARKS

The essence of a gold standard of the kind I envisage for the future makes use of the practical fact that gold is the most important international reserve of the central banks; that central banks now hold a billion ounces of it; that another billion is held in above-ground hoards by individuals or institutions; that official gold stocks are highly coveted by countries as a "patrimony"; that a "mystique" about the metal still exists, though it is not nearly so strong as under prohibition; and that no nation today wants to dispose of huge quantities of its gold stocks. Even at prices exceeding $800 an ounce central banks and treasuries held on to gold.

The present plan turns these facts to advantage by using the familiarity and popularity of gold to help stabilize the world economy. Stabilization of the gold price is the first step. In moving toward that, it would be useful to start with an upper and a lower limit, a selling price and a buying price. Gold sales reduce the money base; gold purchases increase it. This is desirable since it is the first step toward utilization of the golden rudder by which market information is transformed into policy. It is sufficient at first that the market be heeded, and not automatically reversed, by sterilization of gold movements.

The United States will probably have to lead the way. There is no other country at the present time able to take the initiative or to provide the necessary leadership. Other countries may then wish to stabilize their currencies to the dollar within suitable margins. They likewise should allow dollar purchases and sales to affect the monetary bases of their own currencies. They may also wish to adjust their gold/dollar portfolios in directions that indicate their national views about the degree of expansiveness of monetary policy in the United States.

These adjustments are not fundamentally different from those that actually prevailed during the heyday of the Bretton Woods system. The effectiveness of the international monetary system in the quarter-century between 1946 and 1971 should not be underestimated. This was probably one of the most successful periods of comparative peace, growth, innovation, high employment, and political liberation that mankind has every known. Its one problem was that the price of gold was too low.

There are some supplementary guidelines that may be helpful in ensuring the success of the international policy that a full gold standard provides. Monetary policies under fixed exchange rates have to be geared to preserving the balance-of-payments equilibrium. There is no degree of freedom left for inflationary finance. Supply-encouraging fiscal policies can be used for employment stabilization and economic growth, but budgetary policy is effective only in the short run and only in countries where past monetary stability has generated faith in capital markets and government credit. In the intermediate and long run, wage rates have to be the major instrument for achieving employment stability. To the extent that any general nonmandatory wage policy is possible at all, it should be in the form of guidelines that do not interfere with the need for shifts in relative wage rates.

In the spring of 1982, the U.S. Gold Commission made further recommendations that included the issue of gold coins in fractions of an ounce. There would be a strong argument for attempting to stabilize the ounce price of gold at an even fraction for purposes of computational simplicity. That is a useful first step toward a gold standard in which the U.S. public is not prohibited, as it was in the Bretton Woods regime, from holding gold.

I

THE ECONOMICS
OF A MANAGED FLOAT

2

ASPECTS
OF THE OPTIMAL MANAGEMENT
OF EXCHANGE RATES

JACOB A. FRENKEL & JOSHUA AIZENMAN

1. INTRODUCTION

This chapter deals with the problem of the choice of an optimal exchange rate regime for a small, open economy. Previous analyses of the choice between fixed and flexible exchange rate systems centered around questions of stabilization policies, the effect of capital mobility on the efficacy of monetary and fiscal policies, the role of speculation in the foreign exchange market, the nature and origin of exogenous disturbances, and the like. Subsequent discussions originating with contributions in the 1960s by Mundell (1961), McKinnon (1963), and Kenen (1969) have shifted the focus of analysis to the choice of the optimal currency area. The shift of emphasis reflected the recognition of the fact that the optimal exchange rate regime need not be the same for all countries. Rather, a country might find it useful to maintain a fixed rate with some currencies, while having a flexible exchange rate with some other currencies.

The analysis in this chapter recognizes that the spectrum of possibilities open for the various economies is much broader than the one implied by the framework of analysis of the optimal currency

J. A. Frenkel is indebted to the National Science Foundation, grant SES-7814480 A01, for financial support. The research reported here is part of the NBER's Research Program in International Studies. Any opinions expressed are those of the authors and not necessarily those of the NBER.

area. Rather than dividing the world into currencies among which exchange rates are flexible and those among which exchange rates are fixed, one might consider the optimal degree of fixity of exchange rates between each pair of currencies. In this framework the choice of an exchange rate regime between any pair of currencies need not be a fixed or a flexible rate but rather it might be some optimal mix of the two extremes. The optimal mix is referred to as the optimal managed (or dirty) float, and the determinants of the optimal degree of exchange rate management are the subject of this chapter.

The analytical framework that is outlined below builds upon and extends the analysis of recent papers by Fischer (1976) and Gray (1976). Fischer analyzes the choice between the two extreme exchange rate systems in terms of the source of exogenous disturbances. He demonstrates that when the exogenous shocks are real, the variance of steady-state consumption is lower under a fixed exchange rate system than under a flexible rate system. On the other hand, when the exogenous shocks are monetary, the opposite holds, and the flexible rate system is preferred to the fixed rate system. Gray's paper deals with wage indexation in a closed economy and develops the concept of the optimal degree of wage indexation when the system is subject to real and monetary shocks that occur simultaneously. Lack of complete information precludes identifying the effect of each shock separately and thus results in the optimal degree of wage indexation. In what follows we combine the two approaches of Fischer and Gray into a framework that yields an index measuring the optimal degree of fixity of exchange rates, that is, the optimal managed float. Section 2 describes the analytical framework and analyzes the problem for an economy whose production consists only of commodities that are traded internationally. It is shown that the major determinants of the optimal managed float are the variances of and the covariances among the various shocks that affect the economy.[1] In Section 3 we extend the analysis to an economy that produces tradable as well as nontradable goods and examine the dependence of the optimal managed float on the composition of production. Section 4 contains some concluding remarks.

2. OPTIMAL MANAGED FLOAT WITH ONLY TRADABLE GOODS

In this section we analyze the determinants of the optimal degree of exchange rate management for an economy that produces only tradable goods. We start with a presentation of the analytical framework.

2.1. The Analytical Framework

The key characteristic of the analytical framework is the specification of the stochastic structure of the economy. Consider a small economy that is subject to three types of repetitive and serially uncorrelated shocks. These shocks, which are specified below, are referred to as real, monetary, and foreign shocks.

Denote the supply of output by Y_t, and assume that

$$Y_t = y \exp (\mu) \qquad \mu \sim N \left(-\frac{\sigma_\mu^2}{2} , \sigma_\mu^2 \right) \qquad (1)$$

where μ is a stochastic disturbance with a constant variance σ_μ^2. The mean of the distribution of μ is chosen to be $-\sigma_\mu^2/2$ so as to ensure that the expected value of output $E(Y_t)$ equals y. Thus, y is referred to as permanent income, and μ is referred to as the real shock. It can be shown that σ_μ is approximately equal to the standard deviation of current income as a percentage of permanent income.[2]

The second source of disturbances arises from the monetary sector of the economy. Let the demand for nominal balances L_t be

$$L_t = kP_tY_t \exp (\epsilon) \qquad \epsilon \sim N \left(-\frac{\sigma_\epsilon^2}{2} , \sigma_\epsilon^2 \right) \qquad (2)$$

where k is the Cambridge k denoting the desired ratio of money to income, P denotes the domestic price level, and ϵ denotes the stochastic disturbance to the demand for money, where again its time subscript has been omitted. Analogous to the distribution of the real shock, the standard deviation of the monetary shock σ_ϵ is approximately equal to the standard deviation of the income velocity as a percentage of permanent velocity.

The third source of disturbances stems from the foreign sector. Denote the foreign price level by P_t^*, and let it be related to its permanent value p_t^* according to

$$P_t^* = p^* \exp (\chi_1) \qquad \chi_1 \sim N \left(-\frac{\sigma_{\chi_1}^2}{2} , \sigma_{\chi_1}^2 \right) \qquad (3)$$

Thus, χ_1 denotes the shocks due to variability of foreign prices. Again, σ_{χ_1} is approximately equal to the standard deviation of foreign prices as a percentage of their mean.

The domestic price level is linked to the foreign price level through the purchasing power parity, which is assumed to be satisfied except for random deviations. The stochastic deviations from purchasing power parity are denoted by χ_2, and thus

$$P_t = S_t P_t^* \exp(\chi_2) \qquad \chi_2 \sim N\left(-\frac{\sigma_{\chi_2}^2}{2}, \sigma_{\chi_2}^2\right) \qquad (4)$$

where S_t denotes the exchange rate, which is defined as the price of foreign exchange in terms of domestic currency. For further use it is convenient to combine equations (3) and (4) and to express the domestic price level as

$$P_t = S_t p^* \exp(\chi) \qquad (4')$$

where χ denotes the effective foreign price shock that is defined by the sum $\chi_1 + \chi_2$.

Let the flow demand for money ΔM_t^d correspond to a stock adjustment process by which individuals wish to restore stock equilibrium by a constant multiple of the discrepancy between desired and actual money holdings:

$$\Delta M_t^d = \alpha(L_t - \bar{M}_t) \qquad (5)$$

In (5), α denotes the speed of adjustment while $\bar{M}_t$ denotes money holdings at the beginning of the period. The determinants of $\bar{M}_t$ will be discussed later.

Using equations (1), (3), and (4') in (2) we may express the demand for money as

$$L = kp^* S_t y \exp(\mu + \epsilon + \chi) \qquad (2')$$

When the exchange rate is flexible, any stock disequilibrium in the money market will disappear automatically, since the exchange rate will change so as to guarantee that $L_t - \bar{M}_t = 0$. Using equation (2'), it follows that when the exchange rate is flexible the money market clears, and therefore

$$kp^* S_t y \exp(\mu + \epsilon + \chi) - \bar{M}_t = 0 \qquad (6)$$

Thus, the equilibrium exchange rate is

$$S_t = \frac{\bar{M}_t}{kp^* y} \exp[-(\mu + \epsilon + \chi)] \qquad (7)$$

and the percentage change thereof is

$$\ln S_t - \ln S_{t-1} = \ln \left(\frac{\bar{M}_t}{kS_{t-1}p^*y} \right) - (\mu + \epsilon + \chi) \tag{8}$$

For the other extreme regime of the fixed exchange rate system, the exchange rate does not change, and therefore

$$\ln S_t - \ln S_{t-1} = 0 \tag{9}$$

Using (8) and (9), we may define an index γ such that $0 \leqslant \gamma \leqslant 1$:

$$\gamma \equiv \frac{\ln S_t - \ln S_{t-1}}{\ln (\bar{M}_t/kS_{t-1}p^*y) - (\mu + \epsilon + \chi)} \tag{10}$$

In equation (10) the parameter γ characterizes the whole spectrum of exchange rate regimes. In the two extreme systems of a fixed and freely flexible exchange rates, the value of the coefficient γ is zero and unity, respectively. Between these two extremes there is the wide range of possible mixtures of the two extremes. The coefficient γ may be viewed as indicating the fraction of money market disequilibrium that is allowed to be eliminated through changes in the exchange rate. In what follows we will refer to γ as the coefficient of managed float. Equation (10) also implies that the current exchange rate is

$$S_t = S_{t-1}^{1-\gamma} \left(\frac{\bar{M}_t}{kp^*y} \right)^\gamma \exp [-\gamma(\mu + \epsilon + \chi)] \tag{11}$$

2.2. The Objective Function

The optimal managed float strategy is necessary because it is assumed that the government—as well as the private sector—possess information that is incomplete. If information were complete and during each period the various shocks could be observed and identified separately, an optimal policy would be to allow changes in the exchange rates to correct only for the monetary disturbances and not for the real disturbances. This is essentially the main insight from Fischer's paper (1976). In introducing incomplete information it is assumed that during a given period the *joint* outcome of the various shocks is known but not their separate values. Because complete information is not available, policymakers face a signal extraction problem, and some second-best policy is required.

It is assumed that the objective is to minimize the losses due to imperfect information, and that the policymaker seeks to minimize the quadratic loss function H:

$$\text{Minimize } H \equiv E[(c_t - E(Y_t)]^2$$
$$= \text{var } (c_t) + [E(Y_t) - E(c_t)]^2 \qquad (12)$$

where c_t denotes the rate of consumption, which, from the budget constraint, equals the rate of income minus the real value of additions to cash balances

$$c_t = Y_t - \frac{\Delta M_t}{p_t} \qquad (13)$$

The previous relationships imply that

$$c_t - E(Y_t) = y(e^\mu - 1)$$
$$- \alpha k y \left\{ \exp (\mu + \epsilon) - \left(\frac{\bar{M}_t}{kS_{t-1}p^*y} \right)^{1-\gamma} \right.$$
$$\left. \times \exp [\gamma(\mu + \epsilon) + \chi(\gamma - 1)] \right\} \qquad (14)$$

and using (14) in (12) yields the loss function that is to be minimized with respect to the intervention index γ.[3]

Inspection of (14) suggests that in addition to finding the optimal γ, the policymaker might want to pursue what Fischer terms "active" monetary policy by setting the beginning of period holdings of cash balances $\bar{M}_t$ at some desired level. It is assumed that at the beginning of each period the monetary authority changes the money supply so as to compensate for past disturbances. Thus, the money supply is set at that level for which

$$\bar{M}_t = kS_{t-1}p^*y \exp (\delta) \qquad \delta \sim N \left(-\frac{\sigma_\delta^2}{2}, \sigma_\delta^2 \right) \qquad (15)$$

The stochastic term δ in (15) denotes the stochastic shock to the money supply. It reflects the possibility that in setting the money supply the monetary authorities are unable to avoid stochastic deviations from their target.[4] Recalling that the shock to the demand for money is denoted by ϵ, the *net* monetary shock, that is, the shock to the excess demand for money, is $\epsilon - \delta$.

2.3. The Optimal Intervention Index

Having outlined the objective function, we now turn to the solution of the optimal intervention index, which will be denoted by γ^*. To simplify the computations, we approximate the discrepancy between consumption and expected income by the first two terms of a Taylor expansion of equation (14). Thus

$$[c_t - E(Y_t)] \cong [\mu - (1 - \gamma)\alpha k\theta]y \tag{14'}$$

where the expansion is carried out around a zero value of the shocks.[5] In equation (14'), θ denotes the sum of all shocks, that is,

$$\theta \equiv \mu + \chi + \epsilon - \delta$$

and, under full flexibility of exchange rates (when $\gamma = 1$), money market equilibrium implies that the percentage fall in the exchange rate is equal to θ.

Minimization of the loss function requires that the value of γ in (14') is chosen so as to minimize the squared discrepancy between μ and $(1 - \gamma)\alpha k\theta$. This minimization amounts to computing the ordinary least-squares estimate of a regression of μ on $\alpha k\theta$. It follows that the optimal intervention index γ^* is

$$\gamma^* = 1 - \frac{\text{cov}(\mu, \theta)}{\alpha k\sigma_\theta^2} \tag{16}$$

and when all shocks are independent of each other, the optimal intervention index becomes:

$$\gamma^* = 1 - \frac{\sigma_\mu^2}{\alpha k[\sigma_\mu^2 + \sigma_{\chi + \epsilon - \delta}^2]} \tag{16'}$$

where σ_θ^2 is expressed as the sum of the variance of the real shock σ_μ^2 and the variance of the effective monetary shock $\sigma_{\chi + \epsilon - \delta}^2$.[6] The intuition underlying equations (16) and (16') can be provided in terms of the signal extraction problem that is faced by the policymaker given the assumed informational structure. From his knowledge of the intervention rule and from the observed change in the exchange rate, the policymaker can infer the magnitude of the global shock θ. It is assumed that the value of θ is known but not the individual components of the global shock. The signal extraction problem amounts to an attempt to estimate the unobserved value of the real shock μ from the known value of θ (that is inferred from the change in the exchange rate).

Inspection of (16) and (16') reveals that when $\sigma_\mu^2 = 0$ so that the disturbances are composed only of effective monetary shocks, $\gamma^* = 1$ and the optimal exchange rate regime is that of complete flexibility. For the other extreme, for which $\sigma_{\chi+\epsilon-\delta}^2 = 0$ so that the disturbances are entirely of a real origin, the optimal intervention index is set equal to zero and the optimal exchange rate regime is that of fixed rates.[7] In general, when both types of shocks are present, the optimal intervention index is within the range (0, 1) and the optimal exchange rate system corresponds to neither of the extremes of a completely fixed or of a completely flexible rate regime. In that case the optimal system is an intermediate system, that is, a system of an optimal managed float.

The magnitude of the optimal intervention index depends on the characteristics of the shocks. As may be inferred from equation (16), as long as the covariance between μ and $\mu + \chi + \epsilon - \delta$ is positive, the optimal intervention index depends negatively on the variance of the real shock. Thus,

$$\frac{\partial \gamma^*}{\partial \sigma_\mu^2} < 0 \tag{17}$$

High variance of real shocks, ceteris paribus, tends to raise the desirability of greater fixity of exchange rates. Small economies, and in particular developing countries, tend to have concentrated production patterns and thus are likely to have higher variance of real shocks than more diversified economies. Ceteris paribus, these economies will find it optimal to have greater fixity of exchange rates.

Similarly, equation (16) implies that as long as the covariance between the effective monetary shock $\chi + \epsilon - \delta$ and the global shock $\mu + \chi + \epsilon - \delta$ is positive, the intervention index depends positively on the variance of the effective monetary shock. Thus,

$$\frac{\partial \gamma^*}{\partial \sigma_{\chi+\epsilon-\delta}^2} > 0 \tag{18}$$

High variance of the effective monetary shock tends to raise the desirability of greater flexibility of exchange rates.

Equation (16) also implies a definite relationship between αk—the propensity to save out of transitory income—and the optimal intervention index. As long as the covariance between μ and $\mu + \chi + \epsilon - \delta$ is positive, a higher value of αk is associated with a higher value of γ^*:

$$\frac{\partial \gamma^*}{\partial \alpha k} > 0 \tag{19}$$

Thus, high speed of adjustment to asset disequilibrium (high α) and low velocity of circulation (high k) tend to raise the desirability of greater flexibility of exchange rates. This result may be rationalized by noting that the effect of any given value of the real shock on the excess flow demand for money depends positively on αk. Since the desirability of greater flexibility increases with the extent of monetary shocks, and since the monetary disequilibrium that corresponds to a given real shock is larger the higher the saving propensity, it follows that the effect of αk on γ^* is similar to the effect of a rise in the variance of the effective monetary shock.

From equation (16') it is clear that the results in (17), (18), and (19) must hold when the various shocks are independent of each other. Further, inspection of equations (16) and (16') suggests that what is relevant for the optimal intervention index is not the absolute magnitude of the variances of the various shocks but rather their relative magnitude. In general, when the ratio between the variances of the effective monetary shock and the real shock approaches infinity (either because the former approaches infinity or because the latter approaches zero), the optimal exchange rate system is that of freely flexible rates. Likewise, when the same ratio approaches zero (either because the variance of the effective monetary shock approaches zero or because the variance of the real shock approaches infinity), the optimal exchange rate system is that of fixed rates.

Since the optimal intervention index depends negatively on the variance of real shocks and positively on the variance of the effective monetary shock, it is clear that its dependence on the covariance between these two types of shocks is ambiguous, since it depends on the relative magnitudes of the two variances. Using equation (16) it can be shown that

$$\text{sgn} \left[\frac{\partial \gamma^*}{\partial \text{ cov } (\mu, \chi + \epsilon - \delta)} \right] = \text{sgn} \, (\sigma_\mu^2 - \sigma_{\chi + \epsilon - \delta}^2) \tag{20}$$

Thus, if the variance of the real shock exceeds the variance of the effective monetary shock, a rise in the value of the covariance between these shocks results in a higher value of the optimal intervention index and raises the desirability of greater flexibility of exchange rates. This result may be interpreted by noting that when the covariance between the two types of shocks is zero while the variance of the real shocks is large relative to that of the effective monetary shock, the optimal intervention index is low since the optimal exchange rate regime is close to that of a fixed exchange rate. Under these circumstances, a rise in the covariance between the shocks implies that any given real shock is now being accompanied by a monetary shock. The induced rise in the importance of the monetary shock results in a higher value of the optimal intervention index and increases the desirability of greater flexibility of exchange rates. A result similar to that in (20) also applies to the analysis of the dependence of the optimal intervention index on the correlation between the two types of shocks.

2.4. Illustrative Computations

The analysis of the properties and the determinants of the optimal intervention index was based on a Taylor approximation of the loss function. As is obvious, the accuracy of this approximation depends negatively on the magnitudes of the shocks. While the qualitative conclusions do not depend on the accuracy of the approximation, the quantitative estimates might be somewhat affected. To gain insight into the precise quantitative magnitude of the optimal intervention index, we report in Table 2-1 illustrative computations for the case in which the shocks are independent of each other.[8] These computations are performed for alternative values of the propensity to save out of transitory income as well as for alternative assumptions concerning the magnitudes of the various shocks as measured by the standard deviations σ_μ and $\sigma_{\chi + \epsilon - \delta}$. These results illustrate the negative dependence of γ^* on σ_μ—the standard error of the real shock—as well as the positive dependence of γ^* on $\sigma_{\chi + \epsilon - \delta}$—the standard error of the effective monetary shock—and on αk—the propensity to save out of transitory income.

In computing the optimal intervention index in Table 2-1, it was assumed that the covariances among the various shocks were zero. In Table 2-2 we allow for various covariances among some of the shocks, and we report the resulting optimal intervention index. Consider first the comparison between panels A and B of Table 2-2. In panel A all three shocks are assumed to be of the magnitude of

TABLE 2-1. Optimal Managed Float for Alternative Values of Real and Effective Monetary Disturbances and Saving Propensities

	$\sigma_{\chi+\epsilon-\delta}$									
	$\alpha k = .5$					$\alpha k = 1$				
σ_μ	.01	.03	.05	.07	.09	.01	.03	.05	.07	.09
.01	0	.80	.92	.96	.98	.50	.90	.96	.98	.99
.03	0	0	.69	.80	.87	.10	.50	.74	.85	.90
.05	0	0	0	.33	.53	.04	.27	.50	.67	.77
.07	0	0	0	0	.25	.02	.16	.34	.50	.63
.09	0	0	0	0	0	.01	.10	.24	.38	.51

TABLE 2-2. Optimal Managed Float for Alternative Values of Disturbances and Their Covariances

	cov $(\chi, \epsilon - \delta)$									
	A					B				
	$\sigma_\mu=.03; \sigma_{\epsilon-\delta}=.03; \sigma_\chi=.03; \alpha k=1$					$\sigma_\mu=.09; \sigma_{\epsilon-\delta}=.09; \sigma_\chi=.09; \alpha k=1$				
cov (χ, μ)	−.6	−.3	0	.3	.6	−.6	−.3	0	.3	.6
−.6	.33	.66	.78	.83	.87	.35	.67	.78	.84	.87
−.3	.42	.61	.71	.77	.81	.42	.62	.71	.77	.81
0	.44	.58	.67	.72	.76	.45	.59	.67	.73	.76
.3	.46	.57	.64	.69	.73	.46	.57	.64	.69	.73
.6	.47	.56	.62	.67	.70	.47	.56	.62	.67	.71
	C					D				
	$\sigma_\mu=.03; \sigma_{\epsilon-\delta}=.03; \sigma_\chi=.09; \alpha k=1$					$\sigma_\mu=.09; \sigma_{\epsilon-\delta}=.03; \sigma_\chi=.03; \alpha k=1$				
−.6	1.0	1.0	1.0	1.0	1.0	.0	.0	.03	.10	.16
−.3	.98	.99	.99	.99	.99	.0	.06	.12	.17	.22
0	.87	.89	.91	.92	.93	.08	.14	.18	.22	.26
.3	.79	.83	.85	.87	.88	.15	.19	.23	.26	.29
.6	.75	.78	.81	.83	.85	.19	.23	.26	.29	.32
	E									
	$\sigma_\mu=.03; \sigma_{\epsilon-\delta}=.09; \sigma_\chi=.03; \alpha k=1$									
−.6	.94	.95	.96	.97	.97					
−.3	.90	.92	.93	.94	.95					
0	.87	.89	.91	.92	.93					
.3	.84	.87	.88	.90	.92					
.6	.82	.85	.87	.89	.90					

3%, while in panel B all three shocks are assumed to be of the magnitude of 9%. As is apparent, tripling the magnitudes of the shocks while maintaining their ratios constant does not seem to have a significant effect on the optimal intervention index. This illustrates the proposition that the optimal intervention index depends on the ratios of the various shocks rather than on their actual magnitude.

Panels C, D, and E of Table 2-2 illustrate the effects of changing the ratio between the various disturbances. When the magnitudes of the foreign price disturbance or of the domestic monetary disturbance are high relative to the other shocks (panels C and E, respectively) the optimal intervention index is close to unity, and thus the optimal regime is closer to that of a freely flexible rate. On the other hand, when the magnitude of the real shock is high relative to the other shocks (panel D), the optimal intervention index is low and the optimal exchange rate regime is closer to that of fixed exchange rates.

The various panels of Table 2-2 also illustrate the effects of the covariances among foreign and domestic disturbances. Generally speaking, a positive covariance between foreign price shocks and domestic monetary shocks tends to raise the optimal intervention index and thereby lower the desirability of fixed rates. Consistent with the results in equation (19), the effect of a positive covariance between foreign price shocks and domestic real shocks is ambiguous and depends on the sign of the difference between the variance of the real shock and the variance of the effective monetary shock. When this difference is negative, as in panels C and E, a rise in cov (χ, μ) is associated with a decline in γ^*. Likewise, when this difference is positive, as in panel D, a rise in cov (χ, μ) results in a higher value of the optimal intervention index.

2.5. Balance-of-Payments Variability

The logic underlying the optimal degree of exchange rate management is that the optimal response to monetary shocks differs from the optimal response to real shocks. Monetary shocks are best dealt with through exchange rate changes, while real shocks are best dealt with through trade flows. Using the terminology of Mundell (1973) and Laffer (1973), under fixed exchange rates the current account—which equals the balance of payments in the absence of capital flows—cushions the effects of real shocks. As a result, large variability of real shocks yields large variability of the balance of payments. In what follows we examine the variability of the balance of payments under the optimal degree of managed float.

We first note that the discrepancy between consumption and expected income, which is the key element in the objective function (12), can be written as

$$c_t - E(Y_t) = (c_t - Y_t) + [Y_t - E(Y_t)] \tag{21}$$

The first term on the right-hand side denotes the deficit in the trade balance (which equals the balance of payments in the absence of capital flows), and the second term denotes transitory income. Minimization of the loss function amounts to choosing the optimal intervention index so as to minimize the average squared deviation of transitory income from the balance-of-payments deficit. Transitory income is μy, and the balance-of-payments deficit is $(1 - \gamma)\alpha k \theta y$, which measures the fraction of money market disequilibrium that is not allowed to be cleared through exchange rate changes. It follows that the variance of the balance of payments, σ_B^2, can be expressed as the variance of $(1 - \gamma)\alpha k \theta y$. Substituting equation (16′) for the optimal value of γ (under the assumption that the shocks are independent of each other) yields equation (22) as the expression for the variance of the optimal balance of payments σ_{B*}^2:

$$\sigma_{B*}^2 = \frac{(\sigma_\mu^2)^2}{\sigma_\theta^2}\, y^2 \tag{22}$$

or, expressed in terms of the standard deviation,

$$\sigma_{B*} = \frac{\sigma_\mu^2}{\sigma_\theta^2}\, y\sigma_\theta \tag{22′}$$

Thus, given the variability of the global shock θ, a rise in the weight of real variability in total variability increases the variability of the optimal balance of payments. This relationship suggests that, ceteris paribus, countries for which real variability comprises a relatively large share of total variability should hold larger stocks of international reserves in order to be able to facilitate the relatively high variance in the optimal balance of payments.

2.6. The Capital Account

An important limitation of the analysis in the previous sections has been the assumed absence of an integrated world capital market that reflects itself in the capital account of the balance of payments. As a result, the previous analysis identified the trade balance with the balance of payments. While such a simplification might be appropriate for economies with severe limitations on access to world capital markets, it may not represent the conditions faced by developed countries. In what follows, we introduce some elements of the capital account.

It is assumed that the economy faces a perfect world capital market in which it can borrow and lend at a fixed rate of interest. Suppose that the desired ratio of money to securities depends on the rate of interest, and, due to the assumed fixity of the world rate of interest, this ratio is also fixed. Since the economy may be a net debtor or a net creditor in the world capital market, the value of its permanent output need not equal the value of its permanent income. The analysis simplifies considerably by assuming that the world rate of interest is deterministic, since in that case the stochastic characteristics of output are similar to those of income.[9] As a result, the previous analysis, which minimized the squared deviation of consumption from permanent output, remains relevant even though the concepts of income and output need not coincide. The only difference that has to be kept in mind is that when the economy has an access to world capital markets, the previous analysis applies to the current account rather than to the overall balance of payments.

The signal extraction problem is similar to that in Section 2.3. Individuals are assumed to observe the global shock $\theta \equiv \mu + \chi + \epsilon - \delta$, from which they attempt to estimate the real shock component μ and, thereby, the value of transitory income $\hat{\mu}y$ (where $\hat{\mu}$ denotes the estimated real shock given the realization of θ). The least-squares estimate of the real shock is:

$$E(\mu|\theta) = \frac{\text{cov}(\mu, \theta)}{\sigma_\theta^2}\theta \tag{23}$$

which, when multiplied by y, provides the estimated value of transitory income. In the previous analysis we argued that the optimal policy should aim at minimizing the squared discrepancy between transitory income and the current account (which was equal to the balance of payments). Suppose now that, given the rate of interest, portfolio holders wish to add to their holdings of securities a fraction β of their estimated transitory income. Under these circumstances, only a fraction $(1 - \beta)$ of the current account should be offset by monetary flows, and the analogous equation to (14′) becomes

$$c_t - E(Y_t) \cong \left[\mu - (1 - \gamma)\alpha k\theta - \beta\frac{\text{cov}(\mu, \theta)}{\sigma_\theta^2}\theta\right]y + \text{constant} \tag{24}$$

where the constant in (24) is independent of the current values of the shocks and of γ, and where the term $\{\beta[\text{cov}(\mu, \theta)]/\sigma_\theta^2\}y\theta$

represents the desired change in security holdings given the (conditional) estimate of transitory income. Minimizing the squared value of (24) with respect to γ yields the optimal intervention index:

$$\gamma^* = 1 - (1 - \beta) \frac{\text{cov}(\mu, \theta)}{\alpha k \sigma_\theta^2} \tag{25}$$

As is evident, when $\beta = 0$ the optimal intervention index in equation (25) is identical to that in equation (16). Further, as long as the covariance between μ and $\mu + \chi + \epsilon - \delta$ is positive, a rise in the fraction β raises the optimal intervention index. Thus

$$\frac{\partial \gamma^*}{\partial \beta} > 0 \tag{26}$$

The higher the share of transitory income that is absorbed by changes in the holdings of securities, the larger becomes the desirability of greater flexibility of exchange rates. The rationale for that result is quite clear, since a high value of β (which may be viewed as reflecting a high degree of capital mobility) implies that a larger fraction of the real shocks can be cushioned through the international capital market thereby reducing the need for international reserves flows.

Finally, when some of the cushioning is provided by the capital account, the standard deviation of the optimal balance of payments becomes

$$\sigma_{B^*} = (1 - \beta) \frac{\sigma_\mu^2}{\sigma_\theta^2} y \sigma_\theta \tag{27}$$

which is smaller than the magnitude corresponding to the case of no capital mobility. Again, in the special case for which $\beta = 0$, equation (27) becomes identical to equation (22').

2.7. The Supply of Output

Up to this point we have assumed that variations in the supply of output are determined exclusively by the characteristics of the stochastic shock μ. In what follows, we modify the specification of equation (1) and assume a supply function of the Lucas and Rapping (1969) variety. Accordingly, output is assumed to depend on the ratio of realized to expected prices. Thus,

$$Y_t = y \left(\frac{P_t}{E_{t-1}P_t}\right)^h \exp(\mu) \tag{28}$$

where $E_{t-1}P_t$ denotes the expected price level for period t based on the information available at period t - 1; h denotes the elasticity of the supply of output with respect to the ratio of realized to expected prices; and, as before, μ denotes a stochastic disturbance. The specification in equation (28) may be rationalized in terms of models that allow for a confusion between relative and absolute price changes as in Lucas (1973) as well as in terms of models that postulate short-term fixity of nominal wages, for example, Fischer (1977). Using the first two terms of a Taylor expansion, the supply of output in equation (28) can be approximated as

$$Y_t \cong y[1 + \mu + h(\chi + S_t)] \tag{29}$$

where $\hat{S}_t$ denotes the percentage change in the exchange rate, i.e., $\hat{S}_t \equiv \ln S_t - \ln S_{t-1}$.

Under full flexibility of exchange rates, changes in the rate ensure that the money market clears. Thus, analogously to equation (6),

$$kY_t \exp(\epsilon) = \frac{\bar{M}_t}{S_t p^* \exp(\chi)} \tag{30}$$

where, from equation (4'), $S_t p^* \exp(\chi)$ designates the price level. Differentiating equation (30) logarithmically and using equations (15) and (29) for $\bar{M}_t$ and Y_t, the change in the exchange rate may be expressed as

$$\theta \equiv \frac{\mu + h\chi + \chi + \epsilon - \delta}{1 + h} = -\hat{S}_t \tag{31}$$

The equality in equation (31) between the change in the exchange rate and the sum of the shocks θ is confined to the case in which the exchange rate is fully flexible. Under a managed float $-\hat{S}_t = \gamma\theta$, and the supply of output becomes

$$Y_t \cong y[1 + \mu + h(\chi - \gamma\theta)] \tag{29'}$$

Using the previous expressions for the values of consumption and output, the discrepancy between consumption and expected income may be approximated by

$$c_t - E(Y_t) \cong \{\mu + h\chi - [(1 - \gamma)\alpha k + \gamma h]\theta\}\, y \qquad (32)$$

In this formulation, $\mu + h\chi$ may be referred to as a real shock. It is composed of two terms: the first is the genuine output supply shock μ, while the second is induced by the effective foreign price shock χ that is translated into changes in output through the supply elasticity h. Thus, in addition to its direct monetary effect on the price level, χ contributes to output variations. It is noteworthy that in the special case for which h = 0, the value of θ reduces to the one obtained in the previous analysis, and the real shock reduces to μ.

The optimal intervention index, γ^*, is computed so as to minimize the discrepancy between $\mu + h\chi$ and $[(1 - \gamma)\alpha k + \gamma h]\theta$. It follows that

$$\gamma^* = 1 - \frac{b - h}{\alpha k - h} \qquad (33)$$

where b denotes the regression coefficient of the real shock $\mu + h\chi$ on θ, that is,

$$b = \frac{\mathrm{cov}\,(\mu + h\chi,\, \theta)}{\sigma_\theta^2}$$

As is evident, in the special case for which the value of the output elasticity h is zero, equation (33) coincides with (16).

As is revealed by equation (33), the magnitude of γ^* depends on the stochastic structure of the economy and on whether αk—the propensity to save out of transitory income—exceeds or falls short of h—the elasticity of output with respect to the ratio of realized to expected prices. As long as $\alpha k > h$, the relation between γ^* and the variances of μ and $\epsilon - \delta$ is similar to the one analyzed before: a rise in σ_μ^2 lowers γ^*, while a rise in $\sigma_{\epsilon-\delta}^2$ raises it. On the other hand, when $\alpha k < h$, these relations are reversed, and a rise in the variance of $\epsilon - \delta$ lowers it. The rationale for this reversal is that when the value of h is high (relative to αk), changes in the price level that result from monetary shocks induce relatively large changes in output. Thus, when $\alpha k < h$, monetary shocks act more like real shocks. Finally, since the foreign price shock exerts both real and monetary effects, the dependence of γ^* on σ_χ^2 depends on the variances of the real and the monetary shocks as well as on the sign of $\alpha k - h$:

$$\frac{\partial \gamma^*}{\partial \sigma_\chi^2} = (\alpha k - h)[(1 + h)\sigma_\mu^2 - h(1 + h)\sigma_{\epsilon-\delta}^2] \tag{34}$$

3. OPTIMAL MANAGED FLOAT WITH TRADABLE AND NONTRADABLE GOODS

The preceding analysis was confined to an economy whose production consists only of commodities that are traded internationally. This assumption implied that, except for random deviations from purchasing power parities, the domestic price level was tied to the foreign price. In this section we extend the analysis to an economy that produces both traded and nontraded goods. This production structure relaxes the constraint that was imposed by the small country assumption. Due to its relative size, the economy is a price taker in the world traded-goods market, but it is obviously large in the market for its own nontraded goods. Thus, the relative price of nontraded goods may not be viewed as given to the small economy but rather it is determined endogenously by the market-clearing conditions. In extending the analysis, we first specify the stochastic characteristics of the production structure and then proceed to determine the optimal intervention index.

3.1. Equilibrium in the Market for Nontraded Goods

Production of traded and nontraded goods is assumed to be carried along a production possibility frontier that is assumed to be concave to the origin. Denoting the nominal prices of traded and nontraded goods by P^T and P^N, respectively, we define the relative price of nontraded goods by $q \equiv P^N/P^T$. Production of traded goods X^T is assumed to depend negatively on the relative price according to

$$X^T = X^T(q) \exp(\mu) \tag{35}$$

where μ, which denotes the real shock, is defined in equation (1). Production of nontraded goods X^N is assumed to depend positively on the relative price according to

$$X^N = X^N(q) \exp(\omega + \mu) \qquad \omega \sim N\left(-\frac{\sigma_\omega^2}{2}, \sigma_\omega^2\right) \tag{36}$$

where ω denotes a stochastic shock that is *specific* to the production of nontraded goods. Thus, μ may be viewed as an aggregative real shock that moves the transformation schedule in a uniform way, while ω may be viewed as a sector-specific real shock.

On the demand side it is assumed that the demand for the two goods is homothetic and that the share of spending on nontraded goods depends negatively on the relative price. Measuring income as the value of production in terms of traded goods and denoting the share of spending on nontraded goods by ψ, we can describe the equilibrium in that market (when income equals spending as under flexible exchange rates) as follows:

$$\psi(q)[qX^N(q) \exp(\omega) + X^T(q)] \exp(\mu) = qX^N(q) \exp(\omega + \mu) \tag{37}$$

In equation (37), the left-hand side denotes the demand for nontraded goods, while the right-hand side describes the supply. Equation (37) implies that the equilibrium relationship between the relative price and the specific real shock may be expressed as

$$q = q_o \exp(-m\omega) \tag{38}$$

where q_o denotes the equilibrium relative price in the absence of shocks and where m denotes the elasticity of the relative price with respect to the relative price shock, that is,

$$m = \frac{1}{\eta/(1 - \psi) + 1 + \xi^N + \xi^T}$$

where η denotes the elasticity of the share of spending on nontraded goods (defined to be positive) and ξ^N and ξ^T denote, respectively, the elasticities of supply of nontraded and traded goods with respect to their relative price.

3.2. The Optimal Intervention Index

When the exchange rate is freely flexible, the demand for real balances equals the supply at each moment of time. Assuming, as before, that the demand is proportional to income and is subject to a stochastic shock ϵ, money market equilibrium obtains when

$$k[qX^N(q) \exp(\omega) + X^T(q)] \exp(\mu + \epsilon)$$

$$= \frac{\bar{M}_t}{S_{t-1}p^* \exp(\chi) \exp(-\theta)} \tag{39}$$

where $\bar{M}_t$ is defined in equation (15)[10] and where the denominator on the right-hand side denotes the price level P_t^T. The parameter θ denotes the percentage change in the exchange rate that is necessary to ensure stock equilibrium in the money market. By differentiating equation (39) and using (38) for the equilibrium relative price, we note that θ, the percentage change in the exchange rate that is required to clear the money market under a freely flexible exchange rate regime, is[11]

$$\theta = \mu + \chi + \epsilon - \delta + \omega\psi(1 - m) \tag{40}$$

As before, θ denotes the global shock. In this case, however, it also contains terms that reflect the effects of changes in the relative price that result from the various shocks. It is relevant to note that when the specific real shock (ω) is zero, the required change in the exchange rate is, as before, $\mu + \chi + \epsilon - \delta$.

The above analysis characterized the equilibrium under a freely flexible exchange rate regime. When the exchange rate is managed, only a fraction γ of the stock disequilibrium in the money market is allowed to be eliminated through changes in the exchange rate. In terms of equation (39), when the exchange rate is managed, the domestic currency price of traded goods becomes $P_t^T = S_{t-1}p^* \exp(\chi) \exp(-\gamma\theta)$, and the money market remains in stock disequilibrium. Under such circumstances, the value of income diverges from the value of spending by the resultant flow demand for real balances [as indicated by equation (13)]. Consequently, the demand for nontraded goods is not described any more by the left-hand side of equation (37)—which was only appropriate for a freely flexible exchange rate regime. Rather, the demand for nontraded goods is equal to

$$\psi(q)\left[\bar{Y}_t - \frac{\alpha(L_t - \bar{M}_t)}{P_t^T}\right]$$

where $\bar{Y}_t$ denotes the value of output in terms of traded goods. By substituting the previous expressions for $\bar{Y}_t$, L_t, $\bar{M}_t$, and P_t^T and equating the demand for nontraded goods to the supply, we obtain the equilibrium relative price of nontraded goods:

$$q = q_o \exp[(-m\omega) - (1 - \gamma)\theta z] \qquad (41)$$

where

$$z = \frac{m\alpha k}{\psi m\alpha k + (1 - \psi)} < 1$$

Equation (41) reveals that the equilibrium relative price is influenced by both the specific shock ω and the global shock θ. The sensitivity of the equilibrium price to the specific shock depends on the elasticities of demand and supply that determine the value of the parameter m. This sensitivity is independent of the exchange rate regime. On the other hand, the dependence of the equilibrium price on the global shock depends on the intervention index γ. The higher the value of γ, the smaller is the effect of the global shock. In the extreme case for which $\gamma = 1$, the exchange rate is freely flexible and the equilibrium relative price depends only on the specific real shock ω. In that case equation (41) coincides with (38).

To find the optimal intervention index, we turn to the specification of the objective function. We first note that the objective function (12) needs to be specified with greater care once there are traded and nontraded goods. In order to avoid an index number problem, we express the value of consumption and production in terms of the general price index, which is assumed to be a Cobb–Douglas function of the prices of the two goods. Thus, if we denote the values of spending and income (measured in terms of traded goods) by $\bar{c}_t$ and $\bar{Y}_t$, respectively, their corresponding values in terms of the general price index are $\bar{c}_t/q^\psi$ and $\bar{Y}_t/q^\psi$, and the loss function becomes

$$E\left[\frac{\bar{c}_t}{q^\psi} - E\left(\frac{\bar{Y}_t}{q^\psi}\right) \right]^2$$

Substituting the previous expressions for the real values of consumption and income and expanding in a Taylor series we approximate the discrepancy between real consumption and expected real income by

$$\left[\frac{\bar{c}_t}{q^\psi} - E\left(\frac{\bar{Y}_t}{q^\psi}\right) \right] \cong \{(\mu + \omega\psi) - \alpha k[(\mu + \omega\psi)$$

$$+ (\chi + \epsilon - \delta - \theta\gamma + \hat{q}\psi)]\}\frac{\bar{y}}{q_o^\psi} \qquad (42)$$

where $\bar{y}$ denotes the permanent value of income in terms of traded goods and $\hat{q}$ denotes the percentage change in the equilibrium relative price of nontraded goods. In equation (42), $\mu + \omega\psi$ and $\chi + \epsilon - \delta - \theta\gamma + \hat{q}\psi$ may be referred to, respectively, as the real shock and the monetary shock.[12] Using equation (40) as the definition of the global shock θ and substituting from equation (41) for the relative price change, the discrepancy between consumption and permanent income can be expressed as

$$\left[\frac{\bar{c}_t}{q^\psi} - \mathrm{E}\left(\frac{\bar{Y}_t}{q^\psi}\right)\right] \cong [\mu + \omega\psi - (1 - \gamma)(1 - \psi z)\alpha k\theta]\frac{\bar{y}}{q_o^\psi} \qquad (42')$$

Minimizing the loss function amounts to choosing γ so as to minimize the squared discrepancy between $\mu + \omega\psi$ and $(1 - \gamma)(1 - \psi z)\alpha k\theta$. Following the same logic of the signal extraction problem of the previous analysis, individuals who observe the global shock θ (through its effect on the exchange rate) attempt to estimate the real shock component, which in this case is composed of the ordinary real shock μ plus $\omega\psi$, which represents the effect of the specific real shock on the real value of aggregate output in terms of the general price level. Computing the least-squares estimate of relevant regression coefficient yields the optimal intervention index:

$$\gamma^* = 1 - \left(1 + \frac{\psi}{1 - \psi}\alpha km\right)\frac{\mathrm{cov}\,(\mu + \omega\psi, \theta)}{\alpha k\sigma_\theta^2} \qquad (43)$$

As in the earlier sections, the magnitude of the optimal intervention index depends on the structure of the economy. In general, the optimal value of γ^* declines when the variance of the real shock rises. In this context both σ_μ^2 and σ_ω^2 are viewed as real shocks. Also, consistent with the previous results, a higher value of αk is associated with a higher value of γ^*.

The new results of this section concern the relation between the optimal intervention index and the share of the nontraded goods sector (which may characterize the degree to which the economy is open), as well as between the optimal intervention index and the elasticities of demand and supplies of traded and nontraded goods. It can be shown that as long as the covariance between the real shock and the global shock is positive, a higher value of ψ is associated with a *lower* value of γ^*:

$$\frac{\partial \gamma^*}{\partial \psi} < 0 \tag{44}$$

Thus, a high share of spending on (and production of) nontraded goods tends to reduce the desirability of greater flexibility in exchange rates. This result seems to conflict with some of the well-known arguments on the relationship between the openness of the economy and the optimal exchange rate regime—for example, McKinnon (1963). Likewise, by noting that m—the elasticity of the relative price of nontraded goods—depends negatively on η, ξ^N, and ξ^T, it follows that

$$\frac{\partial \gamma^*}{\partial \eta} > 0 \qquad \frac{\partial \gamma^*}{\partial \xi^N} > 0 \qquad \frac{\partial \gamma^*}{\partial \xi^T} > 0 \tag{45}$$

Thus, the higher the degree of flexibility in the structure of an economy, the larger the need for increased flexibility of exchange rates.

These results can be rationalized by noting from equation (41) that, ceteris paribus, a given monetary shock induces a larger change in the relative price of nontraded goods the higher the relative share of that sector and the lower the elasticities of demand and supply. For a given exchange rate, the change in the relative price is reflected in a change in the nominal price of nontraded goods, which, in turn, affects the aggregate price level in proportion to the relative share ψ. The induced change in the price level mitigates the initial disequilibrium and thereby reduces the need for exchange rate flexibility. When all goods are internationally traded so that the internal price structure cannot be adjusted, the necessary changes in the price level can only be obtained through changes in the exchange rate. In contrast, the presence of nontraded goods provides for a flexible internal price structure capable of inducing some of the necessary adjustments in the price level. It follows that the need for exchange rate flexibility is reduced the higher the degree of price level flexibility, which, in turn, depends negatively on the elasticities of demand and supply and positively on the relative share of nontraded goods.[13]

This discussion of the relationship between internal price flexibility and the optimal exchange rate regime has implications for the choice between tariffs and quotas as alternative forms of commercial policy. In some respects the imposition of an import quota (in contrast with the imposition of an import tariff) may be viewed as transforming a traded commodity whose relative price is determined in world markets into a nontraded commodity whose price is determined in the domestic market. It follows that the desirability of exchange rate flexibility is lower for economies with import quotas than for economies with equivalent import tariffs, since the former enjoy a greater degree of internal price flexibility than the latter. Put differently, ceteris paribus, a rise in the degree of exchange rate flexibility provides an incentive to convert quota protection into tariff protection.

Inspection of equation (43) and its comparison with equation (16) reveals that even when the specific shocks are zero, the optimal intervention index for an economy with nontraded goods is smaller than the corresponding coefficient for an economy that produces only traded goods. Therefore, the mere existence of nontraded goods raises the desirability of greater fixity of exchange rates. The explanation is that even in the absence of specific supply shocks changes in demand will be absorbed in part by changes in the price of nontraded goods. The induced change in the price level will mitigate the initial disequilibrium and thereby reduce the need for exchange rate flexibility. Finally, it can be seen that in the special case for which $\psi = 0$, equation (43) coincides with (16).

4. CONCLUDING REMARKS

In this chapter we have analyzed aspects of the economics of managed float. We have shown that the choice of the optimal exchange rate regime depends on the nature and the origin of the stochastic shocks that affect the economy. Generally, the higher the variance of real shocks that affect the supply of goods, the larger becomes the desirability of fixity of exchange rates. The rationale for that implication is that the balance of payments serves as a shock absorber that mitigates the effect of real shocks on consumption. The importance of this factor diminishes the larger the economy's access to world capital markets. On the other hand, the desirability of exchange rate flexibility increases the larger the variances of the shocks to the demand for money, to the supply of money, to foreign prices, and to purchasing power parities. All of these shocks exert a similar effect, and their sum was referred to as the effective monetary shock. We have also shown that the desirability of exchange rate flexibility increases the larger the propensity to save out of transitory income. When we extended the analysis to an economy that produces traded and nontraded goods, it was shown that the desirability of exchange rate flexibility diminishes the higher the share of nontraded goods relative to traded goods and the lower the elasticities of demand and supply of the two goods.

As a general comment it should be noted that in this chapter monetary policy and foreign exchange intervention were treated as being close substitutes. In fact, as a first approximation, in our framework, these two policies are indistinguishable. It is believed that this feature of the model is much closer to reality than would be the other extreme in which monetary policy and foreign exchange policies are viewed as two independent policy instruments.

The special role of the exchange rate should also be noted. In our framework the exchange rate (and thereby the price level) is determined to a large extent by ·considerations of asset market equilibrium. This characteristic is in accord with the recent developments in the theory of exchange rate determination.

An important characteristic of the approach is that the choice of an exchange rate regime is an integral part of a general optimization process. It calls, therefore, for an explicit specification of the objective function as a prerequisite to the analysis. This feature is emphasized since such a specification of the objective function has been neglected by much of the writings in the area.

A limitation of the analysis is that, except for the discussion in Section 2.6, the model did not incorporate explicitly the implications of an integrated world capital market that reflects itself in the capital account of the balance of payments and prevents insulation from stochastic shocks to world interest rates. It should be emphasized, however, that the mere access to world capital markets and the ability to borrow are unlikely to alter the essentials of our analysis, since they are unlikely to eliminate the occasional need for using international reserves. Most countries cannot expect to be able to borrow any amount at a given rate of interest. Rather, the borrowing rate is likely to rise when the country's net debtor position rises. This rise reflects the deterioration of the quality of the loans, which is due to the deterioration of the economy's credit worthiness. As a result, countries will find it useful to hold and use international reserves in order to reduce the likelihood of facing a steeply rising cost of borrowing. In that sense, the holdings of international reserves may be viewed as a form of forward borrowing that is likely to continue even when capital markets are highly integrated.

It should be noted that the present specification of the nature of the shocks is somewhat biased in favor of government intervention since to some extent the shocks have been presumed to originate from the instability of the private sector rather than from the actions of government policies. Furthermore, the concept of the optimal intervention index that is implied by the optimal managed float was developed as a policy prescription for the monetary authorities. This was motivated by realism and could be rationalized in terms of the presumption that, compared with the private sector, the monetary authorities possess superior information concerning their own actions. In principle, however, much of the optimal mix could also be performed by the private sector.

Finally, it is relevant to note that as a practical matter it is unlikely that a policymaker will be capable of implementing policies with sufficient precision so as to distinguish between cases in which, for example, $\gamma^* = 0.2$ and those for which $\gamma^* = 0.3$. Thus, when the optimal intervention index turns out to be about 0.3 or less, it is likely that the practical policy would be that of a fixed exchange rate; likewise, when the optimal intervention index turns out to be about 0.7 or more, it is likely that the practical policy would be that of flexible exchange rates. In that sense, the choice of an exchange rate regime may be viewed as the outcome of the search for a second-best solution, and the analysis in this paper should be interpreted as providing a qualitative guide for such a choice.

NOTES

1. The analytical framework is adapted from Frenkel (1976, 1980). For an early analysis of the optimal exchange rate regime in terms of the structure of the economy see Stein (1963). Modigliani and Askari (1973) have emphasized that the optimal exchange rate regime depends on the nature of the shocks, and that the optimum may be an intermediate system between fixed and flexible rates, for example, sliding parities. A similar emphasis on the origin of shocks is found in Flood (1979), Buiter (1977), and Enders and Lapan (1979) who also emphasize the stochastic nature of the various shocks.

2. $E(Y_t) = y$, $E(Y_t^2) = y^2 \exp(\sigma_\mu^2)$ and $\text{var}(Y_t) = y^2[\exp(\sigma_\mu^2) - 1]$; thus $\sigma_\mu/E(Y) = y[\exp(\sigma_\mu^2) - 1]^{1/2}/y = [\exp(\sigma_\mu^2) - 1]^{1/2} \cong \sigma_\mu$ for small σ_μ. It should be clear that the choice of $-\sigma_\mu^2/2$ as the mean of the distribution of μ is made solely for analytical convenience. None of the results is affected by rescaling the distribution so as to move its mean to zero. To simplify notations we have suppressed in equation (1) the subscript t that is attached to the realization of the shock μ. We will follow the same convention in subsequent specifications of shocks.

3. In a recent analysis of the optimal foreign exchange intervention, Boyer (1978) extends and applies Poole's framework (1970) to the problem at hand. Boyer assumes that real income is fixed and that the objective function is to minimize the variability of prices.

4. It should be noted that the specification of the "active" monetary policy is somewhat arbitrary since, in principle, other rules are possible. For example, one could specify a rule by which the monetary authority sets $\bar{M}_t$ so as to ensure equality between the values of the mathematical expectations of the streams of consumption and income, i.e., $E(c_t) = E(Y_t)$. Further, equation (14) suggests that the monetary authority possesses two instruments for the attainment of its policy goals: a γ policy—the optimal intervention index—and an $\bar{M}_t$ policy—the optimal stock of money at the beginning of each period. The general optimization procedure would then solve simultaneously for the optimal *combination* of $\bar{M}_t$ and γ so as to minimize the loss function. In the following section we report and analyze the results of computer simulations that are based on determining $\bar{M}_t$ according to Fischer's specification of "active" monetary policy. We have experimented with the other two alternative monetary rules. It turns out that, at least for the range of parameters that have been assumed, the resulting optimal intervention index is almost invariant among the various monetary rules for the choice of $\bar{M}_t$, and thus, for ease of exposition, we report only simulations using Fischer's rule. It is also relevant to note that under rational expectations the precise specification of the $\bar{M}_t$ policy is completely irrelevant for the key results; for an explicit demonstration of this point see Aizenman (1980).

5. The expansion is around zero in order to ensure that the approximation would be around the expected value of the function; thus we approximate exp (μ) by $(1 + \mu)$, and thereby we have that $E[\exp(\mu)] = 1$. Likewise, as was shown in footnote 2, $\sigma^2_{\exp(\mu)} \cong \sigma^2_{1+\mu}$. It should be noted that, in computing the loss function, the second moment of the distributions is much more relevant than the mean, and thus the choice of the mean may be made on the basis of convenience.

6. Since the effective foreign price shock χ (which is composed of the shock to foreign prices, χ_1, and the shock to purchasing power parities, χ_2) exerts similar effects as shocks to the excess demand for money, $\epsilon - \delta$, their sum $(\chi + \epsilon - \delta)$ is referred to as the effective monetary shock. Since ϵ represents a change in taste, we assume that the objective function remains invariant with respect to this shock. If the objective function were to depend on ϵ, we would have had to assume that there are no shocks to money demand. In that case the effective monetary shock should be read as $\chi - \delta$ instead of $\chi + \epsilon - \delta$.

7. From (16) and (16'), when the effective monetary shock is zero then $\gamma^* = 1 - (1/\alpha k)$, where αk denotes the marginal propensity to save (hoard) out of transitory income. When $\alpha k = 1$, the loss function is minimized when $\gamma^* = 0$. For $\alpha k < 1$, γ^* is set equal to zero since we rule out negative values.

8. In these computations the optimal intervention index was obtained by using equation (14) in the loss function (12) and minimizing with respect to γ. We are indebted to Michael Bazdarich for helpful assistance in the computations.

9. Flood (1979) analyzes the implications of stochastic interest rates on the choice of the exchange rate system.

10. Since the economy produces both goods, permanent income in this case is defined as the value of production in terms of traded goods when the relative price is q_0.

11. In deriving equation (40) we have used the envelope theorem for movements along the transformation curve, according to which $\psi \xi_N - (1 - \psi)\xi_T = 0$.

12. As may be seen, the real shock does not include the effect of the relative price change, $\hat{q}$, since, due to the envelope theorem, the change in price

does not affect the value of production. The effect of $\hat{q}$ is classified as a monetary shock since it induces a change in the price level (equal to $\hat{q}\psi$).

13. The conventional result that γ^* depends positively on γ reflects the assumption that both the foreign currency price of traded goods *and* the domestic currency price of nontraded goods are given. In that case, changes in the exchange rate are the only source for changes in the price level and, as a result, the required change in the exchange rate is larger the smaller the share of traded goods (that is, the higher is γ). Our analysis shows that this dependence is reversed when the price of nontraded goods is flexible.

REFERENCES

Aizenman, Joshua. "Optimal Managed Flexibility of Exchange Rate." Unpublished manuscript, University of Chicago, 1980.

Boyer, Russell S. "Optimal Foreign Exchange Market Intervention." *Journal of Political Economy* 86 (December 1978).1045-55.

Buiter, Willem. "Optimal Foreign Exchange Market Intervention with Rational Expectations." Unpublished manuscript, London School of Economics, 1977.

Enders, Walter, and Harvey E. Lapan. "Stability, Random Disturbances and the Exchange Rate Regime." *Southern Economic Journal* 45 (July 1979): 49-70.

Fischer, Stanley. "Stability and Exchange Rate System in a Monetarist Model of the Balance of Payments." In *The Political Economy of Monetary Reform*, edited by R. Z. Aliber. Montclair, NJ: Allenheld, Osmun and Co., 1976, pp. 59-73.

———. "Long-Term Contracts, Rational Expectations and the Optimal Policy Rule." *Journal of Political Economy* 85 (February 1977).191-206.

Flood, Robert P. "Capital Mobility and the Choice of Exchange Rate System." *International Economic Review* 20 (June 1979):405-16.

Frenkel, Jacob A. "An Analysis of the Conditions Necessary for a Return to Greater Fixity of Exchange Rates." Report for the Department of State, U.S. Government, Contract No. 1722-520100, 1976.

——— "The Demand for International Reserves Under Pegged and Flexible Exchange Rate Regimes and Aspects of the Economics of Managed Float." In *The Economics of Flexible Exchange Rates*, edited by H. Frisch and G. Schwödianen. Supplement to *Kredit und Kapital*, Heft 6. Berlin:

Duncker and Humblot, 1980. Also reprinted in *The Functioning of Flexible Exchange Rates: Theory, Evidence and Policy Implications*, edited by D. Bigman and T. Taya. Cambridge: Ballinger, 1980.

Gray, JoAnna. "Wage Indexation: A Macroeconomic Approach." *Journal of Monetary Economics* 2 (April 1976):231–46.

Kenen, Peter B. "The Theory of Optimum Currency Areas: An Eclectic View." In *Monetary Problems of the International Economy*, edited by R. A. Mundell and A. K. Swoboda. Chicago: University of Chicago Press, 1969, pp. 41–60.

Laffer, Arthur B. "Two Arguments for Fixed Rates." In *The Economics of Common Currencies*, edited by H. G. Johnson and A. K. Swoboda. London: Allen & Unwin, 1973.

Lucas, Robert E., Jr. "Some International Evidence on Output-Inflation Trade-offs." *American Economic Review* 63 (June 1973).326–34.

Lucas, Robert E., Jr., and Leonard A. Rapping. "Real Wages, Employment and the Price Level." *Journal of Political Economy* 77 (September/October 1969):721–54.

McKinnon, Ronald I. "Optimal Currency Areas." *American Economic Review* 52 (September 1963):717–24.

Modigliani, Franco, and Hossein Askari. "The International Transfer of Capital and the Propagation of Domestic Disturbances under Alternative Payment Systems." *Banca Nazionale del Lavoro Quarterly Review* 26 (December 1973):295–310.

Mundell, Robert A. "A Theory of Optimum Currency Areas." *American Economic Review* 51 (November 1961):509–17. Reprinted as Chapter 12 in his *International Economics*, 1968.

——. "Uncommon Arguments for Common Currencies." In *The Economics of Common Currencies*, edited by H. G. Johnson and A. K. Swoboda. London: Allen & Unwin, 1973.

Poole, William. "Optimal Choice of Monetary Instruments in a Simple Stochastic Macro-Model." *Quarterly Journal of Economics* 83 (May 1970):197–216.

Stein, Jerome L. "The Optimum Foreign Exchange Market." *American Economic Review* 53 (June 1963): 384–402.

3

THE MISMANAGED FLOAT: OFFICIAL INTERVENTION BY THE INDUSTRIALIZED COUNTRIES

DEAN TAYLOR

INTRODUCTION

The world's major central banks have been unsuccessful in managing floating exchange rates. Official foreign exchange intervention has at times produced abrupt changes in exchange rates and has resulted in the loss of billions of dollars.

In an attempt to smooth foreign exchange markets, the central banks generally have resisted exchange rate changes. In some cases this policy of "leaning against the wind" has led to pegging an existing exchange rate when there is a change in its equilibrium value. After losing substantial international reserves, these central banks have given up their support operations, and the exchange rate has dropped precipitously. They then depressed the price of their currency further by buying back reserves.

When judged by Friedman's (1953) profit criterion, the central banks have mismanaged the managed float. The combined losses of the central banks of the nine countries in this study—France,

Work on this study began while I was a National Fellow at the Hoover Institution. Partial support for this research was provided by the National Science Foundation (grant number DAR 7826307). I am indebted to numerous individuals for help in trying to uncover the various methods of concealed intervention.

Canada, Germany, Italy, Japan, Spain, Switzerland, United Kingdom, and the United States—is approximately $12 billion for the 1970s.

The first part of this chapter assesses the performance of the central banks. The second part describes the methods of measuring intervention for the individual countries.

1. CENTRAL BANK PERFORMANCE

Leaning Against the Wind

Generally, countries have followed a policy of "leaning against the wind" by resisting exchange rate changes. When exchange rates have appreciated, countries have accumulated dollars to retard appreciation; when their currencies have depreciated, countries have sold dollars to prop up their home currency. In some cases, resisting exchange rate changes has led to pegging the existing exchange rate when there is a change in its equilibrium level.[1] The authorities can hold out temporarily, but must eventually allow exchange rates to adjust and lose substantial sums in the process.

Figure 3-1 shows the dollar price of each country's currency[2] and the cumulative amount of dollars each central bank purchased on the foreign exchange market.[3] Since most of the countries resist exchange rate changes, the exchange rate and cumulative intervention[4] patterns are similar for each country. In other words, when the price of the currency tends to decline, the central bank buys the domestic currency with dollars; when the price tends to rise, it sells its own currency and accumulates dollars.

Three countries produced abrupt changes in their exchange rates by resisting exchange rate movements and then reversing their actions. Italy, Spain, and the United Kingdom sold substantial amounts of dollars to maintain an existing rate but eventually had to give up the support operations. They then reversed their policy and bought back reserves, depressing the price of their currency. From the time Italy floated the lira in February 1973 until January 1976, the authorities expended $13 billion in reserves to buy lira to support its price. When support of the lira was suspended in January 1976, the exchange rate dropped by about 20%. In the next four years the Italian authorities increased reserves by $25 billion, buying the dollars back at a much higher lira price.

From January 1974, when Spain allowed the peseta to float, until July 1977 the Spanish authorities used $5 billion in reserves to buy pesetas. Despite these support purchases, the price of the peseta began to gradually decline. Thus the authorities only delayed the fall in the exchange rate. In July 1977 they reversed their policy and the exchange rate dropped. During the following years the Spanish authorities increased reserves by $10 billion, buying dollars back at substantially higher prices.

From June 1973 through May 1975, the United Kingdom authorities expended $7.5 billion in reserves to buy pounds in support operations. The pound then began to drop, despite additional support purchases. By October 1976, when the pound had reached its lowest point, the authorities had spent an additional $7.5 billion in reserves. In the following year the authorities reversed their policy, increased reserves by $13 billion, and did not allow the exchange rate to appreciate.

The remaining countries in this study resisted exchange rate adjustments but allowed more movement when there was pressure in either direction. Thus, their cumulative intervention patterns are more similar to their exchange rate movements.

Open and Hidden Intervention

From the era of the pegged exchange rates, the central banks have inherited a tradition of concealing their foreign exchange operations. Under this system, a decline in reserves could produce a run on the currency, since a devaluation would be likely. Even with floating rates, the central banks continue to conceal intervention and have employed additional means to disguise it. Generally, only vague descriptions of the countries' intervention activities are later released. Without concealment, a country's international reserves reflect its intervention. To support its currency price, the central bank buys its currency with reserves; to prevent currency appreciation, it buys reserves with its own currency. In practice, however, intervention is frequently hidden so that it does not show up in the official international reserve figures.

In France, Italy, Spain, and the United Kingdom, nationalized industries effectively intervene by borrowing foreign currency and using it to buy their own currency on the foreign exchange market. In Italy and the United Kingdom, the treasury insures the nationalized industries against any foreign exchange loss, but in France and apparently in Spain the industries must assume the exchange risk. Japan, and to some extent France, intervene with "hidden reserves," which are dollar deposits held at commercial banks. These are not reported as part of the official reserves. In Switzerland, and more recently in Germany, the central banks swap foreign exchange with

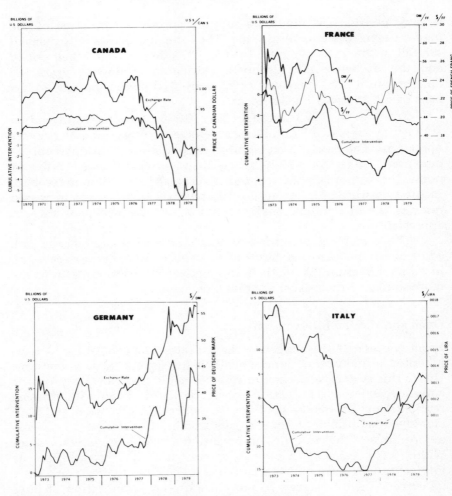

FIGURE 3-1. Exchange rates and intervention.

the commercial banks. Since the official reserves include these swaps, they do not accurately reflect intervention. In Italy and France commercial banks effectively intervene, since the government manages their foreign exchange position. Moreover, many central banks borrow foreign currency but report only their gross reserves rather than their net reserves.[5] A detailed description of how intervention is measured to overcome these difficulties is given in the second part of this chapter.

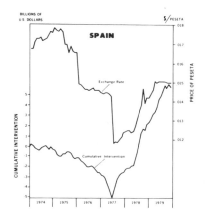

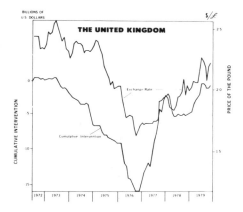

FIGURE 3-1. Exchange rates and intervention *(continued)*.

Friedman's Profit Criterion and Central Bank Losses

Milton Friedman (1953) argues for a simple criterion of successful intervention: whether the central bank makes a profit or loss. Friedman's basis for using profitability to monitor the central bank's performance is that if the central bank buys and bids up the currency price when it is low and sells and bids down the price when it is high, it will both stabilize the price and make a profit.[6]

The Federal Reserve is the only central bank that reports its profits and losses from foreign exchange transactions rather than burying them in the interest earnings on their assets. In congressional testimony, Federal Reserve Board Governor Henry Wallich (1978) used the profit criterion to argue that Federal Reserve intervention was successful:

> One test, which has sometimes been proposed, of whether actual intervention operations serve the purpose of countering disorderly markets by purchase of foreign exchange when the price drops sharply and sales when it rises sharply, is the degree to which intervention is profitable. With the exception of the unwinding of the pre-August 1971 support operations under fixed exchange rates, the recent record of Federal Reserve intervention in this regard is quite positive. In each of the 5 years of intervention operations under the regime of managed floating, the Federal Reserve has realized modest profits on its current operations in foreign currencies, totaling almost $25 million over the period. While profits are not a necessary criterion of successful intervention and certainly not its objective, they nevertheless suggest that Federal Reserve intervention has tended to smooth exchange-rate fluctuations.

Unfortunately, the Federal Reserve figures that Wallich cites exclude the major part of official foreign exchange transactions by the United States between 1973 and 1978, which resulted in a loss of $1.8 billion. Federal Reserve reporting makes the misleading distinction between profits and losses on "current" operations and on liquidations of foreign currency debts outstanding as of August 15, 1971. When exchange rates were first allowed to float in early 1973, the Federal Reserve and the Treasury had $3.1 billion in foreign currency debts, which had been incurred before the first dollar devaluation in 1971. The Treasury had foreign currency bonds and the Federal Reserve owed on its swap lines with other central banks. Some of the debts were paid as scheduled in 1973 and early 1974, but both the Federal Reserve and the Treasury refinanced their obligations with the Swiss National Bank and the Bank for International Settlements by borrowing Swiss francs. They continued to reborrow in the following years. Between 1973 and 1978, the majority of U.S. foreign exchange transactions were connected with these pre-August 1971 foreign currency debts. These debts were finally paid between 1977 and 1979, by which time the Swiss franc had nearly doubled in price. The 16 outstanding Treasury bond issues were refinanced an average of four times. Since the Swiss franc almost continuously appreciated against the dollar between

1973 and 1979, the Treasury lost almost each time that a bond was refinanced. Of 65 transactions to refinance the Swiss franc bonds, 60 resulted in losses as shown in Fig. 3-2. [In the figure, the bars represent the profit or loss that resulted from each decision to refinance rather than repay a Swiss franc bond. The upper half of the chart shows the cumulative total of these losses and the Swiss franc/dollar exchange rate. Losses are shown at the time when the decision to refinance was made; therefore, there is no loss shown at the time of the final payments. The Treasury lost $1,182 million from the decisions to refinance rather than pay the debt when it was due in 1973 and early 1974.] Like the Treasury, the Federal Reserve continually refinanced its Swiss franc debt and made few payments until 1977, with the final payment not taking place until April 1979, as shown in Fig. 3.3. [On the graph, each bar represents a repayment on the swap debt. The swaps normally matured in three months. However, they were repeatedly renewed and only one payment made during the first three years. The white section of the bar represents the original dollar value of the swap. The black section of the bar represents the additional dollar cost of purchasing the Swiss francs to repay the swap. The cost increased the longer the repayment was delayed. By not repaying the swaps in the first year of floating exchange rates, the Federal Reserve lost an additional $607 million.]

Most of the losses from the liquidation of the pre-August 1971 debt resulted from transaction decisions during the managed float, not decisions made when the exchange rates were pegged. The Federal Reserve accounting treats the additional $1.8 billion losses from these transactions as if they were inevitable and not determined by Federal Reserve and Treasury decisions after the dollar was allowed to float in 1973. The Swiss franc/dollar rate would have been more stable if the United States had purchased the Swiss francs in 1973 or early 1974 and bid up the price when it was relatively low.

Although the other central banks do not segregate intervention profits and losses from their other profits and losses, figures can be calculated from information they do publish. The gains and losses from intervention of the nine countries in this study, from the time they floated their exchange rate in the early 1970s until 1980, are shown in Table 3-1. These figures include only the gains or losses from foreign exchange transactions. Losses incurred from the valuation changes in the assets held prior to floating are excluded.

In the calculations, dollars are assumed to be purchased or sold at a constant rate during a month. The profit equals the sum of dollars purchased less the dollar value at the end of the period of

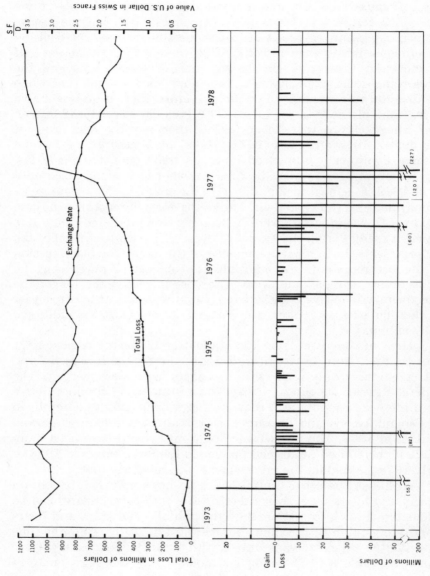

FIGURE 3-2. Losses from U.S. Treasury refinancing Swiss franc debt.

56

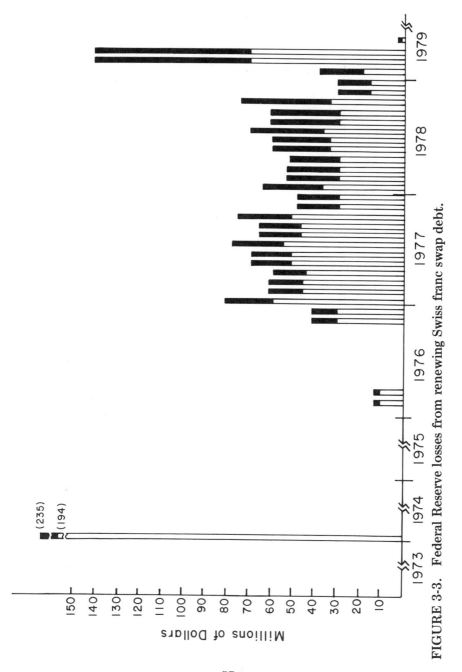

FIGURE 3-3. Federal Reserve losses from renewing Swiss franc swap debt.

57

TABLE 3-1. Gains and Losses from Official Intervention in the Foreign Exchange Market

Country	Period beginning	Period ending	Gain or loss (−) without interest in millions of $	Gain or loss (−) with interest in millions of $
Canada	June 1970	Dec. 1979	−82	−69
France*	Apr. 1973	Dec. 1979	1035 (−2003)	1224
Germany	Apr. 1973	Dec. 1979	−3423	−3394
Italy	Mar. 1973	Dec. 1979	−3724	−2510
Japan	Mar. 1973	Dec. 1979	−331	375
Spain	Feb. 1974	Dec. 1979	−1367	−1537
Switzer-land	Feb. 1973	Dec. 1979	−1209	−788
United Kingdom	Feb. 1972	Dec. 1979	−2147	−3418
United States†	Apr. 1973	Jan. 1980	−2351	−2351

*For France, the loss is calculated assuming intervention is done in dollars and in marks. A profit is shown for for the dollar figure and a dollar equivalent loss, in parentheses, for the mark figure.

†The United States issued dollar bonds with a Swiss franc exchange rate guarantee. This was equivalent to issuing Swiss franc bonds at U.S. interest rates. Consequently, there is no difference in the calculated loss.

the domestic currency sold.[7] Losses are substantial for Germany, Italy, Spain, Switzerland, the United Kingdom, and the United States.[8]

These calculations do not take into account interest differentials on assets denominated in different currencies. As pointed out by Wallich (1980) this could lead to a misleading result:

> Typically, the stronger a currency, the lower its interest rates and vice versa. Hence, a central bank that has losses on a weak currency that it holds is likely to find itself compensated, in some degree, by interest earnings that are higher than would be the earnings on alternative assets in its own currency. Precise accounting would be difficult. But totally to ignore the interest-rate aspect, as seems to be the predominant practice among central banks nowadays, conveys a false impression of gains and losses and of the risks encountered in holding foreign currencies. If interest-rate differentials exactly match exchange-rate movements, of course, there would be no net gains and losses at all.

Wallich is discussing appreciation or depreciation of total dollars held. For example, Germany has reported losses on its external assets of $30.6 billion marks between April 1973 and December 1979. Most of this total, however, is due to the decline in the 1970s of the value of the dollars it held before the mark was allowed to float. This chapter, however, is concerned only with the change in value of dollars accumulated and decumulated from intervention. Only a fraction of the Bundesbank's recorded $30.6 billion loss is due to intervention.

The second column of Table 3-1 shows the losses and profits when the difference in interest on the different assets accumulated and decumulated is included. Assuming that intervention does not affect the money supply, buying and holding dollars (usually U.S. Treasury bills) will mean holding less in domestic assets. Without any borrowing, the difference in interest earned each month is the rate on U.S. Treasury bills times the cumulative dollars purchased (and then converted to the domestic currency), less the product of domestic interest rate and the total amount of domestic currency sold. The sum of the difference for each month, compounded by the domestic interest rate to the end of period, gives the total additional interest earned on the accumulated dollar balance less the interest lost on the domestic assets sold. Canada, France, Italy, Spain, and the United Kingdom, however, have borrowed substantially on the international capital markets to finance their intervention. When borrowing occurs, the difference in interest earned is the product of the dollars accumulated times the U.S. Treasury bill rate, less the interest paid on the cumulative dollars borrowed, less the interest that could have been earned on the domestic currency sold.

The problem when interest is included in the calculations is in determining which interest rates should be used. In this chapter, the U.S. Treasury bill rate is used for the interest rate on accumulated dollar holdings. For the return on domestic assets, the shortest-term government security rate, published in *International Financial Statistics*, is used. The Treasury bill rate is used for Canada and the United Kingdom, the medium-term government bond rate is used for Italy, and the government bond rate is used for the remaining countries, except Spain, where only the discount rate is available. The limited information available on the interest rates on the borrowings indicate that the rate paid is closest to the Baa corporate bond rate in the United States and is therefore used in the calculations.

These calculations are, by necessity, approximations. Some borrowing of foreign exchange occurred in marks and Swiss francs.[9] If the dollar appreciation of this borrowing were accounted for, it would increase the losses of the five countries that borrowed in the international markets. On the other hand, for the countries that have accumulated dollars, Germany, Japan, and Switzerland, the opportunity cost of the domestic interest rate may be too high and the loss overestimated. The combined loss for the nine countries is $12.5 billion. These results are tentative, since information on interest rates is incomplete; however, even with interest rate data more favorable to the central banks, the loss would exceed $10 billion.

The French Paradox

France's intervention appears to have been profitable in dollars but has destabilized the franc/mark exchange rate. The profitability criterion becomes ambiguous with three major currencies: In terms of the franc, the dollar may be high when the mark is low, and the dollar low when the mark is high. When intervention is in dollars but the objective is to stabilize the mark, the profitability rule is reversed: Profiting in dollars destabilizes the mark.

Suppose the mark price of the franc is high during the first period and low during the second period, and the dollar price of the franc is low during the first period and high during the second. If the authorities buy francs with dollars during the first period and sell francs and acquire dollars during the second period, they will destabilize the franc/mark exchange rate as well as make a profit on their dollar/franc transactions. In terms of the mark, they have bought high and sold low, which is destabilizing; in terms of the dollar, they have bought low and sold high, which is profitable.

The French authorities' objective has apparently been to stabilize the franc relative to the mark and other European currencies in the snake. Through the snake, France was linked to the mark three separate times during the 1970s. In March 1973, the French franc floated jointly with the other European currencies. However, France left the snake to float independently in January 1974, rejoined in July 1975, left again in March 1976, and rejoined again in March 1979.

Although France never stated its objective when floating separately from the snake, its repeated membership in the snake indicates a desire to stabilize the franc relative to these currencies. The trade volume France has with the European countries provides an incentive to stabilize exchange rates with them. The capital account, however, provides motivation to stabilize the dollar/franc rate, since most capital account transactions are settled in dollars.

When France was in the snake, the authorities were clearly trying to stabilize the franc relative to the mark. During the periods when France was out of the snake, the behavior of the French authorities indicates that they were again trying to stabilize relative to the mark. The pattern of intervention in Fig. 3-1 suggests that the French monetary authorities have given priority to franc/mark stabilization over franc/dollar stabilization. One dramatic episode with heavy intervention, when the franc/dollar and franc/mark rates were moving in opposite directions, occurred between September 1977 and March 1978, when there was concern that the Leftist Coalition would win the legislative election. During this time the franc was depreciating relative to the mark and appreciating relative to the dollar. The authorities intervened by purchasing francs, thus resisting mark/franc movement but reinforcing the dollar/franc movement. The authorities were clearly responding more to the mark than to the dollar.

Moreover, if France is following a policy of "leaning against the wind" and resisting changes in the franc/mark rate, there should be a positive relationship between exchange rate changes and the intervention figures. For the period between April 1976 and February 1979, when France was out of the snake, the correlation between French intervention and the change in the franc/mark rate over the month is .5, whereas the correlation between French intervention and the franc/dollar rate over the month is -.1 when it would be positive if they were resisting movements in the dollar.

Although France appears to pursue stabilizing the franc/mark rate, the intervention currency is probably the dollar. The funds that the public firms borrow and convert into francs in order to affect the exchange rate are primarily dollars. Historically, central banks have usually held their currency reserves in dollars, and most monetary authorities still use the dollar for intervention.

The Bank of France does not give a breakdown of foreign exchange by currency and reports the data only in French francs. Germany, on the other hand, generally holds at least 95% of its foreign currency reserves in dollars.[10] Countries in the snake apparently use the dollar extensively for intervention. It is therefore most likely that France primarily holds and intervenes with dollars.

The French authorities can use dollars as readily as marks to influence the mark/franc (DM/FF) rate. Assuming that the mark/dollar relationship (DM/$) will be unaffected by France buying and selling francs in the foreign exchange market, the French authorities can decrease the DM/FF rate by buying dollars with French francs, thereby decreasing the dollar/franc ($/FF) rate. Since triangular currency arbitrage will maintain the relationship (DM/$)($/DD) = DM/FF, the dollar/franc rate will decrease proportionately to the mark/dollar rate. Thus, from the viewpoint of stabilization it makes little difference whether the authorities intervene in dollars or marks.

In terms of profitability, however, the currency used to intervene can make a significant difference. In this case, France shows a profit of $1.0 billion if intervention occurred in dollars during the 1970s, whereas it shows a loss of the equivalent of $2.0 billion if it intervened in marks during the same period.

In order to use the profitability criterion to determine whether intervention stabilized the exchange rate, the profit should be calculated assuming that the country intervenes in the currency that it seeks to stabilize. In this case, the profit or loss should be calculated assuming the authorities are intervening with marks, regardless of what currency they actually use for intervention. If, on the average, the francs are sold when their price in marks is high and are bought when their price in marks is low, the calculations would show a profit, and intervention would have a stabilizing effect. However, calculations assuming intervention with marks show a significant loss, of the equivalent of $2.0 billion. Hence, France failed in its effort to stabilize the franc with the mark even though they inadvertently profited in dollars, the intervention currency.

Concluding Remarks

None of the central banks in this study have successfully stabilized exchange markets. Several have incurred substantial losses and have adversely affected exchange rate movements. Some of the central banks have resisted gradual exchange rate movements until pressure on the currency became substantial, then dropped their support, inducing a large movement in the exchange rate. By "leaning against the wind," the central banks are retarding fundamental adjustments and are losing substantial sums in the process.

2. MEASURING INTERVENTION

Canada

Canada reports its reserve figures in U.S. dollars. The Canadian Department of Finance issues monthly reserve data in press releases and daily reserve data with an 18-month delay. This study uses daily data for the years between 1970 and 1976 and monthly data from 1977 onward, with the assumption that dollars are bought or sold at a constant rate during the month.[11]

This chapter adjusts for the following factors that affect the level of reserves but do not reflect intervention:

1. Canada had outstanding forward contracts to purchase 360.3 million U.S. dollars, which were acquired while pegging the Canadian dollar before it was allowed to float upward at the beginning of 1970. This study assumes that these forward contracts matured at a constant rate through the remainder of that year.

2. Canada received SDR allocations for January 1970 of $117.7 million, for January 1971 of $116.6 million, and for January 1979 of $183.9 million.

3. Canada used reserves for repayment of a $68-million debt to the Italian Exchange Office in June 1970 and for repayment of a $94-million Deutsche-mark-denominated loan in June 1973.

4. Canada revalued gold and SDR-denominated assets in May 1972, when gold was revalued to $38.00 per fine ounce and by $184.9 million when gold was revalued to $42.22 per fine ounce.

5. Beginning on July 31, 1974, Canada valued SDR-denominated assets according to the IMF method, using market values of a composite basket of currencies. This study adjusts the data for valuation changes in the dollar value of the SDR-denominated assets.[12]

6. Canada sold gold in March and August of 1976 and transferred gold to the mint in December of 1977 and 1978.

7. Beginning in 1978, Canada arranged credit facilities both with Canadian chartered banks and with U.S. and other foreign banks.[13] The Department of Finance's monthly press releases report the various drawings and re-payments.

8. Beginning in May 1978, Canada issued bonds in the U.S., German, Japan-ese, and Swiss capital markets.

France[14]

Changes in the net foreign assets of the Bank of France only partially reflect official intervention activities. The Exchange Stabilization Fund (FSC from its French initials), rather than the Bank of France, makes the official transactions in the foreign exchange market; therefore, these transactions are not always reflected on the Bank of France balance sheet. Moreover, the government has a policy of having public and semipublic firms borrow foreign funds and then convert them on the foreign exchange market to affect the exchange rate. Finally, the government directs the net foreign exchange position of the commercial banks, which are primarily owned by the government.

The Bank of France is required to publish a weekly financial statement. Since weekly statements would prevent it from concealing intervention, the FSC was established. When the FSC intervenes in the market by using advances from the Bank of France or by selling the Bank of France foreign exchange to obtain francs, its operations show up one-for-one on the Bank of France balance sheet, under "Liquid Reserve Assets" or "Advances to the FSC." However, no transactions with the Bank of France occur when the FSC uses its own resources or its funds from the European Monetary Corporation fund to intervene. Data on the sources of the monetary base reported in the National Credit Council's annual report reflect all FSC inter-vention;[15] thus these data are used in this study.

France borrowed from and then repaid its loans to the European Monetary System in September 1973 and in the first quarter of 1976. Since the FSC has limited resources, the major discrepancies between intervention measured as changes in the monetary base due to changes in reserves and intervention as reflected on the Bank of France balance sheet are due to this borrowing.

Since mid-1974 nationalized industries have effectively intervened by borrowing foreign exchange to purchase francs.[16] This policy adds the financial burden of exchange rate risk, since the majority of these nationalized firms realize their incomes in domestic currency. Presumably the treasury encourages nationalized industries to borrow foreign currency and assume the additional risk. However, the treasury does not guarantee the firms against exchange rate risk.[17]

The exchange rate can be influenced either by immediately converting the foreign exchange funds borrowed or through delaying their conversion up to-one month after receiving the funds.[18] Apparently, the Bank of France or the Ministry of France suggests the date these firms convert the proceeds of their borrowings.[19]

Data for borrowing figures are obtained by computing the net inflow of capital (borrowing minus repayments). The data comes from *Borrowing in International Capital Markets: Foreign and International Bond Issues, Publicized Euro-currency Credits* (World Bank). Each borrowing's repayment schedule is also available. Generally, a fixed fraction of the total amount borrowed is repaid each year starting on a specified date and continues until the obligation is fulfilled. These repayments are deducted from the gross borrowing figures to obtain the net capital flow figure for each month.

In this study, the date on which the foreign exchange is assumed to be converted to francs varies according to whether the franc was under pressure. During the periods of relative stability of the franc, the conversion is 15 days after the offering date, which is assumed to be the date the funds are received. During periods when the government is known to have resisted downward pressure on the franc,[20] the entire proceeds from the borrowings of that month are converted immediately. The four major commercial banks, which carry the bulk of foreign exchange transactions, are government-owned and appear to reinforce the FSC actions rather than speculate for a profit. Data used to measure the changes in the net foreign position of the commercial bank are reported quarterly in the Ministry of Finance's publications, *Statistiques et Études Financières: Balance des Paiments entre La France et l'Exterieur.*

Germany

Until April 1979, Germany was the only country whose international reserve data reflected official intervention in the foreign exchange market. Germany has never had official compensatory borrowing disguised as private capital flows or any other form of hidden intervention.[21] From April 1979 on, however, reserve changes include foreign exchange swaps that occur between the Bundesbank and the domestic banks; consequently, reserve changes are a poor measure of intervention. These swap transactions affect the domestic banking's liquidity system but have no direct effect on the foreign exchange market.[22] The Bundesbank buys dollars with marks from domestic banks. To reverse the swap at the agreed-upon future date, the Bundesbank sells the dollars back to the banks for the same number of marks. In other words, when the Bundesbank buys the dollars from the domestic banks, there is a forward commitment to sell the dollars back to the domestic banks; this forward commitment is, however, not entered onto the Bundesbank's balance sheet. Hence, even though no intervention takes place, net foreign exchange reserves of the Bundesbank increase. The German monetary base increases at the same time, since the mark reserve holdings of the domestic banks have increased.[23]

The Bundesbank intervenes both to influence the dollar/mark rate and to maintain exchange values within the European joint float. The intervention against the dollar appears to be the most important.[24] Although the intervention within the snake may account for some short-term movements in reserves, the Bundesbank has generally resisted changes in the dollar/mark rate. Hence, large changes in reserves are related to movements in the mark's dollar value, as can be seen in Fig. 3-1 in the first section of this chapter.

Since the Bank Agreement of 1972 restricts Germany's right to hold European currencies, most of Germany's foreign exchange is held in dollars.[25] When it becomes necessary to intervene within the snake using a European currency other than the German mark, short-term bilateral loans, which are normally settled at the end of the month following intervention, are used.[26] For example, in order to maintain the European system of narrow exchange rate margins, when the Dutch guilder is weak relative to the German mark, the German central bank would purchase guilders with marks and the Dutch central bank would sell marks (buy guilders). The equivalent operation is achieved by the Dutch selling dollars and the Germans buying dollars, without any consequent pressure on the dollar. Most intervention is apparently in dollars; however, the intervention in dollars is not necessarily directed toward the dollar. The conclusion that the dollar is the most important consideration comes primarily from Bundesbank reaction to movements of the dollar.

In this chapter, changes in the Bundesbank's net external assets are used as the measure of intervention. The Bundesbank uses this same measure in its *Monthly Report* when discussing the foreign exchange market and its own intervention activities. The net external position of the Bundesbank consists of net monetary reserves plus net external loans and other external assets. Net monetary reserves consist of gold, the reserve position at the IMF and SDRs, claims on the European Monetary Cooperation Fund, foreign currency balances less liabilities arising from foreign business, and the counterpart to the revaluation of gold contributed to the European Monetary Cooperation Fund. This study excludes changes due to valuation adjustments, SDR allocations, and foreign exchange swaps with domestic banks.

Information on the foreign exchange swaps between the Bundesbank and the domestic banks is not always reported on a monthly basis, and reported numbers are rounded. Some of the monthly reports include graphs comparing the changes in the net external assets of the Bundesbank that exclude the swap with those that include the swaps. This study estimates monthly intervention figures using these graphs and statements in the text of the *Monthly Report* of the Deutsche Bundesbank. The profit and loss calculations are not very sensitive to errors in estimating the swap figures since the swaps were made only during the last eight months of 1979. Also, any error is offset when the swap is reversed.

For Germany, using data that are reported four times rather than once each month makes some difference in the overall loss figures. Germany reports international reserve assets on the 7th, 15th, 23rd, and last day of each month, but it reports international liabilities less frequently. Using this more frequently reported gross monetary reserve data from March 1973 until the end of November 1978 gives a loss of $250 million less than when the monthly gross monetary reserve data are used. These calculations cannot be extended through 1979, since no information on the swaps is reported on less than a monthly basis.

Italy

Italy intervenes in the foreign exchange market not only by using official reserves but through compensatory borrowing of foreign currency by state-controlled enterprises. Public corporations are instructed to borrow foreign currency abroad on behalf of the Bank of Italy and then sell the foreign exchange for lire, which is used to meet their financing needs. These enterprises then receive full forward coverage for their debt service payment and thus are not subject to an exchange risk.[27]

Italy also intervenes by managing the net foreign position of commercial banks. The government owns the principal banks[28] and the Italian Exchange Office controls the extent to which an Italian bank may take a net debtor or creditor position in foreign exchange.[29] The monetary authorities do not intervene in the forward exchange market.[30]

Monthly data on official reserves as well as compensatory borrowing and changes in the net foreign position of banks are available in Banca d'Italia, *Bollettino*, and *Supplemento al Bollettino*.[31] Changes in the net foreign position of the commercial banks are included below the line in the balance of payments figures. Compensatory capital flows are reported as a separate item.[32]

Italy values foreign currency at the central rate of 581.5 lire to the dollar through November 1973, but since December 1973 it values its foreign currency at market rates on the last working day of each month.[33] A monthly breakdown of foreign currencies by currency is not available; however, the 1973–75 annual reports[34] give a breakdown of currency holdings for eight different dates. Since most of the variations in reserves reflect changes in dollar holdings, most intervention is presumably in dollars. Whereas dollar holdings range from $665 to $2520 million, other currency holdings, about 2/3 of which consist of German marks and 1/3 of Swiss francs, range from $460 to $680 million. Thus, in the calculations all foreign currency is treated as U.S. dollars. This study excludes gold from the reserve figures, because only one important gold transaction occurred. The data in International Financial Statistics show that except for March 1979, the variations in Italy's physical holdings of gold is very small. Since December 1976, Italy has revalued its gold holdings quarterly on the basis of free market prices. The monetary changes as reported in the balance-of-payments figures in the *Supplemento Bollettino* include the figure for the counterpart of the revaluation of the gold. When the gold stock is revalued in the last month of each quarter, the change in its value is matched by a change in the counterpart of the revaluation of gold, except in March 1979, when Italy contributed gold and foreign exchange to the European Monetary Cooperation Fund. The revaluation of the gold stock is 3667.8 billion lire, but the increase in the value of the gold stock is 555.4 billion lire. The difference of 3112.4 billion lire is the value of gold given to the European Monetary Cooperation Fund. Since the reserve figures do not include gold, this difference is deducted from the change in the European Monetary Cooperation Fund account for

March 1979. The gold in the European monetary cooperation fund account was also revalued in July 1979 and October 1979. During these two months the value of Italy's gold holdings did not change, but the counterpart to the revaluation of gold increased by 383.6 billion lire in July 1979 and 526.4 billion lire in August 1979. These amounts are deducted from the change in the European Monetary Cooperation Account.

Until June 1974, the gold-based reserve assets of SDRs and the IMF reserve position are calculated on the basis of a gold price of $35 per ounce and at an exchange rate of 625 lire to the dollar. Subsequently, these assets are evaluated on the basis of the market rate on the last working day of the period.[35]

Short-term liabilities consist primarily of swaps with other central banks. Medium- and long-term positions include foreign and Italian securities in foreign currency, the contraentry liabilities for SDR allocations, borrowing from the IMF under the standby agreement and the oil facility,[36] and other liabilities with the EEC and the Bundesbank.

Monthly lira figures are reported for compensatory borrowing from the second quarter of 1974 onward, whereas quarterly figures are available before that time. This study converts compensatory loans to dollar figures—corresponding to the dollar figures found in the annual reports—by using the average exchange rate during each month.[37] The net position of the commercial banks is valued at market rates on the last working day of the month starting from December 1973 and is valued at the central rate prior to this date.

Intervention is defined as the change in the net foreign position (excluding gold) of the Bank of Italy and of the Italian Exchange Office, plus the change in the net foreign position of the banks, less compensatory borrowing, plus repayments. The net foreign position of the Bank of Italy and the Italian Exchange Office is the sum of foreign exchange, SDRs, the IMF position, and the balance at the European Monetary Cooperation Fund, less the short-term foreign liabilities, plus the medium-term position. The *Bolletino* reports that the global balance of payments is equal to the change in the foreign position of the Bank of Italy and of the Italian Exchange Office plus the change in the net foreign positions of the banks.[38] The *Bolletino* also reports the autonomous balance of payments, which excludes the compensatory borrowings.

The global balance of payments less compensatory borrowing is the same as in intervention defined above. If the autonomous balance of payments less compensatory borrowing is converted to dollars at the average monthly exchange rate and compared to the intervention figures used in this study, the correlation is .98. The two series show discrepancies from month to month, but these discrepancies offset one another over time. This study's intervention series shows net dollar sales from March 1973 through June 1976 at $15.1 billion, while the autonomous balance of payments shows net dollar sales at $15.4 billion. In addition, the intervention series shows the total dollars purchased between June 1976 and December 1979 at $18.2 billion, while the autonomous balance of payments series shows the dollar purchases at $18.0 billion. Both series give the loss from foreign intervention at $3.72 billion.

Japan

Japan uses both official reserves and "hidden reserves"—official government deposits of foreign exchange with Japanese commercial banks—to intervene in the foreign market. There is apparently no intervention in the forward market, and there is no significant borrowing to obtain funds for intervention, since external liabilities are small and relatively stable.[39] Japan can use "hidden reserves" to conceal its spot purchase by using a commercial bank to buy or sell for the central bank in the commercial bank's name. For instance, during the 1973-74 oil crisis, the Bank of Japan bought yen to prevent the exchange rate from falling. When it appeared they were running out of reserves, the Bank of Japan produced $9 billion of "hidden reserves" that had been accumulated when Japan was embarrassed by its surpluses.[40]

Quirk (1977) measures Japan's intervention with two data series: changes in gross international reserves and changes in the Foreign Exchange Fund accounts, the counterpart of the Ministry of Finance's account used for all transactions in the foreign exchange market. The problem with the first measure is that it does not include official deposits of foreign exchange with commercial banks. The second measure also creates problems, since it does not include transactions that are conducted outside the foreign exchange market. The relationship between these measures is $\Delta FXF + XM \cong \Delta R + \Delta OD$: where ΔFXF is changes in the Foreign Exchange Fund accounts, XM extramarket transactions, ΔR changes in gross reserves, and ΔOD changes in official deposits. The data Quirk (1977) uses are published monthly by the Bank of Japan.[41] There are no exact figures for extramarket transactions, which are comprised of earnings on official reserve assets (gold accounts for only 5% reserves) and of receipts from U.S. military purchases. However, extramarket receipts are estimated at $150 to $160 million per month.[42] By excluding extramarket transactions, changes in the Foreign Exchange Fund account result in a bias that underestimates intervention. In his empirical work, Quirk (1977) finds that changes in the Foreign Exchange Fund account were a better measure of intervention than the change in reserves. He shows that substantial use of "hidden reserves" occurs at times such as the 1973–74 oil crisis. Unfortunately, after September 1977, changes in the Foreign Exchange Fund are no longer a good measure of intervention since the Foreign Exchange Fund Bill held by the public is included in this series.[43]

The "hidden reserves" figures are published quarterly (semiannually prior to 1976) in a disguised form by the Bank of Japan in the supplementary tables "Amount of Deposit by Depositors" in *Economic Statistics Monthly*.[44] In the first table "All Banks," the column labeled "Other Deposits" is actually foreign currency deposits and nonresident free yen deposits, which are broken down by depositor. The official government foreign currency deposits appear in this column in row "(f) Government Funds." (The government holds no free-yen deposits, only foreign currency deposits.) The total of the column "Other Deposits" corresponds exactly with that recorded in the third month of the quarter in the monthly data series "Non-resident Free Yen Deposits, Foreign Currency Deposits" in the table "Bank Accounts for all Banks" in *Economic Statistics Monthly*. The foreign currency deposits are reported in yen. Some reporting banks make the conversion using the basic rate, while other banks use market rate.[45] According to these figures, the "hidden reserves" stood at $8.3 billion in June 1973, declined to $5.7 billion in June 1974 after the oil embargo, and then rose rapidly in late 1977 and 1978 to $11.5 billion in December 1978.

A monthly data series of government foreign currency deposits is constructed using the quarterly and semiannual data series on government foreign currency deposits and the monthly data series on free yen and foreign currency deposits. As mentioned above, the total reported in the column "Other Deposits" is identical with the "Non-resident Free Yen, Foreign Currency Deposits" for all banks in *Economic Statistics Monthly*; government deposits account for over 65% of this total. Thus changes in government deposits correspond well to changes in total deposits. The correlation coefficient of the first differences of government and total deposit series is .83.

Using a variant of Friedman's (1962) correlation method, the government foreign currency deposit data series is interpolated from a quarterly—and semiannual—series to a monthly series. The interpolation is obtained by first finding a straight-line trend between values of the government foreign currency deposits reported every three months. Another trend is computed between the corresponding values (for example, the same three-month intervals) of the total foreign currency and free yen deposits. Differences between each deleted value of total foreign currency and free yen deposits and the respective trend values are then found. A fraction of this difference is then added to the trend value of the government foreign currency deposits. This fraction is chosen to maximize the correlation between changes in the Foreign Exchange Fund account (ΔFXF) and changes in official reserves plus government foreign currency deposits (ΔR + ΔOD) for the period that ΔFXF was a valid measure of intervention—March 1973 to September 1977. The fraction .75 gives the highest correlation, which is .92.[46]

Spain

In addition to its official reserves, Spain finances foreign exchange intervention by compensatory borrowing—borrowing from banks and the IMF and borrowing by public enterprises. During 1974 and 1975, government-owned enterprises borrowed relatively little foreign currency, but in 1976 and 1977 this borrowing was considerable; Spain made substantial repayments in 1978, but showed little activity in 1979. No mention of exchange rate guarantee for the public enterprises can be found in the literature.

Figures for official reserves come from *International Financial Statistics*. Because of different valuation procedures, these data do not correspond to the official reserve data presented in *Boletin Estadistico*.[47] The Bank of Spain intervenes only in dollars.[48]

Spain has borrowed from the IMF under the oil facility drawings and compensatory drawings. Data on these borrowings comes from *International Financial Statistics*. A discussion on borrowing by government-owned enterprises is given in the Bank of Spain's annual reports.[49] The 1976 annual report, which gives the most complete information of all the reports, shows that in 1976 Spain greatly increased its compensatory financing. Annual figures that distinguish between autonomous capital movements and those movements that reflect balance-of-payments policy considerations are given.[50] Separate dollar figures are given for capital movements and for external public sector borrowing. Public sector borrowing rose from $30 billion in 1975 to $632 million in 1976.[51] These loans are considered "accommodating" transactions, (or below-the-line transactions) and are treated in the same way as borrowing from the IMF or a change in the Bank of Spain's reserves. In 1977, public sector borrowing reached its peak of $1267.1 million.[52] These dollar figures correspond to the peseta figures under "Capital publico del exterior España."[53] Two monthly data series for public sector borrowing are reported in the *Boletin Estadistico:* Net and long-term public capital flows from the exterior to Spain.[54] The first data series matches the annual data given in the annual reports more closely and is therefore used in this study.

Switzerland

Switzerland intervenes in the foreign exchange market by using only its official reserves; still, its official reserves figures do not reflect official transactions in the foreign exchange market, because they include dollar/franc swaps between the Swiss National Bank and the commercial banks. The swaps were introduced in 1959 and were employed by the banks as a window-dressing device until the early 1970s.

In the last decade the Swiss National Bank has used the swaps to provide additional liquidity to the banks at the end of the quarter. In a swap the Swiss National Bank buys dollars with francs from a commercial bank and simultaneously makes a forward commitment to sell the dollars back to the bank at the same exchange rate. In this operation, the official foreign reserves held by the Swiss National Bank increase even though there has been no intervention. At the same time there is a corresponding increase in the Swiss monetary base, since the Swiss franc reserves held by the commercial banks are increased.

Although the Swiss National Bank's assets and liabilities are reported four times each month in Schweizerische National Bank, *Monatsbericht,* the foreign monetary reserves that it reports include the dollar/franc swaps between the Swiss National Bank and the commercial banks. Due to these swaps, the official reserves, even without intervention, frequently increase substantially at the end of a quarter. For instance, in the fourth quarter of 1976, the swaps increased from less than 2 billion Swiss francs at the end of October and November to 7.7 billion Swiss francs at the end of December. This resulted in a similar increase in the official reserves without any substantial purchases in the foreign exchange market.[55] There are substantial but less dramatic increases in the level of the swaps at the end of most quarters and usually a decline in the following month.

The Swiss National Bank reports the sources of the monetary base with the swaps deducted from the international reserves figures. The swaps are then added to the domestic assets held by the central bank. This treatment of the swaps reflects the idea that the swap operations are an internal monetary policy similar to the Swiss

National Bank purchasing Swiss assets for their portfolio. Thus the monthly changes of these reserves, which exclude swaps, record foreign exchange intervention at prevailing market prices. As explained in the appendix to *Monatsbericht*, August 1975,[56] the changes in international reserves, recorded in the sources of the monetary base, also equal the current account balance plus net capital exports, which equals the amount of intervention in Swiss Francs.[57]

United Kingdom

The official United Kingdom foreign exchange reserves only partially reflect foreign exchange market intervention. Under the "exchange cover scheme" of 1969, nationalized industries and local authorities have been able to borrow foreign currency with an exchange rate guarantee given by the Treasury. When local authorities or public corporations borrow foreign currency under the exchange cover scheme, they surrender the proceeds to the government in exchange for sterling.[58] As a result, the foreign assets of the Bank of England increase without intervention and without any corresponding increase in the Bank of England's foreign liabilities. On the other hand, no corresponding change in official reserves occurs when the Bank of England uses this borrowed foreign exchange to intervene.

The Bank of England recognizes borrowing by the nationalized industries as a means of foreign exchange intervention and reports it along with monthly reserve changes and other transactions. The Bank of England has referred to official reserves less official short- and medium-term borrowing from abroad as net reserves.[59] This borrowing includes net foreign currency borrowing by the public sector under the "exchange cover scheme," borrowing from the IMF under the oil facility or the stand-by credit arrangement, increases in short-term currency swaps with the Group Ten and the Bank for International Settlements, and government Eurodollar borrowings though commercial banks.

The United Kingdom has extensively used these different sources of funds to intervene. After the pound began floating in June 1972, net reserves were $5.7 billion. The authorities used only official reserves to intervene until early 1973. In April 1973, when the exchange cover scheme was reintroduced, public sector borrowing steadily increased from $.4 billion to $3.0 billion by the end of the year. During 1974, foreign currency borrowing by nationalized industries and local authorities increased by $2.6 billion, and the central government borrowed $1.5 billion in the Eurodollar market. By the end of the year, net reserves were a negative $.4 billion. During 1975, $.8 billion was borrowed under the exchange cover scheme and $1.0 billion more by the central government in the Eurodollar market. Net reserves continued to fall to a negative $3.5 billion.

By the end of November 1976, net reserves had fallen to a low of $10.4 billion. During the first eleven months of 1976, the United Kingdom borrowed $2.1 billion from the IMF, $1.5 billion from other monetary authorities, and $3.1 billion under the exchange cover scheme. As the pound then began to strengthen, intervention was reversed, which kept the price of the pound from rising. By the end of 1977, gross reserves increased by $15.4 billion and net reserves became positive, even though official borrowing increased by $2.4 billion. In 1978 the country began repaying its loans, and the borrowing decreased from $18.0 billion to $15.8 billion by the end of 1978 and to $14.6 billion by the end of 1979.

United States

The United States is unique in two respects: Usually it does not hold any substantial foreign exchange reserves, and it is the only country that reports its profit and loss figures for official foreign exchange transactions. Nevertheless, it makes the misleading distinction between profits and losses on "current" operations and on liquidations of foreign currency debts outstanding as of 15 August 1971. Most of the losses from the liquidation of this pre-August 1971 debt resulted from transaction decisions made during the managed float, not when the exchange rates were pegged.

In early 1973, the Federal Reserve and the Treasury had $3.1 billion in foreign currency debts, which had been incurred before the first dollar devaluation in 1971. These debts, which were scheduled to be repaid in 1973 and early 1974, were not paid until 1977 and 1979, by which time the Swiss franc had nearly doubled in price. These refinancing transactions resulted in the loss of $1.8 billion.

In March 1973, the Treasury had $1578 million equivalent in foreign currency bonds outstanding. The Switzerland National Bank and the Bank for International Settlements had $1425 million in bonds with a Swiss franc guarantee. Germany held $153 million. The United States fulfilled its obligation to Germany by 1974, as scheduled. The Swiss franc bonds matured during 1973 and the first few months of 1974. Rather than repay these bonds, the Treasury refinanced the 16 outstanding bond issues an average of four times, as shown in Fig. 3-4.[60] As a result, the Treasury had to pay an additional $1182 million, or 67%, more than if the debt had been repaid when it was due in 1973 and 1974.

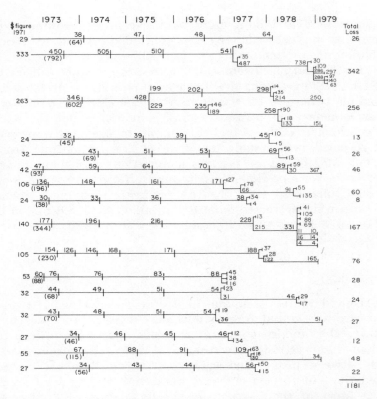

FIGURE 3-4. The increase of the U.S. Treasury Swiss franc debt resulting from refinancing decisions (in $ millions).

Each line shows the increase in the dollar value of Treasury indebtedness. The first figure in each line (for example, $29 million in the first line) is the dollar value in 1971 of each Swiss franc debt issue. The subsequent figure (for example, $38 million in the first line) is the dollar value when the issue matured after the dollar was allowed to float in early 1973—calculated by converting the original amount by the pre-August 1971 exchange rate of 4.087 Swiss francs per dollar and then converting back at the then prevailing exchange rate. The figure immediately beneath the line in the parenthesis (for example, $64 million in the first line) is the amount the Treasury eventually paid. The difference shown under "Loss" is the additional loss that the Treasury incurred by refinancing the bonds rather than making payment when the bonds matured within a year after the dollar was allowed to float in early 1973. The remaining figures (for example, $47, $48, $64 billion in the first line) are the dollar values at each subsequent maturity date. Usually the issues were not paid in full at any one time. For instance, the issue in the second line was refinanced three times and was worth $541 million in 1977; $19 and $35 million were paid in 1977; $487 million was refinanced and was worth $738 million when it matured in late 1978. The total additional loss from refinancing the Treasury Swiss franc debt is $1181 million.

76

In March 1973, the Federal Reserve had swap debts that originated prior to August 1971 of $1555 million equivalent.[61] It owed the Swiss National Bank and the Bank for International Settlements $1165 million equivalent or $4761 million Swiss francs at the pre-August 1971 exchange rate of 4.087 Swiss francs per dollar. The remainder was owed to the Bank of Belgium in Belgian francs. The Federal Reserve kept refinancing these swaps. The Belgian debt was paid by the end of 1976 and had little effect on the losses. The Federal Reserve, however, made few payments on the Swiss franc swap until 1977, and the final payment did not take place until April 1979. Repayment of the Swiss franc swap at the later date resulted in a total dollar cost of $2141 million.[62] If the swaps had been paid within a year after the dollar was allowed to float, the cost of repayment would have been $1534 million.[63] Thus, an additional $604 million loss resulted from the refinancing of the swaps beyond one year after the dollar had floated. The total additional loss to the Treasury and the Federal Reserve from refinancing and borrowing Swiss francs to meet their obligations comes to $1772 million.

According to profit and loss statements in the Federal Reserve *Bulletin*, the sum of the losses for all pre-August 1971 foreign currency debts for the years 1971 to 1979 is $2478 million. The footnotes reveal that only $517 million is attributed to the two dollar devaluations. These calculations show that the difference is almost entirely due to Federal Reserve and Treasury transactions after the dollar was allowed to float in March 1973.

Beginning in 1978, the United States increased its "current" intervention operations. The Treasury established its own swap lines and also issued German mark and Swiss franc foreign currency bonds. The losses between 1973 and January 1980 on current operations are $562 million. The total transaction loss from March 1973 to January 1980 for the Federal Reserve and the Treasury is $2.3 billion.

NOTES

1. In his classic essay on flexible exchange rates, Friedman (1953) feared this result: "A positive disadvantage of government speculation is the danger that government authorities . . . will try to peg the exchange rate thereby converting a flexible exchange rate system into a system of rigid rates subject to change from time to time by official action."

2. The exchange rates, with the exception of Switzerland's, are averages of daily figures for the month as reported by *International Financial Statistics* since July 1974 and by *The Wall Street Journal* for dates prior to July 1974. For France, the commercial rate is used prior to March 20, 1974, when the exchange market was split into a two-tier system. Exchange rate data for Switzerland are based on the monthly average of daily figures taken from Schweizeische National Bank, *Monatsbericht*.

3. Since appreciation or depreciation of nondollar assets may be mistaken for dollar intervention, the composition of reserves is taken into account where possible in this study. Allocation of SDRs and the revaluation of the gold contribution to the European Monetary Cooperation are also taken into account. Reserves for Canada, Spain, and the United Kingdom are reported in dollars; for France, Germany, Japan, and Switzerland, in home currency at acquisition cost; and for Italy, at market value. Complete information for each country is given in the second section of this chapter.

4. If countries only intervened with official reserves, cumulative intervention would equal the total change in their reserves.

5. Since the monetary authorities apparently direct all of these activities, the term "central bank" is used for all institutions used by the government to intervene.

6. Friedman's proposition that destabilizing speculators must lose money has been extensively contended. But as Johnson (1976) points out, "The critics have, however, in the judgment of those who have studied the matter, failed to make their case: their counterexamples have implicitly either selected arbitrarily a small group of especially clever destabilizing speculators who make money at the expense of other destabilizing speculators (the whole group losing in total), or imputed to destabilizing speculators profits that are not realized—and could not be realized—through market closure of the speculation" (see Telser, 1959).

Eastman and Styhold (1957) discuss theoretical problems concerning the profit criterion, assuming the central bank is a monopolist with perfect foresight. The central bank would make zero profit if it could remove currency fluctuations completely. To maximize profit, they would stabilize exchange rates only to the point where the price gave them a monopoly profit. A third rather contorted argument is that a central bank could reduce volatility and lose money if it were able to reverse slightly a cyclical exchange rate movement. This would occur if the central bank sold so much of its currency that it actually depressed the price slightly below the fundamental value, when without intervention the price would be above the equilibrium. In other words, the intervention is in the right direction but is excessive in amount.

Empirically the central banks have intervened in the wrong direction and have delayed equilibrium adjustments. Central banks have some degree of monopoly power, but they are closer to a competitor than to a monopolist. Gross central bank intervention for all banks is $100 billion to $150 billion per year, while gross transactions on the New York Market alone average $25 billion per day. (Quarterly figures for gross intervention are released by the Federal Reserve. The central banks supply intervention figures among themselves but do not release the data. See Federal Reserve Bank of Chicago, *International Letter*, 4 July, 1980 for an estimate of the size of the New York Market.) If central banks did have the ability to predict exchange rates, the monopoly profits would soon dissipate since other speculators would enter the market when central bank did.

Another theoretical argument against the profit criterion is that a central bank could make a profit by deceptively inflating or deflating the economy. If the bank purchased foreign assets and then inflated the money stock by buying domestic assets, the domestic currency would depreciate and the foreign assets would appreciate in terms of the domestic currency. The opposite, selling foreign assets and then deflating the economy, is also possible. It is unlikely, however, that monetary authorities would pursue a policy of producing unanticipated inflation or deflation in order to show a profit on their foreign exchange transactions. If countries were willing to let their monetary policies be dictated by foreign exchange transactions, they would be able to maintain a unified currency system, as under the gold standard with truly fixed exchange rates. It is, in fact, because countries have independent monetary policies that fixed exchange rates are not possible.

7. That is, Profit $= \Sigma_{i=i}^{f}[n_i - n_i(e_i/e_f)]$ where n_i dollars are purchased at the average price e_i. Therefore $n_i e_i$ is amount of domestic currency sold, which is valued in dollars at e_f the price of the dollar at the end of the period.

8. The losses for individual central banks vary according to the starting and ending points used in the calculations. However, as a group, the central banks show losses for various time periods (see Taylor, 1981).

9. See *Borrowing in International Capital Markets;* and *The Economist,* March 27, 1976, p. 99.

10. The *Monthly Report* of the Deutsche Bundesbank gives the portion of reserves held in dollars.

11. Using monthly instead of daily figures for the 1970–1976 period gives $20 million less profit.

12. The sum of the adjustments for daily figures used in this study corresponds to the adjustment figures given monthly by the Department of Finance.

13. A fee of $\frac{3}{8}$ of 1% per annum and of $\frac{1}{4}$ of 1% per annum was paid on the undrawn amount of the Canadian and foreign credit facilities, respectively. These fees were not included in the calculations.

14. Parts of this section are adapted from Taylor and Nascimento (1980). I am indebted to Jean-Claude Nascimento and Debbie Reinhart for research assistance.

15. The European Monetary Cooperation Fund's liability is included in these figures. The revaluation of the gold component is excluded.

16. *Statistiques et Études Financières—Balance des Paiments entre La France et l'Exterieur:* the government has adopted the policy "to prevent drastic changes in official reserve assets or unwarranted levels of depreciation of the French franc," 1976, p. 43; Banque de France *Compte Rendu:* "Many French firms are encouraged by the monetary authorities to borrow foreign exchange in order to facilitate the financing of our balance of payments deficit," 1976, p. 31. I am indebted to Jean-Claude Nascimento for translating the references in this section.

17. *Statistiques et Études Financières—Le Rapport d'Ensemble sur les Enterprises Publiques,* 1976, p. 14.

18. *Statistiques et Études Financières—Balance de Paiments entre La France et l'Exterieur,* p. 59. This delay is two months according to *International Monetary Fund, Exchange Arrangements and Exchange Restrictions.* 1976, pp. 225, 248.

19. *Rapport Annuel du CNC:* "During the year, the conversion of foreign exchange from borrowings abroad have been adapted to the movement of the

franc on the foreign exchange market as much as possible – so, that by the end of the year, a fraction of foreign exchange borrowed during the last quarter of 1977 has been kept in order to be converted into French francs only the 1st quarter of 1978," 1978, p. 46 (translated from the French).

20. Periods of pressure on the French franc are September 1973, January 1974, the first quarter of 1976, July and August 1976, and the first quarter of 1978.

21. Artus (1976), p. 312.

22. Deutsche Bundesbank, *Monthly Report*, September 1979, p. 37.

23. Foreign exchange swaps are also used as an instrument of monetary policy by Switzerland.

24. Artus (1976) found that specifications of intervention policy taking into account the European joint float were unsuccessful. His explanation was that the mark dominated the other snake currencies.

25. Monthly figures on dollar holdings are given in Deutsche Bundesbank, *Monthly Report*.

26. Deutsche Bundesbank, *Monthly Report*, January 1976.

27. International Monetary Fund, *Annual Report on Exchange Restrictions 1978*, p. 255.

28. Hodgman, Donald R., *National Monetary Policies and International Monetary Cooperation*, Boston, Little Brown, 1974, p. 90.

29. International Monetary Fund, *Annual Report on Exchange Restrictions 1978*, p. 228.

30. *Ibid.*, p. 225.

31. The Italian data are often revised at a very late date. Thus the most recent source that contains the data is used.

32. In the Bank of Italy annual reports, the balance of payments is usually reported with compensatory borrowing both as an above the line item and as a below the line item.

33. Banca D'Italia, *Abridged Version of the Report for the Year: 1973*, p.79.

34. *Ibid.*, p. 80; 1974, p. 87; 1975, p. 75.

35. Banca D'Italia, *Abridged Version of the Report of the Year: 1974*, p. 87.

36. No adjustment is made for the dollar appreciation or depreciation of the SDR-denominated assets, since SDR-denominated assets and liabilities are of the same approximate magnitude.

37. Banca D'Italia, *Abridged Version of the Report for the Year: 1975*, p. 76; *1976*, p. 63; *1977*, p. 65.

38. The item "aggiustamenti di cambio" [exchange rate adjustment] also appears below the line. This adjustment accounts for the change in the lira valuation of the foreign assets. The changes in official reserves and the net foreign assets of the banks are reported in lire. The change is obtained by converting the net foreign assets of these institutions from dollars to lire and taking the difference between month-end values. Since the flows recorded above the line are converted into lira at their respective current exchange rates, a correction is needed for the valuation effect of a given stock of reserves at different exchange rates.

39. Quirk (1977), p. 643.

40. *Wall Street Journal*, January 25, 1974.

41. They appear in Bank of Japan *Economic Statistics Monthly*. Foreign Exchange Fund accounts are found in the table "Demand and Supply of Funds in Money Markets," which lists major sources of the monetary base. Reserves are found in the table "Gold and Foreign Exchange Reserves."

42. "Yen Is Not 'Cheap,'" *The Oriental Economist* 44 (October 1976), p. 6.

43. The Ministry of Finance publication *Financial and Monetary Statistics Monthly: Special Issue on Treasury Expenditure* gives monthly figures for the Foreign Exchange Fund Bill held by the public. Sometimes the nonpublic holdings can be quite substantial. For instance, in 1977 the holdings increased by 298 billion yen between September and October and decreased by 321 billion yen between November and December. These figures are of the same magnitude as those reported for the changes in the Foreign Exchange Fund. Because of the delay in publishing, these numbers could not be used to eliminate the public holdings of the Foreign Exchange Fund Bill from this data series.

44. I am indebted to Peter Quirk for referring me to Norman Klath, who told me about these data. Employees of the Bank of Japan have confirmed that these figures represent the government deposits at commercial banks.

45. According to an employee at the Bank of Japan, conversion back to dollars at the market rate for these deposits will give a good approximation of the changes that are occurring.

46. The interpolated data series that is constructed is an improvement over using the change in official reserves, which is the other data series used by Quirk (1977). The correlation between changes in official reserves and ΔFXF is .81.

47. The Bank of Spain uses central rates in converting nondollar foreign exchange into dollar terms. The *International Financial Statistics* uses the market rate. The Bank of Spain also converts SDR-denominated assets at the "prebasket" dollar/SDR rate, while the IFS uses the prevailing dollar/SDR rate. I am grateful to Joaquin Muns for this information.

48. Banco de Espana, *Informe Annual 1976*, p. 139.

49. I am indebted to Maria Caban-Garcia for translating these reports.

50. See the table "Balanza de pagos," Banco de Espana, *Informe Annual 1976*, p. 133.

51. *Ibid.*, p. 135. Of the $632 million, $500 million is from a loan to the government of Spain by an international syndicate of banks. *Ibid.*, p. 136.

52. *Informe Annual 1977*, p. 133.

53. *Ibid.*, p. 131.

54. Table VIII-4, "Prestamos exteriores," and Table XIII-11 "Capital publico a largo plaza del exterior en Espana."

55. These figures come from worksheets that show the construction of the monetary base and have the swap figures for the end of the month. They have been provided by a source at the Swiss National Bank.

56. In German on p. 4; in French on p. 10.

57. The other factors which influence the stock of international reserves are interest payments and revaluations at the end of the year. These figures are not published. According to an employee at the Swiss National Bank, however, the effect of interest payments on the stock of reserves is offset by the revaluations at the end of the year. The exception is 1978, when the revaluation was a negative 4434 million Swiss francs while the interest payments on reserves was 1258 million Swiss francs.

58. Bank of England, *Quarterly Bulletin* (March 1975), p. 43.

59. *Ibid.*, December 1977, p. 420.

60. Information on the value of various notes and certificates of indebtedness and their issue and maturity dates is available in Table PDO-90 Foreign Currency Series Securities in the *Treasury Bulletin*. Each time a security was refinanced the appreciation or depreciation to the time it was repaid or again refinanced was calculated.

61. Dollar equivalent figures are reported in the Federal Reserve *Bulletin* at the exchange rate at the time borrowing.

62. Data taken from tables in the reports "Treasury and Federal Reserve Foreign Operations" in various issues of the Federal Reserve *Bulletin* give enough information to calculate borrowing or repayments in the first month of each quarter and the sum of borrowing and repayments in the last two months of each quarter. In this study, the dollar equivalent payments are converted to Swiss francs at 4.087 Swiss francs per dollar and then back to dollars at the prevailing average monthly exchange rate. In December 1975 the swap debt was revalued from $971 million equivalent to $1167 million equivalent, to account for the two devaluations of the dollar. The dollar equivalent repayments after December 1975 are therefore multiplied times the ratio 971/1167 times 4.087 Swiss francs per dollar to obtain the number of Swiss francs repaid. I am indebted to Linda Deubert for making the calculations in this section.

63. This statement assumes that 397 Swiss francs are paid per month between April 1973 and March 1974 at the average monthly exchange rate.

REFERENCES

Artus, Jacques. "Exchange Rate Stability and Managed Floating: The Experience of the Federal Republic of Germany." *IMF Staff Papers* (July 1976): 24.

Banca d'Italia. *Abridged Version of the Report for the Year.* Various years.

——. *Bulletino.* Various issues.

——. *Supplemento al Bulletino.* Various issues.

Banco de España. *Boletin Estadistico.* Various issues.

——. *Informe Annual.* Various years.

Bank of England. *Quarterly Bulletin.* Various issues.

Bank of Japan. *Economic Statistics Monthly.* Various issues.

Banque de France. *Bulletin Trimestriel.* Various issues.

——. *Compte Rendu.* Various issues.

Connolly, Michael, and Dean Taylor. "Adjustment to Devaluation in a Small Country." *De Economist* 124 (1976):319-27.

Conseil National du Credit. *Rapport Annuel.* Various issues.

Department of Finance (Canada). *Annual Report to the Parliament on the Operation of the Exchange Fund Account* 1977. Various years.

Department of Finance, Information Division (Canada). *Release.* Canada. Various issues.

Deutsche Bundesbank. "The European System of Narrow Exchange Rate Margins." Monthly Report (January 1978):22-29.

———. *Monthly Report.* Various issues.

———. *Report for the Year.* Various issues.

Eastman, Harry, and Steefan Styholt. "Exchange Stabilization Once Again." *Canadian Journal of Economics and Political Science* 24 (May 1958): 266-72

Federal Reserve. *The Annual Report.* Various issues.

———. *Bulletin.* Various issues.

———. "Statements to Congress." *Bulletin* (February 1978):89.

Federal Reserve Bank of Chicago. *International Letter* 425 (July 4, 1980):3.

Financial Times. Various issues.

Friedman, Milton, "The Case for Flexible Exchange Rates," *Essays in Positive Economics,* Chicago, 1953.

———. "The Interpolation of Time Series by Related Studies." *Journal of the American Statistical Association* (December 1962):729-57.

H.M. Treasury (U.K.). *The Reserves.* Monthly press release. Various issues.

International Monetary Fund. *Annual Report on Exchange Restrictions 1978.*

———. *International Financial Statistics.* Various issues.

Johnson, Harry G. "Destabilizing Speculation: A General Equilibrium Approach." *Journal of Political Economy* (February 1976):101-08.

Ministry of Finance (France). *Statistiques et études financières—balance des paiments entre la France et l'exterieur.* Various years.

——. *Statistiques et études financières—le rapport d'ensemble sur les enterprises publiques.* Various issues.

Ministry of Finance (Japan). *Financial and Monetary Statistics Monthly: Special Issue on Treasury Expenditure* (Japan). Various issues.

Quirk, Peter J. "Exchange Rate Policy in Japan: Leaning against the Wind." *IMF Staff Papers* 24 (November 1977):642-64.

Schweizerische National Bank. *Monatesbericht.* Various issues.

Taylor, Dean G. "Official Intervention in the Foreign Exchange Market: or, Bet against the Central Bank." *Journal of Political Economy* 90 (April 1982).

Taylor, Dean, G., and Jean-Claude Nascimento. "Intervention in the Foreign Exchange Market by France" (1980), processed.

Telser, Lester G. "A Theory of Speculation Relating to Profitability and Stability." *Review of Economics and Statistics* 41 (August 1972):295-301.

United States Treasury Department. *Treasury Bulletin.* Various issues.

The Wall Street Journal. Various issues.

"Who Gets Hurt When the Pound Falls Ill." *The Economist* (March 27, 1976):99.

Wonnacott, Paul. "Notes and Memoranda—Exchange Stabilization in Canada, 1950-4, A Comment." *Canadian Journal of Economics and Political Science* 24 (May 1958):262-65.

World Bank. *Borrowing in International Capital Markets* (Report EC-181)/1. Various issues.

"Yen Is Not Cheap." *The Oriental Economist* 44 (October 1976):6.

4

STOCHASTIC DISTURBANCES,
TRADED AND NONTRADED GOODS,
AND THE CHOICE OF THE EXCHANGE REGIME

HARVEY E. LAPAN & WALTER ENDERS

Much of the discussion concerning the relative desirability of fixed versus flexible exchange rates has focused upon the ability of each regime to stabilize an economy in the presence of internal and external disturbances. The consensus opinion—as reflected in Fischer (1977), Laffer (1973), and Mundell (1973)—is that fixed exchange rates are preferable if disturbances are real and internal. The "rest of the world," via domestic Trade Account surpluses or deficits, acts to absorb some of these shocks. Flexible rates, however, are viewed as preferable for those disturbances that emanate from abroad or for internal nominal disturbances. Indeed, if there is only one traded good and no capital mobility, a flexible rate system will perfectly insulate the economy from foreign disturbances.

A second basis for comparing exchange regimes has been the openness of the domestic economy. Papers following the lead of McKinnon (1963) have argued that fixed rates are preferable for relatively open economies, while flexible rates are preferable for relatively closed economies. Shocks to the exchange rate (presumably from external disturbances) will have small effects on the domestic

This material is based upon work supported by the National Science Foundation under Grant Soc-7907066. We would like to thank the National Science Foundation for this support.

price level if the size of the traded-goods sector is small. Highly open economies, on the other hand, should peg the exchange rate in order to maintain the purchasing power of the domestic currency.

While intuitively it seems that both the source of the disturbances and the degree of openness of the economy would be important components in choosing between exchange regimes, it should be noted that few papers have presented a microtheoretic approach in addressing these issues. Helpman and Razin (1979), and Lapan and Enders (1980) have argued that the choice between exchange regimes ultimately hinges on which regime provides higher expected utility for individuals. Thus, it would seem as though tastes of individual agents would be the appropriate yardstick for making comparisons between regimes. Further, consistency requires that the demand or expenditure functions used to describe macroeconomic behavior should be generated from these agents' utility functions. In Lapan and Enders (1980) we utilized a consumption-loan model to derive agents' behavior under uncertainty and then to compare expected utility under the alternative exchange regimes. The basic conclusion of the paper is that the primary determinant of the choice of the exchange regime is not the source of disturbance but, rather, individual attitudes toward risk (the elasticity of the marginal utility of income). However, our previous paper assumed that there was only one good that was traded, and that the economy in question was small. Hence, a flexible exchange regime completely insulated the economy from external disturbances. As there were no nontraded goods in the model, no conclusions concerning the relevance of the openness of the economy were feasible. It is our purpose in this chapter to remedy those omissions and to investigate how relative price movements in traded goods or the presence of nontraded goods affects our earlier conclusions.

In Section 1 we present the basic model and derive the behavior of individuals under uncertainty. Section 2, using the analysis of Section 1, compares the expected utility of fixed rates to that of flexible rates in the case in which all goods are traded. It is shown that regardless of the number of traded goods and regardless of the source of disturbances, the choice between exchange regimes depends only upon individual attitudes toward risk. In Section 3 we introduce nontraded goods into the analysis and demonstrate that the size of the nontraded-goods sector, as well as attitudes toward risk, affect the choice between exchange regimes. Unlike the traditional view embodied in the Optimum Currency Area argument, we show that the presence of a nontraded good raises the likelihood that expected utility will be higher under a fixed exchange rate regime.

1. THE MODEL OF INDIVIDUAL BEHAVIOR

In this section, we derive the micro demand functions for agents who maximize expected utility; these relationships will subsequently be aggregated in order to characterize the macro equilibrium and thus provide a normative comparison of the two regimes. In a previous paper (Lapan and Enders, 1980) we assumed that there was only one commodity and that the country under study was small, so that the foreign currency price of the (traded) good was exogenous. The assumption of a single commodity implies that flexible exchange rates can completely insulate the economy from foreign disturbances and also implies that—in a stationary, deterministic world—there would be no trade. The assumption that the foreign currency price is exogenous implies that the "shock-absorber" effect obtained by linking the two countries together under a fixed exchange rate regime is nonexistent, since output movements in the large country dominate and determine the distribution of prices. Thus, in this section we develop a model that can be used to compare the two regimes for cases in which there are many traded goods and when foreign currency prices are not exogenous.

The basic model we employ uses Samuelson's (1958) consumption-loan framework in which there are two overlapping generations. We assume that:

1. There are two countries, the "home" and "foreign" countries.

2. An individual of generation t works and derives income in period t and consumes in periods t and t + 1; after t + 1, he leaves the economic system.

3. Each generation of the home (foreign) country consists of N ($\bar{N}$) identical individuals. Hence, in any time period, there are 2N "home" residents and 2$\bar{N}$ "foreign" residents.

4. All individuals (of both countries, and all generations) have identical preferences; the utility of an individual born at t depends on his consumption vector in t and t + 1.

5. All individuals of the same generation of a given country have the same income; however, incomes may differ across countries and generations.

6. Commodities are perishable, and money is the only store of value. Further, it is assumed that individuals hold only their domestic currency;[1] thus, "home" residents hold dollars (denoted by M), whereas "foreign" residents hold only pounds (denoted by $\bar{M}$).

Throughout the following analysis, a "bar" over a variable represents the foreign counterpart of the "home" variable.

To provide a systematic exposition of the price determination process, it is necessary to specify the utility function of individuals. Let:

$$C_i^t \ (\bar{C}_i^t) \qquad = \text{consumption of good i in t of a member of the home (foreign) generation of period t} \qquad (1)$$

$$B_i^{t+1} \ (\bar{B}_i^{t+1}) \ = \text{consumption of good i in t + 1 of a member of the home (foreign) generation of period t;} \\ i = 1, \ldots, n \qquad (2)$$

$$P_i^j \ (\bar{P}_i^j) \qquad = \text{home (foreign) currency price of good i in period j} \qquad (3)$$

As noted earlier, it is assumed all individuals have identical preferences;[2] we assume that these preferences can be represented by the following utility function:

$$U_t = U(C^t, B^{t+1}) = \frac{[V(C^t)]^{\theta/2} \, [V(B^{t+1})]^{\theta/2}}{\theta} \qquad (4)$$

where C^t, B^{t+1} are vectors, and $V(\ )$ is assumed to be homogeneous of degree one. Note that $1 - \theta$ is the measure of relative risk aversion.

Since all individuals are assumed to have identical preferences, the demand rules can be solved for a representative individual and then aggregated to determine the macro demands. Note, however, that although the demand functions are identical, the actual quantities consumed by individuals will differ across countries and generations because of differences in income (and prices over time). The individual born at t must choose current consumption C^t before the next period's prices are known but after current prices and income are known. These decisions imply how much wealth (currency) the individual may carry over to t + 1. At t + 1, the individual chooses B^{t+1} to maximize utility, given (then) current prices and his money holdings. Define

$$S^t = \sum P_i^t C_i^t \qquad M^{t+1} = Y^t - S^t \qquad (5)$$

In (5), S^t represents total spending, at t, of a member of generation t, and M^{t+1} depicts the member's demand for (domestic) currency. Since domestic currency is the only store of value, the individual chooses B^{t+1} at t + 1 to maximize utility given M^{t+1}, C^t, P^{t+1}:

$$\underset{B^{t+1}}{\text{Max}} [U_t] = \underset{B^{t+1}}{\text{Max}} \left[\frac{[V(C^t)]^{\theta/2} [V(B^{t+1})]^{\theta/2}}{\theta} \right] \tag{6}$$

subject to

$$M^{t+1} - \sum_i P_i^{t+1} B_i^{t+1} \geqslant 0$$

In (6) C^t is given. Given the homogeneity of $V(\ )$, all commodity demands exhibit unitary expenditure (income) elasticity. Hence, the demands at $t + 1$ are given by

$$B_i^{t+1} = \left(\frac{M^{t+1}}{P_1^{t+1}} \right) g_i(r^{t+1}) \qquad r_i^{t+1} \equiv \frac{P_i^{t+1}}{P_1^{t+1}} \qquad i = 1, \ldots, n \tag{7}$$

$$\sum_i [r_i^{(t+1)} g_i(r^{t+1})] = 1 \tag{8}$$

In (7) and (8), r^{t+1} is the vector of relative prices, in terms of good 1, and M^{t+1}/P_1^{t+1} is real expenditures, measured in terms of good 1. Consequently, $g_i(r^{t+1})$ indicates the effect of relative prices on demand for i (given "real" income), and $r_i^{t+1} g_i(r^{t+1})$ is the share of total expenditures (equal to the marginal propensity to consume because of the homotheticity of preferences) allocated to good i. Substituting (7) into $V(B^{t+1})$ yields the indirect utility function, $V*(M^{t+1}, P^{t+1})$:

$$V*(M^{t+1}, P^{t+1}) = \left(\frac{M^{t+1}}{P_1^{t+1}} \right) H(r^{t+1})$$

$$H(r^{t+1}) \equiv V(g_1(r^{t+1}), \ldots, g_n(r^{t+1})) \tag{9}$$

In (9), $H(r^{t+1})$ depends only on relative prices and indicates how a change in relative prices, given "real" income M^{t+1}/P_1^{t+1}, affects utility. At t, the individual must choose C^t, S^t before P_1^{t+1}, r^{t+1} are known; substituting (9) into (6), and assuming that S^t, M^{t+1}, P^t are given,

$$\underset{C^t}{\text{Max}} E \left[\frac{(V(C^t))^{\theta/2} (M^{t+1}/P_1^{t+1})^{\theta/2} (H(r^{t+1}))^{\theta/2}}{\theta} \right] \tag{10}$$

subject to

$$S_t - \sum P_i^t C_i^t \geqslant 0 \tag{11}$$

In (10), the expectation runs over P_1^{t+1}, r^{t+1}. The optimal consumption rule at t is given by

$$C_i^t = \left(\frac{S^t}{P_1^t}\right) g_i(r^t) \qquad i = 1, \ldots, n \qquad \sum r_i^t g_i(r^t) = 1 \tag{12}$$

where, in (12), the functional form for $g_i(\ )$ is the same as that obtained at $t + 1$. Substituting (12) into $V(C^t)$ yields the indirect utility function at t, $V^*(S^t, P^t)$:

$$V^*(S^t, P^t) = \left(\frac{S^t}{P_1^t}\right) H(r^t) \tag{13}$$

where, again, the functional form of $H(r^t)$ is identical to that for $H(r^{t+1})$. Finally, substituting (13) into (10) and maximizing over S^t,

$$\underset{(S^t)}{\text{Max E}} \left[\frac{(S^t/P_1^t)^{\theta/2} \, (M^{t+1}/P^{t+1})^{\theta/2} \, [H(r^t)H(r^{t+1})]^{\theta/2}}{\theta} \right] \tag{14}$$

subject to

$$Y^t - S^t - M^{t+1} \geqslant 0 \tag{15}$$

yields

$$\bar{S}^t = \frac{Y^t}{2} \tag{16}$$

where Y^t is nominal income at t. Hence, the demand rules at t for a member of generation t are given by

$$C_i^t = \left(\frac{Y^t}{2P_1^t}\right) g_i(r^t) \qquad \bar{C}_i^t = \left(\frac{\bar{Y}^t}{2\bar{P}_1^t}\right) g_i(\bar{r}^t) \qquad i = 1, \ldots, n$$

$$M^{t+1} = \frac{Y^t}{2} \qquad \bar{M}^{t+1} = \frac{\bar{Y}^t}{2} \tag{17}$$

where the "bar" denotes the foreign counterpart of the home-country resident, and M^{t+1} ($\bar{M}^{t+1}$) denotes the demand at t by an individual for the home (foreign) currency. Once P^{t+1} is known, the demands by a member of generation t are given by

$$B_i^{t+1} = \left(\frac{M^{t+1}}{P_1^{t+1}}\right) g_i(r^{t+1})$$

$$\bar{B}_i^{t+1} = \left(\frac{\bar{M}^{t+1}}{P_1^{t+1}}\right) g_i(\bar{r}^{t+1}) \tag{18}$$

$$i = 1, \ldots, n$$

Assuming commodity arbitrage and that all goods are traded,

$$P_i^j = e^j \bar{P}_i^j \tag{19}$$

hence

$$r_i^j = \bar{r}_i^j$$

where e^j is the period j home-currency price of the foreign currency. Thus, relative prices are equalized by trade. Finally, the expected utility of a member of generation t is given by

$$E[U_t] = E\left[\frac{(Y^t/2P_1^t)^{\theta/2} (Y^t/2P_1^{t+1})^{\theta/2} [H(r^t)H(r^{t+1})]^{\theta/2}}{\theta}\right] \tag{20}$$

where, if we are interested in expected utility in the ex ante sense, the expectations run over Y^t, P_1^t, r^t, P_1^{t+1}, r^{t+1}.

Recognizing that there are N ($\bar{N}$) members of each home (foreign) generation, and that at any t, two generations are alive in each country, world demand at t for good i is given by

$$D_i^t = \left[\frac{N(Y^t + 2M^t) + e^t\bar{N}(\bar{Y}^t + 2\bar{M}^t)}{2P_1^t}\right] g_i(r^t) \tag{21}$$

$$i = 1, \ldots, n$$

where the demands by the retired generation at t are obtained from (18) by lagging time one period. Also, the aggregate demand at t for each currency is given by

$$NM^t = \frac{NY^t}{2} \qquad \overline{NM}^t = \frac{\overline{NY}^t}{2} \tag{22}$$

⋮

Turning to the production side, it is assumed that the allocation of resources is stationary over time and independent of the exchange regime.[3] Thus, assume that aggregate home (foreign) production is given by

$$Q_i^j = N\lambda_i^j a_i \qquad \bar{Q}_i^j = \overline{N\lambda_i^j}\bar{a}_i \tag{23}$$

where

$$E[\lambda_i^j] = E[\bar{\lambda}_i^j] = 1 \tag{24}$$

In (23), a_i, $\bar{a}_i$ are constants, and λ_i^j ($\bar{\lambda}_i^j$) represent productivity disturbances to good i at time j in the home (foreign) country. For any good, i, we assume that λ_i^j ($\bar{\lambda}_i^j$) is identically, but independently, distributed over time. Thus, while we allow for correlation at any time t between domestic and foreign output levels, or for correlation across sectors at time t, we assume that there is no serial correlation and that the distribution of λ_i^j ($\bar{\lambda}_i^j$) is unchanging over time.

By assumption, all output at t accrues to the working generation at time t, and the income levels of all members of the same generation of the same country are identical. Thus

$$Y^t = \sum_i P_i^t \lambda_i^t a_i \qquad \bar{Y}^t = \sum_i \bar{P}_i^t \bar{\lambda}_i^t \bar{a}_i \tag{25}$$

Finally, aggregate supply at t of good i is given by

$$\hat{Q}_i^t = N\lambda_i^t a_i + \overline{N\lambda_i^t}\bar{a}_i \tag{26}$$

From (21) and (26), relative prices at t are determined by

$$\frac{\hat{Q}_i^t}{\hat{Q}_s^t} = \frac{D_i^t}{D_s^t} \to \frac{g_i(r^t)}{g_s(r^t)} = \frac{N\lambda_i^t a_i + \overline{N\lambda_i^t}\bar{a}_i}{N\lambda_s^t a_s + \overline{N\lambda_s^t}\bar{a}_s} \tag{27}$$

Note that relative prices are independent of the exchange regime; the difference that arises between the regimes is in the determination of the price level for each country. Under flexible exchange rates, assuming no active monetary policy, the aggregate stock of each currency is unchanging over time; hence, the home (foreign) currency price of good 1 is determined by

$$N \cdot M = N \cdot M^t \quad \text{or} \quad Y^t = 2M \rightarrow P_1^t = \frac{2M}{\sum_i (r_i^t \lambda_i^t a_i)}$$

$$\bar{N} \cdot \bar{M} = \bar{N} \cdot \bar{M}^t \quad \text{or} \quad \bar{Y}^t = 2\bar{M} \rightarrow \bar{P}_1^t = \frac{2\bar{M}}{\sum_i (r_i^t \bar{\lambda}_i^t \bar{a}_i)}$$

(28)

and

$$e^t = \frac{P_1^t}{\bar{P}_1^t} = \left(\frac{M}{\bar{M}}\right) \frac{\sum_i r_i^t \bar{\lambda}_i^t \bar{a}_i}{\sum_i r_i^t \lambda_i^t a_i}$$

(29)

In (28), the equilibrium values of r_i^t are determined from (27) and are independent of the exchange regime. NM ($\overline{NM}$) represent the constant supply of the home (foreign) currency. Note that (29) asserts that the domestic currency price of the foreign currency is directly related to the relative per capita supplies of the domestic and foreign currencies, and inversely related to the ratio of per capita real income levels—as is implied by the monetary approach without currency substitutability.

Under fixed exchange rates, the supply of each currency may vary over time, but—assuming no active monetary policy and a permanently fixed exchange rate—the value (in either currency unit) of outstanding currency is constant. Normalizing e to 1 for convenience, let

$$M^* = NM^t + \overline{NM}^t \quad e = 1 \quad M^* = \text{constant}$$

(30)

From (22) and (25),

$$P_1^t = \bar{P}_1^t = \frac{2M^*}{\sum_i r_i^t (N\lambda_i^t a_i + \bar{N}\bar{\lambda}_i^t \bar{a}_i)}$$

(31)

and the home-country's trade balance at t is given by

$$N(M^{t+1} - M^t) = N\left[\left(\frac{Y^t}{2}\right) - M^t\right]$$

(32)

hence:

$$NM^{t+1} = NM^* \left[\frac{\sum_i r_i^t \lambda_i^t a_i}{\sum_i r_i^t (N\lambda_i^t a_i + \bar{N}\bar{\lambda}_i^t \bar{a}_i)}\right]$$

(33)

$$NM^{t+1} = \bar{N}M^* \left[\frac{\sum_i r_i^t \bar{\lambda}_i^t \bar{a}_i}{\sum_i r_i^t (N\lambda_i^t a_i + \overline{N\lambda_i^t \bar{a}_i})} \right] \tag{33'}$$

Thus, under flexible exchange rates, the value of aggregate domestic consumption must equal the value of domestic income, whereas under fixed rates the country may transfer purchasing power over time. For example, when the value of domestic income is high, some of this purchasing power may be transferred to the next period by acquiring claims against the rest of the world. It is this ability to "buffer" domestic disturbances which is supposed to make fixed exchange rates superior to flexible exchange rates in the presence of domestic disturbances. We investigate the normative implications of the choice of exchange regimes in the next section.

2. PRICE STABILITY, EXPECTED UTILITY, AND THE EXCHANGE REGIME

In the previous section we characterized the full macro equilibrium under each exchange regime, we now turn to a comparison of the regimes. We first compare the stability of the price level and then consider the normative implications of each regime.

Quite clearly, whether domestic (dollar) prices are more stable under fixed or flexible exchange rates will depend upon the relative sizes of the two countries, and the relative variability of disturbances in each country. Consider first the simplest case in which there is only one good ($i = 1$). Then, for flexible rates,

$$P_1^t = \frac{2M}{\lambda_1^t a_1} \tag{34}$$

whereas for fixed rates,

$$\hat{P}_1^t = \frac{2M^*}{N\lambda_1^t a_1 + \overline{N\lambda_1^t \bar{a}_1}} \qquad M^* = NM^t + \overline{NM}^t \tag{35}$$

Since, in considering price variability, we are essentially concerned with the real purchasing power of nominal assets, it is more convenient to work with the reciprocal of the price level;[4] define

$$\pi_1^t = \frac{1}{P_1^t} = \frac{\lambda_1^t a_1}{2M} \tag{36}$$

$$\hat{\pi}_1^t = \frac{1}{\hat{P}_1^t} = \frac{N\lambda_1^t a_1 + \overline{N\lambda_1^t \bar{a}_1}}{2M*} \tag{37}$$

Further, normalize units such that

$$\frac{M}{a_1} = \frac{M*}{Na_1 + \overline{Na}_1} \tag{38}$$

essentially, we assume that real per-capita money balances are equal under the two regimes.

Clearly, under which regime the value of real money balances (the reciprocal of the price level) is more variable depends on the relative sizes of the countries $(N, \bar{N})$, the variability of disturbances, and the correlation between disturbances. As $\bar{N} \to 0$, the home economy is essentially closed, and the choice of the exchange regime is irrelevant. As $\bar{N} \to \infty$, so that under fixed rates prices are exogenous, then $\hat{\pi}_1^t$ will be more variable than π_1^t if, and only if, the variance of $\bar{\lambda}_1^t$ is larger than that of λ_1^t.

For intermediate cases, it is likely that fixed exchange rates yield a more stable price level, unless foreign disturbances are considerably larger or else disturbances are (perfectly) correlated internationally. If $\lambda_1^t \equiv \bar{\lambda}_1^t$, it is clear that there is no "shock-absorber" effect as the peaks and troughs for each economy coincide. However, if $\lambda_1^t, \bar{\lambda}_1^t$ have identical, but independent, distributions, then prices will clearly be more stable under fixed rates $(0 < N < \infty)$. In general, if we define

$$E[(\lambda_1^t - 1)^2] = V_1^2 \qquad E[(\bar{\lambda}_1^t - 1)^2] = \bar{V}_1^2 \equiv \gamma^2 V_1^2$$
$$E[(\lambda_1^t - 1)(\bar{\lambda}_1^t - 1)] = \rho \cdot V_1 \bar{V}_1 = \rho\gamma V_1^2 \tag{39}$$

where γ measures the relative variability of disturbances, and ρ is the correlation coefficient between λ_1 and $\bar{\lambda}_1$, then prices will be more stable under fixed rates if

$$2\mu(\gamma\rho - 1) + \mu^2(\gamma^2 - 1) \leqslant 0 \qquad \mu \equiv \frac{\overline{Na}_1}{Na_1} \tag{40}$$

where μ measures the relative (economic) sizes of the two countries.

For $\gamma \leqslant 1$, it is clear that prices will be more stable under fixed rates ($\rho < 1$); however, even if $\gamma > 1$, domestic prices may be more stable under fixed rates if μ is not "too" large. For example, for $p = 0$, $\gamma^2 = 2$, domestic prices will be more stable under fixed rates for $\mu < 2$. By symmetry, it is clear that prices in the foreign country will be more stable under fixed rates if $\gamma \geqslant 1$. In general, then, for γ near 1, fixed exchange rates will yield more stable prices for each country than would a flexible exchange rate world. This demonstrates the "shock-absorber" role played by fixed exchange rates.[5]

The above analysis was for the case of a single commodity, in which case flexible exchange rates perfectly insulate each country from foreign disturbances. In a multi–traded-good world, flexible rates will not insulate the economy from foreign real disturbance unless these are perfectly correlated across sectors. As we have seen, relative prices are invariant to the exchange regime, and as foreign real disturbances will alter relative prices it is clear that no insulation is possible and that relative prices are equally variable under the two regimes.

To compare the variability of absolute prices under the two regimes, it is necessary to specify a price index; a plausible candidate is that obtained from the indirect utility function, which measures the change in expenditures needed to hold utility constant. Thus, from (14) define the price index P_I^t as

$$P_I^t = \frac{P_1^t}{H(r^t)} \tag{41}$$

where $H(r^t)$ is as defined previously. Following our earlier procedure, we compare the variability of the reciprocal of the price index (that is, the variability of the purchasing power of money balances) under each regime. For flexible rates,

$$\pi_1^t \equiv \frac{1}{P_I^t} = \frac{\left[\sum_i (r_i^t \lambda_i^t a_i) \right] H(r^t)}{2M} \tag{42}$$

and for fixed rates,

$$\hat{\pi}_1^t \equiv \frac{\left[\sum_i r_i^t (N\lambda_i^t a_i + \overline{N\lambda_i^t \bar{a}_i}) \right] H(r^t)}{2M*} \tag{43}$$

While it is, in general, difficult to compare these two expressions (and their variability), consider the special case in which $N = \bar{N}$, $a_i = \bar{a}_i$, and hence $M^* = 2NM$, and in which λ_i^t, $\bar{\lambda}_i^t$ have identical, but independent distributions. For this case, it is clear that the reciprocal of the price level is more stable under fixed rates. To see this, define

$$X_i = a_i r_i \lambda_i H(r) \qquad \bar{X}_i = a_i r_i \bar{\lambda}_i H(r) \qquad (a_i = \bar{a}_i) \tag{44}$$

where $X_i(\bar{X}_i)$ depend on all λ, $\bar{\lambda}$; for convenience, we drop the time superscript. By the symmetry of distributions,

$$E[X_i] = E[\bar{X}_i] \equiv \mu_i \tag{45}$$

where the expectation runs over all λ, $\bar{\lambda}$. Thus, the variance of π_I for flexible rates is given by

$$V(\pi_I) = \frac{1}{4M^2} E \left[\left(\sum_i (X_i - \mu_i) \right)^2 \right] \tag{46}$$

and for fixed rates by

$$V(\hat{\pi}_I) = \frac{N^2}{4(M^*)^2} E \left[\left(\sum_i (X_i - \mu_i) + \sum_i (\bar{X}_i - \mu_i) \right)^2 \right] \tag{47}$$

Letting $M^* = 2NM$, and recognizing that

$$E \left[\left(\sum_i (X_i - \mu_i) \right)^2 \right] = E \left[\left(\sum_i (\bar{X}_i - \mu_i) \right)^2 \right] \tag{48}$$

it follows that

$$V(\hat{\pi}_I) < V(\pi_I)$$

$$\text{if} \qquad E \left[\left(\sum_i (X_i - \mu_i) \right) \left(\sum_i (X_i - \bar{X}_i) \right) \right] \tag{49}$$

$$= E \left[\left(\sum_i X_i \right)^2 - \left(\sum X_i \right) \left(\sum \bar{X}_i \right) \right] > 0$$

Since the X_i, $\bar{X}_i$ have identical distributions, but are not perfectly correlated, it follows that the inequality holds.

Thus, as contended by the adherents of a fixed exchange rate regime, prices are likely to be more stable under a fixed exchange rate system, assuming the countries in question are subject to similar, but independent, disturbances. However, we must be careful in moving from this conclusion to normative conclusions for two reasons. First of all, it is not obvious ex ante that price stability is desirable. It is well known from the micro literature that price variability can raise expected utility. As we demonstrated in our earlier paper for a one-good world in which there are only foreign disturbances (Lapan and Enders, 1980), expected utility will be higher under a fixed exchange rate system—due exclusively to the price variability—if agents are not "too" risk-averse. Moreover, since in the presence of internal—as well as external—disturbances, domestic nominal (real) income will be variable, it is not sufficient to consider only the variability in the price level; one should consider the impact on real income. Under a flexible exchange rate system, movements in the price level are inversely correlated with domestic output, whereas under a fixed exchange system the movements in the price level depend on foreign disturbances as well. Thus, real income may be more stable under flexible rates than under fixed rates, even though the price level may be more stable under fixed rates.

To provide a normative comparison of the two regimes, we return to the indirect utility function developed in (20). For flexible rates, using (28),

$$Y^t = 2M \qquad P_1^t = \frac{2M}{\sum\limits_i (r_i^t \lambda_i^t a_i)} \tag{50}$$

Hence, from (20), utility under flexible rates is given by:

$$U_t = \left(\frac{\sum\limits_i r_i^t \lambda_i^t a_i}{2} \right)^{\theta/2} \left(\frac{\sum\limits_i r_i^{t+1} \lambda_i^{t+1} a_i}{2} \right)^{\theta/2} \frac{[H(r^t)H(r^{t+1})]^{\theta/2}}{\theta} \tag{51}$$

For fixed rates, P_1^j is given by (31); hence, utility under fixed rates is given by

$$\hat{U}_t = \left(\sum\limits_i \frac{r_i^t \lambda_i^t a_i}{2} \right)^{\theta} \left[\frac{\sum r_i^{t+1}(N\lambda_i^{t+1} a_i + \overline{N}\lambda_i^{t+1}\bar{a}_i)}{\sum r_i^t (N\lambda_i^t a_i + \overline{N}\lambda_i^t \bar{a}_i)} \right]^{\theta/2}$$

$$\times \frac{[H(r^t)H(r^{t+1})]^{\theta/2}}{\theta} \tag{52}$$

Clearly the realizations of utility for each generation will differ under the two regimes; however, we wish to compare expected utility under the two regimes. Define

$$Z^t \equiv \sum_i (r_i^t \lambda_i^t a_i) \qquad \bar{Z}^t \equiv \sum_i (r_i^t \bar{\lambda}_i^t \bar{a}_i) \tag{53}$$

Thus, for flexible rates

$$E[U_t] = E\left[\left(\frac{Z^t}{2}\right)^{\theta/2} \left(\frac{Z^{t+1}}{2}\right)^{\theta/2} \frac{[H(r_t)H(r^{t+1})]^{\theta/2}}{\theta}\right] \tag{54}$$

and for fixed rates

$$E[\hat{U}_t] = E\left[\left(\frac{Z^t}{2}\right)^{\theta} \left(\frac{NZ^{t+1} + \bar{N}\bar{Z}^{t+1}}{NZ^t + \bar{N}\bar{Z}^t}\right)^{\theta/2} \frac{[H(r_t)H(r_{t+1})]^{\theta/2}}{\theta}\right] \tag{55}$$

The expectations in (54) and (55) run over λ^t, $\bar{\lambda}^t$, λ^{t+1}, $\bar{\lambda}^{t+1}$. Define

$$J^t = \frac{NZ^{t+1} + \bar{N}\bar{Z}^{t+1}}{NZ^t + \bar{N}\bar{Z}^t} \tag{56}$$

Using the fact that λ^t, $\bar{\lambda}^t$ have identical but independent distributions over time, it is clear by symmetry that

$$\begin{aligned} E[\hat{U}_t] &= E\left[\left(\frac{Z^t}{2}\right)^{\theta} (J^t)^{\theta/2} \frac{[H(r^t)H(r^{t+1})]^{\theta/2}}{\theta}\right] \\ &= E\left[\left(\frac{Z^{t+1}}{2}\right)^{\theta} (J^t)^{-\theta/2} \frac{[H(r^t)H(r^{t+1})]^{\theta/2}}{\theta}\right] \end{aligned} \tag{57}$$

Thus,

$$E[\hat{U}^t] - E[U^t] = \frac{1}{2\theta} E\left[\left(\left(\frac{Z_t}{2}\right)^{\theta/2} (J^t)^{\theta/4} - \left(\frac{Z^{t+1}}{2}\right)^{\theta/2} (J^t)^{-\theta/4}\right)^2 \right.$$

$$\left. \times [H(r^t)H(r^{t+1})]^{\theta/2}\right] \tag{58}$$

The term inside the expectations operator is nonnegative and will be strictly positive for some λ, $\bar{\lambda}$ unless λ_i, $\bar{\lambda}_i$ are perfectly correlated

($N\lambda_i a_i \equiv \overline{N\lambda_i a_i}$). Assuming that domestic and foreign disturbances are not perfectly correlated,

$$E[\hat{U}^t] \gtreqless E[U^t] \text{ as } \theta \gtreqless 0 \tag{59}$$

Since $1 - \theta$ is the degree of relative risk aversion, it follows that a fixed exchange regime will yield higher expected utility for individuals who are not very risk-averse, while a flexible exchange regime will be preferred by individuals who are more risk-averse. Notice that this result is independent of the relative magnitudes of the disturbances at home and abroad, and holds regardless of the number of commodities. Thus, if there are no real domestic disturbances and if all foreign disturbances are perfectly correlated across sectors, then a flexible exchange rate will yield perfect insulation, whereas under fixed rates the domestic price level will be variable; nevertheless, fixed rates will be preferred for $\theta > 0$.

Hence, no normative conclusions can be drawn from analyzing the stability of the price level, or by comparing the magnitude of domestic and foreign disturbances. The explanation for our results is rather straightforward. Under fixed exchange rates, real consumption (utility) for an individual born in t will be correlated between periods, whereas under flexible rates there is no such correlation. Thus, under fixed rates, high domestic output levels at t allow members of generation t to increase (expected) consumption in t, t + 1 by accumulating money balances; under flexible rates this is not possible. The positive correlation in the intertemporal consumption bundle is clearly an advantage to fixed rates and depicts the usual "shock-absorber" role imputed to fixed rates. On the other hand, under flexible rates, the value of real money balances at t + 1 of an individual born at t depends only on t + 1 events, and not on t events, whereas under fixed rates it depends on both t and t + 1 events. This implies that utility will be more variable under fixed rates since the real income in each period t, t + 1 is tied to events in t, whereas under flexible exchange rates there is no such linkage; this result is the direct corollary of the "shock-absorber" role of fixed rates since the ability to transfer real purchasing power intertemporally implies that real income during retirement is dependent upon prior events. Hence, under fixed exchange rates there is more international risk-sharing, whereas under flexible rates there is more intergenerational risk-sharing. In the Appendix, a simple example is presented that illustrates this point.

Thus far, we have seen that if all goods are traded, relative prices are independent of the exchange regime. Moreover, although prices may tend to be more stable under fixed rates, the normative comparisons hinge only on attitudes toward risk; the fact that less risk-averse individuals will prefer fixed rates implies that price stability is not necessarily desirable. We now turn to the role played by nontraded goods to ascertain if the degree of "openness" of the economy is positively related to the desirability of fixed exchange rates.

3. NONTRADED GOODS AND THE CHOICE OF THE EXCHANGE REGIME

In the previous section we saw that the choice of the exchange regime depended only upon individual attitudes toward risk, and not upon the source of disturbances or country size. This seems to contradict the standard argument that asserts that the source of disturbances is of importance in choosing between regimes, and that fixed rates are likely to be preferred among countries of similar size because of the "shock-absorber" role played by linking the regimes—and hence the disturbances—together.

When we turn to discuss the role of nontraded goods, we find that a different, but related, criteria is applied in choosing between regimes. It is generally argued that for relatively open economies, fixed rates are preferable, because internal disturbances will have less impact on domestic prices; hence, for an open economy, prices are, it is argued, likely to be less volatile under fixed rates than under flexible rates. However, for relatively closed economies, flexible rates are supposed to be preferred because of the insulation from foreign disturbances and because the price of nontraded goods—under either regime—is determined in domestic markets.

The introduction of nontraded goods clearly complicates the analysis, because the relative price of nontraded to traded goods will depend upon the exchange regime. As we have seen, when all goods are traded, relative prices (given our assumptions) are independent of the exchange regime. However, since the demand for each good depends upon domestic wealth as well as income, and since under fixed rates domestic wealth changes over time, it follows that relative prices of nontraded goods under fixed exchange rates change (in a systematic way) over time, whereas under flexible rates the (probability) distribution of relative prices is unchanging.

On the other hand, it seems likely that the presence of nontraded goods will make fixed exchange rates appear *more* desirable (unlike the standard contention). The reason for this is straightforward:

under flexible rates, the society may not transfer purchasing power intertemporally. Consequently, the proportion in which traded and nontraded goods are consumed will depend only on domestic output levels; thus, this proportion will vary over time and will not be serially correlated (unless disturbances are). However, under fixed rates, purchasing power may be transferred intertemporally. If all goods are tradable, the desirability of this depends on attitudes toward risk. However, in the presence of nontradables, the inter-temporal transfer of purchasing power is more advantageous, because it allows the society (and hence individuals) to vary the proportion in which traded and nontraded goods are consumed. Consider, for example, a temporary increase in output of the traded good at time t. Under flexible rates, the proportion (in consumption) of tradables to nontradables will increase in t but return to its steady-state level at t + 1. However, under fixed rates, not all of the additional output will be currently consumed; some will be saved (via increases in wealth) for future periods. Thus, the proportion between tradables and nontradables will rise in t and subsequent periods; moreover, in any one period, the change in this proportion will be smaller under fixed rates than under flexible rates. Consequently, fixed rates allow the individual to smooth out the proportions in which goods are consumed, as well as the aggregate consumption bundle.

The ability to adjust the proportion in which goods are consumed is likely to become more important as the degree of substitutability between commodities decreases. If commodities are perfect substitutes, then the fact that one good is nontraded is essentially irrelevant; in essence, all goods are traded, and we can then resort to the analysis of prior sections. On the other hand, if the goods must be consumed in fixed proportions, it is clear that fixed rates must be preferred. Under flexible rates, if at any time output of the tradable exceeds that of the nontradable, the excess traded good is essentially discarded (since there are no capital movements), whereas under fixed rates the excess production can be sold to increase claims for future periods. Conversely, when output of the tradable is low, part of the nontraded good is discarded under flexible rates, whereas under fixed rates money balances can be drawn down to maintain the proportion in which the two goods are consumed. Hence, the smaller the degree of substitutability between traded and nontraded goods, the more likely it is that fixed rates will be preferred.[6]

Unfortunately, the analysis for this case is quite complicated. To simplify the analysis, we specialize the utility function given in Section 1 to the case in which the degree of substitutability between commodities is 1. Thus, let

is quite difficult, since, under fixed rates, the probability distribution of utility for a member of generation t depends on the (ex ante) distribution of M^t. Clearly, disturbances in the nontraded sector, λ_1^j, enter symmetrically for the two cases; however, disturbances in the traded sector (and in foreign prices) play a quite different role. In order to approximate expected utility under the two regimes, let

$$\lambda_1^t = 1 + b_1 V_1^t \qquad \lambda_2^t = 1 + b_2 V_2^t \qquad E[V_i^t] = 0 \qquad (80)$$

In (80), the productivity disturbances, $\lambda_1^t - 1$, depend upon the random variables V_1^t and the parameters b_i.

Further, we assume that the foreign currency price $\bar{P}_2^t$ is generated by a large economy that has the same structural form as the domestic economy:

$$\bar{P}_2^t = \frac{1}{\bar{\lambda}_2^t} \qquad \bar{\lambda}_2^t = 1 + b_3 V_3^t \qquad E[V_3^t] = 0 \qquad (81)$$

As for domestic disturbances, the disturbance in the foreign traded sector, $\bar{\lambda}_2^t - 1$, depends upon the random variable V_3^t, and a parameter b_3. For simplicity, we assume all disturbances are uncorrelated across sectors or time, and that they have stationary distributions:

$$E[V_i^t V_j^k] = \begin{cases} V_i^2 & i = j, t = k \\ 0 & \text{otherwise} \end{cases} \qquad (82)$$

Thus, V_i^2 is the variance of the random variable V_i^t.

Under flexible rates, the foreign currency price of tradables is irrelevant, and the distribution of utility for a member of generation t depends upon the distributions of λ_1 and λ_2, and hence upon the distributions of V_1, V_2 and the parameters b_1, b_2. Consequently, given the distributions of V_1, V_2, the *expected* utility under flexible rates depends upon the parameters b_1, b_2. Define

$$U*(b_1, b_2) = \frac{\alpha^{\alpha\theta}(1 - \alpha)^{(1-\alpha)\theta}}{2^\theta \theta}$$
$$\times E[(\lambda_1^t)^{\alpha\theta/2}(\lambda_1^{t+1})^{\alpha\theta/2}(\lambda_2^t)^{(1-\alpha)\theta/2}(\lambda_2^{t+1})^{(1-\alpha)\theta/2}] \qquad (83)$$

In (83), the expectation is taken over V_1^t, V_1^{t+1}, V_2^t, V_2^{t+1}; thus, from (80), expected utility may be thought of as depending upon the parameters b_1, b_2. While no direct evaluation of (83) is possible, for small b_i it can be approximated by the first three terms of a Taylor series expansion as

$$U^*(b_1, b_2) \cong U^*(0, 0) + \sum_{i=1}^{2} U_i^*(0, 0)b_i$$

$$+ \frac{1}{2} \sum_{i=1}^{2} \sum_{j=1}^{2} [U_{ij}^*(0, 0)b_i b_j] \tag{84}$$

where $U_i^*(0, 0) = \partial U^*/\partial b_i$ evaluated at $b_1 = b_2 = 0$, and $U_{ij}^*(0, 0) = \partial^2 U^*/(\partial b_i \, \partial b_j)$ evaluated at $b_1 = b_2 = 0$.

Differentiating (83), using (80), and evaluating it at $b_i = 0$ yields: [13]

$$U^*(b_1, b_2) \cong \left[\frac{\alpha^{\alpha\theta}(1 - \alpha)^{(1-\alpha)\theta}}{2^\theta} \right] \left[\frac{1}{\theta} + \frac{\alpha(\alpha\theta - 2)}{4} (b_1^2 V_1^2) \right.$$

$$\left. + \frac{(1 - \alpha)[(1 - \alpha)\theta - 2]}{4} (b_2^2 V_2^2) \right] \tag{85}$$

where $b_i^2 V_i^2$ is the variance of λ_i. Note that for $\theta/2 < 1$, expected utility decreases as the variance increases, as expected under risk-aversion.

A similar but more tedious process yields an approximation for expected utility under fixed rates. From (79), the distribution of utility for a person born at t depends on past, as well as current, disturbances (note, however, that disturbances in the nontraded sector enter equivalently under the two regimes). Given the (stationary) distributions of the V_i, ex ante expected utility under fixed rates depends upon the parameters b_1, b_2, b_3. Define

$$\hat{U}(b_1, b_2, b_3) = a \times$$

$$E\frac{(\lambda_1^t)^{\alpha\theta/2}(\lambda_1^{t+1})^{\alpha\theta/2}(M^{t+1})^\theta}{(P_2^t)^{(1-\alpha)\theta/2}(P_2^{t+1})^{(1-\alpha)\theta/2}[(1-\alpha)X^t + 2M^t]^{\alpha\theta/2}[(1-\alpha)X^{t+1} + 2M^{t+1}]^{\alpha\theta/2}}$$

$$\tag{86}$$

$$a \equiv \frac{\alpha^{\alpha\theta}(1 - \alpha)^{(1-\alpha)\theta}(2 - \alpha)^{\alpha\theta}}{\theta}$$

The expectation in (86) is taken over V_1^t, V_1^{t+1} and all V_2^j, V_3^j, $j \leqslant t + 1$.

Proceeding as for flexible rates, we may approximate the expected utility as

$$\hat{U}(b_1, b_2, b_3) \cong \hat{U}(0) + \sum_{i=1}^{3} \hat{U}_i(0)b_i$$

$$+ \frac{1}{2} \sum_{i=1}^{3} \sum_{j=1}^{3} \hat{U}_{ij}(0)b_i b_j \tag{87}$$

where, as earlier, $\hat{U}_i(0) = \partial\hat{U}/\partial b_i$ evaluated at $b = 0$ and $\hat{U}_{ij} = \partial^2\hat{U}/(\partial b_i \, \partial b_j)$ evaluated at $b = 0$. Taking the appropriate derivatives, using (80), and evaluating the expectations at $b = 0$ yields:

$$\hat{U}[b_1, b_2, b_3] \cong \frac{\alpha^{\alpha\theta}(1 - \alpha)^{(1-\alpha)\theta}}{2^\theta} \left\{ \frac{1}{\theta} + \left[\frac{\alpha(\alpha\theta - 2)}{4} \right] (b_1^2 V_1^2) \right.$$

$$+ \left[\frac{(1 - \alpha)^2}{4(2 - \alpha)^2} \right] [\theta(8 - 8\alpha + \alpha^2) - 4(2 - \alpha)](b_2^2 V_2^2)$$

$$\left. + \left[\frac{(1 - \alpha)}{2(2 - \alpha)} \right] [(1 - \alpha)\theta + \alpha](b_3^2 V_3^2) \right\} \tag{88}$$

As for flexible rates, risk aversion ($\theta < 1$) suffices to ensure expected utility decreases as the variance of domestic productivity disturbances increase. Note, however, that, as in our earlier section foreign price disturbances can increase expected utility, even if agents are risk-averse.

To compare the two regimes, it is necessary to compare the differences in expected utility. Using (85) and (88),

$$L \equiv \hat{U} - U^* = \frac{\alpha^{\alpha\theta}(1 - \alpha)^{(1-\alpha)\theta}}{2^\theta} \left\{ \left[\frac{(1 - \alpha)}{2(2 - \alpha)^2} \right] \right.$$

$$\times [2\theta(1 - \alpha)^2 + \alpha(2 - \alpha)](b_2^2 V_2^2)$$

$$\left. + \left[\frac{(1 - \alpha)}{2(2 - \alpha)} \right] [(1 - \alpha)\theta + \alpha](b_3^2 V_3^2) \right\} \tag{89}$$

where L is defined as expected utility under fixed minus expected utility under flexible exchange rates.

Several confirmations of (89) are available. For $\alpha = 1$, there are no traded goods, and the two regimes are identical; from (89), $L = 0$

at $\alpha = 1$, as expected.[14] For $\alpha = 0$, there are no nontraded goods, and the results of our previous section hold; from (89), at $\alpha = 0$, $L \geqslant 0$ as $\theta \geqslant 0$, as reported in our earlier sections. Finally, note that disturbances in the nontraded sector do not affect the choice of regimes, due to the symmetric way in which these disturbances appear in (74) and (79).[15]

A quick glance at (89) indicates that, regardless of the source of disturbances, as α (the size of the nontraded-good sector) increases, the range of values of θ for which fixed rates are preferred also increases. Thus, for α near zero, fixed rates will be preferred for $\theta \geqslant 0$ (relative risk aversion less than, or equal to, 1); however, as α tends to 1, the fixed exchange rate regime will be preferred by almost all individuals with finite levels of risk aversion.[16]

As discussed earlier, the presence of nontraded goods makes fixed exchange rates more appealing because of the ability to vary the proportion in which goods are consumed. Consider, for example, the case in which there are no internal real disturbances, but foreign price disturbances are present (hence, the money supply is random). Perfect insulation occurs under flexible rates, with individuals consuming $(\alpha/2, (1 - \alpha)/2)$ in each period; this would also be the consumption bundle under fixed rates if there were no price variability. The optimal decision rule calls for the individual to spend half his or her nominal income, $[P_1\alpha + P_2(1 - \alpha)]/2$, in each period. Hence, if all goods are traded ($\alpha = 0$), first-period consumption is unaltered by price variability; and, due to Jensen's inequality, the expected value of second-period consumption, $E[P^t/2P^{t+1}]$, exceeds $1/2$. Thus, whether price uncertainty is beneficial depends only upon attitudes toward risk. However, if some goods are nontraded, the price variability will increase the real value of first-period consumption, regardless of risk attitudes. Assuming the individual spends half the nominal income in that first period, the bundle $(\alpha/2, (1 - \alpha)/2)$ is always attainable and would be purchased if relative prices, P_2^t/P_1^t, equalled 1. Consequently, any variation in prices in that period must increase utility (the real value of consumption) for that period, since, if the relative price of the nontraded good exceeds 1, the person becomes a seller of that good, whereas the opposite occurs when its relative price falls below 1. Thus, first-period utility is minimized when relative prices equal 1, and any variation must be beneficial. Of course, the price variability also affects the real value of consumption in period 2, and the impact of this depends on attitudes toward risk. Nevertheless, the net effect of the presence of nontraded goods is to increase the desirability of price variability and hence to increase the attractiveness of fixed rates.

A similar analysis holds for the case of internal disturbances in the traded sector. Of course, these disturbances to productivity lower expected utility if individuals are risk-averse. Nevertheless, if some nontraded goods are present, the real disturbances lead to relative price changes that, as argued above, are beneficial. Consequently, for individuals who have a given relative risk aversion, the ability to vary the proportions of the consumption bundle is an asset and increases the desirability of fixed rates.

4. SUMMARY AND CONCLUSIONS

Traditionally, two criteria have been used in comparing exchange regimes: the source of economic disturbances, and the "openness" of the economy. The former argument asserts that fixed exchange rates are preferable if disturbances are real and internal, whereas flexible rates are preferable for internal nominal, or external, price disturbances. If internal and external disturbances are present and of comparable size, it is argued that fixed rates are likely to be preferred, because the linking together of the economic systems dampens the aggregate variability of the disturbances. The latter argument indicates that fixed exchange rates tend to be preferable for open economies, since domestic disturbances will then have little effect on domestic prices, whereas flexible rates are more desirable for closed economies.

The analysis presented in this chapter challenges both of these contentions. Using a microtheoretic approach, we have shown that when all goods are traded, the choice between exchange regimes depends only on attitudes toward risk; country size, or the sources of disturbances, are unimportant in choosing between exchange regimes. Moreover, we have demonstrated that price stability is not necessarily a desirable outcome. In the context of nontraded goods, we have shown that fixed rates are not necessarily preferable for open economies; the choice hinges upon attitudes toward risk, as well as the "openness" of the economy. Further, we have shown that the larger the size of the nontraded-good sector, the more likely it is that fixed rates will yield higher expected utility—a result that contradicts the prevailing view.

Of course, the analysis pursued here has been special in several ways. Money has been assumed to be the only store of value, so financial assets or real capital cannot be used to transfer purchasing power intertemporally. Also, the specification of preferences has entailed a rather special form; throughout, we assumed that the intertemporal degree of substitutability between aggregate consumption (expenditures) was 1, and for the case of nontraded goods we assumed that the intratemporal degree of substitutability between commodities was 1.

Intuition suggests that the choice between exchange regimes will depend not only upon attitudes toward risk, but also upon the intertemporal and intratemporal elasticities of substitution between commodities. For the case of nontraded goods, the smaller the degree of substitutability between traded and nontraded goods, the more likely it is that fixed exchange rates will be preferred because of the ability to vary the consumption bundle. Hence, the conclusions presented in this paper concerning the role of nontraded goods would have been strengthened by assuming that the degree of substitutability between traded and nontraded goods was less than 1.

As the analysis of Section 2 indicates, the intratemporal elasticity of substitution between traded goods is not crucial. However, intuition again suggests that the intertemporal elasticity of substitution between aggregate consumption (expenditures) should be important. Assuming that there are only foreign price disturbances (and no relative price movements), consumption will be stable under flexible rates but will vary intertemporally under fixed rates. Hence, the larger the elasticity of substitution between intertemporal consumption (and/or, the smaller the degree of risk aversion), the more likely it is that fixed rates are preferred; for very risk-averse individuals, or for individuals whose intertemporal elasticity of substitution is small, flexible rates are likely to be preferred. On the other hand, if disturbances are real and internal, then intertemporal consumption will be more stable under fixed rates. Thus, for this case, it is likely that fixed rates will be preferred by individuals who are not very risk-averse or by those for whom the intertemporal elasticity of substitution is small, whereas flexible rates will tend to be preferred by individuals with considerable risk aversion who possess a large intertemporal elasticity of substitution.

In general, then, the choice between exchange regimes cannot be reduced to issues such as where disturbances occur or the degree of openness of the economy. The ultimate comparison must be based on the expected utility of agents and hence will depend on the properties of the agents' utility function, such as risk aversion and intratemporal and intertemporal commodity substitution. Further research in this area could attempt to generalize the results presented here and also to introduce alternative stores of value. Our preliminary research indicates that, even when real capital (and investment) is introduced to provide an alternative store of value, the comparison between exchange regimes still hinges upon the degree of risk aversion. Hence, we believe that recognition of the different forms of risk sharing under each regime is an important step in providing a systematic comparison of fixed and flexible exchange rates.

APPENDIX: COMPARING FIXED AND FLEXIBLE EXCHANGE RATES

It is important to note that, while our normative conclusions differ from those of Fischer and Mundell, our positive conclusions concerning price and consumption stability are identical to earlier results. A simple example may help illustrate how this difference arises. Consider the case of a single good, Q_1. Using the basic model of the text, domestic and foreign aggregate output, Q_1^t, $\bar{Q}_1^t$, are

$$Q_1^t = N\lambda_1^t \qquad \bar{Q}_1^t = \overline{N\lambda}_1^t \tag{1}$$

Under flexible rates, aggregate domestic consumption C_a^t equals aggregate domestic output:

$$C_a^t = N\lambda_1^t \tag{2}$$

However, under fixed rates, domestic consumption will differ from domestic output; aggregate domestic consumption under fixed rates is given by

$$\hat{C}_a^t = \left(\frac{N\lambda_1^t}{2}\right) + \left(\frac{NM^t}{P^t}\right) \tag{3}$$

M^t and P^t are given by equations (31) and (33) of the text; assuming that there is only one good

$$\hat{C}_a^t = \left(\frac{N\lambda_1^t}{2}\right) + \left(\frac{N\lambda_1^{t-1}}{2}\right)\left(\frac{N\lambda_1^t + \overline{N\lambda}_1^t}{N\lambda_1^{t-1} + \overline{N\lambda}_1^{t-1}}\right) \tag{3'}$$

Comparing (2) and (3′), it is clear aggregate consumption will be more stable under fixed rates if there are no foreign disturbances ($\bar{\lambda}_1^t \equiv \bar{\lambda}_1^{t-1} \equiv 1$), whereas it will be more stable under flexible rates if there are no domestic disturbances ($\lambda_1^t \equiv \lambda_1^{t-1} \equiv 1$). Similarly, if countries are of comparable size ($N = \bar{N}$), and disturbances are similar (λ, $\bar{\lambda}$ have identical and independent distributions), then aggregate consumption will be more stable under fixed rates. This conclusion is in full agreement with the earlier works of Mundell (1973) and Fischer (1977), and reflects the shock-absorber role of fixed exchange rates.

The stability of aggregate consumption cannot, however, be used as a basis for normative conclusions for at least two reasons: (1) the stability of aggregate consumption tells us nothing about the consumption bundle of individuals. and (2) expected consumption levels may differ under the two regimes. To illustrate the latter point, suppose $\lambda_1 \equiv 1$ (no domestic disturbances), and that $N/\bar{N} \to 0$ (domestic economy is small). Clearly, aggregate consumption is more stable under flexible exchange rates; however, expected (aggregate) consumption is higher under fixed rates. Thus, a comparison of the stability of aggregate consumption is not decisive.

Instead of considering aggregate consumption, we now consider the life-time (2-period) consumption bundle of an agent born at t. Under either regime, one-half of current income is spent, the rest saved for consumption during retirement. The intertemporal consumption bundle under either regime is given by

$$(C^t, B^{t+1}) = \left(\frac{\lambda_1^t}{2}, \frac{P^t \lambda_1^t}{2P^{t+1}}\right) \tag{4}$$

The difference between the two regimes depends upon the determination of the intertemporal price ratio. Using the results of Section 1, for flexible rates

$$\frac{P^t}{P^{t+1}} = \frac{\lambda_1^{t+1}}{\lambda_1^t} \tag{5}$$

whereas for fixed rates

$$\frac{\hat{P}^t}{\hat{P}^{t+1}} = \frac{N\lambda_1^{t+1} + \overline{N\lambda}_1^{t+1}}{N\lambda_1^t + \overline{N\lambda}_1^t} \tag{6}$$

Consequently, the intertemporal consumption bundle under flexible rates is given by

$$(C_t, B_{t+1}) = \left[\left(\frac{\lambda_1^t}{2}\right), \left(\frac{\lambda_1^{t+1}}{2}\right)\right] \tag{7}$$

whereas under fixed rates

$$(\hat{C}_t, \hat{B}_{t+1}) = \left[\left(\frac{\lambda_1^t}{2} \right), \left(\frac{\lambda_1^t}{2} \right) \left(\frac{N\lambda_1^{t+1} + \bar{N}\bar{\lambda}_1^{t+1}}{N\lambda_1^t + \bar{N}\bar{\lambda}_1^t} \right) \right] \tag{8}$$

In comparing (7) and (8), we can see that under flexible rates there is more intergenerational risk sharing, whereas under fixed rates there is more international risk sharing. A comparison of the stability of individual consumption in either period under each regime is, in general, not meaningful since the issue is the whole consumption vector. The utility function is the appropriate device to allow us to compare different consumption vectors.

To illustrate, consider a special case in which the domestic economy is small ($N/\bar{N} \rightarrow 0$). Under fixed rates,

$$(\hat{C}_t, \hat{B}_{t+1}) = \left[\left(\frac{\lambda_1^t}{2} \right), \left(\frac{\lambda_1^t}{2} \right) \left(\frac{\bar{\lambda}_1^{t+1}}{\bar{\lambda}_1^t} \right) \right] \tag{8'}$$

If we further assume there are no foreign disturbances ($\bar{\lambda}_1 \equiv 1$), then *aggregate* consumption will be more stable under fixed rates. There is, of course, no direct way to compare the stability of individual consumption under the two regimes, since it is a vector. Note, however, that under flexible rates C_t, B_{t+1} are uncorrelated, whereas under fixed rates they are perfectly correlated. Thus, lifetime consumption $C^t + B^{t+1}$, as well as utility, is more variable under fixed rates, even though aggregate consumption is *less* variable under fixed rates. The normative conclusions depend upon comparing the benefits of having C_t, B_{t+1} positively correlated under fixed rates, with the costs due to the greater variability of utility under fixed rates. Thus, despite the macro results, very risk-averse individuals would prefer flexible rates.

A similar result holds when disturbances are only external ($\lambda_1 \equiv 1$). Under this case, flexible exchange rates provide complete isolation, and personal—as well as aggregate—consumption is stable. Under fixed rates, aggregate consumption is variable, and individual consumption is given by

$$(\hat{C}_t, \hat{B}_{t+1}) = \left(\frac{1}{2}, \frac{\bar{\lambda}_{t+1}}{2\bar{\lambda}_t} \right) \tag{9}$$

Thus, under fixed rates, individual and aggregate consumption are more variable than under flexible rates. However, note that expected consumption is higher under fixed rates than under flexible rates, since $E(\bar{\lambda}_1^{t+1}/\bar{\lambda}_1^t) > 1$. Thus, the price uncertainty (instability) increases average consumption levels. Even though consumption is less stable under fixed rates, individuals who are not very risk-averse will prefer fixed rates. Consequently, no normative conclusions can be drawn from statements concerning the relative stability of macro variables.

NOTES

1. If agents may hold either currency and there is no explicit transactions demand for a particular currency, then the exchange rate is indeterminate, but constant over time (Kareken and Wallace, 1979); hence, fixed and flexible exchange rates would be identical. To avoid this result, we assume agents may hold only their domestic currency as a store of value—essentially, we assume there are capital controls. While Helpman and Razin (1979) argued, correctly, that this is an asymmetric treatment of the two regimes (since governments may engage in capital movements under fixed rates), our results indicate that a flexible exchange regime with capital controls may be superior to a fixed exchange regime—and hence imply that capital controls could increase expected utility in each country.

2. The assumption of internationally identical preferences greatly simplifies the analysis, since it implies relative prices are unaffected by international transfers, and hence, by the choice of the exchange regime. However, flexible rates do not insulate an economy from real foreign disturbances that alter relative prices.

3. While some claim that the choice of exchange regimes may affect the allocation of resources, we assume that this is not the case. Our analysis for the case in which $\theta = 0$ indicates that, when all goods are traded, the allocation of resources is independent of the exchange regime (Enders and Lapan, 1981).

4. Little would be altered if we discussed the variability of prices instead of their reciprocals.

5. It is also true that aggregate consumption in each country is likely to be more stable under fixed rates if the disturbances have similar distributions and countries are of similar size. However, no normative conclusions can be drawn from the stability of aggregate consumption.

6. More specific results can be found in Lapan and Enders (1981).

7. The analysis of the previous section indicates that little is gained by assuming that there is more than one traded good.

8. Essentially, we assume that the ex ante production possibility frontier is linear but that resource allocation decisions are made before the λ_i are known. It is readily seen that the allocation $Q_1 = \alpha$, $Q_2 = (1 - \alpha)$ $(Q_1 + Q_2 \leqslant 1)$ is optimal for a stationary economy and for flexible exchange rates. Under fixed rates, if resources are intertemporally mobile the allocation would change over time, depending on the domestic money supply (see Enders and Lapan, 1981). However, if a stationary allocation must be chosen, then the assumed allocation is optimal. For simplicity, we assume that resources are immobile under both regimes.

9. We assume the home country is small; as seen in Section 2 relative country size does not affect the normative comparisons.

10. This result holds because the elasticity of substitution between goods is unity; for other cases, prices in each sector would depend on disturbances in each sector, but relative prices would depend upon only the ratio of these disturbances. For details, see Lapan and Enders (1980).

11. If the only source of disturbances is in the nontraded sector, the two regimes will be identical when the elasticity of substitution between commodities is unity.

12. A lengthier discussion of the stability of relative prices may be found in Enders and Lapan (1979).

13. The specific calculations used to approximate expected utility under each regime are omitted in order to save space. Full details are available in Lapan and Enders (1980).

14. Note that $\lim_{\alpha \to 1} [(1-\alpha)^{(1-\alpha)\theta}] = \lim_{\alpha \to 0} [\alpha^{\alpha\theta}] = 1$.

15. As noted above, this is true only for the case in which the commodity elasticity of substitution is one.

16. At $\alpha = 1$, the two regimes are identical; hence, for α near one, the differences in expected utility will be small; nevertheless, for α near one, expected utility will be higher under fixed rates for finite θ. Thus, large α raises the likelihood that fixed rates are preferable, though increasing α does not necessarily increase the differences in expected utility. For example, define $D = L/|U(0)|$, i.e., D is the percent difference in expected utilities (relative to the certainty value). For $\alpha = 0$, $D \gtreqless 0$ as $\theta \gtreqless 0$; and as $\alpha \to 1$, $D > 0$ but tends to zero. If disturbances are only internal, D initially increases with α, then decreases as α tends to one; similar results hold for external disturbances if $\alpha < 2/3$. Thus, the larger is α, the more likely it is fixed rates are preferred, and some value of $\alpha \epsilon$ (0, 1) will maximize the percent differences in utility under the two regimes. Clearly, the presence of nontraded goods is an argument in favor, not against, fixed exchange rates.

REFERENCES

Enders, W., and H. E. Lapan. "The Exchange Rate, Resource Allocation, and Uncertainty." *Southern Economic Journal* 47 (1981):924–40.

——. "Stability, Random Disturbances and the Exchange Rate Regime." *Southern Economic Journal* 45 (1979):49–70.

Fischer, S. "Stability and Exchange Rate Systems in a Monetarist Model of the Balance of Payments." In *The Political Economy of Monetary Reform*, edited by Robert Aliber. Montclair, NJ: Allanheld, Osmun and Co., 1977, pp. 59–73.

Helpman, E., and A. Razin. "Towards a Consistent Comparison of Alternative Exchange Rate Systems." *Canadian Journal of Economics* 12 (1979): 394–409.

———."Uncertainty and International Trade in the Presence of Stock Markets." *Review of Economic Studies* 45 (1978):239-50.

Kareken, J., and N. Wallace. "Samuelson's Consumption Loan Model with Country Specific Fiat Monies." *Staff Report of the Federal Reserve of Minneapolis*, No. 24, 1977.

Laffer, A. "Two Arguments for Fixed Rates." In *The Economics of Common Currencies*, edited by H. G. Johnson and A. K. Swoboda. London: Allen & Unwin, 1973, pp. 25-34.

Lapan, H. E., and W. Enders. "Random Disturbances and the Choice of Exchange Regimes in an Intergenerational Model." *Journal of International Economics* 10 (1980):263-83.

McKinnon, R. I. "Optimum Currency Areas." *American Economic Review* 53 (1963):717-24.

Mundell, R. A. "Uncommon Arguments for Common Currencies." In *The Economics of Common Currencies*, edited by H. G. Johnson and A. K. Swoboda. London: Allen and Unwin, 1973, pp. 114-32.

Samuelson, P. A. "An Exact Consumption Loan Model of Interest with or without the Social Contrivance of Money." *Journal of Political Economy* 66 (1958):467-82.

Tower, E., and T. D. Willett. *The Theory of Optimum Currency Areas and Exchange Rate Flexibility*. Princeton: International Finance Section, 1976.

Turnovsky, S. J. "Technological and Price Uncertainty in a Ricardian Model of International Trade." *Review of Economic Studies* 41 (1974):201-18.

II

EXCHANGE RATE POLICIES
FOR DEVELOPING COUNTRIES

5

THE OPTIMAL CURRENCY BASKET
IN A WORLD OF GENERALIZED FLOATING
WITH PRICE UNCERTAINTY

LESLIE LIPSCHITZ & *V. SUNDARARAJAN*

1. INTRODUCTION

Since the advent of generalized floating exchange rates, many countries have elected to peg the value of their currencies to some currency basket. Some have chosen the SDR as their basket, but others have preferred to set up their own baskets which they considered were better suited to their patterns of trade and their particular objectives. In this latter case policymakers have had to decide on the best weights for component currencies in the basket and, presumably, have had to specify criteria for assigning basket weights. Recently a number of articles have been written on this question, and the objective of this chapter is to synthesize two distinct approaches that have emerged in these articles.[1] The approach in the papers by Flanders and Helpman (1979; hereafter referred to as FH) and by Branson and Katseli-Papaefstratiou (1978, 1980; hereafter referred to as BP) focuses chiefly on offsetting the effects of nominal exchange rate fluctuations on the target variable specified by the authorities.[2] It is argued in the following sections that their contribution lies mainly

The authors are grateful to James Healy and Susan Schadler for constructive comments and suggestions. This paper should be construed as representing the personal views of the authors and not the official position of the IMF.

in developing a methodology for choosing sets of weights for (nominal or real) effective exchange rate indices—"elasticity" weights—that are each appropriate to a selected target variable.[3] These weights, however, are conceptually distinct from currency basket weights, and the selection of elasticity weights is merely the first step in the process of choosing weights for a currency basket. FH and BP succeed in accomplishing this first step, but they go on to conclude that it is optimal to use the derived elasticity weights as the weights for the currency basket. This conclusion is the consequence of the suppression of relative prices in their models, reflecting the assumption that variations in the relevant target variable arise solely from nominal exchange rate variations. On this assumption, stabilization can be achieved by changing the home-currency exchange rate to eliminate variations in a suitably measured effective exchange rate index.

In contrast, the paper by Lipschitz and Sundararajan (1980a; hereafter referred to as LS) makes no attempt to derive elasticity weights or to show how these weights will depend upon the objective of policy. It merely assumes as a starting point that such weights can be derived from an empirical model, such as the MERM, and goes on to discuss the optimal currency basket given an appropriate set of weights for the effective exchange rate index.[4] It does, however, focus on the distinction between the weights that are appropriate to the effective (real) exchange rate index and those appropriate to an optimal currency basket to be employed as an exchange rate standard. The distinction is due to the incorporation of price movements as well as exchange rate movements into the analysis and the attempt to view the basket as a means to deal with price uncertainty. Thus, while FH and BP, which derive elasticity weights rigorously, may be regarded as complementary to LS, it is shown in the following sections that the basket weights derived in these former studies are optimal only in a (trivial) special case.

It is argued here that the objective of a currency basket is to provide a rule for exchange rate management in an environment where appropriate discretionary exchange rate changes—managed floating—are impossible because of uncertainty regarding the value of relevant economic variables. Nominal exchange rates are known instantaneously, and there is no uncertainty regarding their values at any point in time. Therefore, the stabilization of a linear function of nominal exchange rates—which is the problem posed both in BP and FH—is a straightforward matter as soon as the coefficients of the linear function are known. As there is no uncertainty, information on the probability distributions of nominal exchange rate changes is quite irrelevant. However, any useful model of trade must include prices as well as exchange rates, and, while particular prices may be quoted continuously, price indices are usually available only after a considerable time lag. Thus, at any particular time, the policymaker is faced with price uncertainty, and in order to conduct exchange rate policy with some trade-related objective in mind, a method, or rule, for dealing with this uncertainty is required. This rule should ideally incorporate all the available information on prices, including the relevant probability distributions, and the determination of optimal basket weights should involve not only the elasticity weights required for deriving the appropriate effective real exchange rate index, but also the rule for dealing with price uncertainty.

Both the BP and the FH studies are incomplete insofar as they abstract from relative price movements. In the next section the standard trade model analyzed in BP is generalized to include relative price movements, and in Section 3 the implications for optimal basket weights are spelled out.[5]

2. THE OBJECTIVE OF THE PEG, THE APPROPRIATE PRICE INDEX, AND THE REAL EXCHANGE RATE

The analysis of this section focuses on three points. First, a concern with the trade-related objectives most frequently mentioned—such as stabilizing the terms of trade or the trade balance at some acceptable level—should lead to a desire to stabilize an appropriate index of the real effective exchange rate rather than some index of the nominal effective exchange rate. Prices are important, and the lack of contemporaneous price data makes it difficult to fine-tune exchange rate policy. Second, the conventional specification of aggregate trade equations in the empirical literature leads to the conclusion that the price indices of importance to the construction of a real effective exchange rate index are overall price indices—such as a world price of traded goods, or an index of GNP deflators, or wholesale prices— rather than some small subset of prices. Third, the arguments in BP, recast to allow the explicit inclusion of prices, lead to the derivation of a set of weights for a real exchange rate index appropriate to the objective of the authorities. The larger part of this section is given to the derivation of these weights, as this is an important first step in the analysis. It is shown in the final section that these same weights are not usually ideal for a currency basket designed to meet the policy objective.

TABLE 5-1. Conventional Trade Model

A. Behavioral equations

Export supply:
$$x = a + s_x (p_x - p_h) \tag{1}$$

Export demand:
$$x = a' + d_x (q_x - q_x^w) \tag{2}$$

Import supply:
$$m = b + s_m (q_m - q_m^w) \tag{3}$$

Import demand:
$$m = b' + d_m (p_m - p_h) \tag{4}$$

B. Definitions

Export prices:
$$q_x = p_x + e \tag{5}$$

Import prices:
$$q_m = p_m + e \tag{6}$$

C. Reduced forms (ignoring the constants)

Exports:
$$x = \frac{s_x d_x}{d_x - s_x}(q_x^w - e - p_h) \tag{7}$$

$$p_x = \frac{d_x}{d_x - s_x} (q_x^w - e) - \frac{s_x}{d_x - s_x} p_h \tag{8}$$

Imports:
$$m = \frac{d_m s_m}{s_m - d_m} (q_m^w - e - p_h) \tag{9}$$

$$p_m = \frac{s_m}{s_m - d_m} (q_m^w - e) - \frac{d_m}{s_m - d_m} p_h \tag{10}$$

Table 5-1 shows a conventional model of trade, and Table 5-2 provides a glossary of symbols. Where trade is broad-based—that is, exports and imports span a wide range of commodities—each of the two foreign price indices, q_x^w and q_m^w, in the model is approximated by a suitably weighted sum of general price indices for trading partner countries. This simplification is prevalent in the empirical

TABLE 5-2. Glossary of Symbols

A. Parameters

a, a', b, b'	= constants
s_x	= export elasticity of supply with respect to relative price term
d_x	= export elasticity of demand with respect to relative price term
s_m	= import elasticity of supply with respect to relative price term
d_m	= import elasticity of demand with respect to relative price term

B. Variables

Note: All lower-case letters represent the natural logarithms of the variable. The corresponding upper-case letters represent the simple value of the variable. Where convenient, lower-case letters may also be regarded as logarithmic indices about a unit value at some base date so that $z = \ln(Z_t) - \ln(Z_0)$.

x	= our export volume
m	= our import volume
p_x	= price index of our exports in domestic currency
p_h	= price index of home goods in domestic currency
q_x	= price index of our exports in foreign currency
q_x^w	= price index in foreign currency of goods available to trading partners that are competitive with our exports
p_m	= price index of our imports in domestic currency
q_m	= price index of our imports in foreign currency
q_m^w	= price index in foreign currency of goods competitive with our imports on world markets
e	= foreign currency units per unit of domestic currency

work.[6] For the export demand function, it is difficult to find unit value indices in the importing country for each of the goods that competes with some specific export, and then to aggregate over this set of indices. For the aggregate import supply function, a similar argument can be made.

Following BP, we can extend the reduced forms (7) to (10) in Table 5-1 to the case of many trading partners. It is assumed, for simplicity, that all trading partner countries have identical elasticities (s_x, d_x, s_m, and d_m). However, foreign price indices and bilateral exchange rates have to be aggregated on a weighted average basis over the i trading parters. Export weights (η_i) are used for the export-related reduced forms, and import weights (ϵ_i) are used for the import-related reduced forms. Taking cognizance of the conventional simplifications mentioned in the preceding paragraph, we simply replace the world price variable q_x^w in equations (7) and (8) with the export-weighted average of foreign prices in foreign currency terms, $\Sigma \eta_i p_i$, and the world price variable q_m^w in equations (9) and (10) with the import-weighted average of foreign prices in foreign currency terms, $\Sigma \epsilon_i p_i$. The nominal exchange rate is replaced by a weighted average—export- or import-weighted, depending on which is appropriate—of bilateral exchange rates. We may now write the reduced forms of the disaggregated trade model as follows:

$$x = s_x k (\sum \eta_i p_i - \sum \eta_i e_i - p_h) \tag{7'}$$

$$p_x = k (\sum \eta_i p_i - \sum \eta_i e_i) + (1 - k) p_h \tag{8'}$$

$$m = d_m k' (\sum \epsilon_i p_i - \sum \epsilon_i e_i - p_h) \tag{9'}$$

$$p_m = k' (\sum \epsilon_i p_i - \sum \epsilon_i e_i) + (1 - k') p_h \tag{10'}$$

where

$$k = \frac{d_x}{d_x - s_x} \quad \text{and} \quad k' = \frac{s_m}{s_m - d_m}$$

As pointed out in BP, k and k' are indices of market power. In the small country case, k tends to unity as d_x tends to minus infinity. Similarly, k' tends to unity as s_m tends to infinity.

From these latter four reduced forms we may examine various trade-related objectives of exchange rate policy. For consistency with the earlier papers cited, we focus on two objectives: the terms of trade, and the trade balance.

The Terms-of-Trade Objective

From (8') and (10'), we may write the terms of trade[7] as

$$p_x - p_m = \sum (k \eta_i - k' \epsilon_i) p_i - \sum (k \eta_i - k' \epsilon_i) e_i - (k - k') p_h \tag{11}$$

Remembering that $\Sigma \eta_i = 1$ and $\Sigma \epsilon_i = 1$, it is easy to show that

$$\frac{p_x - p_m}{k - k'} = \sum w_i^{tt}(p_i - e_i - p_h) \tag{12}$$

where

$$w_i^{tt} = \frac{k\eta_i - k'\epsilon_i}{k - k'} \qquad \text{and} \qquad \sum w_i^{tt} = 1$$

Thus our terms-of-trade objective can be translated into a set of weights attached to bilateral real exchange rates in order to aggregate them into an effective real exchange rate index. The index calculated with these weights--as in equation (12)--is the appropriate effective real exchange rate index for consideration whenever the terms of trade is the objective of policy.

The Trade Balance Objective[8]

Starting with indices of nominal exports and nominal imports, we define the trade balance tb as the logarithm of the ratio of exports to imports, both measured in home currency units:

$$tb = x + p_x - m - p_m$$
$$= (x - m) + (p_x - p_m) \tag{13}$$

From $(7')$ to $(10')$, and remembering that $\Sigma \eta_i = 1$ and $\Sigma \epsilon_i = 1$,

$$\begin{aligned} tb &= s_x k \sum \eta_i(p_i - e_i - p_h) - d_m k' \sum \epsilon_i(p_i - e_i - p_h) \\ &\quad + \sum (k\eta_i - k'\epsilon_i)(p_i - e_i - p_h) \\ &= \sum [k\eta_i(s_x + 1) - k'\epsilon_i(d_m + 1)](p_i - e_i - p_h) \end{aligned} \tag{14}$$

(Note that the bracketed expression is simply a repetition of the familiar Marshall-Lerner condition.) Defining $c = k(s_x + 1) - k'(d_m + 1)$, and dividing both sides by c, yields

$$\frac{tb}{c} = \sum w_i^{tb}(p_i - e_i - p_h) \tag{15}$$

where

$$w_i^{tb} = \frac{k\eta_i(s_x + 1) - k'\epsilon_i(d_m + 1)}{k(s_x + 1) - k'(d_m + 1)}$$

and

$$\sum w_i^{tb} = 1$$

Thus, the trade balance objective can also be translated into a set of weights attached to bilateral real exchange rates in order to aggregate them into an effective real exchange rate index. The index calculated with these weights—as in equation (15)—is the appropriate effective real exchange rate index for consideration whenever balanced trade is the objective of policy.[9,10,11]

3. THE DETERMINATION OF CURRENCY WEIGHTS IN THE BASKET

From the preceding section, it is clear that there is an effective real exchange rate index relevant for each of the alternative objectives of exchange rate policy. The weights in this index are determined by the objective and the magnitudes of the relevant elasticities. For simplicity, in this section the superscripts are dropped, and the appropriate set of weights is given as w_i—whether w_i^{tt} or w_i^{tb}. It is argued that while the foregoing analysis might provide the correctly weighted index of real exchange rates for the specified objective of the exchange rate basket peg, the same weights are not necessarily appropriate for the basket. The reasoning is straightforward. It is impossible to monitor price developments at home and abroad on a continuous basis, yet these price developments are important determinants of the appropriately weighted real exchange rate index. If all prices except the exchange rate were fixed, the effective real exchange rate index would be stabilized simply by fixing to a basket of currencies with the same weights as those derived for the index. However, insofar as there is uncertainty about current price movements, it is useful to build into the basket weights any available information about these price movements.

If the authorities of the home country had perfect contemporaneous price data, there would be no need for a basket. They would simply adjust nominal exchange rates on a day-to-day (or even hour-to-hour) basis to stabilize the real exchange rate.[12] Good leading indicators for prices would also be useful in this exercise. Any systematic method of predicting price movements should be built into the exchange rate policy—either in the determination of basket weights or in a formalization of changes in the rate of exchange of the home currency vis-à-vis the basket. For illustrative purposes, we consider the former case in this section: a systematic relationship between each bilateral exchange rate and the corresponding bilateral relative price is assumed, and this relationship is built into the determination of basket weights. The resultant basket is derived so that the weights on nominal exchange rates are such that they minimize the fluctuations of the effective real exchange rate index that is appropriate to the objective of the authorities.[13]

It is helpful at this stage of the analysis to introduce a numéraire currency—say, the pound sterling—and more compact notation. Let s_i denote exchange rates defined as pounds per i-th currency unit, and s_h pounds per home currency unit. Therefore

$$e_i \equiv s_h - s_i$$
$$rp_i \equiv p_i - p_1$$
$$rp_h \equiv p_h - p_1$$

where country (1) is the United Kingdom, so that relative prices are defined vis-à-vis the numéraire currency country. Note that lower-case letters continue to represent logarithms of the variables.

Returning to equations (12) and (15), it is clear that while a different objective is reflected in each set of weights, the basic form of the equation is the same for either objective and may be written as

$$OB = \sum w_i(p_i - e_i - p_h) \tag{16}$$

with OB representing either the terms of trade or the trade balance, and the w_i's defined accordingly. Substituting the new notation into (16), adding and subtracting p_1, and indicating matrix notation by a circumflex ($\hat{\ }$), (16) may be rewritten as

$$OB = \hat{w}'(\hat{rp} + \hat{s}) - (rp_h + s_h) \tag{16'}$$

Assume that the authorities have decided to fix the value of the home currency to some, as yet undetermined, weighted basket of partner countries' currencies. The definition of the currency basket may be written as

$$s_h = \hat{\beta}'\hat{s} \tag{17}$$

where $\hat{\beta}$ is a column vector of weights on trading-partner exchange rates.

Substituting (17) into (16') eliminates s_h so that

$$OB = \hat{w}'(\hat{r}p + \hat{s}) - (rp_h + \hat{\beta}'\hat{s}) \tag{18}$$

The task of the authorities is to choose $\hat{\beta}$ such that the variance of OB is minimized.[14] This is a straightforward exercise. The first-order conditions give the solution for $\hat{\beta}$:

$$\hat{\beta} = \hat{w} + \Omega^{-1}\Pi\hat{w} - \Omega^{-1}\Gamma \tag{19}$$

where

    Ω = variance-covariance matrix of exchange rates
    Π = covariance matrix of relative prices and exchange rates
    Γ = vector of covariances between exchange rates and the home-country relative price.

From (19) it is quite clear that the case analyzed by BP—that is, where prices are fixed so that $\Gamma = \Pi = 0$ and $\hat{\beta} = \hat{w}$—is a special case of the general solution. However, as noted earlier, this solution is trivial; if prices are fixed and contemporaneous information on exchange rates is given, there is no uncertainty at all in the system.

Clearly the formula (19) can only be used to derive β_2 to β_n. The rank of the matrices Ω and Π in (19) is $n-1$, and Γ is a column vector of $n-1$ elements because both s_1 and rp_1 are constants set at zero by definition. β_1 may be obtained residually from the condition that the β's have to sum to unity.

There are a number of conditions under which a single currency peg will be optimal. The most obvious example of a single currency peg is that in which purchasing power parity holds continuously. In this case, $\Omega^{-1}\Pi$ becomes a diagonal matrix of regression coefficients each set at -1, and the first two terms of equation (19) drop out. Thus we may write

$$\hat{\beta}|_{PPP} = -\Omega^{-1}\Gamma \tag{20}$$

If the home country then picks a numéraire currency country with an inflation rate equal to its own, rp_h becomes a constant and Γ becomes a null vector. Thus the weights β_2 to β_n are zero, and the weight on the numéraire currency (β_1) is unity. Other cases in which a single currency peg is optimal are less amenable to so simple an exposition, and details of these cases are given in LS.

Thus far the discussion has been on an abstract level and has not considered the feasibility of computing optimal weights from the available data. Given a constraint on the optimization process that the real exchange rate has to remain within certain limits around the mean, it is, of course, possible that no optimal basket exists if these limits are narrow. If, for example, the home country inflates much more rapidly than any of its trading partners, its currency would not be able to remain pegged to any weighted average of partner-country currencies without violating this constraint. To remain in the neighborhood of the equilibrium real exchange rate, the home currency would have to be devalued periodically vis-à-vis any currency basket chosen. But assuming that the rate of inflation in the home currency is not higher or lower than the extremes among its partner countries, so that a basket peg is feasible, the parameters on which the optimal basket weights depend are obtainable.

Ignoring the off-diagonal elements in equation (19), the optimal basket weights depend on three sets of parameters: (1) the elasticities w_i, (2) the ratio of the covariance of each relative price and corresponding exchange rate to the variance of the exchange rates, and (3) the covariance between the first relative price (of the home and the numéraire currency country, rp_h) and the exchange rates between the numéraire currency and all other partner-country currencies, divided by the variance of the exchange rates. The first set of parameters can be obtained from a model of trade as outlined in Section 2. The second set turns out to be simply the coefficients of a set of least-square regressions relating relative prices between each partner country and the numéraire currency country to the exchange rate between the two corresponding currencies.[15] The parameters in the third set are easy to calculate from the data, but economic theory provides no clue as to their sign or stability. However, as noted earlier, if the inflation rate in the home country is the same as that in the numéraire currency country—the choice of numéraire is in any event arbitrary—the logarithmic relative price, rp_h, will be zero, and Γ will be a null vector.

On this basis, it is possible to compute the parameters of the optimal basket weights, to apply standard stability tests to these parameters—in the hope that if they were stable in the past they will be stable during the period over which the authorities wish to employ the basket peg—and to construct the optimal basket.[16] It should be noted that the particular methodology employed in this derivation assumes that there is some systematic, nonunitary relationship between exchange rates and corresponding relative prices. This relationship constitutes additional information on prices that helps reduce uncertainty and should therefore be incorporated into the derivation of optimal basket weights. However, the particular methodology employed here should be regarded as merely illustrative of the general argument that price uncertainty is fundamental to the optimal basket computation, and that all information on price movements including any model of future price movements or of the correlation between prices and exchange rates should be incorporated in the computation of the optimal basket.

NOTES

1. See, for example, Branson and Katseli-Papaefstratiou (1978, 1980), Flanders and Helpman (1979), Lipschitz (1979), and Lipschitz and Sundararajan (1980).

2. These studies build upon several earlier papers that came out of the IMF—see, for example, Artus and Rhomberg (1973), Thakur (1975), and Rhomberg (1976). These earlier papers do not deal with basket weights but with the closely related problem of choosing weights for an effective exchange rate index.

3. Throughout this paper, an effective exchange rate refers to a weighted average of nominal exchange rates with the weights determined in relation to some specified objective; an effective real exchange rate refers to a similarly weighted average of bilateral exchange rates each adjusted for bilateral relative price movements.

4. For details of the MERM, see Artus and Rhomberg (1973).

5. The FH model is generalized and extended in Lipschitz and Sundararajan (1980b).

6. See, for example, Houthakker and Magee (1969) and Goldstein and Khan (1978).

7. Of course, for the exchange rate of the home currency to have any effect on the terms of trade, it is essential that the home country have some market power over exports or imports—that is, it cannot be a small country in the standard terminology. See BP or Lipschitz (1979).

8. This section is developed similarly to BP. The resultant weights are analogous to those of the MERM analysis. See Artus and Rhomberg (1973) and Feltenstein et al. (1979).

9. Note that a trade surplus or deficit may be taken as the norm. For example, if in the base year ($t = 0$) nominal exports were 100 and nominal imports 130, we can create an index for each based on unit values in those years. The logarithm of the ratio of these two indices (tb) would have a zero value provided that the ratio of exports to imports remained at 100:130, but it would diverge from zero whenever the ratio changed.

10. The implications of the elasticities approach to purchasing power parity, reflected in equation (15), are spelled out in greater detail in Sundararajan (1976).

11. The weights for the real exchange rate indices in equations (12) and (15) provide useful insights into the appropriateness of the commonly used trade-based weights—export shares, import shares, and trade shares—in various empirical situations. For example, if the objective relates to the trade balance, export shares are appropriate if import supply is completely inelastic ($s_m = 0$) and import shares are appropriate if export demand is completely inelastic ($d_x = 0$).

12. There are, of course, good arguments against trying to fix the real exchange rate. If, for example, the real exchange rate changes owing to real (as opposed to financial) factors, manipulation of a financial variable (like the nominal exchange rate) neither can nor should fix the real exchange rate [see Fischer (1977) and Lipschitz (1978)]. Also, it has been argued that short-run, reversible relative price fluctuations should not lead the authorities to immediate compensating exchange rate adjustment. However, the case considered above is largely concerned with deviations from purchasing power parity among trading partners that do not reflect underlying real changes but are of sufficient duration to have adverse effects.

13. The approach followed in the remainder of this section is similar to that in LS.

14. The task becomes more complicated if the minimization is carried out subject to the constraint that the real exchange rate remain within certain bounds. The quadratic programming problem involved in this case is solved in LS.

15. Even if purchasing power parity holds exactly, these least-square coefficients might turn out to be less than unity because of a simultaneity bias. This is demonstrated in Krugman (1978).

16. This exercise is performed in LS. In addition, the optimal basket is compared to an elasticity-weighted basket by simulation and, as expected, found to be superior.

REFERENCES AND BIBLIOGRAPHY

Artus, J. R., and R. R. Rhomberg. "A Multilateral Exchange Rate Model." *IMF Staff Papers* 20 (1973):591–611.

Branson, W. H., and L. T. Katseli-Papaefstratiou. *Exchange Rate Policy for Developing Countries.* Working paper, Princeton University International Finance Section (1980).

——. "Income Instability, Terms of Trade, and the Choice of Exchange Rate Regime." *Journal of Development Economics* 7 (1980):49–69.

Feltenstein, A., M. Goldstein, and S. M. Schadler. "A Multilateral Exchange Rate Model for Primary Producing Countries." *IMF Staff Papers* 26 (1979): 543–82.

Fischer, S. "Stability and Exchange Rate Systems in a Monetarist Model of the Balance of Payments." In *The Political Economy of Monetary Reform* edited by R. Z. Aliber. New York: Allandheld, Osmun and Co., 1977, pp. 59-73.

Flanders, J. M., and E. Helpman. "An Optimal Exchange Rate Peg in a World of General Floating." *The Review of Economic Studies* 46 (1979):533-42.

Goldstein, M., and M. S. Khan. "The Supply and Demand for Exports: A Simultaneous Approach." *Review of Economics and Statistics* 60 (1978): 275-86.

Houthakker, H. S., and S. P. Magee. "Income and Price Elasticities in World Trade." *Review of Economics and Statistics* 51 (1969):111-25.

Krugman, P. "Purchasing Power Parity and Exchange Rates: Another Look at the Evidence." *Journal of International Economics* 8 (1978):397-407.

Lipschitz, L. "Exchange Rate Policies for Developing Countries: Some Simple Arguments for Intervention." *IMF Staff Papers* 25 (1978):650-75.

———. "Exchange Rate Policy for a Small Developing Country, and the Selection of an Appropriate Standard." *IMF Staff Papers* 26 (1979):423-49.

——— and V. Sundararajan. "The Optimal Basket in a World of Generalized Floating." *IMF Staff Papers* 27 (1980a):80-100.

——— and V. Sundararajan. "An Optimal Exchange Rate Peg in a World of General Floating—Extension and Comments." IMF, unpublished, 1980b.

Rhomberg, R. R. Indices of Effective Exchange Rates. *IMF Staff Papers* 23 (1976):88-112.

Sundararajan, V. "Purchasing Power Parity Computations: Some Extensions to Less Developed Countries." IMF, unpublished, 1976.

Thakur, S. M. "A Note on the Concept of Effective Exchange Rate." IMF, unpublished, 1975.

6

OPTIMUM CURRENCY PEGS
FOR ARAB COUNTRIES

MICHAEL B. CONNOLLY & ABDELHADI YOUSEF

INTRODUCTION

After the breakdown of the Bretton Woods system in 1973, each country was confronted with the problem of choosing an exchange rate system involving either a fixed or floating currency peg of one kind or another. While most developed countries have followed a partially flexible exchange rate system, problems particular to developing countries make it more difficult for them to float their currencies. We take it for granted that a currency peg is an appropriate exchange rate policy for developing countries. Among the more important reasons for this are: a currency peg provides a stable rule for and restraint against monetary growth, the small scale of the market for local money, lack of development of financial markets, confidence and currency substitution, openness of the economy, and so forth (see Connolly, 1983; Mundell, 1961).

In this chapter, the case of fifteen Arab countries (seven oil producers and eight non-oil producers) is investigated in light of two fundamental exchange rate issues facing these countries. First, what is an optimum currency peg for these countries? Second, should

The research reported here does not represent any official position of the International Monetary Fund.

these countries choose a basket currency peg, and what weights should be assigned to the different currencies in that basket?

The criteria established for the empirical portion of this study are based primarily on two factors: first, the inflation and money growth rates that are expected to be imported by the sample countries under different pegging policies; second, the variability of domestic inflation rates in these same countries produced by the currency peg. Thus, decision making will be a matter of choosing the pegging policy providing a more stable domestic inflation where stability is measured both in terms of the rate of inflation and by the standard deviation in that rate.

Section 1 reviews the historical record of fifteen Arab countries and five industrial countries, Section 2 develops the theoretical model in terms of the rate of inflation and its variance, Sections 3 and 4 analyze various alternative currency pegs in light of the imported rate of inflation and its stability. Finally, Section 5 draws some conclusions from the analysis.

1. HISTORICAL PERSPECTIVE

The postwar economic record (1950–79) of the Arab countries has high and low points, especially for oil-producing countries (Table 6-1). From a monetary point of view, money growth rates in the 1950–79 period ranged from relatively low levels of 9.5%, 11.4%, 10.9% in Egypt, Iraq, and Lebanon, respectively, to highs of 24.4% in Kuwait, 27.6% in Qatar, 25.7% in Saudi Arabia, and 37.7% in U.A.E.. Furthermore, these money growth rates have been relatively stable in the low money-growth countries (with a standard deviation of 10%, 9.6%, and 10.6% in Egypt, Jordan, and Iraq, respectively), whereas instability in these rates is higher for the high money-growth countries (standard deviation of 41%, 21%, 29%, and 25% in Kuwait, Qatar, U.A.E., and Saudi Arabia, respectively).

Money growth rates for the period 1973–79 differ from those in the period 1950–79 in that most countries in the sample experienced an increase in their money growth rates. The exception to this is Libya, which maintained almost the same average money growth rate (about 27%). However, the stability in these money growth rates increased for most countries. Among the exceptions are Bahrain, Qatar, Libya, and Saudi Arabia which exhibited only a slightly higher level of instability.

TABLE 6-1. Summary: Fifteen Arab Countries

Country	Inflation rate		Money growth	
	1950–79	1973–79	1950–79	1973–79
Algeria	7.84 (4.52)	9.61 (4.42)	19.55 (8.27)	23.56 (3.23)
Bahrain	9.66 (8.44)	16.17 (7.15)	18.58 (15.34)	22.81 (20.45)
Egypt	3.87 (5.34)	9.84 (2.63)	9.51 (10.31)	23.90 (2.34)
Iraq	2.92 (5.32)	8.18 (3.00)	11.38 (10.62)	28.87 (9.56)
Jordan	10.82 (4.54)	12.83 (3.85)	13.82 (9.65)	21.74 (7.42)
Kuwait	8.32 (2.67)	8.33 (2.67)	24.38 (41.75)	25.57 (11.19)
Lebanon	n.a. (n.a.)	n.a. (n.a.)	10.90 (12.25)	16.96 (9.30)
Libya	6.64 (8.26)	10.95 (9.08)	27.33 (10.97)	27.13 (12.10)
Morocco	5.12 (4.67)	9.61 (4.55)	11.71 (8.19)	18.56 (3.27)
Qatar	n.a. (n.a.)	n.a. (n.a.)	27.56 (21.09)	36.77 (23.59)
Saudi Arabia	8.55 (11.43)	16.53 (13.84)	25.74 (24.89)	51.01 (25.08)
Sudan	7.57 (9.74)	19.20 (19.42)	14.46 (13.00)	28.90 (7.04)
Syria	4.02 (8.20)	12.16 (6.50)	15.16 (11.16)	27.24 (8.53)
Tunisia	4.13 (4.18)	6.32 (1.86)	12.75 (6.58)	15.18 (4.11)
U.A.E.	n.a. (n.a.)	n.a. (n.a.)	37.67 (29.44)	37.67 (29.44)

Note: Standard deviation in parentheses.
Source: Inflation rate and money growth: calculated from *International Financial Statistics, 1980 Yearbook*, International Monetary Fund, Washington, D.C., U.S.A.

137

Average inflation rates for the periods 1950–79 and 1973–79 do not reveal the same pattern found in the money growth rates analysis. Some of the differences between the two are: (1) There is much less dispersion in the average inflation rates compared to deviations in money growth rates. Inflation rates range from a low of 2.9% in Iraq to a high of 10.8% in Jordan for the 1950–79 period, and from a low of 6.3% in Tunisia to a high of 19.2% in Sudan for the 1973–79 period. (2) There is no apparent significant relationship between average rates of inflation and their stability. On the other hand, a significant positive relationship between money growth rates and their stability exists. This is shown in the following equations (t values in parentheses):

Money growth rates (1950–79):

$$\sigma_m = .51 + .81\,\Delta m \qquad R^2 = .42 \qquad\qquad (1)$$
$$(.10)\ (3.30)$$

Inflation rates (1950–79):

$$\sigma_p = 5.25 + .18\,\Delta p \qquad R^2 = .03 \qquad\qquad (2)$$
$$(2.29)\ (.56)$$

where

σ_m = standard deviation in money growth rates
Δm = average money growth rate
σ_p = standard deviation in inflation rate
Δp = average inflation rate

There is no positive association between average inflation rates and their stability, but there is in the case of money growth rates.

The historical record of the Arab countries included in the study is graphically illustrated in Figs. 6-1 and 6-2. Figure 6-1 plots the average rate of inflation on the horizontal axis, and the standard deviation in inflation on the vertical axis. Figure 6-2 plots the average rate of money growth on the horizontal axis, and its standard deviation on the vertical axis. Both graphs summarize in the part the detailed information on each country contained in a Data Appendix in Yousef (1981) and available upon request and are drawn from the summary data provided in Table 6-1.

In Fig. 6-1 no significant findings can be extrapolated from the relationship between average rates of inflation and their standard

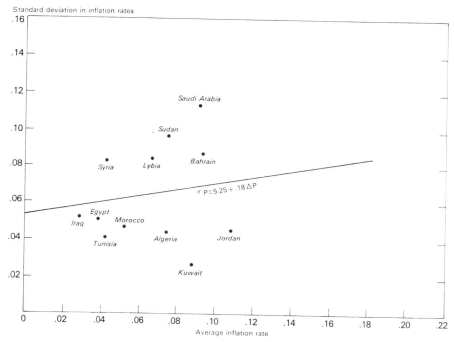

FIGURE 6-1. The relationship between average and standard deviation in inflation rate: twelve Arab countries.

deviations. Most results are mixed as in the case of Iraq and Syria with a dollar peg, which have low but unstable rates of inflation. Similarly, Kuwait, which pegs to a basket of currencies, experienced a relatively high and stable inflation rate. The cases of Libya and Sudan are noteworthy because of the high and unstable inflation rates demonstrated, even though these countries peg to the dollar.

Figure 6-2 illustrates the contrast between the low and stable rate of monetary growth enjoyed by most of the dollar peg countries (Egypt, Iraq, Syria, and Sudan), and the high and unstable rate of money growth experienced by countries not pegging to the dollar. As mentioned, however, there are exceptions such as Libya, which pegs to the dollar but has a high and relatively stable rate of monetary growth. Nevertheless, it should be noted that the advantage of low and stable money growth rates has been shared by some other countries that follow a basket peg (Tunisia and Algeria), as well as by those following the SDR peg (Jordan).

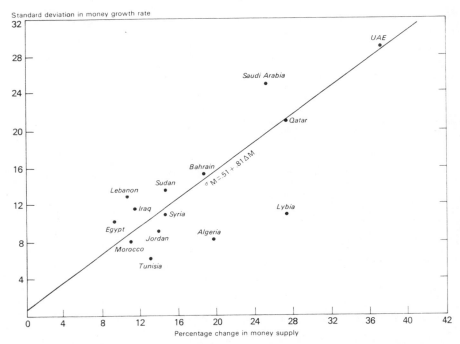

FIGURE 6-2. The relationship between average and standard deviation in money growth rates: fifteen Arab countries.

To complete our historical overview, some remarks about the five industrial countries are now in order. Over the years, higher quality monies with low and stable growth rates drive out lower quality monies that have high and unstable growth rates through currency substitution. The dollar had a good historical record of low and stable growth during the period 1950–79. The pound had a fairly good record for the period 1950–71, but that record changed after 1971, shifting to high and unstable money growth rate. During the 1970s, the rate of growth of the pound was double that of the dollar, and that growth rate was unstable with a standard deviation over three times that of the dollar (see Table 6-2). This, in part, accounts for the disappearance of the sterling zone represented by the decline in the number of countries which peg to the pound from eleven in mid-1973 to only one country today.

The French franc provides a high but stable rate of money growth (11%), with a standard deviation of 2.5% for the period

TABLE 6-2. Summary: Five Industrialized Countries

Country	Inflation rate		Money growth		Real growth	
	1950–79	1973–79	1950–79	1973–79	1950–79	1973–79
United States	3.8 (3.3)	8.2 (2.3)	4.4 (2.3)	6.5 (1.5)	3.49 (2.57)	2.95 (3.15)
United Kingdom	6.6 (5.6)	14.8 (5.3)	6.2 (6.0)	12.7 (5.1)	2.61 (1.95)	2.16 (3.15)
France	6.3 (4.7)	10.2 (2.0)	11.0 (4.2)	11.2 (2.4)	4.86 (1.68)	3.36 (1.69)
Germany	2.8 (2.7)	5.1 (1.6)	9.8 (3.5)	9.3 (3.5)	4.75 (2.86)	2.75 (2.59)
Japan	6.0 (5.5)	10.4 (6.9)	16.8 (7.6)	13.1 (6.2)	8.31 (3.76)	4.95 (3.47)

Note: Standard deviation in parentheses.

Source: Inflation rate and money growth: Calculated from pp. 58–59, *I.F.S. 1980 Yearbook.* Real growth: Germany and U.S., calculations from Gross National Product 1975 prices, line a.r. *1980 I.F.S. Yearbook.* France, Japan, and U.K., calculations from Gross Domestic Products 1975 prices, lines 99 b.r., 99 a.r., and 99 b.p., respectively, *1980 I.F.S. Yearbook.* For France 1978 and 1979, data from February 1981 *I.F.S. Yearbook.*

1973-79. This type of stability in the growth rate is a partial explanation for the survival of the French franc zone. In addition, trade and financial patterns of the former French colonies tend to reinforce the link with the franc, which was not the case with the pound.

The German mark has provided a high and stable growth rate during the entire postwar period. It is ranked between the dollar and the franc, with an average growth rate of 9.8% and a standard deviation of 3.5%. However, real economic growth has been higher in Germany than in the United States. Even so, the higher monetary growth rate did not translate into a higher inflation rate in Germany.

The Japanese yen has provided a high and unstable rate of growth during both periods. That is, 16.8% average money growth with a 7.6% standard deviation from 1950-79, and an average growth rate of 13.0% with a standard deviation of 6.2% from 1973-79. Simultaneously, real economic growth in Japan has been rapid, offsetting the inflationary effects of the high growth rate in money supply over the entire postwar period.

2. A MODEL OF AN OPTIMUM CURRENCY PEG

This section sketches a model of an optimum currency peg in a world of six currencies: the home currency, the dollar, the mark, the franc, the yen, and the pound. The home country trades with the five industrialized countries and seeks to peg its currency for optimum currency arguments. The two broad alternative pegs are a single currency peg versus a basket peg. The choice can be modeled in light of three broad factors.

1. The country's desired inflation rate and its variance.
2. Monetary policies in the five industrial countries.
3. The country's trade pattern and the extent of deviations in exchange rates from purchasing power parity movements.

The three building blocks of the model are the rate of inflation, purchasing power parity (PPP), and the type of currency peg. Each can be specified in turn.

First, the domestic rate of inflation is given by

$$p = \sum_{i=1}^{5} \delta_i(\pi_i + p_i) \tag{3}$$

which states that the domestic rate of inflation in each sample country, p, will depend upon δ_i (the share of trade with each industrial country), π_i (the rise in the home currency price of each of the five industrial currencies), and p_i (the rate of inflation in each of the five countries).

Second, movements in exchange rates between any two currencies is assumed to reflect a systematic component, differentials in the inflation rates between the two countries, and a random component ϵ_{ji} that is an independent, normally distributed random variable with zero mean and variance $\sigma^2_{\epsilon_{ji}}$. Thus, for relative purchasing power parity we have

$$\pi_i - \pi_j = p_j - p_i - \epsilon_{ji} \tag{4}$$

A positive value of ϵ_{ji} means that currency i depreciates relative to currency j by more than warranted due to the difference in inflation rates. This deviation in exchange rates may involve terms-of-trade effects or random monetary shocks to the PPP relationship, for example. (Clearly, $\epsilon_{ji} = 0$ for i = j.)

Third, there are two broad types of currency pegs: a single currency peg, or a basket peg. A single currency peg to currency j involves

$$\pi_j = 0 \tag{5}$$

while a basket peg to the five currencies with weights β_i is represented by

$$\sum_{i=1}^{5} \beta_i \pi_i = 0 \tag{6}$$

In the case of a single currency peg—for example, to the dollar —the domestic rate of inflation in the home country is equal to the U.S. rate of inflation minus a weighted average of deviations in movements of the dollar from purchasing power parity with respect to the four other industrial countries. Thus the domestic inflation rate with dollar peg (dollar is currency j) is given by

$$p = p_j - \sum_{\substack{i=1 \\ i \neq j}}^{5} \delta_i \epsilon_{ji} \tag{7}$$

and, similarly, the variance in the domestic rate of inflation with dollar peg is given by

$$\sigma_p^2 = \sigma_{p_j}^2 + \sum_{\substack{i=1 \\ i \neq j}}^{5} \delta_i^2 \, \sigma_{\epsilon_{ji}}^2 \tag{8}$$

Consequently, with a dollar peg, the expected rate of inflation equals the U.S. rate of inflation, but the actual rate can be higher or lower depending upon deviations in exchange rate movements from purchasing power parity (PPP). If the dollar rises more than is warranted by PPP ($\Sigma \delta_i \epsilon_{ji} > 0$, where j is the dollar), domestic prices will rise less than U.S. prices. Similarly, the variance in domestic prices will equal the variance in the U.S. inflation rate plus a weighted average of the variances in deviations of exchange rates from PPP movements. In a sense, with a dollar peg, a country expects to experience the same price stability pattern as in the United States.

With a basket peg, a country imports a weighted average of inflation rates of countries in the baskets, plus a weighted average of deviations in exchange rates from PPP. The weights applying to the rates of inflation are the currency basket weights β_i, while the weights applying to the deviations in exchange rates from PPP are the *difference* between the basket weight and the trade share of each currency, $\beta_i - \delta_i$. Thus the domestic inflation rate with currency basket peg is

$$p = \sum_{i=1}^{5} \beta_i p_i + \sum_{\substack{i=1 \\ i \neq j}}^{5} (\beta_i - \delta_i) \epsilon_{ji} \tag{9}$$

Similarly, the variance in the domestic rate of inflation with a currency basket is

$$\sigma_p^2 = \sum_{i=1}^{5} \beta_i^2 \, \sigma_{p_i}^2 + \sum_{\substack{i=1 \\ i \neq j}}^{5} (\beta_i - \delta_i)^2 \, \sigma_{\epsilon_{ji}}^2 \tag{10}$$

A strong argument for a trade-weighted basket ($\beta_i = \delta_i$) is that it shields domestic prices from shocks due to deviations in exchange rates from PPP movements. In this case, the right-hand terms in equations (6) and (7) disappear altogether. Or, a Special Drawing

Peg would simply involve setting weights equal to .42 for the dollar, .19 for the mark, and .13 for the franc, yen, and pound, respectively, as established January 1, 1981. A third possibility would be to select weights designed to minimize the variance in the domestic rate of inflation. However, one does not have future data on trade patterns, inflation rates, and deviations in exchange rates from purchasing power parity, so that an educated guess on the future is involved. It is possible, nevertheless, with hindsight, to analyze the currency weights that, if chosen in 1973, would have minimized the variance in the domestic rate of inflation from 1973–79. Such ex post variance-minimizing weights necessarily outperform all other currency pegs, whether single or basket, ex post, in minimizing the variance in domestic inflation; but ex ante, for a postsample period, they may not. With this caution in mind, it is possible to calculate weights so as to minimize the variance in the domestic rate of inflation. To do so, equation (10) would be minimized relative to the β_i subject to the constraint that $\Sigma_{i=1}^{5} \beta_i = 1$, which gives the currency basket with ex post weights that minimize the variance in domestic inflation:[1]

$$B = A^{-1}c \tag{11}$$

where the B and c represent five-element column vectors, and A^{-1} is the inverse of a 5 × 5 matrix.

It would now be possible, on the basis of the above model, to compare alternative currency pegs in the light of their implied rate of inflation and its stability. However, it is fruitful to add one extra element to the model. In a flexible exchange rate system between the five major currencies, the domestic rates of inflation in these countries can be assumed to be composed of (1) a systematic component involving growth in the money stock beyond the long-term real growth rates and (2) an unsystematic component of monetary growth which is assumed to be a random variable μ_i with expectation zero which is independent, normal, and serially uncorrelated. That is, for each of the five industrial countries, the rates of inflation are indicated by

$$p_i = \rho_i + \mu_i \tag{12}$$

where the ρ_i represent the expected, systematic growth in the money stock above (if positive) or below (if negative) the long-term real growth rate in the economy, and the μ_i represent unsystematic, random shocks to the monetary growth process. This conforms to the rational expectations result that the actual rate of inflation will equal the expected rate of inflation plus a white-noise term.

Consequently, it would be possible to conceive of a currency peg based primarily upon expectations regarding future monetary and real growth rates in the industrial countries. Indeed, any currency peg implicitly involves considerations of this sort.

3. ALTERNATIVE SINGLE CURRENCY PEGS

This section compares the hypothetical performance of various single currency pegs for fifteen Arab countries during the period 1973-79. The five single currency pegs compared are the dollar, the mark, the franc, the yen, and the pound. The analysis is done first in terms of the average inflation rate that an Arab country would expect to have imported. The second comparison is in terms of the variability in the rate of inflation over the 1973-79 period. The expected rate of inflation would be equal to the rate of inflation in the country whose currency is used as a peg. The variability in the rate of inflation can be measured by estimating equation (8) using the variance in the rate of inflation in the currency peg country, the trade shares, and the variance of deviations in exchange rates from PPP movements. In this regard, trade shares of oil-exporting countries were adjusted to include the impact of pricing their oil exports in terms of the dollar. The reasoning behind this is based on two factors. First, as long as oil exports are priced in terms of the dollar, they can be considered as trade with the United States. Second, oil exports contribute a larger percentage of total exports of these countries than any other product.

The results of the analysis are reported in Table 6-3, which gives the hypothetical performance of single currency pegs based on the inflation rate of each industrial country, its standard deviation, trade shares adjusted to sum to unity, and deviations in exchange rates from purchasing power parity.

In light of the facts that for all oil-producing Arab countries the United States is the major trading partner, and that the U.S. rate of inflation has been relatively stable (as measured by a standard deviation of 2.3%), it is not surprising that the dollar would provide a more stable peg in terms of the standard deviation in the inflation rates of oil-producing Arab countries. In addition to these countries, Jordan enjoys a more stable dollar peg compared to other single currency pegs. This result can be supported partially by the relatively

TABLE 6-3. Single Currency Pegs Based on Inflation Rates in Industrialized Countries (1973–79)

| Country | Standard deviation in inflation rate with currency pegged to | | | | |
	Dollar	Pound	Franc	Mark	Yen
Algeria*	2.89	7.33	5.59	4.87	16.10
Bahrain	5.50	8.10	5.99	4.98	8.58
Egypt	3.62	6.43	3.86	3.45	10.47
Iraq*	3.01	7.38	5.62	4.47	16.18
Jordan	3.59	6.48	4.22	3.70	10.77
Kuwait*	2.76	7.59	6.06	5.17	17.83
Lebanon	4.00	6.33	3.44	3.36	9.66
Libya*	2.53	7.69	6.27	5.37	17.83
Morocco	5.91	6.94	2.46	4.09	10.33
Qatar*	2.74	7.52	6.01	5.17	16.82
Saudi Arabia*	2.54	7.94	6.61	5.65	18.64
Sudan	4.42	6.15	3.94	4.03	9.12
Syria	4.25	6.51	3.30	3.21	9.60
Tunisia	5.43	6.88	2.80	3.76	10.20
U.A.E.*	2.70	7.62	6.46	6.29	17.22
Average inflation rate in currency peg country	8.2 (2.3)	14.8 (5.3)	10.2 (2.0)	5.1 (1.6)	10.4 (6.9)

Note: Standard deviations in parentheses; δ_i = total trade share.
*Trade shares adjusted to sum to unity.
Source: Direction of Trade, 1980 Yearbook, International Monetary Fund.

high rate of trade Jordan has with the United States and by the stable rate of inflation in the United States.

The French franc would provide the most stable pegging policy in terms of the standard deviation in the domestic inflation rate for Morocco, Sudan, and Tunisia. This is mainly because France is a major trade partner for Morocco and Tunisia. However, it should be noted that the case of Sudan is supported partially by the relatively good performance of the franc in terms of the stability of France's rate of inflation.

The mark would provide a more stable peg for Bahrain, Egypt, Lebanon, and Syria. This is attributed to the low level of variance in the rate of inflation in Germany with a standard deviation of 1.6% as compared to other industrialized countries and to the relatively high shares of trade of these countries with Germany. Neither the pound nor the yen would provide an optimal single currency peg for any of the sample countries.

From a theoretical point of view it is preferable to choose a currency peg in light of the expected monetary policy that is provided by the various major currencies. While the future conduct of monetary policy by the various industrial countries is not known, a long historical record from which lessons can be drawn is available.

Table 6-4, which indicates the hypothetical performance of single currency pegs based on monetary policies of industrialized countries, reports different monetary policies that would have been implicitly imported under five different currency pegs. The procedure used here resembles that of the previous analysis, which was based on inflation rates in currency peg countries. However, the variance in *money* growth rates of the five industrial countries replaces the variance in inflation rates.

Using monetary stability comparisons, the dollar would provide a more stable peg in terms of the standard deviation in inflation rates of twelve countries. These include the seven oil-producing countries (Algeria, Iraq, Kuwait, Libya, Qatar, Saudi Arabia, U.A.E.) and five other countries (Bahrain, Egypt, Jordan, Lebanon, Sudan). The French franc would provide a more stable pegging policy in terms of the standard deviation in the domestic inflation rate for Syria, Tunisia, and Morocco. In this case, the mark, the pound, and the yen are ruled out as being optimal in providing a stable pegging policy.

These results are hardly surprising given the fact that monetary policy in the United States has been somewhat stable since 1973, with an average rate of growth in M1B of 6.5% and a standard deviation of 1.5%. In France, the case is different in that stability is provided with a high but stable rate of growth in money supply (an average of 11% with a standard deviation of 2.5%). This differs again in the case of Germany which has a lower, but relatively unstable, rate of growth in money supply (an average of 9.3% with a standard deviation of 3.5%).

In conclusion, use of the variance in money growth rather than the variance in inflation rates of currency peg countries would increase the appeal of the dollar. This shows up in the increase in the number of countries for whom a dollar peg would provide a more stable policy.

TABLE 6-4. Single Currency Pegs Based on Monetary Policies in Industrialized Countries (1973–79)

Country	Standard deviation in inflation rate with currency pegged to				
	Dollar[†]	Pound	Franc	Mark	Yen
Algeria*	2.34	7.22	5.74	5.78	15.99
Bahrain	5.23	8.01	6.13	5.89	8.36
Egypt	3.19	6.31	4.08	4.66	10.30
Iraq*	2.48	7.28	5.77	5.68	15.06
Jordan	3.17	6.36	4.41	4.84	10.60
Kuwait*	2.18	7.48	6.20	6.05	16.68
Lebanon	3.63	6.21	3.67	4.60	9.47
Libya*	1.88	7.59	6.40	6.22	17.73
Morocco	5.66	6.83	2.78	5.15	10.15
Qatar*	2.15	7.42	6.15	6.05	16.17
Saudi Arabia*	1.88	7.83	6.74	6.46	18.54
Sudan	4.08	6.02	4.14	5.11	8.92
Syria	3.90	6.40	3.54	4.49	9.41
Tunisia	5.16	6.76	3.08	4.90	10.03
U.A.E.*	2.10	7.32	6.30	6.15	17.11
Average money growth in currency peg country	6.5 (1.5)	12.7 (6.2)	11.2 (2.4)	9.3 (3.5)	13.1 (6.2)

Note: Standard deviation in parentheses; δ_i = trade shares.
*With adjusted trade shares.
†For the 1973–79 period, monetary growth in the United States is the percentage change in M1B. Source: *Review*, Federal Reserve Bank of St. Louis, vol. 62, no. 2, pp. 28–39.

4. ALTERNATIVE BASKET CURRENCY PEGS

In this section, a number of multiple currency pegs are presented and compared in terms of their hypothetical performance for the 1973–79 period. The first baskets considered are trade-weighted baskets and the Special Drawing Right basket because they have some common characteristics in shielding a country's domestic inflation rate from disturbances that arise from deviations in exchange rates from PPP movements. In this regard, it should be mentioned that the SDR peg is obviously less efficient than a trade-weighted basket in insulating a pegging country from those deviations, mainly due to the inequality of currencies' weights in the SDR with those of trade shares.

Whether a country is following a trade-weighted or an SDR basket peg, it will be importing the weighted average of inflation or money growth rates of the currencies in the basket. Furthermore, the variance in the domestic inflation rate of the pegging country would be a weighted average of variances in the rates of inflation (or money growth rates) of its major trade partners.

Table 6-5 reports the results of the hypothetical performance of trade-share baskets. The basket exhibits a great deal of stability in terms of the standard deviation in the domestic rate of inflation of a pegging country. This stability in the domestic inflation rate holds regardless of whether the variance in actual inflation rates or the variance in money growth rates of the five industrial countries is used. Further, the hypothetical performance of this basket is better than that of any single currency peg, especially if measured in terms of the standard deviation in domestic inflation rate.

Table 6-6 reports the hypothetical performance of the SDR peg. With the exception of Saudi Arabia, Libya, Morocco, and Tunisia, the SDR appears to be more efficient than any single currency peg in providing a more stable peg. As for Saudi Arabia and Libya, a dollar peg based on monetary policy in the United States would be more efficient than the SDR peg, which is mainly due to the large adjusted trade shares these two countries have with the United States (78% and 74% for Saudi Arabia and Libya, respectively), as well as the highly stable monetary policy in the United States. The case of Morocco and Tunisia, where a franc peg is more efficient than the SDR peg, is explained mainly by their high trade shares with France. As compared to the trade-weighted basket, it can be argued that the loss in stability of domestic inflation rates under the SDR peg is slight and may, therefore, be worth the price. This results from some of the advantages of a common pegging policy (such as the SDR peg). Some of these advantages are reflected in the encouragement of trade and financial relationships between pegging countries.

Finally, Tables 6-7 and 6-8 report the hypothetical performance of a basket weight that would have minimized the variance in the domestic rate of inflation for each country in the sample during the 1973-79 period. The imported inflation columns in Table 6-7 use the derived weights to give a weighted average of inflation imported from the five industrial countries. Obviously, equation (11) would give the weights that minimize the standard deviation in inflation. However, we must be careful in our analysis of these weights. A

TABLE 6-5. Alternative Basket Pegs for Fifteen Arab Countries: Trade Shares and Special Drawing Right Baskets (1973–79)

Country	Total trade shares					Imported inflation*	Standard deviation in inflation with $\sigma^2_{\mu_i} = \sigma^2_{P_i}$	Standard deviation in inflation with $\sigma^2_{\mu_i} = \sigma^2_{m_i}$	Imported money growth
	Dollar	Pound	Franc	Mark	Yen				
Algeria	65.0	2.0	18.0	12.0	3.0	8.39	1.56	1.19	8.0
Bahrain	16.6	29.3	3.9	7.7	42.5	10.91	3.19	3.06	11.52
Egypt	32.8	14.8	20.9	20.9	10.6	9.18	1.40	1.44	9.68
Iraq	61.0	4.0	8.0	11.0	16.0	8.63	1.77	1.45	8.49
Jordan	34.8	20.7	9.9	21.4	13.2	9.39	1.66	1.65	9.72
Kuwait	69.0	7.0	5.0	5.0	13.0	8.81	1.83	1.40	8.10
Lebanon	24.8	16.0	29.4	20.2	9.5	9.42	1.38	1.48	10.06
Libya	74.0	5.0	6.0	10.0	5.0	8.45	1.76	1.27	7.70
Morocco	10.4	7.1	62.8	16.1	3.5	9.49	1.39	1.68	10.57
Qatar	69.0	9.0	7.0	4.0	11.0	9.05	1.81	1.36	8.22
Saudi Arabia	78.0	4.0	3.0	6.0	9.0	8.54	1.90	1.36	7.65
Sudan	15.1	33.9	18.0	17.7	15.4	10.60	2.14	2.15	10.97
Syria	23.0	8.7	34.7	25.7	8.0	8.85	1.20	1.45	9.92
Tunisia	16.9	3.1	55.1	23.0	0.9	8.78	1.26	1.60	10.00
U.A.E.	71.0	9.0	4.0	5.0	11.0	8.96	1.84	1.38	8.11

Note: $\beta_i = \delta_i$ = total trade shares.

*Imported inflation refers to a weighted average of inflation in the five industrial countries where the weights are those of the currency basket, and similarly for money growth.

TABLE 6-6. Special Drawing Right (as of January 1, 1981) (1973–79)

Country	SDR					Imported inflation	Standard deviation in domestic inflation with $\sigma^2_{\mu i} = \sigma^2_{p i}$	Standard deviation in domestic inflation with $\sigma^2_{\mu i} = \sigma^2_{m i}$	Imported money growth
	Dollar	Pound	Franc	Mark	Yen				
Algeria	42.0	13.0	13.0	19.0	13.0	9.02	2.14	2.09	9.31
Bahrain	42.0	13.0	13.0	19.0	13.0	9.02	3.78	3.75	9.31
Egypt	42.0	13.0	13.0	19.0	13.0	9.02	1.68	1.61	9.31
Iraq	42.0	13.0	13.0	19.0	13.0	9.02	1.85	1.79	9.31
Jordan	42.0	13.0	13.0	19.0	13.0	9.02	1.67	1.61	9.31
Kuwait	42.0	13.0	13.0	19.0	13.0	9.02	1.98	1.92	9.31
Lebanon	42.0	13.0	13.0	19.0	13.0	9.02	2.09	2.04	9.31
Libya	42.0	13.0	13.0	19.0	13.0	9.02	2.03	1.98	9.31
Morocco	42.0	13.0	13.0	19.0	13.0	9.02	4.59	4.57	9.31
Qatar	42.0	13.0	13.0	19.0	13.0	9.02	1.94	1.88	9.31
Saudi Arabia	42.0	13.0	13.0	19.0	13.0	9.02	2.13	2.07	9.31
Sudan	42.0	13.0	13.0	19.0	13.0	9.02	2.37	2.32	9.31
Syria	42.0	13.0	13.0	19.0	13.0	9.02	2.49	2.45	9.31
Tunisia	42.0	13.0	13.0	19.0	13.0	9.02	4.14	4.12	9.31
U.A.E.	42.0	13.0	13.0	19.0	13.0	9.02	1.98	1.93	9.31

Note: β_i determined by I.M.F.; δ_i = total trade share.

TABLE 6-7. Currency Basket Pegs That Minimize the Variance in Inflation for Fifteen Arab Countries (1973–79)

Country	Currency weights*					Standard deviation in inflation	Imported inflation
	Dollar	Pound	Franc	Mark	Yen		
Algeria	.54	.04	.21	.17	.04	1.45	8.44
Bahrain	.30	.22	.06	.10	.31	2.78	10.06
Egypt	.33	.12	.22	.23	.09	1.33	8.83
Iraq	.54	.06	.11	.16	.13	1.66	8.60
Jordan	.36	.17	.12	.24	.11	1.56	9.06
Kuwait	.60	.08	.09	.11	.12	1.74	8.83
Lebanon	.28	.13	.30	.22	.08	1.33	9.23
Libya	.61	.07	.10	.16	.06	1.63	8.49
Morocco	.14	.06	.60	.17	.03	1.36	9.33
Qatar	.60	.10	.10	.10	.10	1.71	8.97
Saudi Arabia	.65	.06	.07	.13	.09	1.76	8.58
Sudan	.25	.26	.19	.19	.12	1.91	10.05
Syria	.24	.08	.34	.27	.07	1.18	8.72
Tunisia	.18	.03	.53	.24	.02	1.25	8.75
U.A.E.	.61	.10	.08	.11	.10	1.74	8.90

*Based on inflation in industrialized countries.

misinterpretation of the data is possible for the simple reason that, in order to be useful, all the information regarding inflation, money growth, and deviations in exchange rates from PPP would have had to be known in 1973. Therefore, what is shown in Tables 6-7 and 6-8 are the weights which, if known in 1973, would have provided the most stable pegging policy in terms of standard deviations in domestic inflation rates of pegging countries.

The problem in this case is that the sample period has been used to derive the weights, which by the nature of the calculations would give us the lowest standard deviation in domestic inflation rate. This does not have much meaning in and of itself because we are using ex post currency weights in the basket. To avoid this problem, these ex post weights can remain fixed now; then, we can calculate their performance in light of the subsequent changes of inflation rates, money growth rates, and deviations of exchange rates from PPP movements over the coming period. In this case, a comparison with other single currency or basket currency pegs would be more meaningful.

TABLE 6-8. Currency Basket Pegs That Minimize the Variance in Inflation for Fifteen Arab Countries (1973–79)

Country	Currency weights*					Standard deviation in inflation	Imported money growth
	Dollar	Pound	Franc	Mark	Yen		
Algeria	.63	.03	.19	.12	.03	1.18	8.11
Bahrain	.34	.22	.05	.07	.31	2.66	10.27
Egypt	.41	.12	.20	.18	.08	1.35	9.15
Iraq	.62	.04	.09	.11	.13	1.37	8.27
Jordan	.44	.16	.10	.19	.10	1.52	9.09
Kuwait	.69	.07	.07	.07	.10	1.36	8.11
Lebanon	.35	.12	.28	.17	.08	1.39	9.56
Libya	.71	.05	.08	.11	.05	1.25	7.82
Morocco	.19	.06	.59	.13	.03	1.61	10.21
Qatar	.68	.08	.09	.06	.09	1.32	8.18
Saudi Arabia	.75	.05	.05	.07	.08	1.33	7.77
Sudan	.30	.25	.18	.15	.12	1.90	10.11
Syria	.32	.07	.33	.21	.06	1.37	9.40
Tunisia	.25	.03	.52	.20	.01	1.43	9.82
U.A.E.	.70	.08	.06	.07	.09	1.34	8.07

*Based on money growth in industrialized countries.

5. CONCLUSIONS

The analysis presented in this study suggests, among other things, three propositions in relation to the achievement of an optimum currency peg concurrent with monetary stability in the pegging country. First, if a country has one major trade partner, then a single currency peg appears preferable. Empirical examples supporting this proposition were represented by the cases of Tunisia, Morocco, Saudi Arabia, and Libya. Second, since oil exports contribute a large percentage of total exports of the seven oil countries, and since oil exports are priced in terms of the dollar, a dollar peg, as compared to other single currency pegs, would provide the most stable pegging policy in terms of the standard deviation in the domestic inflation rate of the seven oil-producing countries. Finally, systematic stability, as measured in terms of the standard deviation either in inflation rates or in money growth rates of currency peg countries, is considered an important factor in determining optimum currency pegs for the sample country. As shown in the empirical results, a more stable rate of inflation in Germany offered the mark as the most stable peg for Bahrain, Egypt, Lebanon, and Syria, whereas the dollar proved to be the most stable peg for most countries analyzed when money growth rates were being used instead.

NOTE

1. The matrix system is

$$
\begin{bmatrix}
\sigma_{p_1}^2 & -(\sigma_{p_2}^2 + \sigma_{\epsilon_{12}}^2) & 0 & 0 & 0 \\
\sigma_{p_1}^2 & 0 & -(\sigma_{p_3}^2 + \sigma_{\epsilon_{13}}^2) & 0 & 0 \\
\sigma_{p_1}^2 & 0 & 0 & -(\sigma_{p_4}^2 + \sigma_{\epsilon_{14}}^2) & 0 \\
\sigma_{p_1}^2 & 0 & 0 & 0 & -(\sigma_{p_5}^2 + \sigma_{\epsilon_{15}}^2) \\
1 & 1 & 1 & 1 & 1
\end{bmatrix}
\begin{bmatrix}
\beta_1 \\ \beta_2 \\ \beta_3 \\ \beta_4 \\ \beta_5
\end{bmatrix}
=
\begin{bmatrix}
-\delta_2 \sigma_{\epsilon_{12}}^2 \\
-\delta_3 \sigma_{\epsilon_{13}}^2 \\
-\delta_4 \sigma_{\epsilon_{14}}^2 \\
-\delta_5 \sigma_{\epsilon_{15}}^2 \\
1
\end{bmatrix}
$$

In this system, currency 1 is chosen arbitrarily as the numéraire for which $\epsilon_{11} = 0$.

REFERENCES

Connolly, Michael. "Optimum Currency Pegs for Latin America." *Journal of Money, Credit and Banking* (Feb. 1983).

———. "The Choice of an Optimum Currency Peg for a Small, Open Country." *Journal of International Money and Finance* (Aug. 1982).

Crockett, Andrew D., and Saleh Nsouli. "Exchange Rate Policies for Developing Countries." *Journal of Development Studies* 13 (1977).

International Monetary Fund. "International Financial Statistics." *1980 Yearbook*. Washington, D.C.: IMF, 1980.

International Monetary Fund. "Direction of Trade." *1980 Yearbook*. Washington, D.C.: IMF, 1980.

Klein, Benjamin. "Competing Monies, European Monetary Union and the Dollar." In *One Money For Europe*, edited by Michele Frantianni and Theo Peeters. London: Macmillan, 1978, pp. 69–94.

Mundell, Robert. "A Theory of Optimum Currency Areas." *American Economic Review* (Sept. 1961).

Yousef, Abdelhadi. "An Optimum Currency Peg for Developing Countries: The Case of Fifteen Arab Countries." Ph.D. Dissertation. University of South Carolina, Columbia, South Carolina, 1981.

7

THE IMPACT
OF FLUCTUATING EXCHANGE RATES
ON BARBADOS AND JAMAICA

DELISLE WORRELL

1. EXCHANGE RATE EXPERIENCES

Many of the current economic difficulties of Caribbean and other third world countries are put down to the impact of forces over which they have no control, particularly the economic policies and economic fortunes of major industrialized countries. The instability of world exchange rates is one of the factors that seems to have exacerbated the third world's problems.[1] This chapter will explore the impact of fluctuating exchange rates on the economies of Barbados and Jamaica, two Caribbean countries whose economic fortunes have differed significantly during the 1970s.

Jamaica and Barbados have always followed the policy of pegging their currencies to a major reserve currency, first the pound sterling and later the U.S. dollar. However, for much of the period we are concerned with, their exchange rate experiences were different because the switch from sterling to the dollar took place at different times in the two countries. There was an interval of four years when the currencies were on different standards. Exchange rate experiences have also been different because of domestic decisions to alter the rate. Jamaica has a history of more active exchange rate intervention than Barbados. We will try to isolate these "domestic" exchange rate influences in order to highlight the impact of exchange rate movements over which the local authorities would have had no control.

156

Our procedure will be to describe each country's exchange rate experience, using actual rates for individual currencies of the countries' main trading partners and a "representative" trade-weighted exchange rate. The variance of these exchange rates is measured to see whether instability has had damaging effects on the countries' economic performance. We try to indicate the extent to which variation in the exchange rates of Barbados and Jamaica have originated abroad; we ask whether any exchange rate strategy, other than pegging to reserve currency, might have reduced currency instability. This is followed by attempts to measure the ways in which exchange rate variation have proved harmful.

Jamaica: Exchange Rates

Jamaica's economic experience between 1971 and 1978 can be divided into four phases. The first two years saw the end of a period of economic expansion which was sustained by the growth of the bauxite/alumina industry, manufacturing, and tourism. The first phase also witnessed rapid government expansion and the emergence of worrying balance-of-payments deficits. The energy crisis, economic stagnation abroad, and weakening export markets brought an end to economic expansion in 1973 and 1974. At the same time, the fiscal and balance-of-payments deficits began to widen, leading to expenditure-restraining policies early in 1974. The imposition of a revised bauxite levy in 1974 produced a balance-of-payments surplus, and fiscal and monetary policies were relaxed; however, expenditure growth sowed the seeds of later imbalance. In the third phase, from the beginning of 1975 to the middle of 1977, the government's efforts failed to revive the growth rate, while the balance-of-payments situation deteriorated rapidly in the face of diminishing investor confidence, capital flight, and runaway government expenditure. In April 1977 the government resorted to an IMF program of demand restraint, replaced by an even more rigorous package in May 1978.

The main features of exchange rate trend and variation in Jamaica are illustrated in Fig. 7-1. While the Jamaica dollar was fixed to sterling it appreciated slightly against the U.S. dollar in 1971 and then fell in value by 16% between the middle of 1972 and January 1973, when the parity was switched. There was a 27% devaluation against the U.S. dollar in April 1977,[2] followed by a 5% fall in January 1978. In May 1978 the currency was devalued by a further 15% against the U.S. dollar, with monthly "mini-devaluations" of $1\frac{1}{2}$% (to October) and 1% (thereafter) for the

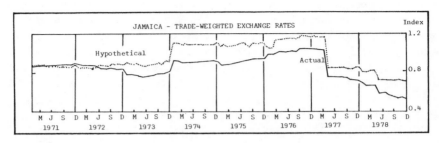

FIGURE 7-1

remainder of that year. The mini-devaluations were terminated in May 1979.

After the link with sterling was severed, the Jamaica dollar remained little changed in value against sterling and regional currencies (which remained with the pound for a while)[3] until March 1975, when the Jamaican currency started to gain rapidly on sterling. This appreciation came to an end in October 1976, by which time the Jamaica dollar had risen 54% against the pound. The gain was wiped out in the next seven months, as the U.S. dollar fell back from its peak value against sterling and Jamaica devalued her dollar. Thereafter, the Jamaica dollar fell steadily against sterling, mainly as a result of the Jamaica government's own devaluations.

Sterling, the U.S. dollar, the Canadian dollar (which moved very much in harmony with the U.S. dollar), and regional currencies account for most of Jamaica's foreign transactions (in 1977, 67% of visible trade, about 91% of tourism, and virtually all visible and capital account payments). The changes summarized in the last two paragraphs therefore account for most of the variation in Jamaica's exchange rate. The SDR may be taken to represent the movements against other currencies; the pattern of change is very similar to that recorded for the U.S. dollar, although there is a little more variation and the overall depreciation is greater.

We use a trade-weighted exchange rate to summarize the fluctuation and trend in the value of the Jamaica dollar. It reflects the importance of the U.S. dollar and sterling, appreciating slightly in 1971 and falling in 1972 (in line with changes in the U.S. dollar value of sterling), remaining little changed until mid-1975, when it began to rise in value. This tendency ended with the first devaluation in April 1977.

Table 7-1 provides a comparison between the variance of the Jamaica currency during the last years of relatively stable world

TABLE 7-1. Jamaica Coefficient of Variation—Actual Exchange Rate

Period	Jamaican currency with respect to					Trade weighted exchange rate	U.S.$/£
	£ stg.	U.S. $	Can. $	TT $	SDR		
1965	—	0.00752	0.00276	—	0.00752	0.00288	0.00752
1966	—	0.00160	0.00278	—	0.00160	0.00284	0.00160
1967	—	0.05159	0.05101	—	0.05154	0.02674	0.00516
1968	—	0.00374	0.00859	—	0.00374	0.00180	0.00374
1969	—	0.28218	0.32888	—	0.28218	0.28259	0.00229
1970	—	0.19210	0.02642	—	0.19210	0.00169	0.00323
1971	—	0.01846	0.01560	—	0.01683	0.00753	0.01846
1972	—	0.04549	0.04889	—	0.02522	0.02150	0.04549
1973	0.03315	—	0.00377	0.03313	—	0.01575	0.03293
1974	0.01936	—	0.01103	0.01941	0.01210	0.00725	0.02015
1975	0.07125	—	0.01220	0.07144	0.03786	0.02696	0.07147
1976	0.07879	—	0.01342	0.02829	0.00728	0.02093	0.08021
1977	0.07707	0.15940	0.14300	0.12504	0.16827	0.14110	0.03366
1978	0.15569	0.09725	0.09725	0.08069	0.12186	0.10481	0.04128

exchange rates and the period of volatility which began around 1972. The coefficient of variation of a trade-weighted exchange rate, calculated from end-of-month observations each year, goes as high as 14% and is generally over 1% in the 1970s. In the 1965–71 period the variation of the trade-weighted exchange rate was greater than 1% only in 1967, when Jamaica followed the U.K. in devaluing its currency against the U.S. dollar.

Increased exchange rate variation in Jamaica has resulted partly from greater variance in exchange rates abroad and partly from the policies of the Jamaican government. There is a fairly close correspondence between the increasing variation of the sterling/U.S. dollar rate and the increasing variation of the Jamaican trade-weighted exchange rate. However, Jamaica's trade-weighted exchange rate also reflects the influence of domestic exchange rate policies, particularly in 1977 and 1978. Those were the years when Jamaica devalued heavily against the U.S. dollar; they were also the only years when the coefficient of variation of the trade-weighted exchange rate exceeded 10%.

Nevertheless, exchange rate variation in Jamaica has never really been very large. Except for 1977 and 1978 the coefficient for the trade-weighted exchange rate has seldom exceeded 5%. Fixed exchange rates vis-a-vis the United States maintained exchange rate stability for the majority of foreign transactions between 1973 and 1976; the variances in terms of sterling, Canadian dollars, and other Caribbean currencies have all been small.

Our next task is to consider alternatives to the exchange rate policy favored by the Jamaica authorities. We will consider the following possibilities: (1) a Jamaica dollar valued by means of a basket of currencies related to the distribution of trade in 1971 and devalued in the same way as the actual rate; (2) the Jamaica dollar adjusted to maintain the purchasing power parity of its trade-weighted value, either by continuous adjustment to a fixed U.S. parity or by means of the currency basket. Would either of these alternatives have served to reduce the variance of the Jamaican currency?

The exchange rate pattern would not have been significantly different had Jamaica employed the currency basket. Figure 7-1 and Tables 7-1 and 7-2 provide comparisons of the variation and trend of the actual rate and a hypothetical rate based on the trade weights. The trend in the rates would have been much the same, assuming that the authorities had devalued at the same time and by the same amounts as they in fact did (but fixing the rates in terms of a basket of trade-weighted currencies). From about mid-1972 the basket-based rate remains a little above the actual rate, but it follows the

TABLE 7-2. Jamaica Coefficient of Variation—Hypothetical Exchange Rates

Period	Jamaican currency with respect to					Trade weighted exchange rate
	£ stg.	U.S. $	Can. $	TT $	SDR	
1971	0.28887	0.02890	0.28889	0.28887	0.01166	0.00482
1972	0.03945	0.00621	0.01120	0.03998	0.01353	0.01872
1973	0.02948	0.00032	0.00514	0.02943	0.00889	0.01446
1974	0.01744	0.00665	0.01133	0.01777	0.01065	0.00471
1975	0.04924	0.02689	0.02362	0.04983	0.02906	0.01243
1976	0.07183	0.00800	0.01804	0.02822	0.00497	0.03396
1977	0.02406	0.00852	0.03043	0.01898	0.00597	0.01989
1978	0.02836	0.01678	0.03911	0.01578	0.01429	0.00968

161

TABLE 7-3. Jamaica—Coefficients
of Variation—Relative Prices

Period	Coefficients
1971	0.01031
1972	0.02127
1973	0.04130
1974	0.01666
1975	0.01151
1976	0.01338
1977	0.02544
1978	0.12518

pattern of that rate very closely throughout. The variance of the trade-weighted rate is a little lower than was the case with the fixed rate. This reflects slightly lower variances for all currencies. However, the orders of magnitude are not much different than for the fixed rate, with variances between 1 and 5% for the most part.

A policy to maintain purchasing power parity throughout would have increased exchange rate variation between 1971 and 1974 and in 1978; it would have caused less variance between 1975 and 1977. This pattern reflects the fact that the policy would have resulted in earlier and more gradual depreciation of the currency. However, it would have left the Jamaica dollar 8.6% higher in value than it was at December 1978.[4] (The exchange rate, considered as an index based on January 1971, would have been the mirror image of relative prices calculated on the same basis; its variance is therefore the variance of relative prices in Table 7-3.)

If we are to judge simply by the variance of the exchange rate, it seems the Jamaican authorities had little to gain by a strategy other than the one actually pursued.[5] The currency basket seems a clearly inferior alternative. It produces results that are not notably different from those of the fixed U.S. parity, and in the process one loses the convenience of a known rate for the majority of foreign transactions. However, the authorities only capitalize on this if they maintain a credible exchange rate policy. Otherwise, the short-term stability of the exchange rate will be bought at the expense of capital flight and a deteriorating foreign payments position. This brings us to the alternative of maintaining purchasing power parity. On the basis of variance alone, it is not evidently a superior alternative. But if the other strategies are not credible, it may nevertheless be the alternative that produces the most favorable balance-of-payments outcome.

Barbados

Like Jamaica, Barbados in 1971 was nearing the end of an expansionary period which had lasted from the mid-1960s. It had witnessed rapid growth in tourism, construction, and light manufacturing, although sugar production (a major export activity) was falling. In 1973 the growth rate slowed, largely because investors were nervous about the introduction of a Barbados currency to replace the East Caribbean dollar in December.[6] This led to capital flight and a drop in investment in 1973, but the situation reversed itself in 1974. However, by then the economy was suffering from the effects of recession in North America, weakening tourist markets, a fall-off in construction, and steep price rises. A slow recovery got underway in 1976, mainly through the resurgence of tourism, but the authorities have continued to face difficulties of fiscal and balance-of-payments adjustment.

Barbados has made only one exchange rate policy move during the period of our analysis. In July 1975 the parity of the Barbados dollar was fixed in U.S. dollars instead of sterling, at a rate close to the average of the U.S./Barbados exchange rate over the previous two years.[7] The rate (two Barbados dollars to one U.S. dollar) is slightly below the January 1971 rate. While it was fixed in terms of sterling, the Barbados currency appreciated sharply against the U.S. dollar until mid-1972, but this gain was completely eroded in the erratic fall in the dollar value of sterling in the following years. Once it had been fixed to the U.S. dollar, the Barbados dollar appreciated strongly against sterling up to October 1976, but the subsequent fall in the value of the U.S. dollar brought the sterling/Barbados rate at December 1978 to a level only 7.4% above that of July 1975 (see Fig. 7-2).

The U.S. dollar and sterling (and Caricom currencies linked to them) between them account for 78% of Barbados' trade and 85% of its tourism transactions; the fluctuations identified in the previous paragraph therefore explain most of the movement in the trade-weighted exchange rate. Overall, that rate appreciated 32% between January 1971 and December 1978, with most of the increase occurring in 1975 (because of the change in parity) and 1976 (because of the continuing depreciation of sterling).

Exchange rate variation has been lower in Barbados than in Jamaica principally because Barbados' exchange rate has been altered

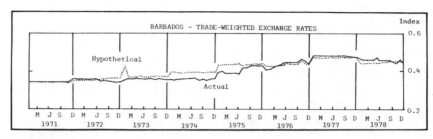

FIGURE 7-2.

less frequently and to a smaller extent. The coefficient of variation for Barbados' trade-weighted exchange rate never exceeds 5% (see Table 7-4). The variance of the trade-weighted Barbados rate has followed trends in the variance of the U.S./sterling rate, though its value has always been lower than that for the U.S./sterling rate (Table 7-4 and Table 7-1, final column).

The floating exchange rate regime has brought some increase in the variance of the value of the Barbados dollar. Up to 1971, the coefficient of variation for the trade-weighted rate, the U.S./Barbados dollar rate, and the Canadian/Barbados dollar rate were all less than 1% in every year except 1967. (The reason for the higher variance in 1967 is that Barbados, like Jamaica, followed the U.K. by devaluing its currency against the U.S. dollar in November of that year.) Since 1972 the variance has generally been higher, and only in 1975 did domestic policy contribute significantly to this.

The use of a currency basket based on 1971 trade weights would have reduced the amplitude of fluctuations in the U.S. dollar/ Barbados dollar rate between 1971 and 1973 and would also have avoided the precipitous decline in the Barbados dollar in the second half of 1973. The currency would have remained above its January 1971 U.S. dollar value, and the new July 1975 rate would have been approached from above (that is, it would have required a slight depreciation). Thereafter the use of the currency basket would have made little difference to the variance. Our conclusions about the use of the currency basket in Barbados are similar to those reached for Jamaica: it has little effect on the already low levels of variation which can be attributed to external causes (compare Tables 7-4 and 7.5). The currency basket therefore seems to be an inferior alternative to the U.S. dollar peg. It offers little benefit in reducing the impact of external fluctuations and it loses the advantage of a fixed rate for the most significant proportion of foreign transactions.

TABLE 7-4. Barbados—Coefficients of Variation—Actual Exchange Rate

Period	Barbados currency with respect to					Trade weighted exchange rate
	£ stg.	U.S. $	Can. $	TT $	SDR	
1965	—	0.00767	0.00244	—	0.00767	0.00273
1966	—	0.00784	0.00280	—	0.00784	0.00041
1967	—	0.05681	0.05601	—	0.05681	0.01584
1968	—	0.00368	0.00849	—	0.00368	0.00510
1969	—	0.00223	0.00240	—	0.00223	0.00409
1970	—	0.00316	0.02773	—	0.00316	0.00029
1971	—	0.01813	0.01544	—	0.01689	0.00460
1972	—	0.04550	0.04861	—	0.04848	0.01460
1973	—	0.03313	0.03294	—	0.03177	0.01015
1974	—	0.01941	0.01462	—	0.02151	0.00813
1975	0.07769	0.02521	0.02235	0.07820	0.05138	0.04416
1976	0.08002	—	0.01317	0.02685	0.00735	0.03494
1977	0.03366	—	0.02380	—	0.01450	0.00523
1978	0.04185	—	0.02387	—	0.03147	0.00134

TABLE 7-5. Barbados—Coefficients of Variation—Hypothetical Exchange Rates

Period	Barbados currency with respect to					Trade weighted exchange rate
	£ stg.	U.S. $	Can. $	TT $	SDR	
1971	0.00907	0.01481	0.01255	0.00908	0.00942	0.00519
1972	0.04265	0.02816	0.01878	0.03383	—	0.01581
1973	0.00967	0.00945	0.01024	0.02135	0.00956	0.04242
1974	0.01471	0.00834	0.01019	0.01633	0.00834	0.00556
1975	0.03980	0.03353	0.02835	0.04219	0.01275	0.00906
1976	0.06676	0.01395	0.02042	0.02910	0.03017	0.02324
1977	0.02234	0.01015	0.03182	0.01015	0.00965	0.00194
1978	0.02388	0.02032	0.04166	0.02033	0.01184	0.00820

TABLE 7-6. Barbados—Coefficients
of Variation—Relative Prices

Period	Coefficients
1971	0.02032
1972	0.02021
1973	0.03874
1974	0.04765
1975	0.01439
1976	0.01285
1977	0.02224
1978	0.01178

The Barbados currency has not been adjusted so as to maintain purchasing power parity. If it had been, it might have depreciated by 39.5% (not allowing for inevitable pass-through of import prices to domestic prices),[8] though its variance would still have been low (see Table 7-6). However, it would not have served to counteract the influence of fluctuations in exchange rates abroad.

2. THE EFFECTS OF UNSTABLE EXCHANGE RATES

Unstable exchange rates create two kinds of problems that might be relevant to countries like Barbados and Jamaica. One problem relates to the costs of covering for exchange rate variation, and the other is the managing of external debt and foreign exchange reserves.

In a world of variable exchange rates, all foreign transactions become more costly. If traders decide to meet their foreign currency needs on spot markets alone, they expose themselves to greater risks of foreign exchange loss. To minimise risk they may go onto the forward exchange market, but here they face higher premiums than they would have under a fixed exchange rate regime. The trading firm therefore has to accept higher costs, either implicitly in the form of a higher probability of foreign exchange loss, or explicitly in the form of increased forward exchange premiums.

The effect of these increased costs depends on the kind of activity which the firm undertakes and the nature of its market. Exporting firms that have to compete with local producers in their countries of destination will find their position eroded. For heavy import users like Barbados and Jamaica, currency instability may be inflationary because there are limited possibilities for domestic substitution. The constraints on potential export growth are perhaps even more harmful. Export promotion is given a crucial role in the development of Caribbean nations. It has been a thorny problem because producers are usually afraid of the complications and unfamiliarity of export markets. Significant gains have been made only where multinational corporations who are already engaged in export markets have been involved. The added complication of managing foreign currency exposure serves merely to aggravate the already serious pains of launching and sustaining a major export drive.

New investment on the whole has become more problematic under the fluctuating exchange rate regime. More sophisticated planning techniques are required and higher levels of skill must be employed to cope with the increased uncertainty in product and factor markets overseas. This high skill requirement aggravates the comparative disadvantage of smaller, less-developed countries in export markets.

The second area of difficulty has to do with reserve and debt management. Fluctuations in exchange rates may reduce a country's ability to meet foreign commitments in a particular currency as they arise. This problem can be alleviated by astute foreign reserve management; it requires that foreign exchange managers take advantage of interest rate and exchange rate movements, switching between currencies to maximize the returns on their foreign asset holdings, and managing the national debt in line with the country's pattern of foreign exchange earnings.

How significant have the above difficulties been in the recent experience of Barbados and Jamaica? In what follows, we look at some of the indicators that should help us to measure the impact of the fluctuating rate regime.

Curiously enough, there seems to have been very little forward exchange trading. We have data for Barbados only, for commercial banks from 1976 onward; the forward position seldom constitutes more than 10% of the spot position. This suggests that forwards are an even smaller proportion of total transactions, because the spot position is net while the forward position is gross, for the most part. (This is because, with a large volume of spot transactions, the position at the end of the day will reflect the net of receipts and payments; on the forward market, on the other hand, there are few transactions, so that there is not usually any offsetting transaction on the same day.) The relative unimportance of forward transactions was confirmed in discussions with commercial bankers, both in Barbados and

Jamaica. The banks act as agents in these transactions, making forward deals in London or New York at the request of clients. They do not themselves try to make a market. Requests for forward cover usually relate to large, single items of machinery and equipment, for example, and are not sought routinely. In Jamaica, the majority of requests for forward cover did not relate to external exchange rate instability at all, but had to do with fears about the devaluation of the Jamaican dollar.

For those limited transactions which did take place on forward markets, traders would have had to pay higher premiums and accept higher discounts in the post-1973 period for the most important currencies in Caribbean payments—sterling and the Canadian dollar. In the case of the U.S./sterling rate, which is the rate of greatest importance for Barbados and Jamaica, the largest month-end discount asked for converting sterling to U.S. dollars in the pre-1973 period was 1.77%. In the post-1973 period a similar transaction at one time would have required a discount of 3.31%.

The costs of foreign exchange transactions can be minimized if debt service payments and other commitments can be scheduled in accordance with the country's potential earnings, both as to timing and to currency. It is impossible to determine accurately how closely this coordination has been achieved, but some hints may be had by comparing the currency composition of reserves, foreign debt, and total transactions. The U.S. dollar is the dominant currency in both cases; it accounted for 76% of Jamaica's foreign debt at the end of 1978. For Barbados at the end of 1978, the U.S. dollar accounted for 73% of all debt and 86% of reserves. The dominance of the U.S. dollar is the major factor containing the costs of foreign exchange transactions. For other currencies the match of earnings and commitments is not very close.

Since 1976 Jamaica has had virtually no foreign exchange reserves on which it might have earned enough to cover foreign exchange costs. After a disastrous balance-of-payments deficit in 1976, gross reserves were down to J$28.7 million at the end of that year, and foreign liabilities have continuously exceeded assets since then. At the end of 1979, Jamaica had net foreign liabilities in excess of J$500 million. In earlier years substantial foreign reserves were available, and at the end of 1974 reserves stood at peak value of J$171.6 million. However, there is no information as to the gains or losses made in managing this foreign exchange portfolio.

Barbados' foreign exchange holdings have fluctuated between BDS$24 million and BDS$102 million during the 1974–78 period.

Virtually all the country's foreign reserves were held in sterling before the Central Bank began operations at the end of 1973. The Bank initiated a policy of switching to the U.S. dollar, with only limited amounts being transferred as long as the U.K. government guaranteed the U.S. value of sterling balances. All new inflows were converted to U.S. dollars once the Barbados dollar value was fixed to the U.S., but some sterling held in longdated stock was retained so as to avoid heavy capital losses. These stocks were liquidated as soon as convenient, and by mid-1976 sterling holdings were minimal.

Thereafter the U.S. dollar was the main vehicle, but there were some experiments with the Canadian dollar and sterling, in search of higher profitability. Substantial amounts of Canadian dollars were held in late 1975 and early 1976, and again in the first quarter of 1978. Also in the first quarter of 1978, sterling holdings accumulated as the pound gained strength in foreign exchange markets. Neither of these experiments was particularly successful, and the Bank recorded losses on foreign exchange for 1976 and 1978.

Some gains were made from the initial switch to U.S. dollars, making for a surplus on foreign exchange operations in 1974. The 1975 surplus was principally a result of asset accumulation, and thereafter losses outweighed gains.

3. CONCLUSION

Our conclusions are tentative, partly because measurement has proved difficult, and partly because of the spotty data we had to contend with. We have noticed virtually no detectable effect of exchange rate variation on trade, costs, and competitiveness. There have been some difficulties with reserve management, and some foreign exchange losses have been recorded.

Nevertheless, we should reserve judgement because the largest costs of exchange rate instability may not be easily quantifiable. They have to do with the information systems and management skills needed to cope with foreign trade and overseas transactions in a world of great exchange rate complexity. Third world countries need to increase their share of world trade; exchange rate difficulties are one additional obstacle in their path.

NOTES

1. Black (1976), Helleiner (1981), Kafka (1978), Williamson (1976) all discuss aspects of the problem.

2. A dual rate was introduced: the depreciated rate (known as the "special rate") was used for most transactions, but the old rate was retained for valuing bauxite levies, for Government transactions, and for a few other specified payments (see IMF, *Report on Exchange Restrictions*, 1977).

3. Barbados was the second to switch to the U.S. dollar (in June 1975); it was followed by Guyana (in December 1975), Trinidad and Tobago (in May 1976), and the East Caribbean Currency Area (in July 1976). Except for Barbados which revalued its currency slightly, the rates were all fixed at what was then the current U.S. dollar value of the local currency.

4. If we were to account for the effect of import prices on domestic prices the devaluation would be even greater. If the authorities had kept the exchange rate in line with relative prices the rate of domestic inflation would undoubtedly have been higher, requiring even larger devaluation to maintain the parity.

5. For alternative views on the rules for exchange rate strategies, see Lipschitz (1979) and Branson and Katseli-Papaefstratiou (1980).

6. The EC dollar remains in circulation in the other English-speaking islands of the Lesser Antilles.

7. There was no change, either in the parity of the domestic currency or in the way it was determined, when the Barbados dollar was first introduced.

8. Barbados' consumer prices rose 39.5% relative to foreign consumer prices. However, if the currency had been depreciated in an effort to keep relative consumer prices constant, domestic prices would have risen relatively faster. Our estimate of the coefficient measuring the impact of import prices on domestic prices is 0.645; if we apply this factor and assume rigid adherence to the relative price rule for setting the exchange rate we get a series which converges at a value well above 100%.

REFERENCES

Black, Stanley. *Floating Exchange Rates and National Economic Policy.* Princeton essay in International Finance no. 119, December 1976.

Branson, William, and Louka Katseli-Papaefstratiou. "Income Instability, the Terms of Trade and the Choice of Exchange Rate Regime." *Journal of Development Economics* (March 1980).

Girvan, Norman, Richard Bernal, and Wesley Hughes, "The IMF and the Third World: The Case of Jamaica." *Development Dialogue* 2 (1980).

Helleiner, Gerald. "The Impact of the Exchange Rate System on the Developing Countries." United Nations, INT/75/015, 1981.

International Monetary Fund, *Report on Exchange Restrictions*, 1977–79.

Kafka, Alexander. "The New Exchange Rate Regime and the Developing Countries." *Journal of Finance* (June 1978).

Lipschitz, Leslie. "Exchange Rate Policy for a Small Developing Country and the Choice of Standard." *IMF Staff Papers* (September 1979).

Williamson, John. "Generalised Floating and the Reserve Needs of Developing Countries." In *The International Monetary System and the Developing Countries*, edited by Danny Leipziger. New York: U.S. AID, 1976.

III

INTERNATIONAL MONEY COMPETITION

8

LESSONS
FROM THE EUROPEAN MONETARY SYSTEM

PASCAL SALIN

The European Monetary System (EMS) began to function on March 14, 1979, and in this chapter we evaluate its progress to date. We shall not describe all its detailed and complex mechanisms since they are well known and, in any case, all its features are not essential for our discussion. Similarly, we shall be interested in its exchange rate arrangements only and not in other ones (for instance, the role of the European Monetary Fund, which is to replace the existing FECOM in the future).

Monetary union consists of organizing monetary authorities in a world of imperfect information. In this chapter we shall not criticize the present organization of monetary systems—for instance, the fact that they are built on a national and hierarchical base, with a central bank controlling the issue of money in each country. Although we do not believe that such an organization allows a first-best solution to the problem of organizing the world monetary system, we shall consider this organization as given and shall focus on the implications of central bank interventions for social welfare. In fact, beyond the declared target of exchange rate stability, one has to evaluate the working of a monetary system, as well as that of any other public system, according to some criteria of social welfare. To carry out this evaluation we first propose a very simple model of currency union (Section 1). In Section 2 we recall the main mechanisms of the EMS, which have to be known in order to use our simple model for evaluation. After having considered the rules and their coherence we examine the actual working of the EMS (Section 3) using not only the official criterion of exchange rate stability but other criteria suggested by our initial model. Finally, we attempt in Section 4 to answer the question, "Does the European Monetary System provide a public good?"

1. A VERY SIMPLE MODEL OF CURRENCY UNION

We assume that a currency union exists between n countries and that there are a national currency and a central bank in each country. For the present time we use the traditional definition of a currency union, namely a system of fixed rates between the participant countries,[1] whereas there are floating exchange rates between these countries and the countries outside the zone. We take the extreme view that floating exchange rates allow perfect isolation, so that, for instance, monetary policies or interest rates in a country are totally independent of what occurs in another country outside the union.

The working of the currency union can thus be described very simply by the following equations:

$$M_{zj} = \sum_i e_{ij} M_i$$

$$e_{ij} = f(M_i, M_j, k_i) \qquad (i = 2, \ldots, n)$$

(1)

where M is the quantity of money, e is the exchange rate, and k is a proxy variable. Subscript z refers to the zone, subscripts i and j to countries i and j belonging to the zone. The currency of country j is the numéraire. When the value of a variable is expressed in terms of this numéraire, there is a second subscript j: thus M_{zj} is the quantity of money in the currency zone in terms of currency j, and e_{ij} is the exchange rate between currency i and the numéraire j. But M_i is the quantity of units of currency i.

The above model of exchange rate determination is the reduced form of a complete macroeconomic model of the zone. As there are n currencies in the zone, there are n − 1 exchange rates between any currency and the one which is chosen as a numéraire, j, so that there are n − 1 equations to determine the exchange rates. In the equation for one given exchange rate (for instance, the one between currency i and currency j) two variables only are explicitly stated— the quantity of currency i and the quantity of currency j. All other variables are encapsulated into the proxy variable k, which may, for instance, be a proxy for interest rates, the quantity of money in other countries, the factors influencing real exchange rates, etc.

Our aim is not to have a discussion of the theory of exchange rate determination but to try to draw some conclusions from what can be accepted as the main features of this theory and to apply them to the theory of currency unions. We shall now make two simple assumptions, namely that $k_i = 0$ in the long run and $k_i \neq 0$ in the short run. In other words, we assume that exchange rates are determined in the long run by the purchasing power hypothesis (PPP)—the law of one price—and a purely monetary determination of prices.

Long-run Working of the System

Let us first examine the long-run working of the system. There are n equations and 2n variables (n quantities of money, M_z, n - 1 exchange rates). For the system to be coherent, n variables have to be exogenous and n variables have to be endogenous.

The working of a floating rate system is quite clear: monetary authorities in each country determine M (or the rate of change of M) independently and there is an endogenous determination of the exchange rates and the quantity of money of the zone (in terms of a given numéraire).

Obviously, a fixed rate system means that the n - 1 exchange rates are exogenous.[2] For the system to be fully determined, another variable has to be exogenous. To that end, several possibilities are open so that there are several different sorts of monetary systems. Monetary authorities may choose as a target variable (an exogenous variable) either M_z or one of the national quantities of money. Let us have a look at each possibility.

Solution (a)

In this system—which is the simplest—one national currency is the "key-currency": all central banks intervene in terms of this n-th currency, except the bank that issues it. The monetary policies of the intervening banks have to be passive (they must not neutralize external influences on the national quantity of money). The dollar standard is an example of such a system. It was a consistent system just because the "Fed" did not intervene in the exchange market. The "benign neglect" policy of the United States, which was frequently criticized by other countries, was necessary for the system to be correctly determined. However, such asymmetrical systems, giving a specific role to one currency and one country, are not easily accepted, except mainly in monetary areas inherited from a colonial organization (franc zone, sterling area, etc.). They have never been proposed, for instance, for the EEC since all countries are assumed to be equal.

Solution (b)

Therefore, the only alternative[3] is to choose M_z as the n-th target variable. Now, M_z cannot be observed directly, but it can be obtained just by summing all the M_i's. In other words there is no institution in charge of managing M_z (for instance, the European quantity of money). Therefore, there are only two practical ways to run Solution (b):

1. Every country determines its quantity of money independently and the system is overdetermined. From time to time one or the other target variables have to be adjusted, which means that it is no longer a target variable: there are either parity changes or changes in monetary policies. What is often named a "currency crisis" is nothing else than the explicit consequence of the working of a system that has been wrongly designed.

2. There is some sort of policy coordination: through mutual agreement each monetary authority determines its quantity of money (or its rate of growth) so that the sum is equal to the target value of M_z. This system of organization—which is often called "monetary cooperation"—is generally considered as the best solution, perhaps because it seems to mean that human beings are able to agree with each other, to be friends and not enemies, as is suggested by the word "cooperation." However, the fact that economic problems are often viewed from a moral point of view does not imply that this system is a first-best solution to the problem of international monetary organization. In our view, it is rather a second-best solution. If, for instance, floating rates are not desired, if there does not exist an (n + 1)th currency, if Solution (a) is not accepted because it is asymmetrical, then there is a *need* for a common determination of M_z: cooperation is "better" than no cooperation, but other systems might be "better."[4]

Either in Solution (a) or in Solution (b), it can be considered that there is only one currency in the monetary area, at least when perfect fixity of exchange rates occurs since it implies that all national currencies are equivalent, except for the unessential aspect of denomination. To make a comparison with industrial organization, one could say that there is one good produced by several firms, namely the different central banks or the different national banking systems. Solution (a) is similar to a hierarchical industrial organization with headquarters—the central bank or the banking system issuing the key-currency—and several subsidiaries—the other central banks or national banking systems—which does not prevent each firm from being a national profit center (the profit being the seigniorage in the case of money).

Solution (b) is similar to a cartel, each firm—that is, each central bank or national banking system—being on the same footing as the others. The cartel decides its common target—for instance, the rate of growth of its production (the quantity of money)—and determines the share of each member. However, as is well known, a cartel is an unstable organization, since there is always the possibility that one or more members might find it profitable to do free-riding.[5] This may be the main explanation for the "monetary crises" we have already mentioned.

There is a further difficulty in Solution (b). In fact, until now we have implicitly assumed that there is perfect information, so that the monetary authorities of the zone can determine the share of each country in the production of money in order to get the desired target of the zone. It is quite obvious that the organization of a decentralized system of production is not that simple. However, we shall not discuss these aspects in this chapter; other aspects of the imperfect information problem will be considered in Section 4.

Short-run Working of the System

If we now turn to the short-run, there are n additional degrees of freedom since $k_i \neq 0$. Once more, several possibilities are open, especially since the k_i's are proxy variables for a certain number of variables which can either be used as targets by the authorities or be endogenous. Let us consider, for instance, the case where the monetary authorities of the zone pursue independent monetary policies in a system of fixed rates. The k_i's then adjust to the exchange rates and the quantities of money. Therefore there is an impact of monetary and exchange policies on variables such as the interest rates and/or the real exchange rates and/or monetary and exchange rate expectations, which may be components of the proxy variables k_i's. However, if the various monetary policies are not consistent in the long run, the variables summarized by k_i have to converge toward their long-run equilibrium values. In comparison with a system of steady long-run equilibrium, the use of independent monetary policies under a fixed rate system introduces variability in variables such as interest rates, real exchange rates, wages, etc. Existing models of exchange rate determination in the short-run make this variability more explicit.

The simple and formal model we used in the present section will help us to evaluate the principles and the working of the European Monetary System.

2. THE MECHANISMS OF THE EUROPEAN MONETARY SYSTEM

Our aim in the present section is not to describe all the features of the complex EMS but to stress only those relevant for our present discussion. As is well known, the main currencies of the EEC participate in the EMS, except for the pound sterling. This system aims mainly at enforcing fixed exchange rates between the participating currencies, at least within a band, whereas exchange rates are floating in relation with outside currencies (although the real system is rather one of dirty floating). The internal fixity of exchange rates implies central bank interventions, and a complex system of indicators has been designed to help in the determination of respective responsibilities of central banks.

The need for intervention could be determined by all sorts of indicators. Two systems have been given particular consideration by the EMS:

1.   A "snake-type" system, like the one that worked under the European snake arrangement at the beginning of the 1970s: there is a need for intervention when the bilateral exchange rate between two currencies reaches its upper or lower limit. In such a system it is clear that both currencies are concerned in intervention, but discussion is open about the choice of the intervening central bank(s). This decision can be made by day-to-day negotiations or via permanent rules.
2.   A "basket-type" system, which is a system where the need for intervention is determined by the fact that *one* currency reaches its upper or lower limit in relation to the basket of currencies (the European Currency Unit, ECU, for instance). It is clear that the corresponding central bank has to intervene, but it is not clear in which currency it has to intervene. Here again, discretionary decisions or institutional rules can be used.[6]

The choice between a snake-type system and a basket-of-currencies system was debated at some length before the introduction of the "new" system. In the end, a kind of mixed system was adopted. In effect, the intervention of central banks is not obligatory until a currency fluctuates at least 2.25% above or below its parity in terms of another currency in the system. In that sense, then, it is merely the old system of the snake which has been carried forward. But a new concept has been added: the divergence indicator. The divergence indicator is reached when a currency reaches a certain limit of fluctuation with respect to the ECU. Because the probability of reaching a given limit of fluctuation is not as great for a currency that is weighted lightly in the ECU as for one that is weighted heavily, the divergence indicator is not the same for each of the currencies that make up the ECU. The divergence indicator acts as a simple signal; it does not trigger any automatic action. If action *is* then taken by the country concerned, it can be in the form of intervention in the exchange markets, or of a change in monetary or fiscal policies, or of an adjustment in the currency's parity.

So the "new" system is not new in relation to the old snake system as far as exchange rate policies are concerned, except for the addition of the divergence indicator, which is supposed to set off an alarm, so to speak, before the bilateral fluctuation limits are reached. But it is interesting to note that this new element of the system is a *discretionary* one. It is more or less agreed that the divergence indicator should normally open the way to consultations between countries. The extent to which this divergence indicator works as a signal provoking effective action will determine whether the exchange system is more a snake-type system or more a basket-of-currencies type.

We shall now compare the new system to the old system of the snake. Obviously, it would not be necessary to make such a comparison if the divergence indicator had no role to play, as the "new" system would be identical to the old one. We shall therefore assume, somewhat arbitrarily, that the divergence indicator does play an important role.

Choosing Those Responsible for Policy Adjustments

Under the traditional snake, where divergences of exchange rates were measured in bilateral terms, a currency was by definition at its permissible ceiling in relation to another currency only if the latter were at its floor in relation to the former. The question of deciding which country (or countries) was bound to intervene (that is, to be responsible for the adjustment) was particularly delicate even though it was clear which currencies were involved. In the absence of automatic institutional rules, consultation among central banks was required; in the European Community, these consultations were aimed, for example, at determining the "Community exchange rate of the dollar," which involved a decision about the position of the snake in relation to a third currency—that is, which currencies were "too high" and which were "too low." The lack of institutional rules fixing *automatically* the respective responsibilities of the different central banks was the cause of constant haggling and, finally, of the breakdown of the system—in place of the cooperation that was always invoked but never achieved.

To the extent that the divergence indicator plays a predominant role in the "new" European Monetary System, this system offers the advantage of indicating clearly which central bank in a given case has the responsibility for adjusting. But there is still wide room for discussion and negotiation about the actions to be taken.

Moreover, when the fluctuation limits between two currencies are reached, the problem of the division of responsibility between central banks is partially resolved by making the position of each currency in relation to the ECU an element to be considered within the framework of the consultations among the monetary authorities. In other words, if the German mark, for example, is at its ceiling in relation to the franc—that is, the franc is at its floor in relation to the mark—central bank intervention is mandatory to keep the snake within agreed limits. So one looks at the position of the franc and the mark in relation to the ECU. If the franc is far below its ECU parity, while the mark is not above its ECU parity, the Community authorities would ask the Bank of France to intervene by buying francs and selling marks (or possibly some other currency). The underlying idea in this system is that the ECU will point to the party most "responsible" for the exchange rate disequilibria, who therefore should intervene. But this notion of responsibility is highly debatable. Instead of asking who is most "responsible" for divergences from the average behavior—which is thus considered a priori as the norm—it would make more sense to ask this question: just what behavior should be imposed on the central banks to achieve the optimum result? The answer is obvious: one approaches the optimum by reducing inflation. To the extent that exchange rate fluctuations— except in the short term—are a reflection of comparative monetary policies (that is, more or less inflationary), then an efficient system is one that imposes adjustment measures on the countries that are most inflationist, and whose currencies are thus subject to greater depreciation. It is not so much a question of holding such countries "responsible" for exchange rate disequilibria, as of keeping them from transmitting their inflationary tendencies to other countries within their zone.

The essential characteristic of a monetary zone based on fixed exchange rates—even though rates may be allowed to fluctuate within given margins—is that there cannot be a sustained divergence of inflation rates among the member countries. Therefore one can create a "European zone of stability"—which is what the European countries say they are trying to do—only by imposing constraints on the countries that are potentially the most inflationist. The "mechanisms" that are actually being set up simply do not answer this need, so that all the talk about the new European Monetary System favoring the creation of a zone of stability in Europe is not supported by the facts. The same sort of claims were made on behalf of the snake, and we know the outcome of that. Public opinion, which has once again been promised a miraculous system to ensure stability in Europe, will therefore once again be disappointed.

The question of which central banks are to intervene in the market has an important bearing on the potentially inflationary character of the European Monetary System. However, the significance of this problem is attenuated somewhat by the fact that interventions presume short-term credits among central banks, since no central bank is likely to hold a sufficiently diversified portfolio of European currencies to enable it always to intervene in the required currency without having to borrow. If the Bundesbank, for example, is called upon to support the Danish crown, it will accumulate crowns, which it will quickly ask the Danish central bank to repay in marks. This will fairly rapidly produce the same situation as if the Danish central bank had initially intervened by selling marks and buying crowns. In the same way, if the Bundesbank has to sell Danish crowns it will borrow them from the Danish central bank against a transfer of marks, but it will later have to repurchase the marks and repay the Danish crowns. So it would have amounted to the same thing for the Danish central bank to have been the initial seller of crowns and buyer of marks. But it is always easier for a country to sell its own currency and to accumulate foreign currencies than the other way around. Consequently, an exchange system in which the respective responsibilities of the various central banks are not clearly defined carries an inflationary bias to the extent that the more inflationary central banks are not required or motivated to buy their own currencies.

In short, the present European Monetary System is somewhat new to the extent that the divergence indicator plays a fundamental role. Because of the discretionary nature of the system, though, no country is bound to stick to precise rules. This is the characteristic that has led people to describe the system in terms that sound favorable, such as "flexible." But if the limits of bilateral fluctuation between currencies turn out to be frequently reached, then there is no difference between the new system and the old one.

At any rate, the complex mechanisms that have been set up are really just technical gadgets; the fundamental reality is the existence of fixed exchange rates among national monetary systems. Would it be considered malicious to wonder whether these complex arrangements are simply cosmetic changes aimed at concealing from the public the fact that it is the same old system?

Freedom of Intervention

We have put one important question aside until now, namely that of the freedom of central banks to intervene inside the permissible margins of fluctuation. We have assumed that intervention was obligatory when the limits were reached, but what about intervention at some point short of that?

If the central banks are free to intervene whenever they wish—as seems to be the case—there is the risk that the simultaneous intervention of several banks will be mutually contradictory. This is currently called the "n - 1 problem." This simply means that, in a zone of n currencies, there are only n - 1 exchange rates in relation to the one currency that serves as the numéraire. If all the n central banks intervene and all aim to alter the rate of their currency in the same direction, they obviously will not succeed and will waste their reserves in a hopeless battle.

The ECU: Caricature of a Currency

It has been claimed that the ECU, created in 1979, is a new currency, launched by the European monetary authorities. To judge how true that is, and to appreciate the exact role of the ECU, we have to consider first of all its main characteristics.

The ECU is defined as a basket of European currencies. More precisely, to calculate the value of an ECU in terms of another currency, one must add up the value, in that same currency, of 0.828 DM, 1.55 French francs, 0.0885 pounds sterling, 109 lira, 0.286 Dutch guilders, 3.80 Belgian francs, 0.217 Danish crowns, and 0.00759 Irish pounds. Thus, to calculate the value of an ECU in French francs on a given day, one adds up the value in francs of each of the above quantities of different currencies. The weight of each currency depends on the economic dimensions of its country (GNP and intra-European foreign trade). So if a currency depreciates in terms of goods—that is, in relation to a certain price index representing a certain basket of goods—then the ECU depreciates in relation to the basket in proportion to that currency's relative weight in the basket. Of course, the value of an ECU in relation to a currency of the basket which defines it changes along with the fluctuations in exchange rates between that currency and other currencies. If the purchasing power parity hypothesis was verifiable at any time, then exchange rates should vary according to the different inflation rates and the ECU would depreciate in relation to goods at a rate equal to the average European inflation rate (that average rate having been calculated according to the same weighting of currencies as used in defining the ECU). In fact, one will note some fairly substantial short-term disparities between the published exchange rates and the exchange rates corresponding to purchasing power parities, so that the value of the ECU, either in terms of currencies or in terms of goods, is as uncertain as any exchange rate.

As we have seen, the ECU serves as a signal for central bank intervention on the exchange markets, and it constitutes the numéraire used in calculating the obligations and debts between the European central banks and FECOM.[7]

If we compare the role played by the ECU with the definition of money, we see that the ECU is not yet a currency. In effect, money is undifferentiated buying power, exchangeable at any time, with anyone, for anything. But for the present only the central banks hold ECUs, and they are exchangeable only for European currencies. Once again, the point has been overlooked that there is no sense in monetary union unless it improves the public welfare and is not simply a gadget for the use of the central banks. Money exists only through, and for, the marketplace. Yet the ECU so far is only a *numéraire.* That is a role that money can play, but it does not always play that role, and it can stop doing so altogether without losing its character as money. There is nothing to stop people from drawing up their private instruments in ECUs if they like, but one cannot have a deposit in ECUs with European banks.

Even for the central banks, the ECU's role is merely symbolic. In effect, they are converting part of their balances through the intermediary of FECOM. When a central bank obtains a credit from FECOM for its interventions on the foreign exchange markets, it is obvious that it can only use its ECU credits by converting them into European currencies, because nongovernmental entities do not hold

ECUs and so they cannot be traded on the market. In short, the ECU is only a mechanism for requiring the central banks to hold a portion of their reserves in European currencies, to diversify their portfolios. But there is no indication that this corresponds to what the central banks would spontaneously have chosen to do. FECOM has simply the role of imposing portfolio constraints on the central banks in the interest of "European solidarity." As the ECU by definition will evolve as the average of the European currencies, the central banks will thus be indirectly forced to hold in their reserves the currency of some of their partners which is depreciating rapidly, instead of holding, for instance, gold or dollars or marks. It is hard to see how this will benefit the public, especially the citizens of countries with more stable currencies.

It is perhaps regrettable to let this ECU be mistaken for what might be a true European common currency. The introduction of a new currency involves potentially large publicity costs, as is often the case in making a new "brand" known. One can imagine the ECU evolving one day into a real currency, held in the private sector. In view of that possibility, one can consider all the current efforts on behalf of the ECU as aimed at promoting a "brand image," not via the usual advertising techniques but through political marketing. This viewpoint is defensible, but the fact remains that the ECU, as defined, *is not a true currency.* Representing a basket of currencies, its value in terms of goods evolves in a less favorable manner than that of the less inflationary currencies, but in a manner more favorable than that of the more inflationary currencies. Why choose to hold ECUs if one is certain that a European currency, such as the DM at the moment, represents a better reserve of buying power?

One could imagine holding the ECU or a reserve currency if the risk attached to that were less than for all the other currencies. But there is no reason why the ECUs volatility should be less than that of the national currencies whose average, after all, it reflects.[8]

Another hypothesis that cannot be entirely excluded is that the European monetary authorities might in future permit the citizens in each country to hold not only their national currency but also the ECU, to the exclusion of any other currency. In the most inflationary countries, this would be an attractive substitution possibility. But it would have to be recognized that holdings of the ECU might become more widespread because of the absence of a right to hold other curencies. Monetary competition would be only partial, as a country's monetary authorities would only give up the legal-tender notion in favor of a currency produced by a cartel of producers to which they belong.

3. THE ACTUAL WORKING OF THE EMS:
APPARENT SUCCESS AND HIDDEN COSTS

Insofar as the aim of the EMS is the fixity of exchange rates, it could be argued that it has been more or less successful. In fact, some parity adjustments did take place, since there was a 2% reevaluation of the mark and a 3% devaluation of the Danish crown on September 23, 1979; another devaluation of the Danish crown (5%) on November 29, the same year; devaluation of the Italian lira by 6% in March 1981; and devaluation of the French franc (3%) and of the Italian lira (3%) and a reevaluation of the German mark (5.5%) and the Dutch guilder (5.5%) on October 4, 1981.

Therefore, it would be an extreme view to hold that the EMS allowed perfectly fixed exchange rates, and from this point of view one can be astonished by the fact that, for instance, the decisions taken in September 1979 were officially considered as proof of the good working of the EMS. In fact, if ever words have any meaning, a parity change in a system of fixed rates means that this system did not work well. We shall not dispute the fact that it is better not to have waited for a longer time before deciding parity adjustments which were unavoidable, so that the European countries did not suffer from the traditional "monetary crises" which had been so frequent in the past. However, it is strange to interpret a parity change as a success for a system of fixed rates, since it can only mean one of the two following things:

1.   either the rules of a fixed rate system have not been correctly played, which implies that the working of the system has been "bad";

2.   or, the system has not been correctly designed.

However, one may argue that these parity changes have not been too numerous and that they have not been of great dimension. It is true that during the year after the first realignment of parities in 1979 there was no further change (except for the Danish crown). Therefore, insofar as the objective of the EMS is the fixity of exchange rates, the system has apparently been successful. But such a statement is not sufficient and one has to ask an additional question: what was the cost of this apparent success?

The EMS has been presented as a mechanism capable of achieving monetary stability in Europe. If monetary stability means zero inflation or lower inflation, this claim is questionable. In fact, the inventors of the EMS have been very inventive in introducing precise and sophisticated techniques in the system, but they have forgotten to include any rule to determine the long-run common rate of inflation and to determine it at a low level. In terms of our model above, there is no rule for the determination either of M_z or of the M_i's so that there is an important risk that the system may become overdetermined, each monetary authority deciding its monetary policy more-or-less independently.

If the European monetary authorities are unable to cooperate in order to implement converging national monetary policies (implying, if possible, a decreasing rate of inflation), as seems to be the case, the inconsistencies between the different monetary policies might shake the very existence of the EMS. Such an end can be considered as likely, as has been the case with the snake arrangement for this same reason, in spite of the apparent success of the EMS at its beginning.

In fact, we have recalled that a fixed rate system has some degree of flexibility in the *short-run* due to the possible changes in the variables k_i. However, an "excessive" variability of k means a social cost. Now, the theory of the short-run determination of exchange rates is not sufficiently reliable—and probably never will be—for anyone to be able to make precise computations about the cost of this variability in comparison to what it could have been in other systems. The builders and defenders of the EMS are very skillful in that they gave an observable variable—the fixity of the exchange rate—as a criterion of success, whereas the cost of the performance is unknown. They have also been skillful enough as to find a way of refusing the only possible criticisms: if national monetary policies are inconsistent, devaluations and reevaluations which occur in the more-or-less long run ought to be considered as proofs of the fact that the system of *fixed* rates did not work well. But the idea has been imposed that it means that the system is flexible, which is considered a priori as a "good" thing.

In trying to evaluate the working of the EMS, in spite of the fact that we cannot have sufficient information—for instance, on the optimal variability of k—we may be unable to do more than choose some indicators, for instance, inflation rates, real exchange rates, or interest rates.

Let us first have a look at recent inflation rates in the member countries of the EMS (Table 8-1). There has been an acceleration of inflation in all countries since the introduction of the EMS so that one can be skeptical about the ability of the EMS to create a zone of monetary stability in Europe. It is true, for instance, that Germany adopted a less restrictive monetary policy in 1979 than before, although it is difficult to know whether it did so to help the working of the EMS—which would mean a cost of the EMS—or to give

TABLE 8-1.   Retail Prices

Country	1977	1978	1979	1980
Germany	3.7	2.7	4.1	5.5
France	9.4	9.1	10.8	13.7
Italy	17.0	12.1	14.8	21.0
Belgium	7.1	4.5	4.5	7.6
Netherlands	6.4	4.1	4.2	6.7

a positive answer to the (unjustified) demands from its European partners in favor of a German expansionary policy.

Under the EMS the inflation rates remained considerably different from country to country. Thus, in 1980, the French inflation rate was 13.7% and the German rate was 5.5%. It was certain that the exchange rate would have to be changed one day or another.

Maintaining fixed rates in a situation of diverging inflation rates had consequences on real exchange rates, as may be suggested by Table 8-2, which gives effective real exchange rates for some European countries in recent years. From this table, one can see that:

1.   The changes of real exchange rates in the long run (March 1973 to December 1980) are limited, which is in agreement with the PPP hypothesis.

2.   In 1980—that is, in a period where there has been no exchange rate adjustment in the EMS—there were rather important changes in real exchange rates. For instance, there was a 7.3% decrease in the German real exchange rate and a 5% decrease in the Belgian real exchange rate. These figures are high in comparison with the long-run evolution of real exchange rates. These changes have a cost, since they imply changes in relative prices.

The case of Germany in 1980 is interesting from another point of view: in fact, the mark has been close to its lower limit of fluctuation for a long time, contrary to what could have been expected from a simple application of the PPP theory to the determination of exchange rates in the short run, which only means that PPP does not hold in the short run and that other forces were present (for instance, expectations, a wrong evaluation of the equilibrium exchange

TABLE 8-2. Real Effective Exchange Rates

Period	Germany	Belgium	Denmark	France	Italy	Netherlands
1977	102.7	100.0	97.5	96.6	92.4	104.0
1978	103.4	99.9	103.7	97.3	90.9	103.9
1979	104.2	97.3	101.8	99.2	90.7	100.5
1980	101.2	92.2	93.7	101.0	92.0	97.9
1980						
Jan.	104.5	94.9	95.7	99.9	93.1	100.1
Feb.	103.5	94.0	94.8	99.9	93.8	99.3
Mar.	102.0	93.0	94.2	100.3	92.5	98.6
Apr.	101.4	92.9	93.5	100.4	92.0	98.6
May	102.1	93.5	94.2	100.3	92.8	97.1
June	101.8	93.4	94.3	100.4	92.9	97.0
July	101.4	92.9	96.0	101.3	92.8	97.9
Aug.	100.6	91.6	95.7	101.6	92.9	97.8
Sep.	100.0	92.0	94.1	101.5	93.3	97.6
Oct.	98.9	91.1	93.4	101.3	92.7	96.6
Nov.	97.5	90.2	92.6	100.5	93.8	96.0
Dec.	96.9	89.9	92.2	100.5	93.5	95.3

Note: Index 100 in March 1973. The index of the real effective exchange rate is the index of the effective exchange rate adjusted for inflation differentials, measured by wholesale prices of non-food manufactures. Annual figures are averages of months.
Source: Morgan Guaranty, *World Financial Markets*, Jan. 1981.

rate in the parity adjustment of 1979, etc.). Whatever the cause of this situation, Germany has been obliged to accept higher interest rates than those that could be considered as consistent with inflationary expectations. Excessively high *real* interest rates also mean a cost for the economy.

According to common opinion, the "low" German exchange rates were unrealistic and floating exchange rates would have allowed still lower exchange rates, so that fixed rates prevented excessive fluctuations in the DM exchange rate. However, we believe, on the contrary, that the fact that these low exchange rates could not be perfectly explained supports the idea that a fixed rate system introduces costly rigidities. In other words, by limiting the fluctuations of the exchange rate, one does get a higher stability of the exchange rate—by definition—but at a cost that is not well known, precisely because the short-run determination of exchange rates is not well known. Numerous variables are interdependent, and in a floating rate system the exchange rate would fluctuate as an answer to changes in other variables—for instance, interest rates, inflationary expectations for various currencies, etc. If the variability of some variables is constrained by public intervention, other variables have to carry a greater part of the burden of adjustment. Thus, when keeping an exchange rate that is not in harmony with inflation differentials, expectations on exchange rates and inflation rates, monetary and credit policies, and all sorts of other variables, one cannot, for instance, obtain the interest rates that would permit equilibrium on credit markets.

Thus, the apparent "good" working of the EMS hides disequilibria somewhere in the macroeconomic system. These disequilibria cannot last for long and adjustment has to occur—for instance, via exchange rate changes or via changes in monetary policies.

4. DOES THE EUROPEAN MONETARY SYSTEM PROVIDE A PUBLIC GOOD?

The EMS is a system of fixed rates. Fixed rates between different currencies, issued by different banking systems, are possible because of public intervention on the exchange markets. As the justification for public intervention is the provision of a public good, one may ask whether the EMS provides people with a public good.

A public good has to be provided by the public sector if the market will not provide it because the return would be too low for the potential producers in comparison with the costs they would incur, even though the social return is higher than the social cost of providing it. The non-exclusion principle explains such a situation. Economic stability certainly enters the category of public goods since it cannot be provided only to those who pay for it. However, the words "economic stability" are rather vague. In fact, it does not mean perfect fixity of variables; rather, we shall define economic stability as a situation in which the gap between the actual value of a variable and its equilibrium value is a minimum.

Therefore, according to this definition, exchange rate stabilization does not mean fixity of actual exchange rates since the equilibrium exchange rate may be changing. In fact, and as we have seen, a fixed rate system is a special case of a broader category, that of systems where the producers of currencies—the central banks in the present organization of the world—announce in advance the long-run trend and possible variations of exchange rates between their currencies. The role of this announcement effect is to decrease uncertainties in production and trade decisions, and it may be considered as a public good. However, the designers of international monetary systems do not usually consider other systems of pre-determined long-run exchange rates than the special case of fixed rates. This is true for the EMS.

In our view, the public-good argument is the only valid criterion to evaluate any exchange rate regime. Fixed parities or broader bands, for instance, are not desirable per se. They are desirable only if they increase social welfare, which cannot be appreciated just by considering the evolution of exchange rates, but that of the over-all economic system.

As we have already seen, the EMS is a system where:

1. In the short run, exchange rates are maintained within a limited and publicly known band.
2. In the long run, exchange rates are adjustable.

In terms of our model, there is an independent determination of the various quantities of national currencies, M_i, and, therefore, of M_z.

Adjustment takes place in the short run via the variables k_i. In the long run, it takes place either via the quantities of money, M_i, which then become endogenous, according to the principles of a fixed rate system, or via exchange rate adjustment. It must be stressed that adjustment via M_i or e_i depends on discretionary decision and not on predetermined rules.

Knowing the explicit rules and the effective working of the EMS, we may now be able to answer the question: does the EMS allow the production of a public good, in the form of more economic stability?

In a world with perfect information, there would be no specific role for the central banks as regards exchange rates, in comparison with what the market could do. In a world of imperfect information —as is the case, in fact—the intervention of central banks is justified if they can provide more economic stability than the market alone could do, or if they can provide the same degree of stability at a lower cost.

The conditions under which the market and the central banks can work may be different either as regards the knowledge they have about the working of the macroeconomic system or as regards the information they have about the precise value of the relevant variables.

There is no reason to believe that the central banks have a better explicit or implicit macroeconomic model of exchange rate determination either in the short run or in the long run, and it is well known that the market can provide, due to speculation, as good a stabilization service as the central banks can. It may even be argued that private speculators would perform a better stabilization service since they have a private interest in getting a profit through efficient forecast, which may not be the case for a central banker more-or-less linked to short-run political considerations.

However, the main difference between both may not lie in their views about the working of the macroeconomic system, but in the information they may have on the future value of some important variables. The main reason for that is that central banks benefit from a monopoly position in the creation of national currencies. Therefore, a central bank does not have to guess its own future monetary policy and, if it wishes to do so, can decide it in advance and hold to it. This information is not sufficient to obtain a precise idea of the future value of the exchange rate or of determinants of the exchange rate since a central bank does not determine the production policy for other currencies. However, it may be in a better position than a private speculator to get information from the other central banks about their future policies. This is a reason to believe that interventions by central banks on the exchange market can increase social welfare since they have better information than the market, at least on one important determinant of exchange rates—monetary policies.

However, at this point, some remarks have to be made:

1. From the theory of public goods it can be said that the public sector is in
    a better position than the market to provide some specific goods, for
    instance if exclusion is not possible. However, the case we are studying
    does not enter into this category, and it would be wrong to infer from
    what we have just said that the social welfare can be maximized via inter-
    ventions of central banks on the exchange market. In fact, central banks
    can have better information than the market on future monetary policies
    and, therefore, on the future value of exchange rates in the long run
    because there is no perfect competition on the money market since
    the central banks have a monopoly in the production of money. There-
    fore, the fixity of exchange rates in the EMS or any system of fixed rates
    (or, more broadly, the exogenous determination of exchange rates by
    central banks) may not correspond to a first-best solution, but to a second-
    best solution, given the constraint that there is no perfect competition for
    the production of money. However, we shall not discuss the issue of the
    competitive production of money here.

In that sense it cannot be said that central bank interventions
on the exchange market correspond to the provision of a public good.
Certainly, if the exchange rate, or the over-all macroeconomic system,
is more stable due to interventions by the central banks, all individuals benefit from these interventions, and there is no possibility of
excluding anyone from the advantages of a more stable economy.
But this does not mean that this public good has necessarily to be
provided by the public sector since it is not necessarily true that it
can thus be produced at a lower cost or in a greater amount. Thus,
the case of economic stabilization or exchange rate stabilization has
nothing in common with, for instance, the case of national defence
in which no individual would have an interest in paying voluntarily
to get defence services, but in which all people can gain from being
obliged to pay for defence expenditures.

2. Even if we accept that we must limit ourselves to the narrow framework
    in which the production of money is monopolized by the public sector,
    it does not follow that central bank interventions on the exchange market
    make people better off than they would otherwise be.

In fact, we did see that the only difference between the central banks
and the market as regards the available information is the information
the central banks can get concerning their own intentions about the
quantity of money, since they have control of the supply of money.
Does it imply that they have better information on the long-run or

short-run evolution of exchange rates? The answer could be positive if one assumed that the central banks and the market had the same explanatory models of exchange rate determination so that the relative advantage of central banks in the information about monetary policies would remain. But let us put things otherwise; given the fact that central banks have better information than the market about future monetary policies, there are several ways in which they can supply this information and, thus, give a public good to individuals:

> They can use this information to evaluate the long-run and short-run values of the equilibrium exchange rate and try to minimize actual discrepancies, as we have already seen.

> They can provide directly the specific information they have, namely that concerning the future monetary policies they intend to pursue.

In the present case of the EMS, the central banks transform the monopoly they have in the production of money into a monopoly in the ownership of some information. We assumed previously that the market and the central banks were equally efficient in using given information to forecast the exchange rate. However, it may happen that, at least in some specific instances, the market is more efficient (has a better model of exchange rate determination). Therefore, competition in the use of given information could increase social welfare.

We can thus compare two different systems, taken as examples:

> The first is the EMS arrangement, where the central banks more-or-less keep the information they have for their own use but claim to defend a given parity, at least in the short run;

> The second would be a system without any exchange rate arrangement but in which the central banks would announce monetary targets for the future and where people would be confident in these targets. The exchange rates would be flexible, but people would have the maximum possible information about the determination of exchange rates.

Since the second system is closer to a competitive system than the first, there are reasons to believe that it would be more stabilizing.

3. One of our initial principles was that exchange rate determination was simpler to evaluate the longer the period under examination. More precisely, we believe that everyone could accept the following principle: the shorter the period under consideration, the lower the explanatory power of the relative growth rates of the quantity of money in the respective countries.

From this it follows that the relative advantage of central banks over the market in stabilizing the exchange rate is smaller the shorter the period under consideration, even when the central banks keep information on their monetary policies to themselves.

In turn, this implies that, in the case in which the central banks do not give free information to the market about their future monetary policies, they can provide a public good by giving reliable information on the future course of "predetermined" exchange rates, which implies that they are ready to take any necessary action to make this future course effective. A special case of such a situation is that of fixed rates, but we have exactly the same sort of situation if the central banks announce, for instance, a certain rule of evolution of exchange rates. However, it must be clear that the public good is provided only as far as the central banks supply good information on future exchange rates in the long run. It can then be concluded that the EMS arrangements are in no way optimal since the central banks claim that they defend fixed rates within bands in the short run, but do not take any firm commitment for the long run; as we pointed out, they even consider as an improvement in comparison with the snake arrangement that long-run exchange rates are more flexible.

However, one could consider that central banks contribute to the stabilization of exchange rates in the short run, so that they provide a public good to some degree. In fact, we cannot be certain of that since we know that the determinants of the exchange rate in the short run are numerous and it may well happen that the short-run *equilibrium* exchange rate is much more volatile, so that the stabilization, via the band, of the *actual* exchange rate may imply a social cost and not a social gain. In other words, public intervention is justified only if there is some sufficient information and if it can provide a public good which would not be provided otherwise. These conditions are not warranted in this special case.

We thus come to the conclusion that the EMS exchange rate arrangement is not optimal. In fact, if we put aside the solution of a truly competitive system in the production of money, a (second-best) solution would imply perfect flexibility of the exchange rate without intervention in the short run, whereby some information would be given to the market for the long-run value of the exchange rate, either because all central banks would use a policy of monetary targets or because they would be committed to the attainment of predetermined values of the exchange rate for the long run and would be able to hold their commitment. The EMS arrangement is quite the reverse.

What we mean by "predetermined exchange rate in the long run" is not necessarily "fixed rates." In fact, fixity of exchange rates is a quite unessential problem. If, for instance, information on the future course of exchange rates was perfect, there would not be any reason to prefer fixed rates. Fixity would mean only that there is a link between the national inflation rates, which has no justification, especially if the "common" inflation rate is high. In fact, social welfare can be increased by central banks via two different ways:

By giving good information on the future of exchange rates and/or monetary policies.

By following monetary policies to minimize the inflation rate.

Exchange rate fixity does not imply that any of these functions is correctly performed, particularly if there is no firm commitment to maintain the fixity of exchange rates.

NOTES

1. In fact, we believe that currency unification does not necessarily imply fixed rates: See Salin, *European Monetary Unity: For Whose Benefit?* (Ipswich, Mass.: Ipswich Press, 1980).

2. In fact, there is a broader class of exchange rate systems where the rate of change of the exchange rate is exogenous (for instance, the central bank announces a weekly or a monthly change):

$$\frac{de}{dt} \frac{1}{e} = f(t)$$

where t stands for time. The function $f(t)$ can be a constant, in which case the rate of change of the exchange rate is constant. A fixed rate system corresponds to the special case where $(de/dt)(1/e) = 0$.

3. We do not consider, here, the case where there is an $(n + 1)$th variable. An example of such a system is the gold standard. This system is coherent and all countries are on an equal footing. It has also often been proposed that a man-managed $(n + 1)$th currency—an international currency—be created, but there are risks of mismanagement which do not exist in the gold standard.

4. In the present paper we have not considered all possible categories of exchange rate systems. We have proposed a more exhaustive classification in Salin, "The Political Economy of Alternative Approaches to Monetary Integration," Firenze, Colloquium on New Economic Approaches to the Study of International Integration, June 1979.

5. We have developed the idea of the European monetary organization as being of a cartel-type in Salin, *European Monetary Unity.*

6. The description of the EMS in the present section is extracted from Salin, *European Monetary Unity*.

7. European institution more-or-less similar to the IMF.

8. The wide fluctuation in the value—in terms of a given national currency —of a European composite currency like the ECU has been confirmed by the simulations presented in Chapter III of the OPTICA report, entitled "Inflation and Exchange Rates: Empirical Aspects and Propositions of Political Economy in the European Community", a report of experts prepared for the Commission of the European Communities (II/855/76) by G. Basevi, P. Salin, H. E. Scharrer, N. Thygesen, and P. de Grauwe.

9

COMPETING INTERNATIONAL MONIES AND INTERNATIONAL MONETARY ARRANGEMENTS

BENJAMIN KLEIN & MICHAEL MELVIN

It is obvious that the international monetary system has been in an unsettled state for several years. Although we no longer have a world dollar standard, there is no clear successor waiting to become the world's dominant money. We are said to have a system of floating exchange rates, yet for optimal currency area reasons we know that regional regimes of pegged rates exist. Given the desire for pegged rates, we see the EEC countries searching for an optimal arrangement. What are the prospects for a European dollar standard or mark standard, or how might we expect a new currency like the proposed Europa to fare?

Before investigating these questions, as well as others, we consider the determinants of a currency's international role. Many earlier works, including various monetary reform proposals, are characterized by oversimplified views of the nature of competition in the market for monies. In particular, important analytical distinctions between monetary stability and monetary predictability, between interest-bearing and noninterest-bearing money, between money used as a medium of exchange or unit of account and money used as a store of value, and between a dominant domestic money

---

This paper is a restatement and extension of the ideas presented in Klein (1978).

and an international money, are either ignored or blurred. This incomplete theoretical analysis leads to faulty empirical conclusions and policy recommendations. The analysis to be presented here, as well as the historical evidence, suggests that new dominant monies evolve very slowly in the market place and are not easily substitutable once established.

The first section considers the nature of competition between alternative monies. Using the theoretical framework provided by Klein (1974a), the "inflation uncertainty competitive effect" is discussed in an international context. Section 1 also considers the important issue of producing consumer confidence in money and then investigates the prospects for the usual currency reform propositions. Following a discussion of the natural monopoly aspects of money production, an unusual reform proposal, the private production of money, is considered in Section 2. The analysis presented in the first two sections is drawn together in Section 3 as past, present, and proposed future international monetary arrangements are evaluated.

1. THE NATURE OF COMPETITION BETWEEN ALTERNATIVE MONIES

Inflation as a Basis for Competition

When considering the basis for competition between alternative monies, it is crucial to distinguish between the mean and the variance of the inflation rate. A fundamental determinant of a money's liquidity services is the predictability of its future exchange value in terms of real goods and services. If it were a low inflation rate rather than a highly predictable rate that was the driving competitive force in the market, we would expect gold, with its significant increase in real purchasing power over the recent past, to be an important, if not dominant, competing money. Yet gold is far from being a dominant international money. In fact, the volatility of the real exchange value of gold has demonetized it to such an extent that gold is now best viewed as essentially just a commodity like any other internationally traded commodity.

The average inflation rate is unlikely to be an important competitive force because much of the money stock, broadly defined, yields a competitive rate of interest. Demand is therefore invariant to the anticipated inflation rate as interest payments on money will reflect anticipated inflation. This leads us to our second important distinction: between interest-bearing money and noninterest-bearing money. It is only currency and bank reserves—that is, high-powered money—that do not yield interest and therefore may possibly be expected to be demand-sensitive to varying inflation rates.

While domestic demand for money studies must take non-interest-bearing money into account, in the international context foreign holdings of a nation's high-powered money are trivial. Bergsten (1975) estimates that "between 10 and 50 percent of total U.S. liquid liabilities to foreigners are usually in the form of noninterest-bearing demand deposits" (p. 211). However, treating demand deposits as "noninterest bearing" vastly overstates the fraction of liabilities to foreigners that bears no interest. Recent empirical work indicates that, in the United States, bank deposits can usefully be assumed to be paying implicit competitive interest (see Klein, 1974b), and we would expect this also to be the case for liabilities issued by banking institutions located in the highly competitive financial centers of Europe. Certainly Eurodollar deposits have almost zero high-powered money backing and yield a market rate of interest.[1] Therefore, we should expect such dollar-denominated deposit hold-ings to be totally invariant to the U.S. inflation rate. Dollar price uncertainty and not the level of the dollar inflation rate is what is theoretically relevant as a determinant of demand.

The empirical evidence for the existence of this inflation-uncertainty competitive mechanism is generally weak. One difficulty in isolating the effect is that the two distinct elements of inflation, its average rate and its variability, are generally highly positively correlated. This is, however, not always the case, as the recent experience with gold clearly indicates.

Before reviewing some of the more interesting empirical work, we must mention that there also exist substantial theoretical difficulties in identifying the inflation-uncertainty competitive effect. Earlier work on the effects of price predictability in a competing monies framework (Klein, 1974a) has indicated that increased price uncertainty has theoretically ambiguous effects on the demand for money. The two effects of an increase in price uncertainty (which lowers the "quality" or monetary service stream from money) are (1) an increase in the demand for money necessary to produce any given monetary service flow (the substitution in production effect) and (2) a decrease in the demand for money due to an increase in the implicit price of monetary services (the competitive comple-mentarity in consumption effect). If we assume that the monetary service flow is proportional to the real stock of money held, then the predicted relationship between price uncertainty and money demand is related to the price (interest) elasticity of demand for money.[2] With a generally interest-inelastic domestic demand for money, the predicted relationship is positive. The empirical work done in this area indicates that the effect of inflation variability on money demand depends upon whether we analyze moderate or high inflation samples. Klein (1977) finds the hypothesized positive effect for the United States over the last century, while Frenkel (1977) estimates a zero effect of uncertainty for the German hyper-inflation and Blejer (1979) finds a negative effect for the rapid inflation samples of postwar Argentina, Brazil, and Chile. Cassese (1980) provides an interesting synthesis, as he finds evidence (albeit weak) of a negative effect for three high inflation countries (Argentina, Brazil, and Chile) along with evidence of a positive effect for three moderate inflation countries that maintained exchange rates pegged to the U.S. dollar (El Salvador, Guatemala, and Honduras). These seemingly contradictory findings are consistent with the competing money framework developed by Klein in that the relationship between money demand and price uncertainty should move from positive to zero to negative as the interest elasticity of money demand increases. With a linear money-demand curve, we would expect to be in a more elastic region during hyperinflation.

Since money demand studies have focused on domestic demand functions, it is not surprising to find little evidence regarding the competitive (negative) effect of inflation uncertainty on money demand outside of hyperinflations. However, the international demand for money services, in a context of competing international monies, is likely to be much more interest-elastic than the domestic demand so that we would expect to find the competitive effect.[3] We have seen the beginnings of a literature on currency substitution which is building an additional theoretical base on which to examine the price-uncertainty competitive effect. So far, however, the empirical currency substitution literature has not dealt with the concept of inflation uncertainty and has emphasized interest elasticities to infer the degree of substitutability between competing monies.[4] Thus the international demand for monetary services from competing monies has yet to be estimated in a manner that would allow investigation of the inflation-uncertainty competitive effect.

In a related area, the literature on the currency of denomination of international trade contracts has considered the price-uncertainty competitive effect. It is clear why inflation predictability will have an effect on the currency of denomination of international trade contracts. Since contracts are not generally written in real terms, traders are concerned with the real value of the future nominal amount to be paid. As Cornell (1980) points out, in a world with inflation uncertainty the exporter cannot eliminate risk by simply contracting in his domestic currency. This inflation uncertainty will result unambiguously (in a world with no relative price changes) in both parties to a contract preferring to contract in the currency with the most stable rate of inflation. Thus trade between two countries with highly variable inflation rates should be denominated in the currency of a more stable third country, while trade between a stable currency country and an unstable currency country should be denominated in the more stable currency.

Cornell offered evidence that there exists a significant negative correlation between inflation variability and the choice of a currency in foreign trade contracting. However, one may question the validity of his findings since he correlates 1975 export data with the standard deviation of the inflation rate as computed by Logue and Willett (1976) over the 1960–70 period. There is an additional problem in that a check of the original sources for the export data (Rao and Magee, 1980; Page, 1977) reveals that the export data are from different years. Table 9-1 presents data from Page on the proportion of export contracts written in the exporter's currency for 1975.

TABLE 9-1. Foreign Trade Contracting and the Variability of Inflation

Country	Proportion of export contracts invoiced in exporter's currency (1975)	Standard deviation of inflation	
		1960–70	1965–75
Austria	.55	1.27	2.30
Belgium	.50	1.35	3.56
Denmark	.54	2.38	3.01
Finland	.26	2.64	4.88
France	.69	1.24	3.53
Netherlands	.50	1.82	2.26
W. Germany	.89	.92	2.09

$p = .960 - .240\ \sigma_{60-70}$ $\bar{R}^2 = .57$ D. W. = 2.13.
  (6.74) (−2.97)

$p = .967 - .131\ \sigma_{65-75}$ $\bar{R}^2 = .35$ D. W. = 2.82.
  (4.69) (−2.05)

(t statistics in parentheses.)

Column 2 gives the standard deviations of the inflation rate calculated by Logue and Willett for the 1960–70 period, while Column 3 presents new data on the standard deviations calculated over the 1965–75 period.

To explore the relationship between inflation variability and the choice of a contracting currency in international trade, the export data was regressed on both of the inflation variability proxies. Looking at the regression results at the bottom of Table 9-1, we see that there is a significant negative relation between the standard deviation of a country's inflation rate and the proportion of that country's exports denominated in the home currency. Thus Cornell's earlier findings are reinforced here, so that there is evidence supporting the price-uncertainty competitive effect in the choice of currencies used for international trade contracting.

Magee and Rao (1980) have emphasized the role of a currency's real intertemporal stability in determining its use as a standard of deferred payment (including the invoicing of international trade specifying future payment). International reserve holdings also serve as a store of value, and we can, in fact, find some evidence of the price-uncertainty competitive effect in an examination of reserve holdings over time.

The dollar is still clearly the world's major reserve currency. Aside from anecdotal evidence occasionally provided by central bankers or foreign exchange market observers, we do not see any clear-cut evidence of a shift away from dollars. Figure 9-1 reproduces a table from Heller and Knight (1978) showing the currency composition of official foreign exchange reserves for 76 IMF member nations between 1970 and 1976. Note that the dollar component remained fairly steady between 77 to 84% of total holdings. Of course, one might argue that official reserves are not subject to the price-uncertainty competitive effect to the extent that private holdings are, in that there are other factors beside wealth maximization entering the central bank objective function. But, as will be discussed below, the decline in sterling from 8.6 to 1.8%, and the rise in mark holdings from 2.1 to 6.7%, is not an indication of central bank passivity.

The next section will emphasize the distinction between the use of money as a medium of exchange and the use of money as a store of value. Since intertemporal stability relates primarily to the store of value function, it is not surprising that there is some evidence of a competitive effect regarding the effect of inflation uncertainty on the store of value demand (observed in the currency of denomination of foreign trade contracts and international reserve holdings),

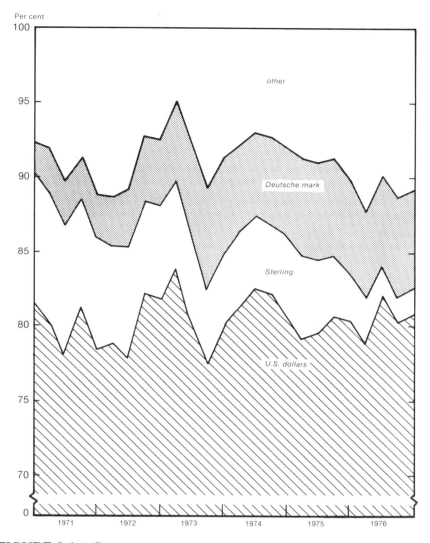

FIGURE 9-1. Currency composition of official foreign exchange reserves: 76 countries.

SOURCE: H. Robert Heller and Malcolm Knight. *Reserve Currency Preferences of Central Banks.* Princeton Essays in International Finance No. 131, Princeton (1978). Reproduced by permission.

205

yet there appears to be a positive effect of inflation uncertainty on the medium of exchange as estimated by the money demand functions cited for moderate inflations (the lack of such an effect for rapid inflation samples will be discussed further in the next section).

Competing Currencies, Consumer Confidence, and Currency Reform

Proponents of international currency reforms often seem to assume a degree of competition between international monies that simply does not exist in the real world. The proposal to achieve European monetary union by creating a parallel European currency, the Europa, is a good example of this phenomenon. Advocates of this proposal believe that because the Europa is to be price indexed and hence inflation-proofed, it will quickly drive the European national currencies out of circulation. Historical evidence suggests this will not be the case as monetary confidence and new dominant monies evolve very slowly in the marketplace and are not easily substitutable once established.

Since national currencies, as opposed to deposits, are noninterest bearing and individuals holding them are paying an inflation tax, we would expect this element of money demand to be sensitive to alternative inflation rates and thus should observe some switching in an inflationary environment to an indexed currency like the proposed Europa. However the degree of competition present and thus the amount of switching to be expected is likely to be much less than the Europa's advocates would suggest.

If we assume that alternative monies (including a newcomer like the Europa) are perfect substitutes, then the pronouncements of the Europa's supporters would of course come true. While the degree of substitution between currencies is an empirical question, the nonpecuniary factors determining the choice of currency used are likely to be nontrivial across countries.

The historical evidence that we are aware of suggests that the switching by the public to a new medium of exchange appears to be highly inelastic with respect to the currency's inflation rate. Even in the extreme cases of the post–World War I hyperinflations or in the moderately rapid but decades-long Latin American inflations, individuals did not switch to competing currencies. Although in these cases individuals often drastically reduced their real holdings of the inflating currency, competing currencies were not held as alternative media of exchange.

One might want to argue that in certain cases competing currencies do not develop because of government regulations prohibiting their existence. Yet it is difficult to believe that legal restrictions, including legal tender requirements, are really very effective competitive constraints.[5] There is much historical evidence in other areas that price controls and trade restraints are, in general, evaded at least partially, even if attempts are made to enforce them strictly. In any case, the evidence suggests that there was no significant black-market pressure toward substitute media of exchange. Cagan (1950, p. 101) notes that, of the seven hyperinflations he studied, only for 1923 Germany did substantial amounts of unauthorized currencies issued by local governments and private organizations circulate. But, unbelievable as it may seem, these illegal substitute currencies were denominated in the hyperinflating unit! Also, Barro's (1972) estimates of the fraction of transactions conducted without domestic money during hyperinflation, that is conducted with a substitute money *or by barter*, are quite low. For example, at an inflation rate of 10% *per month* this fraction was only 0.05.[6]

A careful distinction must be made between the use of money as a store of value and the use of money as a medium of exchange. The vehicle currency role of the dollar as a medium of exchange is determined by transactions costs, while a currency's real intertemporal stability explains its vehicle currency role as a store of value. It is clear that during these hyperinflations large quantities of foreign currencies (e.g., dollars and pounds) were legally held as stores of value.[7] There is also some essentially anecdotal evidence cited by Graham (1930) that the foreign monies gradually began to be used as units of account in Germany. It is likely that such large amounts of foreign exchange were held not only because they were a hedge against inflation (any unregulated interest-bearing foreign or domestic asset could have served this function better), but because the hyperinflating countries also happened to be politically unstable. In this sort of climate, it is understandable that individuals would wish to be uncharacteristically liquid in a stable country's currency.

In any event, foreign monies were not held in these cases to satisfy a medium of exchange demand for money. The evidence appears to indicate that what is generally used as a medium of exchange is highly inelastic with respect to the inflation rate. Perhaps this is because the decision to change what is used as the commonly accepted medium of exchange must involve a large subset of the population and hence implies very large transaction costs. Such social agreements and customs are therefore very costly to change rapidly, even if the immediate benefits to each individual separately appear large (cf. Tullock, 1975).

To sum up, we have seen that to make analytical sense of the argument that competitive substitution toward an alternative money is dependent upon the level of the inflation rate, we must concentrate solely on the currency or noninterest-bearing high-powered element of money. In that case, however, the substitution argument becomes empirically trivial. Once a dominant money is established, the medium of exchange demand appears to be essentially nonsubstitutable in a wide number of circumstances. The empirical evidence indicates that there is little, if any, pressure toward substituting into alternative media of exchange on the basis of price stability or predictability. Hence the concern that a European parallel currency indexed against inflation will be accepted by the market at such a rapid rate that it will quickly drive out all nonindexed national monies and hence create political difficulties is completely unfounded.[8] What is much more likely is that the Europa will not be accepted at all. The existence of any significant amount of competitive switching between dominant monies has not, as yet, been empirically verified and, in fact, there is much evidence to the contrary within a wide band of noncrisis situations. The analysis of the potential attractiveness of a European parallel currency that largely considers differential yields of alternative monies to reach a conclusion of rapid and wide acceptance completely ignores the overwhelming empirical evidence on the degree of rigidity that historically is present in these matters.

One reason for rigidity in accepting new monies is the importance of consumer confidence in a money—that is, the credibility of the money issuer in fulfilling explicit or implicit promises regarding supply. Monetary confidence cannot be created overnight merely by an announcement of a promise regarding future behavior. It must be built up gradually with successful performance over time. Economists have too frequently believed that money merely is whatever "society" (operationally defined as the relevant policymaker) wishes it to be. But institutions are not perfectly malleable, and a real effective demand for a money cannot be produced by official proclamation. As the recent New York City experience illustrates, official promises can always be withdrawn. Furthermore, as anyone who remembers the periods preceding exchange rate adjustments during the fixed rate period knows, market participants require more than governmental assurances at a particular moment. Demand depends upon the existence of consumer confidence in the money, and confidence creation is not a free good. Commodity money produces consumer confidence by placing a physical constraint on money production and hence on the possible unanticipated depreciation.

Building confidence in any particular "brand-name money" may be considered as an investment in "brand-name capital." This may be done by "guaranteeing" convertibility of the money into commodities or high confidence monies so that the stocks of such commodities or monies held as reserves represent the confidence-creating investment. But, of course, convertibility guarantees are not the only way to produce confidence. We observe the major vehicle currencies in the world today as having "earned" that role by successful past performance. It is the importance of this past monetary behavior that implies the very gradual evolution of a currency to "high-confidence" status. Thus the introduction of a new brand name to the market, be it Europa, SDR, or whatever, involves some selling costs analogous to those born by a producer of consumer goods introducing a new product. Just as a purchaser of new automobile tires requires quality assurance in the form of a warranty or contractual obligation on the seller, the money demander seeks quality assurance from the new money supplier. Tires with a long reputation for sound performance will not find consumers as interested in legal quality guarantees, and so it is with monies. The fact that nominal fiduciary monies may be costlessly produced on the margin implies nothing about the marginal cost of creating real cash balances. The latter, of course, refers to the confidence-creating or selling costs needed to build real balances.

We may end this section by concluding that the majority of the currency reforms proposed are utopian in that they assume that institutional and information constraints can be altered costlessly.

2. IMPLICATIONS OF THE
NATURAL MONOPOLY ASPECTS OF MONEY PRODUCTION

The confidence-creating selling costs associated with creating real balances are generally fixed costs such as holding stocks of precious metals or high-confidence currencies, maintaining an army, purchasing an impressive marble building, or spending resources in any fashion that allows the creation of the equilibrium level of confidence. The marginal production costs of increasing real balances are negligible. Thus we have a familiar economic problem in that setting price equal to marginal cost gives us a price less than average cost so that there is a short-run profit incentive to overissue.[9]

Seigniorage and a Declining Cost Industry

By setting the price of the money at a level so that some seigniorage is earned, the money supplier has something to lose by "messing up." An unanticipated increase in the nominal quantity of a competitive firm's money will result in a loss of confidence in that money and a corresponding fall in demand and thus seigniorage earnings. Seigniorage, then, represents a necessary price paid by the money demander to assure quality and may be viewed by the seller as the opportunity cost of overissuing his money; that is, he may increase short-run profit by intentional depreciation in exchange for lower long-run profit.

The large fixed-cost and small or zero marginal-cost of creating money suggests that the money industry is essentially a natural monopoly or that it is economically efficient for there to be a single money within a trade area. Vaubel (1977) recognizes this when he says:

> Since the cost of using money falls as its domain expands, the quality (and, hence, the value) of the product money and, consequently, the marginal value productivity of the factors engaged in its production increase so that the money industry must be viewed as a (permanently) declining-cost industry. Moreover, since a competitive long-run equilibrium cannot be reached, if costs continue to decline even at levels of output equal to the size of the market, currency competition must be expected to destroy itself: money is a "natural monopoly." Since it is, finally, undisputed that lines of production that are subject to permanently declining cost must at some stage be nationalized (or in the international context, be "unified"), the fact that currency competition will lead to currency union must be regarded as desirable (p. 458).

It is in this sense that European monetary union offers potentially large economic benefits. While such statements are easy to make, pinpointing the nature of the benefits is more difficult. Mundell (1961) lucidly stated the theoretical problem of optimum currency areas twenty years ago, yet definitive theoretical work establishing the costs that are present in a flexible multiple-money arrangement has yet to be done.

Basically, the problem is that the theoretical microeconomic (information-transaction cost) foundation for the existence of money is still lacking. Instead of solely relying on the obvious increased computational and money conversion costs of a multiple money system, it is more persuasive to examine the historical evidence in this area. The evidence indicates that monetary arrangements have almost always consisted of a single money or of multiple monies convertible into a single dominant money.[10] The only important example we are aware of where distinct monies circulated side-by-side domestically at flexible exchange rates for any significant length of time is the flexible bimetallic (silver and copper) exchange standard that existed in China from about 1650 to 1850.[11] The only other multicurrency examples that can be cited are brief, atypical, wartime, or postwar arrangements such as the simultaneous circulation of gold and greenbacks in the United States during the Civil War.

The Prospects for Privately Produced Monies

We have recently witnessed an interest in the private production of money. Several authors, most notably Hayek, have discussed the hypothesized benefits to society of having a competitive supply of money. Hayek (1978) boldly asserts:

> I have now no doubt whatever that private enterprise, if it had not been prevented by government, could and would long ago have provided the public with a choice of currencies, and those that prevailed in the competition would have been essentially stable in value and would have prevented both excessive stimulation of investment and the consequent periods of contraction (p. 14).

Yet, as the brief historical review above sketches, the world has long been characterized by dominant monies produced by governments. Hayek wonders, "why people should have put up for so long with governments exercising a power over 2,000 years that was regularly used to exploit and defraud them" (p. 29). Indeed, what is the mechanism that explains the governmental monopoly in money production?

The key to this puzzle is gained by first realizing the natural monopoly aspects of money production given by the high fixed costs and small marginal costs associated with producing real money balances. As discussed above, the competitive money producers must earn a seigniorage return sufficiently high to ensure that the present value of the future stream of seigniorage exceeds the enormous potential gain from a short-run unanticipated increase in the money stock. Thus the private unregulated contractual solution would imply an extremely high "premium" or seigniorage to assure producer performance. Only by the threat of loosing this substantial seigniorage return if the money demanders are cheated can we expect private-wealth maximizers to produce a stable, high-confidence money. Thus the fact that the private contractual solution yields an extremely high-equilibrium return for the producer implies that the government production of money may be more efficient.[12]

The long history of governmental monopoly in money production is not the result of societal ignorance. The "need" for this monopoly power is not a "myth," as Hayek suggests, that has become "so firmly established that it did not occur even to the professional students of these matters ever to question it" (p. 29). A private solution to the production of money could, no doubt, be established. Such a solution could also yield the high-confidence, stable-valued money desired by Hayek and others, but only at a very high cost. Thus the history of money production observed over the past 2,000 years is due to economic efficiency and not to 2,000 years of ignorance or coercion.

3. INTERNATIONAL MONETARY ARRANGEMENTS

Using the framework for analysis developed above, we can now make several comments on international monetary arrangements. First, let us consider the role of the dollar as the dominant international money. To our knowledge there exists no concrete evidence indicating a significant decrease in the international role of the dollar. As illustrated in Figure 9-1 above, the dollar has steadily comprised about 80% of the official foreign exchange reserves of IMF member nations.

A logical next step is to consider what determines the composition of official portfolios. After examining the IMF data on official reserves, Heller and Knight (1978) conclude that the major determinant of the currency composition of reserves is the exchange rate arrangement. A country that pegs to a single currency can eliminate exchange risk by keeping its foreign exchange reserves in that currency.[13] "A country which pegs to a composite basket can eliminate the exchange risk on its reserves by distributing its holdings across different currencies according to the weights in the basket, and a floating rate country can reduce its risk by diversifying its portfolio according to the weights in some effective exchange rate index" (p. 12).

Heller and Knight found an important exception to the relation between exchange regime and currency holdings within the European Snake countries (they were looking at the 1970–76 period). Rather than hold large mark reserves, these countries committed themselves to intervening in dollars so that they held more dollars than would be expected on the basis of their exchange rate regime.

This finding is not surprising if we carefully consider the benefits to the European nations of adopting an explicit dollar standard. As discussed in Section 2, the natural monopoly aspects of money creation indicate the efficiency of having a single money within a region. This suggests that there are large economic gains from a common money. The growing interdependence among the countries of Western Europe and also the United States and Japan should only increase the economic pressure toward the establishment of a single dominant money. It is the very fact that cases of competing currencies or multiple monies circulating within the trade area are so rare, if at all existing, that is the strongest element in the economic case for a unified money. But it is also this fact which suggests that a new parallel currency such as the Europa is not likely to be successful.

A dominant money is necessary if effective European monetary coordination is to exist. If this money is not to be the mark, the obvious alternative is the dollar. European adoption of a dominant dollar standard is therefore a logical and practical way to effect European monetary union. The essential economic benefit of a monetary union could readily be obtained by fixing convertibility of each of the European national currencies at a given exchange rate into a dominant U.S. dollar and permitting denomination of European bank deposits in dollars. In fact, much of the post–World War II period can be described as a movement toward such an international dollar standard. We would, perhaps, be continuing to move at a rapid rate in this direction if the United States had not "messed up" in the late 1960s and early 1970s by producing a large unanticipated increase in the dollar money supply. It was this unanticipated money supply increase and the corresponding large "involuntary" holdings of dollar reserves by some European central banks (and Japan) to maintain dollar parity that effectively halted the move to an international dollar standard and produced the political and economic forces for the creation of a substitute, independent European monetary unit such as the Europa.

But it is more important to recognize that the dollar standard did, in a sense, give the Europeans the best of both worlds. They had some of the major benefits of a united currency area without having to give up the seigniorage on the currency stock which the Europa proposal would largely require. The inflation tax on high-powered money, rather than necessarily being socially inefficient, is likely to be part of an optimal tax package. Given real transaction and distortion costs of levying and collecting all taxes, we would expect an excise tax on money holdings to be part of an efficient general equilibrium tax scheme, especially since the demand for high-powered money is generally price (interest) inelastic.[14]

Realizing, of course, that Europeans are attempting to establish a European currency and move further from a dollar standard, we might well ask what does the future hold for the dollar? First, we should acknowledge that the dollar gained its dominant international position, as sterling before it, not by legalistic coercion, but voluntarily in the market place. The combination of past and prospective performance induced the world to demand dollars as an international money. It is this same past and prospective performance criteria that can cost the dollar, as it did sterling, its dominant position. As Figure 9-1 illustrates, within the short period from 1970 to 1976, sterling declined from 8.6 to 1.8% of official foreign exchange reserves of IMF member countries. This is a far cry from the U.K. position early in the century.

Since past performance largely determines confidence in monies, it is not surprising that the poor performance of the dollar in the 1960s and 1970s has not eroded the dollar's dominant position.[15] In terms of the analysis of this article, the dollar has not seriously depreciated its "brand-name capital" yet, but the fortunes of the pound remind us that this position is hardly a perpetual right.

An important question is, where do we substitute if we want to reduce the dollar's role? Heller and Knight's data indicate that the mark has been rising in terms of official reserve portfolio share, and we know that the Swiss franc has been a popular currency due to its stability, but can we expect either of these currencies to assume the role of dominant money?

The fact that the Germans and the Swiss have resisted this movement is evidence of perhaps two phenomena. First, the dominant money producer, with a large domestic relative to foreign sector, finds that international shifts in demand for his money will have small repercussions on domestic operations relative to the effects a more open economy would face. Second, the seigniorage return to being the dominant international money must be small, at least relative to the costs imposed on the country.

Considering the first suggestion, it is obvious that given the respective size of the U.S. and German money supplies, a given capital flow will have a greater effect on German than U.S. monetary conditions. Empirical studies also indicate that the United States is fairly insensitive to foreign shocks relative to other countries.[16]

Regarding the seigniorage issue, the fact that we have not observed countries competing for the role of dominant money seems to provide evidence that the seigniorage return is low. In this case, recent action by the United States (and the United Kingdom before it) of disinvesting or consuming its monetary confidence capital may be a wealth-maximizing policy.

One reason why this seigniorage has perhaps been low for the dollar is that it has been possible for foreigners to obtain a partial "free ride" on the dollar brand name by denominating bank deposits in dollars and then not having to maintain any significant noninterest-bearing dollar reserves against these deposits. If, in fact, the brand-name depreciation of the dollar is causally related to the growth of the Eurodollar market, then we would infer that the growth of such competitive substitutes for the dollar significantly reduced the expected future seigniorage to the United States from supplying the dominant money. Thus the United States had an incentive to follow a short-run policy of intentional depreciation of the dollar brand name as the expected loss of future seigniorage this implied had been revised downward by changing international institutions. Likewise the United Kingdom may have been following a rational policy after World War II of intentionally depreciating the pound, in anticipation of the dollar's international role in the postwar world.

Since there is plausible evidence that countries have not been competing for reserve currency status, it is understandable that the European nations have been actively seeking an alternative system. Had the United States maintained the monetary confidence it had invested in the dollar, there would have been little incentive for the creation of a European currency. While we have already argued the advantages of a European dollar standard, one might wonder why a German mark peg is not the obvious solution for the European Economic Community. After all, if the countries are seeking to import price stability, then why not peg to the mark? The problem is that some governments would prefer a more expansionary monetary policy than that permitted by a mark peg. This, of course, is another reason for pegging to the dollar, as such countries would find a dollar peg easier to follow. The evidence from the snake period indicated the problems of maintaining a peg with Germany, as Germany accumulated a sizeable portion of the EEC's official reserves (47% by July 1975).

While the snake has been replaced by the European Monetary System (EMS), it is not at all clear that the new system will survive in a better fashion than the snake. March 1981 was supposed to mark the beginning of a European Monetary Fund with the member countries pooling 20% of their reserves and using the European Currency Unit (or Europa) as a reserve asset. At an informal meeting of the EEC finance ministers in Luxembourg in September 1980, it was agreed that while the EMS has provided a period of exchange rate stability, "technical problems" surrounding the proposed European Currency Unit and the powers of the European Monetary Fund made it impossible to begin the Fund in March 1981.

Some observers believe that the transition to the second stage of the EMS has been delayed solely for political reasons. The *Financial Times* reported that:

> The decision was taken privately last year by Herr Schmidt and President Giscard and later rubber-stamped by the European Council. Neither leader wanted the sensitive issue of national sovereignty involved in the second stage of the EMS further to complicate his election campaign last autumn in West Germany, this spring in France.[17]

Regardless of the reason for the delay, it should be obvious that the $2\frac{1}{4}\%$ fluctuations around parity allowed by the EMS can never be maintained as long as the various governments follow diverse monetary and fiscal policies. The adjustments provoked by the diverse domestic policies suggest problems in that "the system has been under considerable strain and the original intention, that the burden of intervention and policy adjustments would be shared equally between strong and weak countries, has not been fulfilled" (Shepheard, 1979, p. 35). We see that just as during the snake period, the more inflation-prone countries have at times found the maintenance of a fixed rate regime with the mark quite difficult to keep. This, of course, indicates the desire for a dominant money that allows a more politically acceptable (higher) rate of inflation than the mark.

We have already discussed in Section 1 what we might expect from the creation of a parallel currency such as the proposed Europa. It is unlikely to provide any significant monetary services in the short run. While advocates of a European currency claim that such a price-indexed, and hence inflation-proof, currency would drive the European national currencies out of circulation, the analysis of this chapter, as well as historical evidence, suggests that this will not be the case. As we have discussed, monetary confidence and new dominant monies evolve very slowly in the market place and are not easily substitutable once established. Vaubel (1977), drawing on Klein's earlier work on competing monies (Klein, 1974a), has addressed this issue by stating:

> If the currencies that are to compete with each other are of very different importance already from the start (as is the case for the EEC member currencies) or if new (private?) currencies are to be introduced, only serious mismanagement can prevent the established and more widely-used currencies from outcompeting the others; indeed, the issuers of the more widely-used currencies can (as their market share grows) successively raise the rate of inflation of their currencies without having to fear that the process of substitution might be halted or reversed (p. 457).

While Vaubel's statement goes too far in stating that the inflation rate can be varied "without having to fear that the process of substitution might be halted or reversed," he is nevertheless emphasizing the wide range of policy variance open to the dominant money producer before money demanders begin to substitute into other currencies.

One can see similarities between the arguments supporting the creation of a European currency and the arguments that led to the creation of SDRs. Besides making the assumption that "money is merely what society wants it to be," the proponents of SDRs were also implicitly assuming that the IMF had unlimited brand-name or monetary confidence capital. However, as we have seen in the years since the creation of the SDR, their use is still quite limited as confidence in these assets has never reached the heights envisioned by their creators.[18] The key theoretical point is that real SDRs, like the real value of any new European parallel currency, cannot be merely "created outright," that is, net wealth cannot be created out of nothing. Thus we should not make the utopian assumptions that institutional and informational constraints can be altered costlessly or that a money, especially a newly proposed money, possesses unlimited monetary confidence and that its demand and market share will therefore depend solely on its current price or the inflation rate in terms of the money.

4. CONCLUSIONS AND SUMMARY

Competition between alternative international monies does not occur primarily on the basis of average inflation rates but rather on the basis of the predictability of these rates. The empirical evidence regarding substitutions among currencies on the basis of this "inflation-uncertainty competitive mechanism" is generally weak. As reviewed in Section 1, domestic money demand studies suggest that, outside of hyperinflations, an increase in inflation uncertainty will increase money demand. While there is no definitive empirical work dealing with inflation uncertainty in the context of competing international monies, there is some related evidence emphasizing the store of value function of money. Specifically, there is evidence of a substitution from sterling to marks in official portfolios while the official portfolio share of the dollar has remained quite steady. There is also evidence of a significant negative correlation between inflation variability and the choice of a currency in foreign trade contracting.

The second part of Section 1 presented an analysis of the importance of consumer confidence in money and how the costs of producing this confidence imposes constraints on currency reforms or new monies. Since the majority of currency reforms assume institutional or informational constraints can be altered costlessly, it is concluded that such reform proposals are utopian.

In Section 2, the natural monopoly aspects of money creation were discussed. Given the enormous potential gain to the money producer from a short-run unanticipated increase in the money supply, the competitive money producer must earn sufficient seigniorage to ensure a policy of providing a stable-valued money. Since the private unregulated supply of money would require an extremely high seigniorage, it is suggested that the government production of money may be more efficient.

In the final section, various past, present, as well as proposed future international monetary arrangements were considered. While the dollar is clearly the world's major currency, it is recognized that the dollar gained its dominant international position voluntarily in the market place, and this same market can take away the dominance (as it did with sterling). However, if the dollar should seriously lose favor, it is not at all clear what would replace it. We have not seen countries competing for the dominant-currency position. In fact, we seem to have observed just the opposite. Two distinct reasons are offered why non–U.S. countries have resisted the assumption of a larger reserve-currency role. First, the dominant money producer with a fairly open economy will find that international shifts in the demand for his money will have large repercussions on domestic operations. Second, the seigniorage return to being the dominant international money must be small, at least relative to the costs imposed on the country. It is in this latter sense that the U.S. policy of depreciating the value of the dollar "brand name" may be rational, as the growth of competitive substitutes such as Eurodollar deposits may have significantly reduced the expected future seigniorage to the United States from supplying the dominant money.

Regarding the likely future for the European Monetary System, it is suggested that as long as the member countries follow diverse economic policies, any fixed parity will be difficult to maintain. Should a new European currency eventually be established, it is unlikely to provide any significant monetary services in the short run. Advocates of a Europa currency claim that by price indexing the currency the various European currencies would be driven out of circulation. However, our analysis suggests that monetary confidence and thus new dominant monies evolve very slowly in the market place and are not easily substitutable once established.

A major lesson of history is that while the dominant medium of exchange does change over time, such change occurs gradually and is largely the result of market-based performance, not government coercion or pronouncements.

NOTES

1. While Eurobanks are not required to hold legal reserves against deposits, they do in fact maintain working balances in U.S. commercial banks. The U.S. banks then hold a fraction of these demand deposit liabilities to Eurobanks in the form of noninterest-bearing reserves. As Dufey and Giddy (1978) point out, there is a weaker relation between the desired working balances of Eurobanks kept in the form of U.S. deposits and total Eurodollar deposits than between domestic commercial bank reserves and deposits for three reasons: (1) Many Eurobanks are branches of U.S. domestic banks and so can rely on parent-bank reserves for contingency purposes. (2) Eurobanks can and do rely primarily on borrowing in the interbank money market (New York and Eurodollar) when they need funds to meet deposit outflows or loan demand. (3) As the total volume of transactions increases, the proportion of working balances tends to decrease.

2. If the demand for money is semilogarithmic in the interest rates, as assumed in Klein (1977), and rotates around the point of unitary elasticity, then the price-uncertainty variable will enter the demand for money as a function of the price of money (measured as the difference between the interest rate on money substitutes and the rate paid on money). This implies a multiplicative functional form regarding the price of money and the price-uncertainty variable. This interactive term will increase due to higher inflation (as the nominal interest rates are increased via a Fisher effect) as well as due to an increase in price uncertainty, so that the data will be weak regarding the separate effects of inflation and inflation uncertainty.

3. While no evidence is offered with regard to domestic versus foreign demand elasticities, Vaubel (1980) finds that "demand for a currency from foreigners is at the margin more sensitive to changes in relative expected yields (and possibly risks), the larger the currency's international role (in proportion to its total supply)" (p. 20).

4. See Bordo and Choudhri (1980), Brillembourg and Schadler (1979), or Miles (1978).

5. The designation "legal tender" means that creditors cannot legally refuse the money as payment for a claim; that is, they cannot use the courts and police to force discharge of a contract in an alternative money. However, there is much evidence that relatively informal legally unenforceable contractual practices predominate in business and that reliance on explicit legal sanctions is extremely rare. See Klein (1974a, p. 448) and Hayek (1978) for further discussion and references to the historical evidence on the existence of nonlegal-tender circulating monies. Perhaps the most spectacular example is the Maria Theresa thaler, which for more than a century circulated as the principal medium of exchange in the Red Sea area, particularly along the southern coast of the Arabian Peninsula and the Horn of Africa. The thaler was introduced in the Arabian Peninsula through commercial relations in the early nineteenth century and remained the dominant unit of account and medium of exchange even though in 1858 it ceased to be legal tender in Austria.

6. On the contrary, the post–World War II German inflation, which was significantly milder than these hyperinflations, was unique in terms of the relative amount of domestic currency that apparently was replaced as a medium of exchange. For a period of time, cognac and cigarettes were substituted for the dominant money in almost all transactions. This was, of course, due to the presence of extraordinary price controls that were very rigidly enforced by the occupying armies, not because of a high inflation rate in terms of the money.

7. Graham (1930) and Bresciani-Turroni (1968) estimate the ratio of foreign to domestic real money holdings in October 1923 Germany to be between 5 and 13. Although reported estimates vary a great deal from month to month and are rather unreliable, these figures should give us some general idea of the large magnitude of foreign currencies held. See Statistiches Reichsamt (1924, pp. 69-70) for an account of the German legislation attempting to regulate this large amount of foreign exchange.

8. See, for example, OPTICA Report 1976.

9. If the demand for money function is linear, then as discussed in Section 1 we would expect a price-inelastic demand in the range near the "optimum" zero price so that price uncertainty will increase real demand and the money supplier will have a large short-run profit incentive to overissue. It appears then that the "optimum quantity of money" may not be socially optimal if there are added real costs of creating institutions to prevent this short-run overissue from occurring.

10. Cipolla (1967, Chap. 2) documents the fact that dominant monies existed over large areas and long time periods as early as the fifth century when the Byzantine gold solidus had a dominant position throughout the Mediterranean.

11. Even this Chinese experiment may be an example of a market-induced optimum currency arrangement along industrial and hence regional groupings. See Chen (1975).

12. A recent paper by Girton and Roper (1981) provides an example of the utopian assumption of costless contracting. After mentioning the analysis

in Klein (1974a), which underlies the current paper, they state: "We differ from Klein in that we assume banks can costlessly write binding contracts if they so desire, these contracts can be costlessly enforced, and default can be insured against" (p. 23). Such an assumption is completely opposite to the entire spirit of the current chapter and makes such real-world phenomena as commodity money or the existence of seigniorage appear to be obviously inefficient.

It is extremely unlikely that quality-assuring contracts for the production of money can be easily written and enforced. This is especially true when one considers the difficulty in measuring money and prices, which would be required in order to verify the agreed-upon real value of a money.

See Klein and Leffler (1981) for discussion of the role of market forces in assuring quality and the conditions under which government supply is the likely quality-assuring solution.

13. While the very existence of foreign exchange risk has been questioned by some writers, the importance of such risk is hardly a settled issue. For a discussion of the issues and new empirical evidence, see Melvin (1980).

14. Because of different transaction costs, the efficient inflation tax may vary across countries. (For example, a larger percentage of taxes may be more efficiently collected by inflation in Italy than in the United States.) In such a case, policymakers must trade-off the economic gains of increased monetary union with the increased costs of collecting taxes by alternative means if inflation is limited to the U.S. rate.

15. Vaubel (1977) suggests the analogy that, "To some extent the choice between currencies is comparable to the choice between languages or telephone networks or industrial locations; the more economic agents choose the product or location X, the more attractive it becomes for others so that success breeds success (and failure failure) in a gradual and cumulative agglomeration process" (p. 457). Thus Vaubel is suggesting that the positive externalities generated by countries and firms choosing the dollar as the dominant international money will result in substitutions into other currencies occurring very slowly at first. However, as the move away from an international money continues, we would expect a sort of "snowball" effect as the shifts out of the currency will impose negative externalities on those who still hold the currency as a dominant money (Vaubel's "failure breeds failure").

In terms of the present discussion, we analyze Vaubel's assertions as indicating that the price-uncertainty competitive effect is positive due to the low price elasticity of demand for the dominant money. However, if the dominant money producer chooses to consume his brand-name capital, then the degree of substitutability between the competing international monies will be observed to increase and the corresponding increase in the price elasticity of the demand for the dominant money will eventually lead to a negative price-uncertainty competitive effect.

16. As mentioned above, Vaubel (1980) concluded in a recent empirical study of international shifts in the demand for money, that "demand for a currency from foreigners is at the margin more sensitive to changes in relative expected yields (and possibly risks), the larger the currency's international role (in proportion to its total supply)." Thus the sheer magnitude of the U.S. money supply serves to insulate the United States, to a certain extent, from international shocks.

Brillembourg and Schadler (1979) developed and estimated a model which "views national currencies as competing assets in an international market for money services." They found that "although rates of return on other currencies significantly affect the demand for the U.S. dollar, these effects are small compared with that of its own rate of return. This suggests that in determining the effect of their own policies, the U.S. monetary authorities need not be as concerned as European authorities about the effect of foreign monetary shocks on the demand for their currency."

17. See *Financial Times*, February 26, 1981, p. 2.

18. The difficulty in establishing the IMF Substitution Account is further evidence of the limited demand for SDRs. Briefly, the Substitution Account would allow countries to deposit "excess" reserve currency balances (primarily dollars) in exchange for SDRs. The major reason for such a facility is to allow a means of diversifying reserve holdings without directly affecting the exchange markets.

The fact that such a proposal was first made at the 1971 annual meeting of the IMF indicates the lack of support for the issue. Still, the issue has been kept alive by the unpredictably poor performance of the dollar. Given the limited use of SDRs relative to dollars, and the fact that SDRs yield an interest rate equal to only 80% of an average of the short-term rates prevailing in the market for five major countries, it is unlikely that the Substitution Account will ever become significant, even if it is eventually adopted.

REFERENCES

Barro, Robert. "Inflationary Finance and the Welfare Cost of Inflation." *Journal of Political Economy* 80 (September/October 1972):978–1001.

Bergsten, C. Fred. *The Dilemma of the Dollar*. New York: Council on Foreign Relations, 1975.

Blejer, Mario I. "The Demand for Money and the Variability of the Rate of Inflation: Some Empirical Results." *International Economic Review* 20 (June 1979):545–49.

Bordo, Michael D., and Ehsan U. Choudhri. "Currency Substitution and the Demand for Money: Some Evidence for Canada." *Journal of Money, Credit and Banking* 14 (February 1982):48–57.

Bresciani-Turroni, Constantino. *The Economics of Inflation*. New York: Kelley, 1968.

Brillembourg, Arturo, and Susan M. Schadler. "A Model of Currency Substitution in Exchange Rate Determination, 1973-78." *IMF Staff Papers* 26 (September 1979):513–42.

Cagan, Phillip. "The Monetary Dynamics of Hyperinflation." In *Studies in the Quantity Theory of Money*, edited by Milton Friedman. Chicago: University of Chicago Press, 1950.

Cassese, Anthony. "The Variability of Inflation and the Demand for Money Under Different Monetary Regimes." Paper presented at Western Economic Association Meetings in San Diego, CA., June 1980.

Chen, Chau-Nan. "Flexible Bimetallic Exchange Rates in China, 1650-1850: A Historic Example of Optimum Currency Areas." *Journal of Money, Credit, and Banking* 7 (August 1975):359-76.

Cipolla, Carlo M. *Money, Prices and Civilization in the Mediterranean World: Fifth to Seventeenth Century*. New York: Gordian Press, 1967.

Commission of the European Communities. OPTICA Report 1976, "Inflation and Exchange Rates: Evidence and Policy Guidelines for the European Community." Brussels, February 1977.

Cornell, Bradford. "The Denomination of Foreign Trade Contracts Once Again." *Journal of Financial and Quantitative Analysis* 15 (November 1980): 933-44.

Dufey, Gunter, and Ian H. Giddy. *The International Money Market*. Englewood Cliffs, New Jersey: Prentice-Hall, 1978.

Frenkel, Jacob A. "The Forward Exchange Rate, Expectations, and the Demand for Money: The German Hyperinflation." *American Economic Review* 67 (September 1977):653-70.

Girton, Lance, and Don Roper. "Theory and Implications of Currency Substitution." *Journal of Money, Credit, and Banking* 13 (February 1981): 12-30.

Graham, Frank K. *Exchange, Prices, and Production in Hyperinflation: Germany, 1920-23*. Princeton: Princeton University Press, 1930.

Hayek, F. A. *Denationalization of Money*. London: Institute of Economic Affairs, 1978.

Heller, H. Robert, and Malcolm Knight. *Reserve Currency Preferences of Central Banks*. Princeton Essays in International Finance No. 131, Princeton (1978).

Klein, Benjamin. "The Competitive Supply of Money." *Journal of Money, Credit, and Banking* 6 (November 1974a):243-53.

——. "Competitive Interest Payments on Bank Deposits and the Long-Run Demand for Money." *American Economic Review* 64 (December 1974b): 931-49.

——. "The Demand for Quality-Adjusted Cash Balances: Price Uncertainty in the U.S. Demand for Money Function." *Journal of Political Economy* 85 (August 1977):691-716.

——. "Competing Monies, European Monetary Union and the Dollar." In *One Money for Europe*, edited by Michele Fratianni and Theo Peeters. London: Macmillan, 1978.

—— and Keith B. Leffler. "The Role of Market Forces in Assuring Contractual Performance." *Journal of Political Economy* 89 (August 1981):615-42.

Logue, Dennis, and Thomas Willett. "A Note on the Relation Between the Rate and Variability of Inflation." *Economica* 43 (May 1976):151-58.

Magee, Stephen P., and Ramesh, K. S. Rao. "Vehicle and Nonvehicle Currencies in International Trade." *American Economic Review* 70 (May 1980): 368-73.

Melvin, Michael. "Foreign Exchange Risk and the Risk Premium: Myth or Reality." Mimeo, 1980.

Miles, Marc A. "Currency Substitution: Perspective, Implications, and Empirical Evidence." In *The Monetary Approach to International Adjustment*, edited by Bluford H. Putnam and D. Sykes Wilford. New York: Praeger, 1978.

Mundell, Robert A. "A Theory of Optimum Currency Areas." *American Economic Review* 51 (September 1961):657-65.

Page, S. A. B. "Currency of Invoicing in Merchandise Trade." *National Institute Economic Review* 81 (August 1977):77-81.

Rao, Ramesh K. S., and Stephen P. Magee. "The Currency of Denomination of International Trade Contracts." In *Exchange Risk and Exposure*, edited by Richard M. Levich and Clas G. Wihlborg. Lexington, Mass.: Lexington, 1980.

Shepheard, Jan. "Exchange Rates and the EMS: Six Months On." *Accountancy* (November 1979):34-35.

Statistiches Reichsamt. *Germany's Economy Currency and Finance.* Committees of Experts for the Reparation Commission, Berlin, 1924.

Tullock, Gordon. "Competing Monies." *Journal of Money, Credit, and Banking* 7 (November 1975): 491-97.

Vaubel, Roland. "Free Currency Competition." *Weltwirtschaftliches Archiv.* 113 (1977): 433-61.

———. "International Shifts in the Demand for Money, Their Effects on Exchange Rates and Price Levels, and Their Implications for the Preannouncement of Monetary Expansion." *Weltwirtschaftliches Archiv.* 116 (1980):1-44.

IV

ALTERNATIVE MONETARY SYSTEMS:
THE GOLD STANDARD AND THE FUTURE

10

THE CLASSICAL GOLD STANDARD: LESSONS FROM THE PAST

1. INTRODUCTION

Widespread dissatisfaction with almost two decades of worldwide inflation has prompted interest in a return to some form of gold standard as a possible cure to the inflation disease.

What was the gold standard that so many people look back to with nostalgia?

What was the record of the gold standard in providing stable prices and overall economic stability?

This chapter focuses primarily on what is referred to as the "classical gold standard" which prevailed in its most pristine form between 1880 and 1914, although aspects of it persisted in various forms until the 1971 breakdown of the Bretton Woods system. The chapter examines the operation of the gold standard as an institutional device to ensure long-run price level stability as well as a device to ensure automatic balance-of-payments adjustment.

Section 2 discusses some fundamentals of the gold standard. Section 3 considers some extensions of the basic gold standard

This paper was written while the author was a Visiting Scholar at the Federal Reserve Bank of St. Louis. My thanks go to Ted Balbach, Sandy Batten, Steve Ferris, Cliff Luttrell, Gary Santoni, and Anna Schwartz for useful suggestions and to Glen Vogt for excellent research assistance.

model. Section 4 is a brief narration of the history of the gold standard. Section 5 presents some empirical evidence on the performance of the economies of the United States and the United Kingdom under the gold standard. Finally, in Section 6 we consider the case for a return to the gold standard.

The evidence presented here suggests that, in many respects, economic performance in the United States and the United Kingdom was superior under the classical gold standard to that of the subsequent period of managed fiduciary money. In the pre-World War I gold standard era, both the price level and real economic activity were more stable than in the subsequent six and a half decades, and, moreover, the classical gold standard period was characterized by a smoothly adjusting balance-of-payments mechanism.

Yet despite this favorable record, it is important to stress that much of the successful operation of the pre-World War I gold standard was due to the presence at the same time of other conditions, notably the prevalence of world peace, the free mobility of capital, and the concentration of world capital and money markets in London. The well-known defects of a commodity money standard—notably, high resource costs of maintenance, an inherent price cycle, and the subservience of internal to external balance considerations—suggest that a properly managed fiduciary money standard would be superior to a return to gold.

2. SOME FUNDAMENTALS

What Was the Gold Standard?

Essentially, the gold standard was a commitment by participating countries to maintain fixed prices of their domestic currencies in terms of a specified amount of gold, and to maintain those fixed prices by being willing to buy or sell gold to anyone at that price. Thus, for example, over the period 1821–1914, Great Britain maintained a fixed price of gold at £3 17s 10½d; while the United States, over the period 1834–1933, kept the price of gold at $20.67 per ounce (with the exception of the Greenback era, 1861–79).

Why Gold?

Gold has all the desirable properties of money stressed by earlier writers in economics. It is durable, easily storable, portable, divisible, easily standardized, and attractive to the holder. Also, it is relatively scarce. Changes in the stock are limited, at least in the short run, by high physical costs of production, making it difficult for governments to manipulate.[1] Because of its physical attributes, it emerged as one of the earliest forms of money.

More importantly, gold is an example of commodity money, and a commodity money standard—regardless of the commodity involved—has a very desirable property that it ensures through the operation of the competitive market mechanism: long-run price stability.[2]

Under a commodity money standard, the exchange value of a unit of commodity money, or what it will buy in terms of all other goods and services, will equal its long-run cost of production.

Consider the example of a closed economy, which is a gold producer, that uses gold coins as money.[3] In that simple world, the price level (some average of the prices of all goods and services produced and consumed in the economy) will be determined by the equality of the quantity demanded and supplied of money.[4]

The supply of gold money is determined by the supply of gold in the economy and the use of gold for nonmonetary purposes. The supply of gold in the long run is determined by the opportunity cost of producing gold—the cost in terms of foregone labor, capital, and other factors of production engaged in producing an additional unit of gold. The fraction of gold devoted to nonmonetary uses is determined by the relative price of gold and all other commodities. The demand for gold money is determined by the community's wealth, tastes, and the opportunity costs of holding money relative to other assets (the interest rate).

In the long run, competition in the gold-producing industry will ensure that the exchange value of gold in terms of all other goods (the inverse of the price level) will equal the opportunity cost of producing an additional unit of gold.

To see how this works, consider what happens when an initial equilibrium is disturbed by a technological advance that improves productivity in the nongold sector of the economy. This technical improvement leads to a rise in real economic activity, an increase in the demand for money (gold coin), and, with a given stock of money, to a fall in the price level. This fall in the price level, or alternatively the increase in the exchange value of gold, means that producers in the gold-producing industry will be earning economic profits. These profits will encourage new entrepreneurs to enter the industry, as well as existing owners to increase production, both factors leading to an increase in gold production.[5] At the same time, the community will switch gold used for nonmonetary purposes to monetary uses (for example, it will melt down jewelry and have it coined). These forces will increase the gold money supply tending to raise the price level back to the old equilibrium.[6]

Thus periods of deflation will set into play automatic forces tending to increase the supply of gold money and restore price stability. In a similar manner, periods of inflation—caused, for example, by gold discoveries increasing the gold money supply— will, by reducing the exchange value of money, cause the community to shift gold from monetary to nonmonetary uses and will reduce current production in the gold-producing industries. Both factors will tend to reduce the gold money supply and cause the price level to decline.

Thus, under a gold standard one would expect to observe long-run price stability, although price levels may rise or fall for years at a time.

The Price Specie Flow Mechanism

When we remove the closed economy assumption and consider a world with a number of countries on a gold coin standard, we introduce a mechanism ensuring uniform price movements across countries.

Consider two countries each on the gold standard, for example, the United States and the United Kingdom. As mentioned above, each country fixed the price of its currency in terms of gold; the United States fixed the price of one ounce of gold at $20.67, while the United Kingdom fixed it at £3 17s 10$\frac{1}{2}$d. An implication of fixing the price of gold in the two countries is that the dollar/pound exchange rate is perfectly determined. This fixed exchange rate of $4.867 per pound was referred to as the par exchange rate.

Actually, as the gold standard operated, the exchange rate was not perfectly fixed; it was bounded on either side by the gold points— the cost of transporting gold between the United States and the United Kingdom. Thus, for example, if the United States reduced its demand for U.K. goods and hence for pounds to pay for them, this would tend to reduce the dollar price of the pound. When the dollar price of the pound declined, say to $4.80, it would pay to melt down English gold sovereigns into bullion, ship the bullion to the United States, and then convert it into U.S. gold coins.

Under the gold standard fixed exchange rate system, any disturbance affecting the price level in one country would be wholly or in part offset by an automatic balance-of-payments adjustment mechanism called the price specie flow mechanism.

Consider again the example where technical advance in the United States lowers the U.S. price level. The fall in U.S. prices will be reflected in the prices of exports, which will decline relative to the prices of imports, determined largely by prices in the rest of the world. This change in the terms of trade (the ratio of export to import prices) will cause foreigners to demand more U.S. exports, and domestic residents to demand less imports. This will create a balance-of-payments surplus, causing gold to flow into the United States from the United Kingdom.[7] The gold inflow will increase the U.S. money supply tending to offset the fall in prices. In the final equilibrium, price levels in both countries will be somewhat lower than otherwise.

Thus the operation of the price specie flow mechanism served to keep price levels in line across the world over relatively short periods of time (for example, within the year).

An alternative interpretation to the price specie flow mechanism described above is called the monetary approach to the balance of payments.[8] According to this approach, through the process of arbitrage—the buying and selling of similar commodities in different markets—the prices of all internationally traded goods, both exports, imports, and close substitutes, will tend to be the same around the world expressed in similar currency units. Moreover, the prices of domestic goods and services (nontraded goods) will be kept in line with prices of internationally traded goods by domestic arbitrage.

Hence, instead of U.S. prices first falling in response to an excess demand for money and the terms of trade changing, what happens is that the excess demand for money will be satisfied directly by the import of gold (through a balance-of-payments surplus), with no change in the terms of trade.

3. SOME EXTENSIONS OF THE SIMPLE GOLD MODEL

The Use of Fiduciary Money

The pure gold coin standard described above had one very detrimental feature. It involved very high resource costs to maintain a full commodity money standard. The costs of finding, mining, and minting gold are high.[9] Consequently, as nations developed they evolved substitutes for pure commodity money, both government-provided paper money, referred to as fiat money, and privately produced fiduciary money—bank notes and bank deposits. As long as governments maintained a fixed ratio of their notes to gold, and commercial banks kept a fixed ratio of their liabilities to gold (or to government notes and gold) then a gold standard could still be maintained. Such a standard prevailed over the pre–World War I period. As long as nations maintained the fixed price of gold, long-run price stability would be ensured by the two mechanisms outlined above.[10]

To see this, consider an example where the monetary authorities in one country under the gold standard increase their issuance of paper money to finance expenditures on major public works. The increase in the domestic money supply will quickly lead to an increase in the domestic price level. This will raise the price of exports relative to imports and lead to a balance-of-payments deficit as domestic residents purchase more foreign goods and foreign residents purchase fewer domestic goods.[11] The deficit will be financed by a gold outflow. The gold outflow will reduce the domestic money supply, tending to restore the price level back to its original level.[12, 13]

One aspect of the gold standard system was that one unit of a country's gold reserves would support a multiple number of units of domestic money (for example, the U.S. ratio of money to the monetary gold stock was 8.5 in the 1880–1913 period). This meant that gold flows could have powerful effects, in the short run, on the domestic money supply, spending, and prices.[14]

International Capital Flows

So far, our discussion abstracts from the role of capital flows between countries. In the pre-World War I gold standard era, much of international trade was financed by credit—by the issuing of short-term claims in the London money market.[15] In addition, much of the development of the less-developed economies of the world was financed by the long-term loans of investors in England, France, and other advanced countries.[16] Allowing for the influence of capital flows complicates the analysis but reduces the burden of gold flows in the adjustment mechanism.

Consider again the example where a country finances public works expenditure by printing money. Now, in addition to the increased domestic money supply raising domestic price levels, it also reduces, in the short run, domestic interest rates.[17] The reduction in interest rates on domestic short-term commercial paper relative to interest rates in other countries will induce investors to shift their funds to foreign money markets. This again will produce a gold outflow, reducing the amount of adjustment required by the terms of trade. Also, to the extent that short-term capital serves as a substitute for gold as an international reserve asset and/or domestic financial intermediaries hold balances with correspondents abroad, a lesser gold outflow would be required than otherwise.

Finally, consider the role of long-term capital movements. In the pre–World War I era when the rate of return on real capital was higher in the United States (also in Canada, Australia, and Argentina) than in the United Kingdom (and other European countries, especially France), British (and other European) investors invested heavily in U.S. industries and utilities by purchasing long-term securities. The demand by British investors for U.S. securities (other things equal) created an excess demand for dollars at the par exchange rate (or, equivalently, an excess supply of pounds). As a result, the price of the dollar increased to the gold import point in the United States (the price of the pound fell to the gold export point in the United Kingdom). Thus gold would flow to the United States from the United Kingdom. The gold inflow to the United States would raise the U.S. money supply above what it would have otherwise been, leading to a rise in the U.S. price level. The resultant rise in export relative to import prices would lead to an increased demand by U.S. residents for imports (primarily manufactured goods from the United Kingdom).

Thus the transfer of capital was effected by a transfer of real resources from the United Kingdom to the United States. Indeed, in the pre–World War I era it was the normal pattern for a developing country such as the United States to run a persistent balance-of-payments deficit on current account (imports of goods and services exceeding exports of goods and services) financed primarily by long-term capital inflows.

The Role of Central Banks under the Gold Standard

Under a strict gold standard such as described in Section 2, there is no need for a central bank. All that is required is that some governmental authority maintain the fixed domestic currency price of gold by buying and selling gold freely.[18] Indeed, many countries on the gold standard before World War I (for example, the United States and Canada) did not have central banks. Most European countries, on the other hand, had central banks—institutions which in most cases had evolved from large commercial banks serving as bankers to the government (for example, the Bank of England, founded in 1697) and institutions serving as lenders of last resort to the banking community.

Under the classical gold standard, central banks were supposed to follow the "rules of the game"—to speed up the adjustment of the domestic money supply and price level to external gold flows. The classical model of central bank behavior was the Bank of England, which over much of the 1870–1914 period did play by the rules.[19] Whenever Great Britain was faced with a balance-of-payments deficit and the Bank of England saw its gold reserves declining, it would raise "bank rate," the rate of interest at which it would be willing to discount money market paper. The rise in "bank rate," by causing other interest rates to rise, was supposed to produce a reduction in holdings of inventories and a curtailment of other investment expenditure. The reduction in investment expenditure would then lead to a reduction in overall domestic spending and a fall in the price level. At the same time, the rise in "bank rate" would stem any short-term capital outflow and attract short-term funds from abroad.

One problem that periodically arose in the nineteenth century was a balance-of-payments deficit (referred to as an external drain), caused, for example, by a poor domestic harvest, which was also accompanied by a domestic recession and an attempt by the public to convert bank notes and deposits into hard currency[20] (called an internal drain). The domestic recession would then be aggravated if the Bank of England raised bank rate to protect its gold reserves.[21]

As a response to persistent criticism of such policies, after 1870 the Bank of England gradually changed its operating procedures and followed what is known as Bagehot's Rule: "when facing an external drain raise bank rate, when facing an internal drain lend freely."[22]

For most other countries on the gold standard there is evidence that interest rates were never allowed to rise enough to contract the domestic price level—that they did not follow the "rules of the game"[23] Also, many countries followed policies of sterilization of gold flows—attempting to neutralize the effects on the domestic money supply of gold flows by open market purchases or sales of domestic securities.[24, 25]

Reserve Currencies and the Role of Sterling

An important complication to the gold standard story is the role of key currencies.[26] Many countries under the prewar gold standard held their international reserves in the form of gold and in the currencies of several major countries.

The center of the international payments mechanism was England, with the Bank of England maintaining its international reserves primarily in gold. Most other countries kept reserves in the form of gold and sterling assets. Two other major European capitals also served as reserve centers in the period between 1900 and 1914 — Paris and Berlin, each of which held reserves in gold, in sterling, and in each of the other country's currency. Finally, a number of smaller European countries held reserves in the form of francs and marks.

In addition to the use of other currencies as reserve assets, there developed in the gold standard world an elaborate network of short-term financial arrangements, between private financial institutions, centered in the London money market.

This extensive network of reserve currencies and short-term international finance had two important implications. First, England (the Bank of England) could act as umpire (or manager) to the world gold standard system without having to hold excessive gold reserves.[27] The Bank of England altering bank rate could have major repercussions around the world.[28] Second, much of the balance-of-payments adjustment mechanism in the pre–World War I period did not require actual gold flows, but transfers of sterling and other currency balances in the London, Paris, Berlin, and New York money markets.[29] In addition there is evidence that short-term capital flows accommodated the balance-of-payments adjustment mechanism in this period.[30] Indeed, the pre–World War I gold standard has often been described as a sterling standard.[31]

External versus Internal Balance Considerations

One implication of adherence to the gold standard is that any individual nation state must subsume internal balance (domestic price and real output stability) to external balance (balance-of-payments equilibrium) considerations. Thus, in the case of a country running a balance-of-payments deficit, the "rules of the game" require domestic deflation until "purchasing power parity"[32] is restored at the par exchange rate. Such deflation could be accompanied by reduction in real output and declines in employment, especially in the short run, before contracts can be renegotiated. In addition, worldwide deflation, as occurred in the 1870s, 1880s, and 1890s as part of the long-run adjustment mechanism of a commodity money standard, could be accompanied by real distress.[33] This so-called "iron discipline" of the gold standard is regarded as one of the key reasons why many countries were reluctant to return to gold after World War I.

4. CHRONOLOGY OF THE GOLD STANDARD 1821-1971

This section briefly sketches the chronology of the gold standard from the end of the Napoleonic Wars to the collapse of the Bretton Woods system.

The Classical Gold Standard 1821-1914

In the eighteenth century, England and most countries were on a bimetallic specie standard based primarily on silver.[34] When Great Britain restored specie payments in 1821 after the Napoleonic War inflation episode, it returned to a gold standard.[35] Throughout the period 1821-80, the gold standard steadily expanded as more and more countries ceased using silver.[36] By 1880, the majority of countries in the world were on some form of a gold standard.[37]

The period from 1880 to 1914, known as the "heyday" of the gold standard, was a remarkable period in world economic history, characterized by rapid economic growth, the free flow of labor and capital, virtually free trade, and, in general, world peace. These external conditions, coupled with the elaborate financial network centered on London are believed by many observers to be the sine qua non of the effective operation of the gold standard.[38]

The Gold Exchange Standard 1925-31

The gold standard broke down during World War I,[39] was succeeded by a period of "managed money," and was briefly reinstated from 1925 to 1931 as the Gold Exchange Standard. Under the Gold Exchange Standard, in addition to using gold as an international reserve asset, countries other than the United States and Great Britain would hold reserves in terms of both gold and dollars or pounds, while the United States and the United Kingdom would each hold reserves in terms of gold. In addition, most countries engaged in active sterilization policies to protect their domestic money supplies from gold flows.

The Gold Exchange Standard broke down in the 1930s following Britain's departure from gold in 1931 in the face of massive gold and capital flows and was again succeeded by "managed money."

Bretton Woods System 1944-71

The Bretton Woods system was an attempt to return to a modified gold standard. Under Bretton Woods, the U.S. dollar became the world's key reserve currency, with all other countries[40] settling their international balances in dollars, but with the United States still maintaining the fixed price of gold at $35.00 per ounce and keeping substantial gold reserves and setting external accounts with gold bullion payments and receipts.

In the post–World War II period, persistent U.S. deficits helped finance the recovery of world trade from the aftermath of depression and war. However, the steady growth in the use of U.S. dollars as international reserves and persistent U.S. deficits steadily reduced U.S. gold reserves and the gold reserve ratio, which in turn reduced confidence in the ultimate ability of the United States to redeem its currency in gold. This so-called confidence problem,[41] coupled with the aversion of many countries to paying seigniorage[42] to the United States as well as paying an "inflation tax"[43] to the United States in the post-1965 period, ultimately led to the breakdown of the Bretton Woods system in 1971. The decision by the U.S. authorities in 1971 that they would no longer peg the price of gold represented the final abandonment of the gold standard.

THE RECORD OF THE GOLD STANDARD

This section briefly examines some evidence for the United Kingdom and the United States over the period 1800–1979 on the stability of the price level and real output under both the gold standard and managed money. In addition, evidence is presented on the operation of the long-run commodity theory of money and the automatic balance-of-payments adjustment mechanism.

Wholesale Price Index

Figures 10-1 and 10-2 portray the behavior of the wholesale price index from 1800–1979 for both countries.

From 1797 to 1821, during and immediately following the Napoleonic Wars, the United Kingdom was on a fiat (or paper) standard; it officially joined the gold standard in 1821, maintaining a fixed price of gold until 1914. There is very little change in the U.K. price level from the first year of the gold standard, 1821, to the last, but over the whole period there was a very slight downward trend in prices, with prices declining on average by 0.4% per year. Within that approximate 100-year span, however, periods of declining price levels alternated with periods of rising price levels—a pattern consistent with the commodity theory of money. Prices fell until

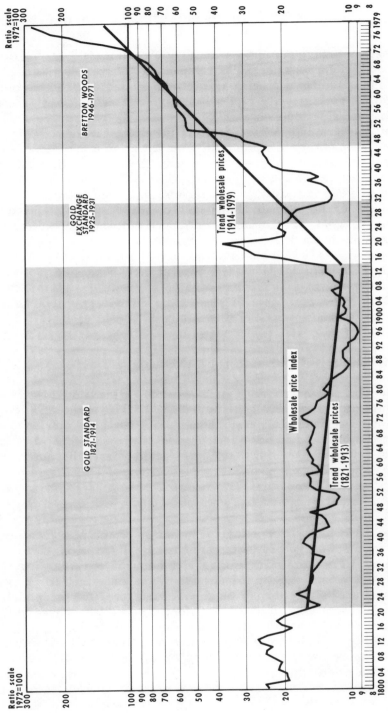

FIGURE 10-1. Wholesale price index, United Kingdom.

SOURCE: Prepared by Federal Reserve Bank of St. Louis.

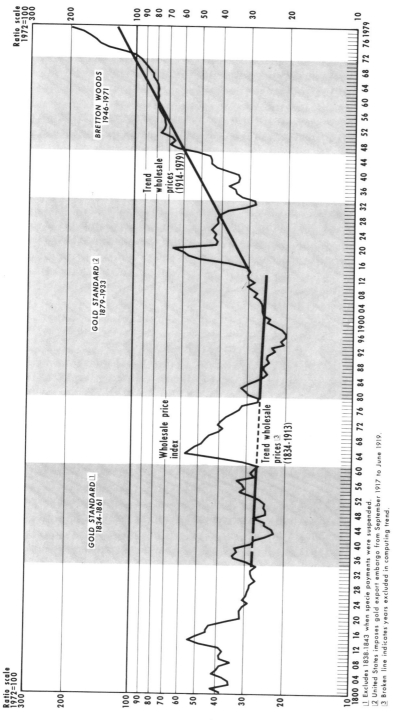

FIGURE 10-2. Wholesale price index, United States.

SOURCE: Prepared by Federal Reserve Bank of St. Louis.

1 Excludes 1838-1843 when specie payments were suspended.

2 United States imposes gold export embargo from September 1917 to June 1919.

3 Broken line indicates years excluded in computing trend.

the mid-1840s, reflecting the pressure of rising real incomes on the limited stock of gold. Following the Californian and Australian gold discoveries of the late 1840s and early 1850s, prices turned around and kept rising until the late 1860s.[44] This was followed by a 25-year period of declining prices, again reflecting both rising real income and expansion of the number of countries on the gold standard. This deflation ended after technical advances in gold processing and major gold discoveries in the late 1880s and 1890s increased world gold supplies.

The United States followed a pattern similar to the United Kingdom, experiencing a very slight downward trend in the price level, with prices declining on average by 0.14% per year from 1834-1913. The country adopted the gold standard in 1834 (it had been on silver for the preceding 35 years) and remained on it at the same price of gold until World War I, with the noted exception of the Greenback episode from 1861-78.[45] During that period, the country abandoned the gold standard and prices increased rapidly until 1866. To restore convertibility to gold, prices had to fall sufficiently to restore the prewar purchasing power parity. This occurred in the rapid deflation from 1869 to 1879.

The period since World War I has not been characterized by price stability except for the 1920s under the Gold Exchange Standard, and the 1950s and early 1960s under the Bretton Woods system. Indeed, since the end of the gold standard, price levels in both countries have on average been rising. The U.K. price level increased at an average annual rate of 3.81% from 1914 to 1979, while the U.S. price level increased by an average annual rate of 2.2%.

Purchasing Power and Monetary Gold Stock Trends

Figures 10-3 and 10-4 present further evidence on the operation of a commodity money standard and on the long-run price-stabilizing character of the gold standard.

Figure 10-3 shows the purchasing power of gold for the world (measured by the ratio of an index of the price of gold to the wholesale price index for the United Kingdom) in relation to its trend, compared to the world monetary gold stock in relation to trend for the period 1821-1914.[46]

The purchasing power of gold index presented here varies inversely with the wholesale price index presented in Fig. 10-1. This inverse association between the two series is a reflection of the fixed price of gold over this period.[47] The trends of both series were rising over the whole period. The upward trend in the purchasing power

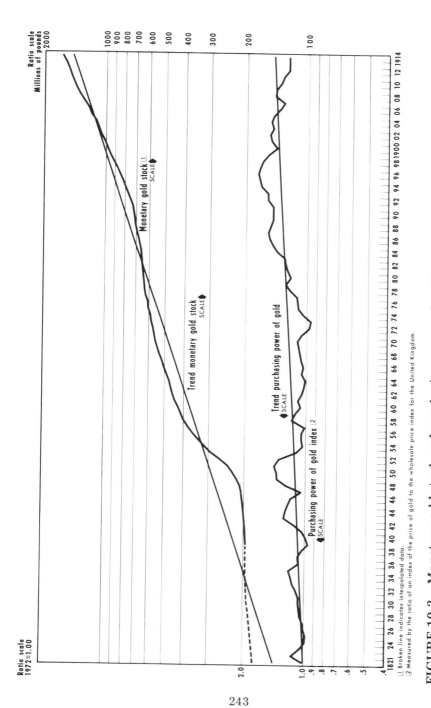

FIGURE 10-3. Monetary gold stock and purchasing power of gold index, world.

SOURCE: Prepared by Federal Reserve Bank of St. Louis.

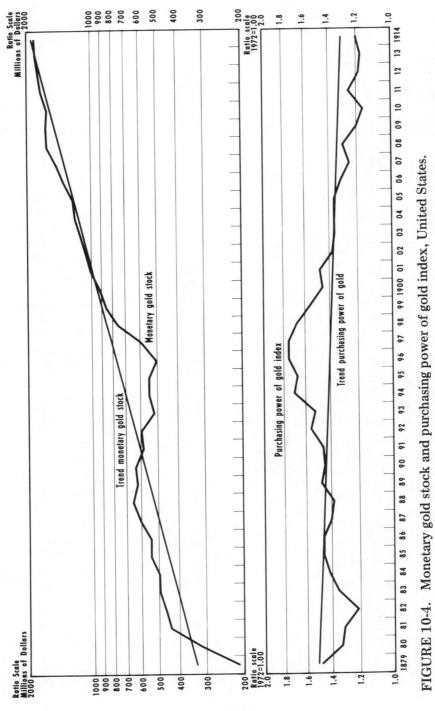

FIGURE 10-4. Monetary gold stock and purchasing power of gold index, United States.

SOURCE: Prepared by Federal Reserve Bank of St. Louis.

of gold series reflects a more rapid growth of world real output and, hence, in the demand for monetary gold than could be accommodated by growth in the world's monetary gold stock.

In comparing deviations from trend in the purchasing power of gold to deviations from trend in the world monetary gold stock, one would expect that deviations from trend in the monetary gold stock would produce corresponding changes in the price level, and for a given nominal price of gold would inversely affect the purchasing power of gold. A comparison of deviations from trend of both series reveals this negative association with deviations from trend in the world monetary gold stock leading deviations from trend in the purchasing power of gold.[48]

In addition, according to the operations of a commodity money standard, movements in the purchasing power of gold would be expected to precede movement in the monetary gold stock with a lead—a rising purchasing power of gold would induce both a shift from nonmonetary to monetary uses of gold and increased gold production. Such a positive association between deviations from trend of the two series is observed.[49] Thus the 1820s and 1830s were largely characterized by the purchasing power of gold exceeding its long-run trend. This was followed by a rapid increase in the world monetary gold stock after 1848 as the output of the new Californian and Australian mines was added to the world's existing stock. Subsequently, the purchasing power of gold declined from its peak above trend in the mid-1850s and was succeeded by a marked deceleration in the monetary gold stock after 1860. The same pattern can be observed comparing the rise in the purchasing power of gold in the 1870s and 1880s and with the subsequent increase in the monetary gold stock in the mid-1890s.

Figure 10-4 compares the U.S. purchasing power of gold in relation to its trend with the U.S. monetary gold stock in relation to its trend over the 1879–1914 gold standard period.[50]

In this period the trends of the two series moved in opposite directions. The declining trend in the purchasing power of gold series reflecting more rapid growth in the U.S. monetary gold stock than in real output over the whole period was a consequence of two developments: the accumulation of monetary gold from the rest of the world early in the period following the resumption of specie payments, and the effects of gold discoveries in the 1890s.

As in Fig. 10-3, a negative association between concurrent deviations from trend in the monetary gold stock and the purchasing power of gold is observed.[51] Also, similar to the evidence in Fig. 10-3, deviations from trend in the purchasing power of gold preceded deviations from trend in the monetary gold stock with a lead.[52] Thus, declines in the purchasing power of gold from 1879 to 1882 preceded declines in the monetary gold stock below trend in the late 1880s and early 1890s, while rises in the purchasing power of gold after 1882 can be associated with a rising monetary gold stock after 1896. Finally, a declining purchasing power of gold in the mid-1890s can be associated with a falling monetary gold stock after 1903.

One important implication of the tendency for price levels to revert toward a long-run stable value under the gold standard was that it ensured a measure of predictability with respect to the value of money—although prices would rise or fall for a few years, inflation or deflation would not persist.[53] Such belief in long-run price stability would encourage economic agents to engage in contracts with the expectation that, should prices of commodities or factor services change, the change would reflect real forces rather than changes in the value of money.

Belief in long-term price-level stability has apparently disappeared in recent years, as people now realize that the long-run constraint of the gold standard has vanished.[54] As a consequence, it has become more difficult for people to distinguish between changes in relative prices and changes in the price level. Such absolute vs. relative price confusion has increased the possibility of major economic losses as people fail to respond to market signals.[55]

Real Output Stability

Next, we present evidence on real output stability for the United Kingdom and the United States. It is frequently argued that, under the gold standard, when countries had to subordinate internal balance considerations to the gold standard's "iron discipline," real output would be less stable than under a regime of managed fiduciary money. Figures 10-5 and 10-6 show the deviations of real per capita income from its long-run trend over the period 1870–1979.

In Fig. 10-5, for the United Kingdom, both a single trend line for the 1870–1979 period as a whole and separate trend lines for each of the pre- and post–World War I subperiods are shown. The U.K. data was split into two subperiods because the trend line for the entire period results in real output after 1919 being virtually always below trend. This suggests that World War I permanently reduced the trend growth rate of real per capita income in the United Kingdom, and hence the two periods should be handled separately. Examining the deviations from trend (using the subperiod trends) suggests that real per capita income was less variable in the pre-World War I

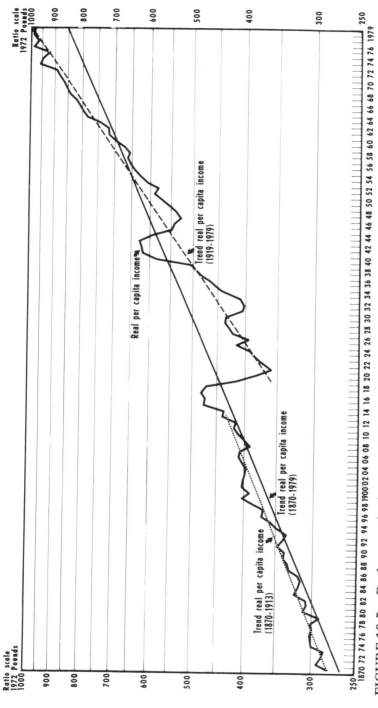

FIGURE 10-5. Real per capita income, United Kingdom

SOURCE: Prepared by Federal Reserve Bank of St. Louis.

247

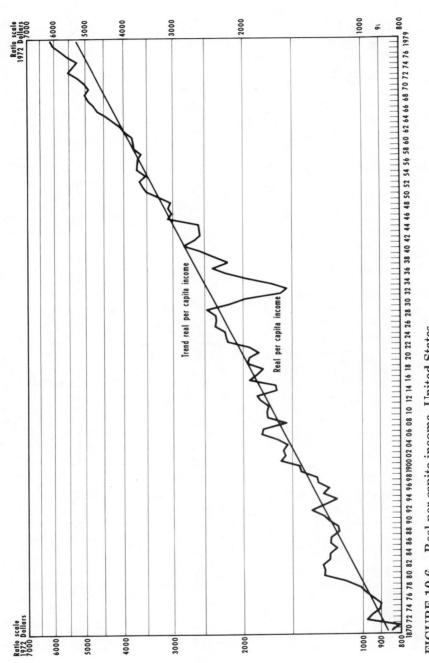

FIGURE 10-6.   Real per capita income, United States

SOURCE: Prepared by Federal Reserve Bank of St. Louis.

248

period than subsequently. The mean absolute value of the percentage deviations of real per capita income from trend was 2.14% from 1870-1913 and 3.75% from 1919-79 (excluding 1939-45).

As in the U.K. case, U.S. real per capita income was more stable under the gold standard from 1879 to 1913 compared to the entire post-World War I period. The mean absolute values of the percentage deviations of real per capita income from trend were 6.64% from 1879-1913 and 8.97% from 1919-79 (excluding 1941-45).

Moreover, unemployment was, on average, lower in the pre-1914 period in both countries than in the post-World War I period. For the United Kingdom, the average unemployment rate over the 1888 to 1913 period was 4.30%, while over the period 1919-79 (excluding 1939-45) it was 6.52%. For the United States, average unemployment rates by subperiod were: 1890-1913, 6.78%; 1919-79 (excluding 1941-45), 7.46%.

Thus, the evidence for the two countries suggests that the managed fiduciary money system superceding the gold standard generally has been associated with less real economic stability.

Balance-of-Payments Adjustment Mechanism

Finally, in Fig. 10-7 we present some evidence on the balance-of-payments adjustment mechanism under the gold standard. For the United States, over the 1880-1913 period, we compare year-to-year gold movements with year-to-year changes in the wholesale price index.[56]

First, we observe that gold outflows and inflows tend to succeed each other and average out close to zero over the whole period. In addition, positive (negative) price changes are generally succeeded by negative (positive) price changes. This behavior is consistent with the role of the gold standard as constraining individual countries to keep their price levels and money supplies in line with those of the rest of the world.[57]

Second, according to the price specie flow mechanism, we would expect: (1) that gold inflows (outflows) would be followed by increases (decreases) in domestic price levels: and (2) that increases (decreases) in domestic price levels would be followed by gold outflows (inflows).

In Fig. 10-7, we observe that changes in gold flows tend to precede or be synchronous with changes in the price level, but it is hard to discern a lagged inverse relationship between changes in the price level and gold movements.[58]

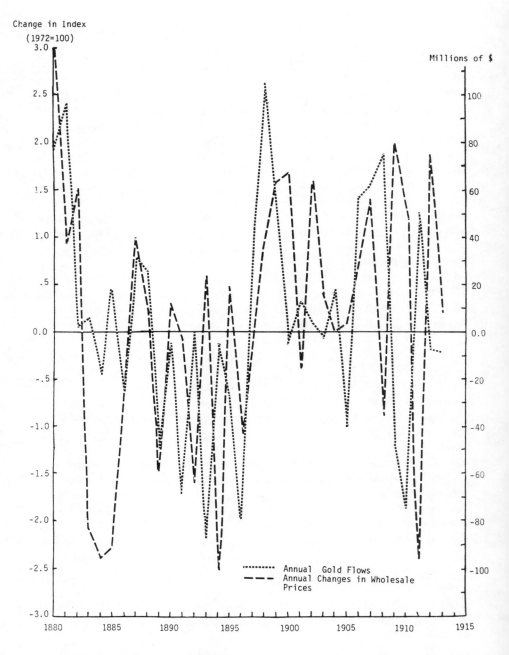

FIGURE 10-7. Annual gold flows (+ net imports, − net exports) and annual changes in wholesale prices, United States, 1880–1913.

250

The inability to discern the predicted negative relationship between either leading or contemporaneous price level changes and gold flows suggests that the price specie flow mechanism may not be a complete explanation for the balance-of-payments adjustment mechanism. Indeed, the alternative monetary approach argues that, since gold flows are caused by excess demand or supply in the money market, we must specify clearly a model isolating the determinants of the demand and supply for money. In such a model, gold flows may be caused by factors other than relative price level movements (for example, differences in real growth rates and interest rates), hence making it difficult to interpret the meaning of the simple relationship presented here between one country's gold movements and changes in its price level.[59]

6. LESSONS TO BE LEARNED FROM THE GOLD STANDARD EXPERIENCE: SHOULD WE RETURN TO GOLD?

1. The pre-World War I gold standard was the closest thing to a worldwide commodity money standard. Hence, the record for that period is of great importance to the question of whether or not we should return to some form of commodity standard such as a gold standard.

The evidence is clear that long-run price stability was a dominant feature of the period. This contrasts favorably with the record for much of the period since World War I which has, with the exception of the Great Depression, been in the main characterized by persistent inflation. Also, real output did vary considerably from year to year under the gold standard, but clearly no more than in the entire period since World War 1.[60] Further, though the pre-World War I period was punctuated by occasional monetary crises, and especially for the United States by monetary instability,[61] this instability was largely due to the structure of the U.S. monetary system rather than the gold standard system. The National Banking System with its pyramiding of reserves on the New York banks enhanced the likelihood of monetary instability when gold outflows were also accompanied by attempted conversions by the public of bank notes and deposits into gold.[62]

Finally, we have presented evidence for a smoothly adjusting balance-of-payments adjustment mechanism in the gold standard period.[63]

2. Despite this favorable record, it must be emphasized that much of the smooth operation of the pre–World War I gold standard was due to the presence at the same time of other conditions. The prevalence of world peace, the free mobility of labor and capital, and the absence of exchange controls were of paramount importance.[64] Perhaps of supreme importance was the role played by London in the gold standard story. The concentration of world capital and money markets in London, as well as the use of sterling as a key currency, enabled the system to function smoothly with very limited gold reserves and to withstand a number of severe external shocks.[65]

The significance of these other factors was pounded home after the demise of the gold standard in World War I. World War I destroyed the London capital market and wiped out England's overseas assets as well as the elaborate fabric of financial arrangements centered on London. Moreover, the advent of economic nationalism in the postwar period—manifested by the erection of barriers to factor mobility, exchange controls, as well as individual countries sterilizing gold flows to preserve internal balance—made it difficult to return to the external discipline of the gold standard. The attempt to return to gold in 1926 failed primarily because these other favorable conditions no longer held.[66] The last attempt to return to a form of gold standard was the Bretton Woods system, which inevitably failed because of the inability of the United States to maintain the gold standard link.

3. In the choice between the pre–1914 gold standard and the use of discretionary monetary policy since World War I, there is evidence that the gold standard provided a more stable monetary environment than in the succeeding period, taken as a whole, for both countries.[67] However, monetary policy since World War II has been more stable for the United States than it was under the gold standard, though not for the United Kingdom. But, as mentioned above, greater monetary instability in the United States under the gold standard may very well reflect the behavior of the U.S. monetary system rather than the gold standard itself.

The beneficial qualities of the gold standard become more apparent when we realize that leaving the gold standard, by reducing long-term price-level predictability, increased the costs to economic agents of distinguishing between absolute and relative price changes and hence increased the probability of major economic losses as agents fail to respond properly to market signals. According to this line of argument, both persistent inflation or deflation, resulting from cutting the link with gold, would produce economic losses.[68]

Perhaps if we view episodes such as the Great Depression and the recent inflation as aspects of the same phenomenon—the reduction of information subsequent to the decrease in price level predictability —we can then see how important the gold standard really was.

This is not to argue in favor of an imminent return to a gold standard. Operating a commodity money standard such as a gold standard involves significant costs: the resource costs of maintaining the standard; the inherent commodity price cycle; and the subservience of internal to external balance considerations. A fiduciary money standard based on a monetary rule of a steady and known rate of monetary growth could provide both greater price level and output stability than a return to the gold standard. The key problem is to ensure that the monetary authorities maintain the rule.

DATA APPENDIX

Figure 10-1: United Kingdom

1. Wholesale Prices 1800-1979 (1972 = 100)

Data for 1800-1938 and 1946-1975 from Roy W. Jastram, *The Golden Constant* (New York: John Wiley and Sons, 1977), Table 2, pp. 32-33; 1939-1945 from B. R. Mitchell, *European Historical Statistics 1750-1970* (New York: Columbia University Press, 1975), Table I1, p. 739; 1976-78 Central Statistical Office, *Economic Trends Annual Supplement 1980 Edition* (London: Her Majesty's Stationery Office, 1979), p. 112, series: Wholesale Prices for All Manufactured Products, 1976 figure used was an average of the CSO 1976 value and Jastram's 1976 value; 1979 from CSO, *Monthly Digest of Statistics* (London: Her Majesty's Stationery Office, Nov. 1980), p. 159, series: same as 1976-78.

2. Trend Wholesale Prices

(a) 1821-1913. Trend computed by running the following regression:

$$\ln (WPI)_t = 10.77 - .0044{*}t \qquad t = 1821, \ldots, 1913.$$
$$(12.44) \quad (-9.47)$$

(b) 1914-1979. Trend computed by running the following regression:

$$\ln (\text{WPI})_t = -70.52 \ \ + .0381*t \qquad t = 1914, \ldots, 1979.$$
$$(-13.63) \quad (14.33)$$

Figure 10-2: United States

1. Wholesale Prices 1800-1979 (1972 = 100)

Data for 1800-1975 from Roy W. Jastram, *The Golden Constant* (New York: John Wiley and Sons, 1977), Table 7, pp. 145-46; 1976 from U.S. Dept. of Labor, Bureau of Labor Statistics, *Wholesale Prices and Indexes Supplement 1977*, Table 4, series: All Commodities; 1977 from Dept. of Labor, BLS, *Monthly Labor Review* (April 1978), Table 26, series: All Commodities; 1978 from same publication as 1977 (April 1979), Table 27, series: same as 1977; 1979 from Dept. of Labor, BLS, *Supplement to Producer Prices and Price Indexes Data for 1979*, Table 4, series: All Commodities.

2. Trend Wholesale Prices

(a) 1834-1913, excluding 1838-43, 1861-79. Trend computed by running the following regression:

$$\ln (\text{WPI})_t = \ 5.86 \ - .0014*t \qquad t = 1834, \ldots, 1837, 1844,$$
$$(4.47) \quad (-1.98) \qquad \ldots, 1860, 1880, \ldots, 1913.$$

(b) 1914-1979. Trend computed by running the following regression:

$$\ln (\text{WPI})_t = -38.05 \ \ + .0217*t \qquad t = 1914, \ldots, 1979.$$
$$(-11.85) \quad (13.12)$$

Figure 10-3: World

1. United Kingdom Purchasing Power of Gold 1821-1914 (1972 = 1.00)

1821-1914 from Roy W. Jastram, *The Golden Constant* (New York: John Wiley and Sons, 1977), Table 3, pp. 36-37.

2. Trend U.K. Purchasing Power of Gold 1821-1914

Trend computed by running the following regression:

$$\ln (\text{UKPPG})_t = -7.78 + .0043*t \qquad t = 1821, \dots, 1914$$
$$(-9.10) \quad (9.34)$$

3. World Monetary Gold Stock 1821-1914

Data for 1821-1838 represent exponential interpolation between values for 1807, 1833 and 1839. These values, along with the 1839-1914 value from League of Nations, *Interim Report of the Gold Delegation and Report of the Gold Delegation* (New York: Arno Press, 1978), Table B, col. (1), series: Monetary Stock of Gold, end of year, millions of pounds at 84/11 1/2 per fine oz.

4. Trend World Monetary Gold Stock 1821-1914

Trend computed by running the following regression:

$$\ln (\text{WMGS})_t = -40.77 + .0251*t \qquad t = 1821, \dots, 1914$$
$$(-45.45) \quad (52.28)$$

Figure 10-4: United States

1. Purchasing Power of Gold 1879-1914 (1972 = 1.00)

Data for 1879-1914 from Roy W. Jastram, *The Golden Constant* (New York: John Wiley and Sons, 1977), Table 8, pp. 147-48.

2. Trend Purchasing Power of Gold 1879-1914

Trend computed by running the following regression:

$$\ln (\text{USPPG})_t = 8.58 - .0043*t \qquad t = 1879, \dots, 1914$$
$$(2.65) \quad (-2.55)$$

3. Monetary Gold Stock 1879-1914

Data for 1879-1914 from Phillip Cagan, *Determinants and Effects of Changes in the Stock of Money 1875-1960* (New York: Columbia University Press, 1965), Appendix F, Table F-7, col. (1), current par value = $20.67/oz. Cagan's sources include the following: 1879-1907, *Annual Report, Mint*, 1907; 1908-1913, *Circulation Statement of United States Money;* 1914, Banking and Monetary Statistics, FRB, 1941.

4. Trend Monetary Gold Stock 1879–1914

Trend computed by running the following regression:

$$\ln (USMGS)_t = -86.72 + .0492*t \qquad t = 1879, \ldots, 1914$$
$$ (-15.88) \quad (17.10)$$

Figure 10-5: United Kingdom

1. Real Per Capita Income 1870–1979 (1972 pounds)

(a) *Nominal Income* 1870–1979. Data for 1870–1975 from Milton Friedman and Anna J. Schwartz, forthcoming *Monetary Trends in the United States and the United Kingdom: Their Relation to Income, Prices, and Interest Rates 1867–1975*, National Bureau of Economic Research, 1980 (hereafter cited as Friedman and Schwartz, *Monetary Trends*), Chapter 4, Table 4-A-2, col (2). Nominal income for 1976–79 computed as GNP at factor cost less consumption of fixed capital. 1976–78 GNP at factor cost from CSO, *Economic Trends Annual Supplement 1980 Edition*, Table 36, col (2); 1979 GNP at factor cost from CSO, *Monthly Digest of Statistics* (Jan. 1981), Table 1.2, col. (2). 1976–79 Consumption of fixed capital from OECD, *National Accounts of OECD Countries* 1 (Paris, 1981), p. 70, series #36: Consumption of the Fixed Capital.

(b) *Implicit Price Deflator* 1870–1979. (1972 = 100) Data for 1870–1975 from Friedman and Schwartz, *Monetary Trends*, Chapter 4, Table 4-A-2, col (4); 1976–79 from International Monetary Fund, *International Financial Statistics* (Jan. 1981), p. 404; deflator calculated as P = 100* [nominal GDP)/(real GDP)], real and nominal GDP appearing in *IFS*.

(c) *Population* 1870–1979. Data for 1870–1965 from C. Feinstein, *National Income, Expenditure and Output of the United Kingdom, 1855–1965*, Table 44, col. (1); 1966–1975 from CSO, *Annual Statistical Abstract;* 1976–1979 from CSO, *Monthly Digest of Statistics* (Nov. 1980), p. 16.

2. Trend Real Per Capita Income

(a) 1870–1979. Trend computed by running the following regression:

$$\ln (Y/P*N)_t = -14.38 + .0107*t \qquad t = 1870, \ldots, 1979$$
$$ (-24.07) \quad (34.39)$$

(b) 1870-1913. Trend computed by running the following regression:

$$\ln (Y/P*N)_t = -13.27 + .0101*t \qquad t = 1870, \ldots, 1913$$
$$ (-21.40) \quad (30.84)$$

(c) 1919-1979. Trend computed by running the following regression:

$$\ln (Y/P*N)_t = -26.45 + .0168*t \qquad t = 1919, \ldots, 1979$$
$$ (-30.17) \quad (37.47)$$

Figure 10-6: United States

1. Real Per Capita Income 1870-1979 (1972 dollars)

This series is the result of splicing together two series, the earlier based upon data from Friedman and Schwartz, *Monetary Trends* and the later based upon data from Citibase databank.

For 1870-1950, a real per capita income series was computed using the following data: nominal income, Friedman and Schwartz, *Monetary Trends*, Chapter 4, Table 4-A-1, col. (2); implicit price deflator, 1971 = 100, Chapter 4, Table 4-A-1, col. (1); population, U.S. Department of Commerce, *Historical Statistics* (1960). This series was then adjusted in the following way:

$$(Y/P*N)_t = \exp [N(FS_t) + (N(CB_{1950}) - N(FS_{1950}))]$$
$$t = 1870, \ldots, 1949$$

where FS_t = Friedman-Schwartz value in time t and CB_t = Citibase value in time t. The adjusted series was then joined to the 1950-1979 series computed from the following Citibase data: GNNP—nominal NNP, average of quarterly figures, seasonally adjusted; GDNNP—NNP implicit price deflator, average of quarterly figures, 1972 = 100; POPCIV—civilian population, average of monthly figures. For t = 1950, \ldots, 1979, $(Y/P*N)_t = (GNNP*100)_t/(GDNNP*POPCIV)_t$.

2. Trend Real Per Capita Income 1870-1979

Trend computed by running the following regression:

$$\ln (Y/P*N)_t = -24.30 + .0166*t \qquad t = 1870, \ldots, 1979$$
$$ (-38.16) \quad (50.21)$$

Figure 10-7

1. Δ Wholesale Price Index 1880-1913

Computed as $\Delta WPI_t = WPI_t - WPI_{t-1}$. Wholesale Price Index same as Figure 1, Panel A, (1).

2. Gold Flows 1880-1913

Data for 1880-1913 from Dept. of Commerce, Bureau of the Census, *Historical Statistics of the United States*, series: U-6.

Other data used

1. U.S. Unemployment Rates 1890-1979

Data for 1890-1900 from Stanley Lebergott, "Changes in Unemployment 1800-1960," in *The Reinterpretation of American Economic History*, ed. Robert W. Fogel and Stanley L. Engerman, New York: Harper & Row, 1971, p. 80, Table 1; 1900-1957 from Dept. of Commerce, Bureau of the Census, *Historical Statistics of the United States* (1960), series D-47; 1958 from Dept. of Labor, BLS, *Monthly Labor Review Statistical Supplement* (1959), Table 1-1; 1963 from same publication as 1958, 1963, Table 1-1; 1964-1979 from Dept. of Labor, BLS, *Monthly Labor Review* (Jan. 1981), Table 1.

2. Great Britain Unemployment Rates 1888-1979

Data for 1888-1976 from B. R. Mitchell, *European Historical Statistics 1750-1970* (New York: Columbia University Press, 1975), Table C2, series: UK:GB; 1967-1972 from CSO, *Monthly Digest of Statistics* (March 1973), Table 21, series: Percent unemployed of total employees for Great Britain; 1973-77 from same publication as for 1967-72 (Oct. 1978), Table 3.9, series: same as that for 1967-72; 1978-1979 from same publication as 1967-72 (Nov. 1980), Table 3.10, series: same as that for 1967-72.

3. U.S. Money Supply 1879-1979

Data for 1870-1975 from Friedman and Schwartz, *Monetary Trends*, Chapter 4, Table 4-A-1, col. (1); 1976-1979 from Board of Governors of the Federal Reserve System, Statistical Release: Money Stock Measures, H.6, series M2, annual average of monthly figures, seasonally adjusted, acquired through Citibase databank.

4. U.K. Money Supply 1870–1979

Data for 1870–1975 from Friedman and Schwartz, *Monetary Trends*, Chapter 4, Table 4-A-2, col. (1); 1976–79 from CSO, *Financial Statistics* (London: Her Majesty's Stationery Office, p. 144, series: M3, not seasonally adjusted, end of second quarter.

NOTES

1. Of course, in earlier times, governments have manipulated gold by debasement, clipping, etc. Such practices, however, were the exception rather than the rule. See Schwartz (1973).

2. For a lucid discussion of the theory of commodity money see Friedman (1953).

3. The government mints coins and certifies their value but does not own the gold mines.

4. This can be alternatively and simply restated in terms of the familiar equation of exchange of the quantity theory of money: (1) $P = MV/y$; where P stands for the overall price level, M the supply of money, V the velocity of circulation, and y the level of real national output. The demand for money—the quantity of real cash balance desired $[m^d = (M/p)^d]$ will be the inverse of velocity (Py/M) given the level of real output; hence we can also express our equation for the price level as: (2) $P = M/m^d$.

5. In addition, exploration for new sources of gold and attempts to mine existing sources more efficiently will be encouraged.

6. Also rising prices will be accompanied by rising wages and other costs making gold mining a less profitable activity. This analysis assumes constant costs, with increasing costs the price of gold will be higher and the price level lower.

7. In this simple example, the increased British demand for U.S. goods lowers the pound to the gold export point, British importers convert pounds into bullion and ship them to the United States, converting them to U.S. gold dollars to pay for the U.S. goods.

8. See Johnson (1976).

9. Friedman (1960) estimated the cost of maintaining a full gold coin standard for the United States in 1960 to be in excess of $2\frac{1}{2}\%$ of GNP.

10. In the absence of exogenous shocks affecting the gold-producing industry.

11. The money-financed government expenditure may also raise real income (at least temporarily), as well as prices, leading to an increased demand for imports.

12. In the case of wartime money-financed government spending, governments usually left the gold standard rather than have their spending checked by a gold outflow.

13. According to the monetary approach to the balance of payments, the excess supply of money would be directly cleared through the balance-of-payments deficit without significant changes occurring in the terms of trade.

14. It also meant that changes in the composition of the money supply between high-powered money (gold coins and government paper) and bank-provided money (notes and deposits) could be a source of monetary instability.

15. See Bloomfield (1963).

16. See Bloomfield (1968).

17. This is the so-called liquidity effect. To induce the community to hold a larger fraction of their wealth in the form of money rather than interest-bearing securities, the price of securities must rise (the interest rate fall).

18. However, a substantial gold reserve is required to do this effectively.

19. Although most other central banks apparently did not; see Bloomfield (1959).

20. The attempt by the public to convert notes and deposits into coin would put pressure on the country banks to reduce their reserve balance with correspondent banks in London. The reduction in deposits with the London banks would in turn lead to a further contraction in the loans (or the selling of other earning assets). The rapid attempt to liquify earning assets sometimes led to the failure of merchant banks or other financial market institutions, leading to a general money market panic.

21. Noted examples of this are the crises of 1847, 1857, and 1866.

22. A key reason for the recurring money market crises in the middle of the nineteenth century was the Bank's rigid adherance to the Bank Charter Act of 1844. Under the Bank Charter Act, the Bank was allowed a fixed outstanding paper note issue of £14 million. Whenever its gold reserves expanded the Bank could expand its note issue by the same amount, whenever its gold reserve declined it had to reduce its note issue pari passu. See Whale (1943).

23. Noted examples are France and Belgium. See Whale (1937) and Bloomfield (1959).

24. Usually, gold outflows were offset by open market purchases of domestic securities. For U.S. experience see Friedman and Schwartz (1963). For other countries see Bloomfield (1959).

25. Such behavior could not persist, however, if a country wished to maintain its link with gold, because if the disequilibrium producing the gold flow were permanent, for example, the domestic price level were higher than world prices, then gold outflows would continue until all of the country's gold reserve were exhausted. (In the case of an inflow, it would continue until the monetary base consisted entirely of gold.)

26. Much of this discussion derives from Lindert (1969).

27. Indeed England's total gold reserves in 1913 only accounted for 9.5% of the world's monetary gold stock while the Bank of England's holdings accounted for 3.6%. See Keynes (1930).

28. It likely caused monetary crises in the United States in the 1837–43 period and 1873. See Temin (1969) and Friedman and Schwartz (1963).

29. Also in the period after 1900, instead of gold being actually transported between centers, the practice of "earmarking" gold holdings in major centers gained importance.

30. See Bloomfield (1963).

31. See Palyi (1972) and Williams (1968).

32. The ratio of the domestic country's price level (value of money) to that of its principal trading partners.

33. Although the evidence for the United States and the United Kingdom is that real output growth was not significantly lower in periods of deflation than in periods of inflation before 1914. See Bordo and Schwartz (1981, Table 1).

34. Under a bimetallic standard, each of two precious metals, gold and silver, serves as legal tender, and the two metals were kept by the mint in a fixed proportion to each other. The relationship between the official exchange rate of gold for silver and the market rate will determine whether either one or both metals is used as money. Thus, for example, in 1834, the United States raised the mint ratio of silver to gold from 15:1 to 16:1, hence valuing silver slightly less highly relative to gold than the world market. As a result little silver was offered for coinage and the United States was in effect on the gold standard. See Yeager (1976), p. 296.

35. Ibid, p. 295.

36. The switch from silver to gold reflected both changes in the relative supplies of the two previous metals with the gold discoveries of the 1840s and 1850s and growing preference for the more precious metal as world real-income rose.

37. With the exception of China, which stayed on silver. See Friedman and Schwartz (1963).

38. See Palyi (1972) and Yeager (1976).

39. The U.S. alone, remained on the gold standard, except for a brief embargo on gold exports from 1917 to 1919.

40. With the exception of the sterling bloc.

41. See H. G. Johnson (1967).

42. Seigniorage refers to the return earned by the U.S. monetary authorities on the issue of outstanding paper money liabilities. It is measured by the interest foregone by foreign holders of U.S. money balances.

43. The "inflation tax" refers to the depreciation in real purchasing power of outstanding money balances.

44. For a discussion of the effects of the gold discoveries on world price levels, see Bordo (1975).

45. Also to be excluded from the gold standard are the turbulent years 1838-1843, during which period specie payments were generally suspended.

46. The United Kingdom was chosen as representative of the pre-1914 world because it was a large open economy with few trade restrictions. Hence the wholesale price index would be dominated by internationally traded goods.

47. Indeed, this inverse relationship prevailed virtually until the late 1960s. Since the freeing of the price of gold in 1968, the purchasing power of gold has varied directly with the wholesale price index. This primarily reflects rising demand for gold as a hedge against inflation and increasing world political and monetary instability.

48. The highest statistically significant negative correlation in the 1821–1914 period, occurred with deviations from trend in the monetary gold stock leading deviations from trend in the purchasing power of gold by two years. The correlation coefficient, −.644, was statistically significant at the 1% level.

49. The highest statistically significant positive correlation in the 1821–1914 period occurred with deviations from trend in the purchasing power of gold leading deviations from trend in the world monetary gold stock by 25 years. The correlation was .436, statistically significant at the 1% level.

50. An important difference in comparing the behavior of the U.S. monetary gold stock with that of the world as a whole is that short-run movements in the United States series would reflect, in addition to changes in gold production and shifts between monetary and nonmonetary uses of gold, gold movements between the United States and other countries.

51. The highest statistically significant negative correlation, in the 1879–

1914 period occurred with the contemporaneous relationship between deviations from trend in the monetary gold stock and deviations from trend in the purchasing power of gold. The correlation coefficient, -.656, was statistically significant at the 1% level.

52. The highest statistically significant positive correlation, in the 1879–1914 period occurred with deviations from trend in the purchasing power of gold leading deviations from trend in the monetary gold stock by 14 years. The correlation coefficient was .793 which was statistically significant at the 1% level. The highest statistically significant positive correlation, in the 1879–1914 period, occurred with deviations from trend in the *world* purchasing power of gold leading deviations from trend in the *world* monetary gold stock by 16 years. The correlation coefficient was .863 which was statistically significant at the 1% level. The considerably longer lead observed over the 1821–1914 period lead in note 49 above likely reflects a longer adjustment period in the early part of the nineteenth century.

53. See Klein (1975) for evidence of long-run price stability for the United States under the gold standard. His evidence that positive (negative) autocorrelations of the price level are succeeded by negative (positive) auto-correlations is consistent with the hypothesis that the price level reverted back to its mean level. A consequence of this mean reversion phenomenon was that year-to-year changes in the price level were substantial for each country. However, the standard deviations of year-to-year changes in the wholesale price index were still considerably lower in the pre–World War I gold standard era compared to the post–World War I managed fiduciary money era. For the United Kingdom, the standard deviations are: 1821–1913, 6.20; 1919–79 (excluding 1939–45), 12.00. For the United States, the standard deviations are: 1834–1913 (excluding 1838-43 and 1861–79), 6.29; 1919–79 (excluding 1941–45), 9.28.

54. Indeed, evidence presented by Klein (1975) shows a marked decline since 1960 in long-term price-level predictability.

55. See Hayek (1972); Friedman (1977), pp. 451–472; and Leijonhuvud (1981).

56. We do not present the British data because of difficulty in choosing comparable gold flow data.

57. The correlation between contemporaneous changes in wholesale prices between the United Kingdom and the United States in this period was .632, significant at the 1% level. This positive relationship between changes in the two countries' price levels may reflect the process of arbitrage in traded goods (the WPI is weighted heavily toward traded goods) as well as rapid adjustment of the price specie flow mechanism.

58. Correlation of gold flows with wholesale price changes produced a positive and significant at the 1% level correlation of .538, with gold flows leading price changes by one year. All other correlations ranging between gold flows leading price changes by two years, to price changes leading gold flows, were insignificant. Using the implicit price deflator, the correlation of gold flows leading price change by one year was .446, significant at the 1% level.

59. For evidence favorable to the monetary approach to the balance of payments in the pre–1914 period, see McCloskey and Zecher (1976) and Wood and Mills (1978).

60. The standard deviations of year-to-year percentage changes in real per capita income for the United States were: 1879-1913, 5.80; 1919–79 (excluding 1941–45) 7.03. For the United Kingdom: 1870–1913, 2.62; 1919–79 (excluding 1939–45) 4.44. For sources of the data used, see the Data Appendix.

61. The standard deviations of year-to-year percentage changes in the money supply (broadly defined) for the two countries were, by subperiods, as follows. The United States: 1879-1913, 5.13; 1919-79 (excluding 1941-45), 5.60; 1946-79, 2.92. The United Kingdom: 1870-1913, 3.04; 1919-79 (excluding 1939-45), 6.38; 1946-79; 6.29. For sources of the data see the Data Appendix.

62. Much of the instability could have been avoided by the institution of 100% reserve backing of all monetary liabilities. See Friedman (1960).

63. At least for the advanced countries. For evidence on the developing countries such as Argentina, whose history was punctuated by frequent suspensions of specie payments, see Ford (1960).

64. Though some would argue that the existence of the gold standard was responsible for these other conditions; for example, see Kemmerer (1944) and Palyi (1972).

65. Periodic harvest failures and periodic political crises such as the Baring crisis of 1890 and the Moroccan crisis of 1911.

66. Other reasons usually cited for the failure of the Gold Exchange Standard are: the decision by Britain to return to gold at an overvalued exchange rate; the decision by France to return to gold at an undervalued exchange rate; German reparations, which disrupted the international payments mechanism; the unwillingness of either New York or London to act as umpire to the system; the frequent sterilization of gold outflows. See Brown (1940) and Yeager (1976).

67. See note 61 above.

68. Inflation or deflation periods while on the gold standard—periods such as 1869-96, and 1879-1914—will not produce the same effects, because agents realize that the price trends will eventually be reversed.

REFERENCES

Bloomfield, A. *Monetary Policy under the International Gold Standard.* New York: Federal Reserve Bank of New York, 1959.

———. *Short-Term Capital Movements under the Pre-1914 Standard.* Princeton, N.J.: Princeton Studies in International Finance, 1963, No. 11.

———. *Patterns of Fluctuation in International Investment before 1914.* Princeton, N.J.: Princeton Studies in International Finance, 1968, No. 21.

Bordo, M. D. "John E. Cairnes on the Effects of the Australian Gold Discoveries, 1851-73: An Early Application of the Methodology of Positive Economics." *History of Political Economy* 7 (Fall 1975):357-59.

Bordo, M., and A. J. Schwartz. "Money and Price in the Nineteenth Century: Was Thomas Tooke Right?" *Explorations in Economic History* 18 (April 1981):97-127.

Brown, W. A. *The International Gold Standard Reinterpreted, 1914-1934.* New York: National Bureau of Economic Research, 1940.

Ford, A. G. *The Gold Standard 1880 to 1914, Britain and Argentina.* Oxford: Clarendon Press, 1960.

Friedman, M. *A Program for Monetary Stability.* New York: Fordham University Press, 1960.

———. "Commodity Reserve Currency" in *Essays in Positive Economics.* Chicago: University of Chicago Press, 1953.

———. "Nobel Lecture: Inflation and Unemployment." *Journal of Political Economy.* June 1977.

—— and A. J. Schwartz. *A Monetary History of the United States 1867–1960.* Princeton, N. J.: Princeton University Press, 1963.

Hayek, F. *A Tiger by the Tail.* Hobart Papers. London: Institute of Economics Affairs, 1972.

Jastram, R. W. *The Golden Constant: The English and American Experience, 1960–1976.* New York: Wiley, 1977.

Johnson, H. G. "Theoretical Problems of the International Monetary System." *Pakistan Development Review* 7 (1967):1-28.

———. "The Monetary Approach to Balance of Payments Theory." In *The Monetary Approach to the Balance of Payments*, edited by J. Frenkel and H. G. Johnson. Toronto: University of Toronto Press, 1976.

Kemmerer, E. W. *Gold and the Gold Standard.* New York: McGraw-Hill, 1944.

Keynes, J. M. *A Treatise on Money, Volume 2: The Applied Theory of Money (1930). The Collected Writings of John Maynard Keynes.* Cambridge: MacMillan/St. Martin's Press for the Royal Economic Society, 1971.

Klein, B. "Our New Monetary Standard: The Measurement and Effects of Price Uncertainty, 1880-1973." *Economic Inquiry* (1975).

Leijonhuvud, A. "Costs and Consequences of Inflation." In *Information and Co-Ordination: Essays in Macro Economic Theory.* London: Oxford University Press, 1981.

Lindert, P. *Key Currencies and Gold.* Princeton Studies in International Finance No. 24. Princeton, N.J., 1969.

McCloskey, D. N. and J. R. Zecher. "How the Gold Standard Worked, 1880-1913." In *The Monetary Approach to the Balance of Payments*, edited by J. Frenkel and H. G. Johnson. Toronto: University of Toronto Press, 1978.

Palyi, M. *The Twilight of Gold 1914 to 1936: Myths and Realities.* Chicago: Henry Regnery, 1972.

Schwartz, A. J. "Secular Price Change in Historical Perspective." *Journal of Money, Credit and Banking* 5, Part II (1973):243–269.

Temin, P. *The Jacksonian Economy.* New York: W. W. Norton, 1969.

Whale, P. B. "The Working of the Pre-War Gold Standard," *Economica*, N-S, 4 (1937):18–32.

———. "A Retrospective View of the Bank Charter Act of 1844." *Paper in English Monetary History.* Oxford: Clarendon Press, 1943.

Williams, D. "The Evolution of the Sterling System." In *Essays in Money and Banking in Honour of R. S. Sayers.* Oxford: Clarendon Press, 1968.

Wood, G. and T. Mills. "Money-Income Relationships and the Exchange Rate." *Federal Reserve Bank of St. Louis Monthly Review* (August 1978).

Yeager, L. *International Monetary Relations: Theory, History and Policy.* Second edition. New York: Harper & Row, 1976.

11

EXPECTATIONS
AND THE GOLD STANDARD

JOHN F. O. BILSON

Recent macroeconomics has emphasized the importance of expectations in the analysis of alternative monetary systems. In the gold standard literature, critics argued that the classical price-specie flow mechanism was incorrect because price fluctuations and gold flows were not large enough to be considered as an effective international adjustment mechanism. The first purpose of this chapter is to demonstrate that expectations based upon the gold standard "rules of the game" and the price-specie flow mechansim act as a strong stabilizing force over both price-level movements and gold flows. Consequently, the stability of the gold standard system may be due in part to these expectations.

The second purpose is to assess the virtues of the gold standard as a modern monetary system. While the idea of restoring convertibility of paper money into a real asset is a good one, the particular institutional arrangements of the gold standard and the structure of the gold standard portfolio are shown to be an inappropriate base for a modern monetary system. An alternative system in which money is valued in terms of a broad portfolio of assets is also discussed.

1. INTRODUCTION

The stability of the international monetary system during the gold standard period has led to a continuing search for the particular characteristics of the system that made it work.[1] In a period marked by rapid economic growth, how did the members of the system adjust to changes in their economic environment without the inflation, unemployment, and balance-of-payments difficulties that characterize the interwar and postwar international monetary systems?

One of the first clear statements of how the gold standard worked is found in this famous passage by Hume:[2]

> Suppose four-fifths of all the money in Great Britain to be annihilated in one night, and the nation reduced to the same condition, with regard to specie, as in the reigns of the Harrys and Edwards, what would be the consequence? Must not the price of all labour and commodities sink in proportion, and everything be sold as cheap as they were in those ages? What nation could then dispute with us in any foreign market, or pretend to navigate or to sell manufactures at the same price, which to us would bring sufficient profit? In how little time, therefore, must this bring back the money which we had lost, and raise us to the level of all of the neighbouring nations? Where, after we arrived, we immediately lose the advantage of the cheapness of labour and commodities; and the farther flowing in of money is stopped by our fulness and repletion.

This passage is an eloquent description of the price-specie flow mechanism. A monetary contraction is assumed to cause an initial fall in domestic prices relative to world prices. Indeed, the passage shines with its belief in price flexibility; even the most ardent modern monetarist would hesitate to contemplate the consequences of an 80% reduction in the money supply without at least mentioning the possibility for some transitional unemployment. (Hume did, of course, discuss the short-run effects of monetary changes elsewhere, but the passage clearly suggests that he felt that the short run was short). It is, then, the induced competitive advantage that leads to an inflow of gold and the restoration of long-run purchasing power parity.

Since prices were stable during the gold standard, later writers felt that the price-specie flow mechanism did not capture the adjustment dynamics of the system. The evidence suggested that the price levels of the gold standard countries tended to move roughly in line, and that deviations from purchasing power parity did not trigger large commodity or payments flows. A number of alternative theories were proposed. Marshall (1926), in an early exposition of the asset market approach, stressed the fact that financial markets were more integrated than commodity markets and that movements in interest rates were the adjustment mechanism. An exogenous fall in the money supply would have its immediate impact on interest rates, which would rise and thereby attract capital into the country. In the *Treatise On Money*, Keynes introduced the idea, later developed more fully in the *General Theory*, that variation in real income, rather than prices, bore the main burden of international adjustment. Although an advance over the simple price-specie flow mechanism these contributions suffer from the same problem as Hume's model: they do not explain how the adjustment was achieved with so little movement in the balance of payments. This point was stressed by Angell (1926), when he wrote that

> It is perfectly obvious that neither the magnitudes nor the directions of the international flows of gold were adequate to explain those close and comparatively rapid adjustments to payments disequilibria, and of price relationships, which were witnessed before the war.

One factor neglected by these early writings on the gold standard is the stabilizing effect of expectations based upon the rules of the game. Consider Hume's example of a fall in the money supply leading to a fall in the price level. Commodity speculators, secure in the knowledge that the forthcoming payments surplus will increase the price level, will purchase goods at the low price in order to sell them later at the higher price. In order to exploit this arbitrage opportunity fully, they will borrow abroad and attempt to sell domestic goods in the world market. This countercyclical speculative demand will result in a smaller initial decline in prices and hence a smaller competitive advantage in international markets. Since the competitive advantage is more limited, so will be the flow of gold into the country. Expectations based upon the rules of the game consequently stabilize both prices and payments flows. These points will be developed more fully in the next section.

2. PRICE–SPECIE FLOW WITH RATIONAL EXPECTATIONS

Scammell (1965) has summarized the "rules of the game" of the gold standard system in four essential conditions:

> (i) A gold value must be fixed for the currency of every country within the system;
> (ii) There must be free movement of gold between countries within the system;
> (iii) The monetary system of all member countries must be such

that the domestic money supply is linked more or less automatically to movements in gold in and out of the country; [and]
(iv) That within each country there must be a high degree of wage flexibility.

A model satisfying these conditions requires a money market equilibrium condition and a balance-of-payments equation. For the money market equilibrium condition, we use

$$g = k + p - \phi \dot{p}^e \qquad (1)$$

where g is the log of the stock of monetary gold, p is the price level (expressed as gold per unit of commodities), $\dot{p}^e$ is the expected rate of inflation of the price level, and k is a shift factor reflecting all other influences on the demand for or supply of money. Changes in k may be the result of increases in real interest rates, in real income, or in the money multiplier. This equation takes account of the third of Scammell's conditions: it posits a direct relationship between the demand for money and the stock of monetary gold. Underlying this equation is the idea that the central bank under a gold standard has the same operating rules as a commercial bank; if reserves (gold) fall, then loans (domestic credit) must be reduced in order to maintain liquidity. For the economy as a whole, the positive correlation between the two assets items in the balance sheet will result in a positive correlation between reserves (gold) and deposits (money supply). This practice differs from the strategy of "sterilized intervention" practiced by many central banks during the Bretton Woods system in which the balance of payments was not allowed to influence the money supply.

In the gold flow equation, the flow supply of gold is negatively related to both the price level and the outstanding stock of gold:

$$\dot{g} = \gamma(\bar{p} - \beta g - p) \qquad (2)$$

This equation applies within either an open economy or a closed economy context. In the closed economy, equation (2) represents the flow supply of gold into the monetary system. As the price level increases, the cost of extracting gold from the ground increases, and gold is in greater demand for nonmonetary purposes. An increase in the outstanding stock will also lead to increasing marginal cost through the depletion effect. Hence the flow supply of gold for the world is negatively related to both the price level and the existing stock.

In the open economy, equation (2) is a price-specie flow version of the balance of payments condition. In this case, the term $\bar{p} - \beta g$ represents the foreign price level; as gold flows into the home country, the gold stock in the foreign country falls and induces a deflation. The β parameter is related to the size of the home country relative to the rest of the world: if the domestic country is small, β will be zero and foreign prices will not be influenced by the size of the domestic gold stock; if the home country is the world, the parameter will be infinite so that the flow of gold must be zero and domestic prices equal to $\bar{p}$.

Following Dornbusch (1976), the expected rate of inflation is initially set as an arbitrary function

$$\dot{p}^e = \theta(\bar{p} - \beta g - p) \tag{3}$$

Later, θ will be set at a value that will ensure that the expected rate of inflation in (3) is equal to the actual rate. For the moment, if domestic prices are below world prices, domestic residents will anticipate an inflow of gold and an increase in prices. As the gold stock does increase, and Hume's "fulness and repletion" is restored, the expected rate of inflation will decline.

Using equations (1) and (3), the domestic money market equilibrium condition becomes

$$g = k + p - \phi\theta(\bar{p} - \beta g - p) \tag{4}$$

Solving for the price level, we have

$$p = \frac{\phi\theta\bar{p} - k}{1 + \phi\theta} + \frac{g(1 - \phi\theta\beta)}{1 + \phi\theta} \tag{5}$$

Equation (5) represents the combinations of the price level and the gold stock that will clear the domestic money market. In the short run, the stock of gold is fixed and the price level is the adjustment variable. Over time, the gold stock will adjust according to equation (2).

Equation (5) and equation (2) are illustrated in Fig. 11-1 as the MM and $\dot{g} = 0$ loci, respectively. Since we are interested in the effect of expectations on the stability of the gold standard system, it is also useful to have an additional locus, M'M', which abstracts from the expectations effect by setting either θ or ϕ equal to zero. In contrast to MM, which has a slope less than unity, the M'M' locus

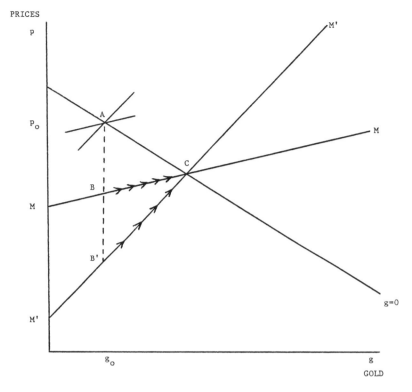

FIGURE 11-1

The MM locus joins the combinations of prices and the gold stock that maintain equilibrium in the money market. The M'M' locus represents the equilibrium points in the absence of expectations. Starting from point A, the economy experiences an unanticipated increase in the demand for money. Since the gold standard is initially fixed, the price level falls to B or B' and then rises to point C as gold flows into the economy. The figure demonstrates that both the price level and the balance of payments will be more stable in the presence of expectations.

has a unit slope. The difference between the two slopes reflects the expectations effect: to the left of the $\dot{g} = 0$ locus, the home economy is in a position of "tight money" relative to the long run. In the short run, the money market will be kept in equilibrium by prices falling below the long-run level. In the absence of expectations, the lower level of prices only clears the market by increasing the real value of the existing stock of gold. However, with expectations, market participants will recognize that the temporary fall in the price level will lead to an increase in the stock of monetary gold in the future and that, in association with the increase, prices will inflate back up to their long-run value. The expected inflation of prices will increase nominal interest rates and will act as an additional element, eliminating the excess demand for money. Consequently, prices will not have to fall by as great an amount as they would have to if the expected rate of inflation were independent of the price level.

This point may also be seen by tracing through the path of prices and the gold stock following an increase in the demand for money. Assume that the initial equilibrium is at A, with price p_0 and gold stock g_0, and that the increase in the demand for money leads to a new long-run equilibrium at C in Fig. 11-1. In the short run, the stock of monetary gold is fixed and all of the adjustment must be born by the price level. If the expectational elements are present, the price level immediately falls to B; whereas, without expectations, the price level would be fallen to B'. Hence, as stated above, the initial fall in prices is less with expectations than it would be in their absence. Further, it is also noticeable that the point B is closer to the $\dot{g} = 0$ locus than the point B', so that the flow of gold into the monetary section is less: the economy will move more gradually up from B to C than it will from B' to C because the relative price of gold has increased by a smaller amount. This implies that both the size of the initial price disturbance and the subsequent reversal in the rate of inflation will be reduced by the presence of expectations concerning the "rules of the game."

Figure 11-1 is also useful for describing the role of interest rates during the gold standard period. Properly stated, the price index should include the prices of equities and bonds, and it is likely that these prices are the ones that adjusted most rapidly to changes in monetary conditions. If we think of the price index as the price of a consul, then the mechanism described in Fig. 11-1 is very similar to the Keynesian analysis of the speculative demand for money. In effect, the increase in the demand for money causes the price of consuls to fall until the yield increases by a sufficient amount to make wealth holders prepared to hold the existing stocks of equities and gold. Other prices with smaller adjustment velocities would then begin to decline as higher interest rates encouraged savings and discouraged investment. An analysis of this extended model could be undertaken by replacing the assumption of instantaneous price adjustment with the assumption that some prices are sticky. As in Dornbusch (1976), the flexible prices would then "overshoot" in order to clear the money market in the short run and the MM locus would represent combinations of aggregate prices and the gold stock that are consistent with domestic price stability.

This mechanism offers an alternative interpretation of the standard analysis of the relationship between gold flows and interest rates. In the standard analysis, the Bank of England was assumed to increase the discount rate in order to attract gold, whereas the rational expectations model suggests that the rise in interest rates reflects an anticipated rate of inflation of domestic prices which is associated with the maintenance of equilibrium in the domestic money market. The anticipated inflation is directly related to the anticipated flow of gold into the domestic money market.

To determine the rational value of the expectations coefficient, we note that equations (2) and (3) imply that

$$\dot{p}^e = \left(\frac{\theta}{\gamma}\right)\dot{g} \tag{6}$$

while total differentiation of the money market equilibrium condition yields

$$\dot{p} = \left(\frac{1 - \phi\theta\beta}{1 + \phi\theta}\right)\dot{g} \tag{7}$$

For expectations to be equal to the actual rate of inflation, the expectations coefficient must be such that the bracketed terms in equations (6) and (7) are equal. Imposing this condition yields the following quadratic equation in θ:

$$\gamma - \theta(1 + \phi\gamma\beta) - \theta^2\phi = 0 \tag{8}$$

Without getting into too many details, the following qualitative conclusions may be drawn from an analysis of the quadratic equation. First, as long as the country is small (or, in the world context, the marginal depletion cost is not too high), an increase in the gold supply elasticity will increase the expectations coefficient. This is a plausible result since if gold flows rapidly between two countries, it is likely that price adjustment will also be rapid. Second, an increase in the semielasticity of the demand for money will lower the expectations coefficient. The reason for this result is that a more interest-elastic demand for money will allow for less initial adjustment of the price level in response to a monetary disturbance;

hence there will be less incentive for gold flows, and hence slower price adjustment. Finally, an increase in the size coefficient (or the depletion cost coefficient) will decrease the expectations coefficient since a given gold flow will result in a greater increase in prices in the other countries.

In both the world and the international setting, the conclusion to be drawn from these results is that the gold standard system contained a system of self-fulfilling expectations that helped to stabilize prices, interest rates, and gold flows. It is not surprising, therefore, that commentators found it difficult to find physical evidence of the operation of the system. Nor is it surprising that a system that offered so much stability for so little activity should be fondly contemplated by current monetary reformers. In the next section, I will argue that while the gold standard system was a good monetary system, it is not the best possible system for the modern world and that a modified, value-based, monetary system would appear to be a superior alternative.

3. THE GOLD STANDARD TODAY

In contrast to the Bretton Woods system, the gold standard was not created out of a mixture of economic theory and political reality.[3] Instead, it evolved as central banks nationalized the industry of creating money, and it was based upon the private industry structure that it had prohibited. The private banks or, still earlier, the goldsmiths, issued certificates of deposit for gold and these notes were subsequently accepted as money. As the textbooks tell it, the banks then began lending certificates of deposit in exchange for private promisory notes and offering to pay interest on gold deposits. For the purposes of the following discussion, the most important aspect of this system is that the notes were created as a bond, not as an equity share. In other words, the owners of the bank were the residual recipients of profits and losses and the money holders were only entitled to the quantity of gold mentioned on the certificate. This tradition has continued down to the present day: a dollar was once considered as a claim on a certain amount of gold, but it has never been considered as an equity claim on the assets of the Federal Reserve Board. In fact, the assets are presumed to be "owned" by the U.S. Treasury, which receives all excess profit from the operations of the Federal Reserve.

In the private sector, a very similar arrangement exists in the provision of traveler's checks. Private companies sell traveler's checks—

a promise to pay the bearer a certain amount of money—as non-interest bearing bonds. As in the traditional approach to the demand for money, it is consequently obvious to think of the demand for traveler's checks as being positively related to the volume of transactions and negatively related to the rate of interest. These relationships are based upon the idea that the liquidity yield must offset the interest cost. Traveler's checks are very profitable, of course, and there are a number of companies that would like to enter the industry. Apart from advertising, however, it is difficult to see how an entrant could offer more favorable terms within the existing institutional arrangements. If an entrant attempted to pay interest on traveler's checks, the resulting bookkeeping would lower their liquidity value.

Of the various ways of circumventing this problem, the most interesting from the point of view of monetary reform is to change the structure of the system from a bond-based to an equity-based system. Instead of offering to exchange money for a single asset (or commodity) at a fixed price, the money could be created as an equity claim on a portfolio of assets. Since the structure of this system resembles that of a modern mutual fund, the financial instrument might be called a mutual fund traveler's check, or MFTC. The idea behind an MFTC is very simple: the customer would buy MFTCs from the fund at a price equal to the dollar value of the existing notes. The dollars would then be converted into interest-bearing assets and all of the return on the assets would be reinvested in the portfolio. Over time, as the dollar value of the portfolio increased, the exchange rate between the MFTC and the dollar would also rise. For example, if the fund invested in short-term money market instruments, the exchange rate would rise at the nominal rate of interest. Since the nominal rate of interest generally reflects the expected rate of inflation, MFTCs would provide a reasonable hedge against inflation.

Relative to traditional traveler's checks, MFTCs have the major advantage that they bear a competitive rate of interest. There would, of course, be some inconvenience attached to the fact that merchants would have to take account of another exchange rate, but this would not be an important drawback for the large corporations involved in the industry. The main barrier to the introduction of MFTCs is that competing currencies are typically prohibited by the world's central banks. One easy solution to this problem is to turn the major currencies themselves into MFTCs.

A number of additional steps have to be taken before a major currency like the dollar could be converted into an MFTC. First, it would be necessary for the Federal Reserve portfolio to contain a base of real assets—equity shares, real estate, and commodities—in order for the price level to be determinant. Second, the structure of the portfolio must be chosen so as to achieve a socially desirable tradeoff between risk and return. Although it appears to be reasonable to choose a portfolio with a low level of consumption risk, an "active" countercyclical monetary policy could be obtained by introducing some degree of market risk into the portfolio. If, for example, the market basket was chosen for the Federal Reserve portfolio, then a decline in the real value of the stock market would result in an inflation of consumer goods prices. If wages were fixed in dollars, a countercyclical movement in real wages could be created which would stabilize employment, earnings, and equity prices. A full treatment of these issues is, however, beyond the scope of this chapter.

The equity money proposal shares the idea from the gold standard model that money should have a value backing. In other respects, however, equity money is far more desirable than gold standard money. In common with other debt systems, the gold standard always faces the risk that the owners of the bank or corporation will fall into bankruptcy. For example, the Bank of England held a portfolio in the period preceding World War I that consisted of a small porportion of gold and a large proportion of government debt, held primarily in the form of consuls. Any factor that led to a decline in confidence in the government's ability to finance the debt, including World War I, would rapidly lower the gold value of the Bank of England's debt portfolio and consequently make it impossible for the Bank to meet its gold pledge. Hence the gold standard, in both its public and private versions, had a characteristic tendency for bank panics when interest rates rose. The equity money scheme does not share this characteristic, since the exchange rate between the currency and gold would adjust when the gold value of the portfolio declined. Although a catastrophe like World War I would still result in a large decline in the value of the currency, the uncertainty associated with a bank panic would be avoided.

A second benefit from the equity standard is that the central bank could hold a well-diversified portfolio, rather than be concerned with the maintenance of the convertibility of the currency into gold. In pure financial terms, gold is not a particularly desirable asset for the monetary portfolio because its return tends to be negatively correlated with the market. During the 1973 oil price increase, for example, gold prices rose and the gold price of commodities fell. Hence the deflationary effects of the oil shock would be accompanied by a further deflation from the monetary standard.

In contrast, the equity model has a stronger potential for counter-cyclical movements in the value of money.

Most of the argument can be summarized by returning to the earlier point that the gold standard was created from the model developed in the commercial banking system. In creating a new monetary system, the model of a successful commercial entity should again be employed rather than resting on historical simplifications. The most successful of today's financial corporations are the mutual funds—they pay the highest yield and they avoid the problem of risk by continually changing the exchange rate between their certificates and the dollar in order to take account of changes in the market value of the portfolio. There is no reason why the world's central banks should not convert themselves into mutual funds. All that would be required is that the bank state the value of the currency in terms of the number of units of a convertible asset that the share in portfolio could purchase. For example, the Federal Reserve could fix the exchange rate between the dollar and the Swiss franc at the ratio of the number of units of high-powered money outstanding to the value of the Federal Reserve portfolio in terms of Swiss francs. Within a reasonable bid-ask spread, the Fed would agree to exchange dollars for Swiss francs at this rate. All revenue on the portfolio would be reinvested in the portfolio. If these simple rules ‚were followed, the rate of inflation in the United States could be reduced to a low level within a reasonably short period of time.

4. CONCLUSION

Liquidity is a characteristic of an asset that is relatively easy to create and cheap to produce. The early goldsmiths created liquidity by converting gold into certificates of deposit, which were a superior medium of transactions. Although the certificates were liquid, their value was derived from the value of the assets included in the banker's portfolio. Over time, value backing of currencies has been derided and currencies have been said to have value because they are accepted as a means of payment. Although this is true, it is becoming increasingly difficult to estimate the real value of a dollar as a means of payment and, as a result, the demand function for dollars has become increasingly unstable and the rate of inflation has increased and become more variable. The greater possibilities for currency substitution, the rapid development of transactions technology, and the ineptitude of central banks suggests that these trends will continue into the future.

Faced with these possibilities, it is reasonable for potential monetary reformers to return to a system that worked. The gold standard worked because it possessed a systematic potential for price stability and because all market participants understood that potential. However, the gold standard had its problems during its years of operation and it would encounter even greater problems today. The solution, then, is to take the best features of the system and blend them with the characteristics of the modern international monetary system. An equity standard accomplishes both of these objectives.

NOTES

1. Recent papers on the gold standard include Aghevli (1975), Barro (1979), Bloomfield (1959, 1963), Collery (1971), Friedman and Schwartz (1963), Lindert (1969), McCloskey and Zecher (1976), Scammell (1965), Triffin (1964), and Williamson (1964). This must be considered as an incomplete list of more recent work, since a full review of the gold standard literature would run into volumes.
2. Hume (1752), as reprinted in Cooper (ed.) (1969).
3. Many of the issues in this section of the paper are discussed in more detail in Bilson (1981).

REFERENCES

Aghevli, Bijan B. "The Balance of Payments and Money Supply under the Gold Standard Regime: U.S. 1879-1914." *American Economic Review* (March 1975):40-58.

Angell, J. W. *The Theory of International Prices.* Cambridge: Harvard University Press, 1926.

Barro, Robert J. "Money and the Price Level under the Gold Standard." *Economic Journal* (March 1979):13-33.

Bilson, John F. O. "A Proposal for Monetary Reform." Working Paper, Hoover Institution, March 1981.

Bloomfield, A. I. *Monetary Policy under the International Gold Standard.* New York: Federal Reserve Bank of New York, 1959.

———. *Short Term Capital Movements under the International Gold Standard.* Princeton: Princeton Studies In International Finance, 1963.

Collery, Arnold. *International Adjustment, Open Economies, and the Quantity Theory of Money.* Princeton: Princeton Studies in International Finance, 1971.

Cooper, Richard N. *International Finance.* Baltimore: Penguin Books, 1969.

Dornbusch, Rudiger. "Expectations and Exchange Rate Dynamics." *Journal of Political Economy* (December 1976).

Friedman, Milton, and Anna Schwartz. *A Monetary History of the United States 1867-1960,* Princeton, N.J.: Princeton University Press, 1963.

Keynes, J. Maynard. *A Treatise on Money.* New York: Harcourt, Brace and Company, 1930.

—— (ed.). *Official Papers of Alfred Marshall.* London: Macmillan, 1926.

Lindert, Peter. *Key Currencies and Gold, 1900-1913, Princeton Studies in International Finance,* No. 24. Princeton, N.J.: Princeton University Press, 1969.

Marshall, Alfred. *Official Papers.* London: Macmillan, 1926.

McCloskey, Donald N., and J. Richard Zecher. "How the Gold Standard Worked, 1880-1913." In *The Monetary Approach to the Balance of Payments,* edited by Jacob A. Frenkel and Harry G. Johnson. London: Allen and Unwin, 1976.

Scammell, W. M. "The Working of the Gold Standard." *Yorkshire Bulletin of Economic and Social Research* (May 1965):32-45.

Triffin, Robert. *The Evolution of the International Monetary System.* Princeton: Princeton Studies in International Finance, 1964.

Williamson, Jeffrey G. *American Growth and the Balance of Payments 1820-1913.* Chapel Hill: University of North Carolina Press, 1964.

12

THE EVOLUTION
OF THE INTERNATIONAL MONETARY SYSTEM

HENRY C. WALLICH

One piece of wisdom was left to posterity when the attempt to redesign a blueprint for the international monetary system was abandoned in 1974. The International Monetary Fund's Committee of 20, that had labored for two years on the project, concluded that the international monetary system would continue to evolve. No truer word has been spoken on this seemingly immortal topic. The system certainly has been and is in continuing evolution. Some of its evolution has been along structural lines, changing the nature of its organization. Among present departures in this area are the work on a substitution account, the European Monetary System, and the effort to strengthen IMF surveillance. Drift toward a multi-currency reserve system could bring a further structural change. Reviving interest in gold has also revived suggestions, impractical in my view, for a new fixed price of that commodity.

Policies carried on within the international monetary system as it currently exists have also been evolving. There have been movements along various spectra of options. One such spectrum runs from fixed to freely floating rates. Here, the initial move toward free floating has been in some degree reversed in the direction of more management. Within a second spectrum, running from preference for appreciation to preference for depreciation, a shift of preferences toward strength rather than weakness of national currencies has been observable. Finally, in the spectrum of options for dealing with payments deficits by adjustment or by financing, a move toward greater emphasis on adjustment may be ahead for many countries in this second round of OPEC-induced payments deficits. I would like to deal briefly with all of these elements of monetary evolution.

1. THE SDR

The Articles of Agreement of the International Monetary Fund call for the SDR (Special Drawing Right) to become the world's principal reserve asset. In concept, this is to be achieved by gradual allocation of SDRs to IMF member countries; in the course of time these SDRs will take the place of gold and of national currencies in countries' reserves. This conception reflects the situation prevailing during the middle 1960s, which reflected concern over an impending liquidity shortage. It was believed that the supply of gold available for use in national reserves would be insufficient to meet reserve needs, while the progressive expansion of the use of the dollar as a reserve medium would eventually undermine the dollar's convertibility into gold. To meet the supposedly oncoming shortage of liquidity, the SDR was established as an extension of gold, sometimes referred to as "paper gold," making its issuer, the International Monetary Fund, an embryonic world central bank.

Events have not borne out the expectations of that earlier period. The supply of world liquidity did not dry up. By most standards, it became excessive, partly as a result of large payments deficits on the part of the United States which caused other countries to acquire dollars, but more fundamentally through the experience that reserves could easily be replenished and indeed replaced by the credit facilities offered by private financial markets. As it became increasingly realized that excess liquidity rather than liquidity shortage was becoming the problem, the principal motive for SDR creation and allocation disappeared. There remained the desire of a number of countries, mostly developing countries, for a costless increase in reserves and relatively cheap credit, which could be met by the holding and use, respectively, of SDR. (Countries pay interest to the IMF for SDR they use, but not for those they hold as part of their original allocation.) Under these circumstances, the allocation of SDRs was suspended in 1972 but resumed in 1979. Some of the industrial countries expressed a concern that continued allocation of SDR in the absence of a liquidity need would convert the instrument into an aid device, weaken the IMF, and undermine the prospects of the SDR as a reserve asset.

Meanwhile, however, important changes were being made in the terms and conditions governing the SDR. They were designed to, or at least had the effect of, making it more attractive principally to countries receiving SDRs through international payments but also to some extent to countries using them for that purpose. Several features of the SDR had made it cumbersome and unattractive. One was the reconstitution obligation, requiring users to maintain over a five-year period an average balance in SDRs of 30% and later of 15% of their average allocations. Another was the low interest rate paid to recipients of SDRs in international payments (60 and later 80% of the average Treasury bill rate in five currencies). Still another was the difficulty of computing the value and interest rate of an instrument constituting an average of 16 currencies and five interest rates. To make the SDR more attractive, the reconstitution requirement was eliminated, the interest rate raised to the market level, and the number of currencies in the basket reduced from 16 to 5. The acceptance limitation—that is, the maximum of SDRs that a country as a member of the IMF was committed to accept if offered in payment—remained at three times the original allocation, reflecting the basically skeptical attitude of creditor countries toward the SDR.

A major opportunity to broaden the use of the SDR was put aside when the plan for a substitution account in the IMF failed of acceptance at the meeting of the IMF Interim Committee in Hamburg on April 25, 1980. The substitution account was to absorb supposedly unwanted dollars from major official holders and to replace them with SDRs. This would have reduced the role of the dollar in official reserves and increased the role of the SDR. The dollars received by the account were to have been invested in U.S. Government securities. The interest on these securities would have financed the interest payment on the SDR. The account would have been an independent entity within the IMF. The IMF would have had no responsibility for the SDR issued by the account or the interest due on them. The obligations of the account would have been backed exclusively by its dollar assets.

The difficulty to be overcome was to maintain adequate coverage for the liabilities of the account and the interest thereon, by means of the dollar assets and dollar interest earnings of the account. A decline of the dollar against the SDR would have put the account into deficit, and a decline of dollar interest rates below the amounts needed to service the SDR interest would have put the account into income deficiency.

The United States, as the debtor in the scheme, and the potential creditors of the substitution account were unable to agree on a method to guarantee the equivalence of these balances and interest flows or on a sharing of the risks in case they should diverge. The United States viewed the scheme as a long-run restructuring of the world monetary system to the benefit of all, which implied an equal sharing of risks and costs. The potential creditors seemed to regard the scheme as a bail-out for the dollar, in which case costs and risks should fall principally on the United States. The implication of the deadlock was that the dollar-holding countries were not sufficiently eager to replace their dollars with SDRs, and the United States was not sufficiently eager to consolidate its liquid dollar liabilities into long-term dollar obligations. Both sides preferred the risks and opportunities of the existing situation. It was a kind of back-handed compliment to the dollar that, from the point of view of the Europeans, of course, proved justified when the dollar subsequently appreciated far above the exchange rate level at which SDRs would have been substituted for dollars if that substitution had taken place soon after the abortive Hamburg Interim Committee meeting.

But while the SDR suffered a setback at the official level, new opportunities seemed to open up in the private sector. Under conditions of floating exchange rates, a feature became apparent that had not been considered during the fixed exchange rate period in which it was first developed. This feature was its capability as an exchange risk diversifier. As long as exchange rates were expected to remain stable, this feature did not attract much attention. When floating rates began to induce some official and private holders of foreign currency balances to diversify, the SDR was seen to offer ready-made diversification in major currencies. Wide swings in exchange rates, including strength of the dollar and weakness of some of the currencies that had attracted diversification, may have reduced the confidence of market participants in the belief that they could anticipate rate movements and do better by mixing their own portfolio than by accepting the fixed SDR mix. Aided by this developing attitude, private obligors, banks and nonbanks, have begun to issue their own SDR liabilities on a modest scale. These "SDR claims" are not to be confused, of course, with the SDR proper issued by the IMF or with the SDR claims that would have been issued by the substitution account. They are simply the obligations of the issuer denominated in a new synthetic currency, the SDR. As such, their appeal rests on the credit standing of the issuer and the degree to which the interest rate paid matches market rates on assets denominated in the component currencies.

While this new function of the privately issued SDR is still in its infancy, it does seem to offer at least conceptually the possibility of greatly broadening the role of the SDR as a unit of account, even though not as an increase in the world's paper gold supply. Moreover, since many central banks hold Euromarket CDs and similar paper in their reserves, it is not unlikely that in the course of time they may come to own CDs denominated in SDR, issued by the same prime banks. The possibility thus exists that privately issued SDR claims may become an important reserve asset, making it unnecessary for the IMF-issued variety to expand greatly in volume in order to assume that role.

2. THE EUROPEAN MONETARY SYSTEM (EMS)

The European Monetary System constitutes another direction of structural evolution, toward creating a zone of exchange rate stability and incidentally limiting the role of the dollar in intervention by the participating countries. The system now has been in operation for over three years. Neither the hopes nor the fears associated with its creation seem to have been more than very partially validated so far. The system per se does not seem to have produced the greater discipline on its members that would have helped to bring down national rates of inflation. But neither has it led to exaggerated exchange rate rigidity or payments controls. In some measure it can be held responsible for the higher inflation now prevailing in countries where inflation was low, before the recent oil price increases, because it has kept some of the high-inflation members of the EMS from depreciating and has thus compelled the low-inflation members to import more inflation. By the same token, it has held down inflation in the high-inflation group.

Some of the smaller members may have felt that their currencies were pulled along excessively by the German mark. Some also may have felt under a constraint to match German interest rates more than they would have wanted to for domestic purposes. That, of course, is what discipline means.

For the United States, the EMS has not had the result that some may have feared—a coordinated European dollar policy aiming at control over the value of the dollar. At times it has had the anomalous effect of pulling up, relative to the dollar, the currencies of some countries whose rates of inflation were no less than those of the United States, in circumstances when the U.S. current account was improving. Since the EMS, under the terms of its charter, is to evolve in the direction of tighter cohesion, its effects may change over time. Suggestions have been made that arrangements similar to the EMS could be devised for the dollar area or for the Pacific Basin. The benefits derived so far by the European system do not suggest that there is something here that urgently requires application elsewhere. But, in any event, the problems encountered in the European system, less difficult there, would almost certainly become much more visible in a Western Hemisphere or Pacific Basin context, such as widely differing rates of inflation—the United States and Canada on one side, Latin American countries on the other—and a history of wide exchange rate fluctuations that would be difficult to confine—United States and Japan, Japan and other Pacific Basin countries.

3. INTERNATIONAL LIQUIDITY

Creation and control of international liquidity has always been regarded as an important feature of the international monetary system. During the 1960s, there was concern about inadequate liquidity under a system that seemed to be throwing increasing burdens on the U.S. dollar. The creation of the SDR was the response that eventually turned out to be at least premature. During the 1970s, concern was primarily with excessive liquidity. International reserves could readily be obtained by borrowing from the private market. Reserve requirements, on the part of OPEC and of countries that sought to keep their currencies from appreciating under the floating system by buying dollars, became very large.

Traditional analysis would imply that high liquidity is an inflationary threat. Inflation has indeed been rampant, but it is not easy to trace it back to excessive international liquidity. One reason is that much of the additional liquidity has accumulated in the hands of countries that normally pursue strong antiinflationary policies and thus are unlikely to take advantage of their high liquidity. Countries likely to overspend internationally do not have excessive reserves, perhaps precisely because they have not followed strongly antiinflationary policies.

Recently, high liquidity has been "absorbed," in a sense, by the rising volume of international trade and mounting payments imbalances. Liquidity, in other words, is not as excessive as it might appear. This reduces the need to be immediately concerned about how to curb excessive liquidity creation. Nevertheless, for the long run the danger exists and policies bearing on international liquidity—such as the creation of SDRs by the IMF, the possible treatment of gold reserves of the Fund and of national authorities, as well as possible control of the Euromarkets—will have to take account of it.

4. IMF SURVEILLANCE

The IMF has the power, and indeed the obligation, to exercise surveillance over the exchange rate policies of its members. The Fund has been given the power also to monitor the monetary and fiscal policies of its members, since these are important determinants of exchange rates. Finally, as a third parameter of surveillance, the Fund can examine members' policies with respect to the financing of their payments deficits. The surveillance process covers countries in surplus, influence over whose policies has always been a weak part of the adjustment mechanism. To implement the surveillance process, the United States has proposed that countries with large imbalances submit to the IMF proposals for dealing with them, that the Fund assess the performance of individual countries in a global context, that the Managing Director more often take the initiative in arranging consultations with members, and that the IMF examine how payments imbalances have been financed.

The Fund has approached its task of surveillance with a great deal of caution. It is significant, however, that the United States has declared itself willing to accept this degree of IMF influence. Historically, the United States has been resistant to any thought of IMF influence over its freedom of domestic decision-making. One may view this evolution of U.S. thinking as evidence that the United States increasingly realizes that its domestic policies may benefit from balance-of-payment discipline, as well as from finding greater activity of the IMF in this area to be in the U.S. interest generally.

5. A MULTICURRENCY RESERVE SYSTEM

The drift toward a multicurrency reserve system is not an organized process. It seems to be happening, in some degree, as a result of diversification efforts on the part both of some central banks outside the G-10 group of countries and of some private sector participants. Such a move is not surprising under a system of floating rates. A diversified portfolio, whether of common stocks or of currencies, has less risk for a given rate of return than investment only in a single company or a single currency. In choosing the desired composition of their currency portfolio, holders presumably will give weight to the distribution of currencies in which they conduct their imports and in which their debts are denominated. That would still leave a very sizable demand for dollar assets. Indeed, the share of the dollar in monetary authorities' portfolios of foreign exchange holdings since 1973 has been fairly constant at about 80 to 85%.

The world has had experience with multicurrency reserve systems before. Gold and silver, sterling and dollar, gold and dollar, with an admixture of French francs, have all been tried by force of circumstances and have been found to be unstable as holders switched from one asset to the other. A new edition of the old text probably would not turn out very differently. It might be noted additionally that the countries whose currencies are candidates for reserve-currency status at first were far from enthusiastic about the prospect. More recently they have been pushed to a more positive stance mainly by the desire to obtain financing for the payments deficits resulting from higher oil imports. This motivation is not necessarily a commendation of a multicurrency reserve system.

An alternative to a multicurrency reserve system would be an SDR-based system. An SDR-based system, employing the newly established five-currency basket, seems far preferable. To be sure, the lack of progress made by that instrument since its creation in 1969 might give one pause. One should think that, if the SDR were a promising financial instrument, the private market would have created and popularized its counterpart, the SDR claim. So far, very few borrowers outside those from the IMF have wanted to borrow in SDRs, and few depositors have sought SDR deposits. A demand for such instruments, if it were manifested, could, of course, be accommodated by the private banking system as well as by other financial institutions.

The fact that the interest rate on the SDR has been kept artificially low is not a complete answer. It applies only to the SDR that is issued as a liability of the IMF. The potential role of SDR-denominated claims and liabilities is much wider. Borrowers and lenders could put on such instruments any interest rate commensurate with interest rates in the underlying basket or part thereof, or even an independent interest rate.

Nor is it a valid explanation of the failure of the SDR claim to find customers so far that its rate of return, taking 100% of the computed interest and the appreciation or depreciation against particular currencies into account, has been less than the total return on the strongest currencies. Ex post, the same can be said about any successful asset—it tends to outperform the total return on an average portfolio. But that does not prevent most investors from preferring diversified to highly concentrated portfolios. In the exchange market, any currency may be expected so to position itself that its total return, interest plus expected appreciation, is equal to that of other currencies allowing for factors of convenience and political risk. Ex post it will undoubtedly turn out that some currencies appreciated or depreciated in ways not expected, making total returns unequal. An investor gifted with superior foresight could take advantage of this. But the average investor or monetary authority will be better off with the lower risk of a diversified portfolio, of which the SDR claim, and to a lesser extent the ECU, are prime instances.

A means of easing the transition to a multicurrency reserve system and of avoiding the market effects of sales of dollars for other currencies is sometimes suggested. It consists in an arrangement whereby the monetary authorities of potential reserve-currency countries would make available their currencies to foreign monetary authorities against payment in dollars outside the exchange market. The same avoidance of market disturbance, but with less risk for the buyer and less exposure to reserve-currency status for the seller, could be achieved if a central bank in that situation were to issue SDR liabilities. As long as SDR claims are not widely acceptable among central banks, a central bank issuing such liabilities would probably have to stand ready to convert them back into dollars or into its own currency at the prevailing exchange rate. Eventually, SDR claims might move in official or private market channels much as bank liabilities denominated in national currencies do today. The risk for the issuing bank, which acquires dollars, would in any event be less if it issues SDR liabilities against these dollars than if it issues its own currency.

6. NO RETURN TO THE GOLD STANDARD

The rise in the price of gold has encouraged suggestions that the monetary problems of the world could be solved by putting gold back in the center of the picture, fixing its price (by committing to buy and sell at this price), and starting a new ballgame. The implausibility of these proposals is easily seen if one notes their consequences. Suppose a single country were to fix a price for gold. It is most unlikely that that price would be one at which the market neither wants to sell nor to buy gold on balance. If the price is too low, the country will find itself selling out its gold reserves to the market. If the price is too high, the country will find itself acquiring large amounts of gold and pouring out liquidity. The experience of the gold pool of the 1960s, which, after all, operated in a world still accustomed to stability, is a faint foretaste of that situation. The experience of the United States during the 1930s is also indicative. Following the rise in the price of gold from $20.67 to $35.00 per ounce, U.S. gold holdings rose from 195 million ounces in January 1934 to 419 million ounces in January 1939, although some of the movement probably reflected war fears.

If several countries were to fix the price of gold, they would then effectively have fixed their exchange rates against each other. We would be back in the Bretton Woods system, but with much higher rates of inflation and greater variation of inflation rates. Exchange rates would quickly get out of line, and the gold pegs would be broken.

Such a result could be avoided only if countries were to subject their domestic policies to a severe discipline designed to keep their domestic price levels and their balance of payments in line with arbitrarily fixed exchange rates. That would mean the full discipline of the gold standard. Some of the proponents of a return to gold seem to desire the imposition of such discipline. Whether that kind of harsh discipline is desirable, or whether it would just make us repeat the experience of 1931–33, its achievement today seems altogether out of reach. For some countries, moreover, the discipline might work in reverse—forcing them to inflate when they do not want to inflate.

The more likely consequence of the rise in the price of gold to date is a reduction in discipline, if gold-holding countries were to take advantage of their new-found wealth. Looser fiscal policies and monetary policies, and looser balance-of-payments behavior, could all be financed if present gold profits were mobilized by a write-up of gold assets. It will take some effort to prevent this from happening in particular circumstances.

7. BETWEEN FIXED AND FREELY FLOATING RATES

Since generalized floating began in March 1973, the degree of acceptance of free floating has varied from country to country and from time to time. To the extent that there ever was acceptance of perfectly clean floating, there clearly has been a movement away from that position. At the same time, however, there seems to have been some convergence of views internationally that exchange rates cannot be determined by fiat or market intervention but must be left to the determination of fundamental factors such as the rate of inflation, the current account, capital movements, and the rate of interest. It is recognized, of course, that these fundamentals are in good part themselves determined by national policy actions.

The difficulty of controlling exchange rate movements by intervention was demonstrated, for instance, in 1977, when foreign central banks bought approximately $35 billion without being able to prevent the decline of the dollar. Japan, over the period January 1979 to January 1980, reduced its reserves by about $12 billion without preventing a substantial depreciation of the yen.

Nevertheless, in a minor key, market intervention has come to be recognized as a means of countering not only day-to-day disorder, but disorder also in a broader sense. The history of exchange rate movements during the period of floating suggests that exchange rates often overshoot on the upside as well as on the downside. Whether this simply reflects speculative bubbles and bandwagon effects, or differences in the speed with which asset markets and goods markets clear, a case has been seen to exist for countering excessive market movements. The United States today stands alone in limiting intervention to instances of high disorder.

8. APPRECIATION VERSUS DEPRECIATION

Much of the Bretton Woods thinking about exchange rate policy derived from a fear of competitive depreciation. If this fear ever prevailed during the period of generalized floating since 1973, it has proved to be superfluous. The much more general tendency among countries has been to aim at a strong currency.

Many factors have contributed to this. Nowadays, a country suffering from unemployment can deal with it by domestic expansion. It needs no recourse to exchange depreciation to promote employment by stimulating exports. A declining exchange rate, on the other hand, has been observed to contribute to inflation and also to reduce the scope for domestic expansionary measures that would create adverse exchange rate expectations. Vicious circles of inflation and depreciation have acquired an ominous reputation, while virtuous circles of appreciation and lower inflation have seemed worthy of emulation.

As regards the dollar, the case for strength has gained from its reserve-currency role. Weakness of the currency in which the world carries its reserves, in which it trades and invests, is bound to create uncertainty, instability, and a propensity to systematic changes. Not all currencies can rise at the same time, but during a period of world-wide inflation all countries can pursue domestic policies designed to strengthen their currency to their own and the common good.

9. FINANCING VERSUS ADJUSTMENT

When the first OPEC price increase hit the world and created the prospect of a period of enormous deficits, it was widely recognized that a universal effort to eliminate these deficits by internal contraction or depreciation would be futile and possibly disastrous. Now that OPEC-induced deficits have mounted again, the same issue reappears, but with different accents. Countries that relied heavily on financing their deficits instead of adjusting them away during the earlier round will find it preferable, and perhaps necessary, to lean the other way this time. Their debt burdens, and the limited capacity of banks to accumulate obligations of particular countries, makes this advisable. Thus, within the spectrum that runs from adjustment to financing of deficits for countries already heavily in debt, the accent should shift in the direction of earlier adjustment and less financing. Given that the OPEC-imposed deficits in the aggregate cannot be reduced quickly, this would mean that countries that are able to finance their deficit would have to accept larger deficits.

10. THE INTERNATIONAL MONETARY FUND

The continued effective functioning of the International Monetary Fund is an important condition for weathering the difficult period that is likely to be ahead in international markets. The IMF has been involved in almost all the dimensions of the international scene examined in this chapter. There is no need, therefore, for a special discussion of its role. In terms of international discipline, the IMF is probably the most influential international institution in existence. Whatever there is of an "international monetary system" is rooted in one way or another in the IMF. That the system has not been weakened more than it has is in good part attributable to the IMF. The IMF is still far removed from a world central bank role. But, unless the European monetary fund should in time accede to that role, the IMF is the most likely candidate.

11. CONCLUSION

As we view the evolution of the international monetary system, we have reason to reject the allegation that the system is in the process of disintegration. It is true that fixed rates have come to an end, that we may be moving to a multiple-currency system, and that the appearance of shifting trends, such as sketched in this chapter, in lieu of stable rules of international financial behavior, may convey the impression of disintegration. But on the whole, the system has produced good results. The first oil crisis has been weathered, trade has expanded, international capital flows have been enormous. The ultimate calamity—worldwide trade restrictions and a freezing over of international payments as happened during the 1930s—has been conspicuously avoided.

APPENDIX

LIST OF PARTICIPANTS

CAROLINA CURRENCY CONFERENCE

Joshua Aizenman, *University of Pennslyvania*
John F. O. Bilson, *University of Chicago*
Stanley Black, *Vanderbilt University*
Michael David Bordo, *University of South Carolina*
Charles Cathcart, *Citibank*
Emil Claassen, *Université de Paris-Dauphine*
Michael B. Connolly, *University of South Carolina*
Michael Darby, *University of California at Los Angeles*
Walter Enders, *Iowa State University*
Robert Flood, *Board of Governors, Federal Reserve System*
Michele Fratianni, *Indiana University*
Jacob A. Frenkel, *University of Chicago*
Hans Genberg, *Graduate Institute of International Studies, Geneva*
Margaret Green, *Federal Reserve Bank of New York*
H. Robert Heller, *Bank of America*
Thomas Humphrey, *Federal Reserve Bank of Richmond*
B. F. Kiker, *University of South Carolina*
Anthony Lanyi, *International Monetary Fund*
Harvey E. Lapan, *Iowa State University*
Leslie Lipschitz, *International Monetary Fund*

Michael Melvin, *Arizona State University*
Robert A. Mundell, *Columbia University*
Bluford Putnam, *Chase Manhattan Bank*
Blaine Roberts, *University of South Carolina*
Don Roper, *University of Utah*
Pascal Salin, *Université de Paris-Dauphine*
Alexander Swoboda, *Graduate Institute of International Studies, Geneva*
Dean Taylor, *State University of New York at Albany*
Henry Wallich, *Board of Governors of the Federal Reserve System*
Joseph Whitt, *University of South Carolina*
Glyn Williams, *University of South Carolina*
D. Sykes Wilford, *Chase Manhattan Bank*
John Wilson, *Board of Governors of the Federal Reserve System*
DeLisle Worrell, *Central Bank of Barbados*
Abdelhadi Yousef, *International Monetary Fund*
J. Richard Zecher, *Chase Manhattan Bank*

DISCUSSANTS' COMMENTS

COMMENTS BY JOHN F. WILSON ON DEAN TAYLOR:
"THE MISMANAGED FLOAT:
OFFICIAL INTERVENTION BY THE
INDUSTRIALIZED COUNTRIES"

Dean Taylor's basic thesis is that central banks are almost always losers in their exchange market intervention, except in certain special cases such as France, where apparent gains are explained as deviations related to efforts to stabilize the franc/mark exchange rate. It is a particularly strong thesis, because Dean's statistical results suggest that virtually *all* the major central banks have "lost money" in their intervention activities, irrespective of what the period of measurement is. That is, since these calculations are influenced by starting- and ending-points, they tend to show central banks as peculiarly inept "speculators" in the foreign exchanges. Even "random intervention" would allegedly produce more favorable profit and loss results than the more-or-less systematic leaning-against-the-wind style of the central banks. Since Dean takes Friedman's 1953 article, with its pure profit-loss criterion, as a starting point for rationalizing *any* exchange market activities by the authorities, on this standard they come off looking pretty bad.

Before turning to the main point, I notice that the current version of this work lays a great deal of emphasis on the large losses sustained by U.S. authorities in liquidating the System's and Treasury's pre-1971 commitments in Swiss francs. There is no doubt that this was the case; overall, these realized losses came to something like $1.8 billion and they are a matter of public record. No doubt, also, that the magnitude of these losses was influenced by foreign exchange management decisions taken after the advent of floating rates, but even so there are dangers in laying too much stress on this particular experience. One response, of course, is that if we are focussing mainly on the intervention activities of central banks *following* early 1973, it has to be taken into account that the U.S. short position in Swiss francs fundamentally antedates the floating rate period. As is known, this debt was originally associated with a very basic change in the exchange rate regime—the shift away from the Bretton Woods system—and that alone makes it somewhat noncomparable to subsequent experience. It should not be cited as primary evidence that central banks inevitably make wrong decisions. Additionally, if the short position maintained by the United States going into the era of floating rates is to be considered in this analysis, then why not consider also the long positions (foreign exchange stocks) maintained by other countries at the same time? Taking other countries' stock holdings of dollars in early 1973 into account would vastly change some of the calculations I am about to mention.

Coming back to the main focus, there are several main issues raised by Dean Taylor. The most fundamental, in a floating rate environment, is whether central banks should intervene at all and, if so, what their objectives should be. This question goes not only to Friedman's fundamental article, but also to volumes of literature from the last twenty years. Unfortunately, a proper discussion of this question would use up a lot more than my allotted time, and I suspect it would lead in the same inconclusive directions as the many written treatments. As an empirical matter, under the new U.S. administration it appears that exchange market intervention will be used much more sparingly than it has in the previous eight years, but of course it is still early on, the dollar is strong these days, and it remains to be seen whether this new line will be followed with utter consistency when the devil is at the door. Irrespective of what course the United States follows in the future, it is clear that other central banks will continue to intervene in the exchange markets. Many of them, in fact, are obliged to in certain circumstances, at least as long as there continue to be attempts, such as the European Monetary System, to create "zones of currency stability."

Even if one sidesteps the philosophical problem about intervention and accepts the profits-and-losses criterion, my basic comment on Dean's chapter is that the results are not necessarily so adverse to central bank actions as the conclusions he reaches. Much depends on how "intervention" is measured and the time period chosen to render these judgments. To start, let us take the basic formula used in Chapter 3 to measure profits and losses:

$$\text{Profit} = \sum_{i=1}^{f} \left[n_i - n_i \left(\frac{e_i}{e_f} \right) \right]$$

It measures, in essence, profits and losses in dollar terms by comparing net dollar intervention over some time period against its domestic currency equivalent, period-by-period, with the total then retranslated to dollars at the end of the exercise. So if some country buys dollars over a long period, leaning against the wind while its own exchange rate appreciates, the formula will show a loss via the final-period translation. The same result obtains if the country sells dollars and its own currency continues to depreciate. Whether it comes up with a profit or loss, naturally, depends on a comparison of the current exchange rate with the weighted-average rate on its net purchases or sales in the past. An important thing to note is that the computation produces results that blend realized and unrealized profits and losses, and with the information given in Chapter 3 these two elements cannot be disentangled. Dean's treatment makes it look very much as though all the losses are "realized" and irretrievable, whereas this is not at all the case. I will return to the importance of this distinction shortly.

As I suggested before, how intervention is measured is quite important. Dean has made a truly back-breaking effort to develop such a measure from the reserves data of various central banks, together with estimates of foreign currency borrowing by some—and the way central bank reserves interact with other—entities, such as the Exchange Equalization Account in the United Kingdom or the way "hidden reserves" might be moved back and forth in commercial bank accounts, as in the case of Japan. I might note that I asked some of my country-specialist colleagues at the Board to look over his approximations—which are made with sometimes intractable national data—and for the most part they thought he had performed a conscientious labor. What I will do is present two tables with some of my own estimates perhaps leading to different conclusions. However, I do not want to argue that the figures underlying my own computations are necessarily a more accurate reflection of the situation than Dean's. They are alternatives, based on different definitions, and my main purpose is to show how hard it is to reach unambiguous conclusions.

Table 1 gives alternative profit and loss calculations using Dean's formula, but based on some of my own estimates about the magnitude of foreign exchange dealings by central banks in recent years, using three different "starting points" and a common terminal point of December 1980. Even a quick perusal of these figures will illustrate the sensitivity of the results to changes in sample and according to country. While Dean's figures tend to show almost all central banks as chronic losers, this alternative set does not necessarily support such a view. The most striking difference is in the case of Japan, but as you can see—even on Dean's definitions—some other central banks also look like profit-makers at least some of the time. I have given only rough calculations for a few selected "terminal dates"; what cannot be seen directly is the large amount by which purported profits and losses shift around from period to period, resulting both from ongoing foreign exchange transactions and the large changes in exchange rates we have experienced in the recent past. The mere fact of these wide swings, in my view, is an argument against the proposition that the accumulated dealings of any central bank are inevitably profit making or loss making. Taking the case of Japan, for instance, if we use Dean's formula it would appear that the Japanese had "lost" somewhat more than $1 billion on their transactions from early 1973 through the end of 1975, because on net they had sold dollars over this period and the yen had depreciated. By the end of 1978, however, the Japanese would be showing a "profit" of close to $3 billion on their accumulated intervention. This result runs somewhat counter to intuition for the 1976–78 period because the dollar fell sharply and it was known that the Japanese were making dollar purchases to resist yen appreciation. The answer to the paradox resides in the fact that in this framework the *earlier* dollar sales now appear to generate a profit for the Bank of Japan, which is more than sufficient to outweigh hypothetical losses from their 1977-78 activities. In other words, if profits and losses in Dean's type of computation are the only criterion, then one might conclude that the Japanese had done very well. Their sales of dollars in the early 1970s appear remarkably farsighted, in spite of the short-term book losses they might have shown for a while. Even the dollar purchases of the 1977-78 period look pretty good in hindsight, since the yen has depreciated since that time and the profit-loss picture has improved considerably. From this perspective, rather than serving as a model for what has been

TABLE 1. Approximate "Profits and Losses" for Various Time Periods ($ millions equivalent)*

France

To end		From 2/73	1974	1976
1975		200	200	
1978	0 (A)	−200	−200	−400
1980		600	600	300
3/81	700 (A)			
	900 (B)			

Germany

To end		From 2/73	1974	1976
1975		100	0	
1978	900 (A)	−500	−1400	−1000
1980		−400	−1200	−900
3/81	600 (A)			
	600 (B)			

Canada

To end		From 2/73	1974	1976
1975		0	−0	
1978	−0 (A)	−400	−400	−300
1980		−400	−400	−400
3/81	−0 (A)			
	−400 (B)			

Italy

To end		From 2/73	1974	1976
1975		−600	100	
1978	−2300 (A)	−2700	−300	−300
1980		−2200	800	600
3/81	−3600 (A)			
	−1600 (B)			

Japan

To end		From 2/73	1974	1976
1975		−1300	−0	
1978	6900 (A)	2800	−2700	−3100
1980		5000	800	400
3/81	5100 (A)			
	3000 (B)			

Switzerland

To end		From 2/73	1974	1976
1975		100	0	
1978	−1600 (A)	−2900	−3000	−500
1980		−2000	−2100	−0
3/81	−1000 (A)			
	−800 (B)			

United Kingdom

To end		From 2/73	1974	1976
1975		−300	−0	
1978	−400 (A)	−1800	−1400	−2000
1980		−3900	−3900	−5900
3/81	−200 (A)			
	−2700 (B)			

Note : Case (A) assumes no foreign exchange transactions after 1975. Case (B) assumes no foreign exchange transactions after 1978.

*Estimates rounded to nearest $100 meq.

wrong with central bank behavior, the Japanese experience might illustrate what has been right.

As you know, central banks tend to lean against the wind with their interventions. Since we never know just when the wind might shift directions, this circumstance lends a certain "loss-producing" bias to the kinds of calculations Dean has carried through. If we look at any month's or any quarter's transactions in isolation, as long as the direction of exchange-market pressures does not change quickly it is probable that revaluations of such positions will tend to show "losses" in subsequent periods. To illustrate this, and also to show the way that simple exchange rate swings can alter the apparent profit-loss results of earlier net intervention, I have included some additional data in Table 1. The figures labeled (A) show computed profits or losses under the assumption that each central bank ceased doing all foreign exchange transactions at the end of 1975. Those labeled (B) make the same assumption with respect to the end of 1978. In other words, swings in these results will be pure revaluation effects of some given level of net dollar purchases or sales prior to a certain date, depending entirely on subsequent exchange rate movements with the dollar. Of course the (A) and (B) profits and losses will coincide with the basic data in the table for the two terminal points mentioned.

I hope the perspective given by these two cases will highlight the importance of distinguishing realized "gains and losses" in private and official portfolios from the unrealized or book-revaluation component. What they show is how a central bank can sit tight and do nothing while their purported gains and losses can swing all over the map.

If we adopt this perspective, several central banks come off looking very much like winners on their earlier activities. In addition to France and Japan, even the Germans wind up showing "profits" on their earlier position-taking; again, this runs counter to the conventional wisdom. Using Dean's formula, the Bundesbank might have appeared foolish to be buying dollars in 1977/78, but, as these data suggest, in longer-run terms dollar purchases then might have been a pretty good investment. Even though four of the seven central banks for which I have estimated figures still show net "losses" as of March 1981 on their cumulative activities through end-1978, you might also note that in two of the cases this loss has *diminished* since the end-1978 calculation.

Figures such as these must temper a conclusion that central banks are inevitably wrong in their intervention decisions, even if we accept the pure profit-loss standard. I do not mean to suggest, however, that they are invariably right. Several of my calculations—that for Italy is a good example—produce results that are qualitatively similar to Dean's, even if the actual magnitudes are not the same. Some central banks have indeed sustained dollar-equivalent losses on their activities. Perhaps some of them have also resisted fundamental changes in their exchange rates for too long, but it is clear that not all of them are in this same boat together.

This matter of resisting "fundamental changes" in exchange rates—which seems to be one of Dean's premises—is rather troublesome. Most readers will already be aware that inside central banks we are not much better informed about what a fundamental exchange rate change is than are outside observers. I am unaware of conscious attempts, by the Fed or by other central banks, to resist such fundamental changes. Most central banks tend to pursue their leaning-against-the-wind strategy fairly cautiously, playing it by ear most of the time and intensifying their activity if it appears that market bandwagons are getting carried *away* from fundamentally correct rates. But what a fundamentally right exchange rate is, is subject to a lot of doubt. Of course, some kinds of foreign exchange activity also are very much unrelated to contemporary rate movements (for instance, interest collections on asset stocks or those connected with government or military activities). In addition, when there are side-constraints—such as the obligations of central banks in currency arrangement such as the EMS—all kinds of counterintuitive transaction patterns can result. But to stick to the profit-loss criterion, it should be pointed out there are various ways central banks could make or lose money, not all of which assume they are intervening on the "correct" side of exchange-rate trends or in any particular relation to the fundamentals.

I have tried to illustrate some of the ways this can happen in the data in Table 2. Basically, I have tabulated a set of "counters" for central banks' interventions, covering the 94 months running from March 1973 through December 1980, which summarize whether the *direction* of intervention was potentially profitable or unprofitable. All of these, as we will see, depend very much on ex post information and judgments.

One simple-minded approach is to assume that "correct" exchange rates follow a linear trend over this entire period, so for each rate against the dollar I have computed such a trend (based on monthly data) and counted up the number of instances where estimated dollar purchases and sales were "profitable" with regard

TABLE 2. Direction of Foreign Exchange Transactions in Relation to Certain Profit/Loss Criteria (number of instances, 3/73 to 12/80)

Country		Actual XR vs. trend*	Short-run rate movements			Liquidation opportunities
			1 month	3 months	6 months	
Japan	P	45	27	31	31	45
	U	39	56	51	49	49
Canada	P	47	27	40	36	37
	U	47	66	51	52	57
U.K.	P	49	38	39	35	12
	U	42	52	49	50	81
France	P	52	36	33	36	53
	U	28	43	44	38	31
Germany	P	37	23	28	33	56
	U	47	60	53	45	34
Italy	P	32	39	39	33	6
	U	59	51	49	52	86
Switz.	P	41	37	42	36	25
	U	34	37	30	33	62
U.S.†	P	47	30	38	50	—
	U	41	57	47	32	—

Note: P = profitable; U = unprofitable.
*Trends computed as $XR = a_0 + a_1$ time.
†Based on movements of weighted-average dollar, FRB index.

to trend. By "profitable" I mean if a central bank was purchasing dollars when the dollar's exchange value was below its long-run trend, and vice versa, irrespective of the short-run direction of movement. As is evident, in most of the eight cases, central banks intervened in the desirable manner more frequently than in the wrong. Incidentally, I have not computed transaction amounts in this experiment but have only counted *signs*.

An alternative approach is to look at whether any one month's transactions might be reversed at a profit in some following period, irrespective of the longer-run evaluation. As I noted before, leaning against the wind may lend some bias to loss making for the short run, so I have tallied up cases where horizons extend out to one, three, and six months. In the middle three columns of the table, therefore, I have called "profitable" intervention cases of dollar purchases (sales) where the exchange rate moved in such a way that the position could be sold out (repurchased) at a profit in some subsequent period. For the most part, note that all the way out to six months most interventions by most central banks seem to be unprofitable on this measure, but hardly by an overwhelming margin. There are many instances where rate movements in subsequent periods were favorable to profit making.

Finally, I thought it would be an interesting exercise to take the transactions estimates from Table 1 and count up how often during the 94-month sample each central bank's total cumulated position could have been sold out with a profit or loss. (Let me assume for the sake of argument that the implied extra intervention would have had no effect on the existing exchange rate.) These calculations are shown in the last column of Table 2. Here, too, it appears that during the floating rate period most of these central banks had lots of hypothetical opportunities to flatten their positions at a nice profit. The Germans had relatively more than the others; the Italians, regrettably, seem to have had but few.

I have provided these additional calculations mainly in the intention of highlighting the basic ambiguity in the data and stressing the difficulty of making hard judgments about how central banks have done in the exchange markets. As I stated at the outset, all of this leaves aside the basic question of whether profits *ought* to be the basic objective function of central banks in such activities; there are many—including Governor Wallich in the quotation Dean uses in his paper—who argue that there are other welfare objectives which should also be taken into account. If exchange rate volatility has welfare costs and if intervention can do something to calm markets and reduce volatility, perhaps there are gains in this direction which outweigh apparent monetary losses or enhance the profits. But that is another argument. All that I have attempted to do is cast some doubts on the alluring thesis that whenever central banks act they make big mistakes. Sometimes yes, but my reading of the data suggests that "sometimes no" is also a sustainable conclusion.

That said, I would be remiss in not expressing the hope that Dean will moderate his maintained hypothesis in the future. But if not, I will happily look forward to perhaps giving another rejoinder on some future occasion. Whichever the outcome, I do want to stress that Dean has taken on a tough job in grinding through the data necessary for the kind of study he has given, and I should conclude by complimenting him again on tackling this formidable task.

COMMENTS BY JOSEPH WHITT, JR. ON
L. LIPSCHITZ AND V. SUNDARARAJAN:
"THE OPTIMAL CURRENCY BASKET IN A WORLD OF
GENERALIZED FLOATING WITH PRICE UNCERTAINTY"

Lipschitz and Sundararajan (hereafter, LS) provide a theoretical analysis of the policy problem of choosing an optimal currency basket. During the current period of generalized floating of exchange rates, some countries have chosen to peg their exchange rates to a basket of currencies, such as the SDR, instead of pursuing alternative policies such as pure floating or pegging to the currency of a single major trading partner.

LS use a conventional partial-equilibrium (elasticity approach) model of international trade, extended to include many countries and many commodities. The policy problem is the choice of optimal currency basket weights for a single country within the system.

To derive an optimal currency basket, it is necessary to specify the objectives that the country seeks to achieve through exchange rate policy. For LS, the objective is either to stabilize the terms of trade or to stabilize the trade balance at some acceptable level. LS demonstrate that both objectives can be expressed in terms of stabilizing a weighted average of real exchange rates.

Given either of these objectives, LS suggest that an ideal exchange rate policy would involve continual intervention by the government in order to move nominal exchange rates, thereby keeping a weighted average of real exchange rates at the optimizing level. The real exchange rate between two currencies is a ratio involving foreign nominal prices, domestic nominal prices, and the nominal exchange rate between the currencies. Implicit in the formulation by LS is an assumption that, at least in the short run, nominal prices at home and abroad are either fixed or sticky.

If nominal prices are fixed or sticky, then changes in nominal exchange rates induced by government intervention will be translated into changes in real exchange rates. If in addition the government has full contemporaneous information about domestic and foreign prices,

307

then it can keep the various real exchange rates at their optimized levels by continual intervention in the foreign exchange market, in order to offset known movements in domestic and foreign prices.

According to LS, such an ideal intervention policy is not feasible, because the government receives information about domestic and foreign nominal prices only after a time lag. Because of the time lag, the government must, in effect, forecast the currently prevailing nominal prices at home and abroad, using all available information, and then set the nominal exchange rate in hopes of attaining its target for the real exchange rate. Because the government's forecast of currently prevailing nominal prices is not completely accurate, the actual real exchange rate will generally differ from the government's target.

LS then derive the optimal basket weights, which provide a guide for the government's intervention activity. The weights are chosen to minimize the difference between the actual real exchange rates and the targets, given the limited information available to the government.

Before discussing the basket weights in more detail, I would question the general approach used by LS. Consider an analogy with the debate over the Phillips curve in macroeconomics.[1]

Supporters of a stable, nonvertical Phillips curve have argued that systematic monetary policy, such as expanding the money supply during recessions and reducing it during booms, would enable the government to stabilize real output and unemployment at desired targets.

However, the reevaluation of the Phillips curve by Lucas, Sargent, and others who apply rational expectations has indicated that systematic, predictable monetary policy has little scope for altering real variables, because workers and businesses adjust their behavior in ways that nullify the effects of predictable monetary policy.

In the chapter by LS, government manipulation of nominal exchange rates is capable of altering real exchange rates. However, the monetary approach to the balance of payments and exchange rates[2] indicates that choosing the nominal exchange rate puts considerable restrictions on the monetary policy that can be followed; in a sense, exchange rate policy is almost equivalent to monetary policy. By analogy with the Phillips-curve case, I would suggest that systematic, predictable exchange-rate policy has little scope for altering the real exchange rate, because workers and businesses adjust their behavior in ways that nullify the effects of such a policy.

The policy of pegging the exchange rate to a basket of other currencies is an example of a systematic, predictable exchange-rate policy because once the government has set the weights in the basket, its future policy is determined. According to LS, different choices of the weights in the basket lead to predictable differences in future real exchange rates. However, the analogy with the debate over the Phillips curve suggests that workers and businesses would change their behavior in response to changes in the basket weights, thereby offsetting any effects on future real exchange rates.

To be more specific, LS derive the following expression [their equation (19)] for the optimal basket weights:

$$\hat{\beta} = \hat{w} + \Omega^{-1}\Pi\hat{w} - \Omega^{-1}\Gamma$$

where

$\hat{\beta}$ = column vector of optimal basket weights.

$\hat{w}$ = column vector of basket weights as derived by Branson and Katseli-Papaefstratiou (1980) under the assumption of fixed prices.

Ω = variance-covariance matrix of exchange rates.

Π = covariance matrix of relative prices and exchange rates.

Γ = vector of covariance between exchange rates and home country relative price.

As noted by LS, if prices are fixed, then $\Pi = \Gamma = 0$ and the optimal weights $\hat{\beta}$ reduce to $\hat{w}$, the same weights found by Branson and Katseli-Papaefstratiou. However, LS argue that if prices are not fixed, then the optimal basket weights should take account of the covariances contained in Ω, Π, and Γ.

The additional elements in equation (19) can be interpreted as regression coefficients. The elements of $\Omega^{-1}\Pi$ are the coefficients of a set of least-squares regressions relating relative prices between each partner country and the *numéraire* currency country to the various exchange rates. The elements of $\Omega^{-1}\Gamma$ are the regression coefficients relating the relative price between the home country and the *numéraire* currency country to the various exchange rates.

In the derivation by LS, the covariances contained in Ω, Π, and Γ must be stable for different choices of the basket weights by the government. By analogy with the debate over the Phillips curve, however, I would suggest that the covariances contained in Ω, Π, and Γ would be expected to shift in response to different choices of the basket weights, thereby making the analysis by LS invalid.

NOTES

1. For a recent review of this debate, see Anthony M. Santomero and John J. Seater, "The Inflation-Unemployment Trade-Off: A Critique of the Literature," *Journal of Economic Literature* 16 (June 1978):499–544.

2. For a useful collection of papers on the monetary approach to the balance of payments, see Jacob A. Frenkel and Harry G. Johnson, (ed.), *The Monetary Approach to the Balance of Payments* (Toronto: University of Toronto Press, 1976).

REFERENCES

Branson, W. H., and Katseli-Papaefstratiou, L. T. "Income Instability, Terms of Trade, and the Choice of Exchange Rate Regime." *Journal of Development Economics* 7 (1980):49–69.

Lipschitz, Leslie, and Sundararajan, V. "The Optimal Currency Basket in a World of Generalized Floating with Price Uncertainty." *IMF Staff Papers* 27 (March 1980):80–100.

COMMENTS BY STANLEY BLACK ON
MICHAEL B. CONNOLLY AND ABDELHADI YOUSEF:
"OPTIMUM CURRENCY PEGS FOR ARAB COUNTRIES" AND
ON LESLIE LIPSCHITZ AND V. SUNDARARAJAN:
"THE OPTIMAL CURRENCY BASKET IN A WORLD OF
GENERALIZED FLOATING WITH PRICE UNCERTAINTY"

In commenting on these two papers, I think the first discussant would have said "Vive la difference!" For each paper is supposed to analyze the "optimum" currency peg, each chooses a different objective for exchange rate policy, and each appears to come up with an opposite conclusion! Connolly and Yousef (hereafter, CY) assign the exchange rate to take care of domestic price stability, while leaving the money supply to adjust endogenously to the balance of payments and assuming that output is stable at full employment. Lipschitz and Sundararajan (hereafter, LS) assign the exchange rate to an external objective such as the terms of trade or trade balance, while presumably assigning monetary and fiscal policy to the domestic targets. In CY's treatment, the exchange rate is assigned to a nominal target, while it aims at a real target in the LS analysis. While LS would presumably not argue that the exchange rate can *set* a real variable, frequent evidence of overvaluation proves that it can *influence* real variables. CY conclude that small, open economies should peg to the dollar, while LS, in another place [*IMF Staff Papers*, 27 (1), March 1980] find the pound sterling to have the dominant role, at least in an illustrative calculation.

Starting with the LS chapter, let me commend it for systematically bringing relative price factors into the analysis of the appropriate exchange rate basket. The basic idea is absolutely right, and the elasticity weights could be recalculated for other relevant objectives of exchange rate policy such as stability of the domestic price level.

Given the elasticity weights, the LS equation (19) for the optimal basket is an ingenious derivation which, however, raises a few questions, based on the numerical example given in their 1980 *IMF Staff Papers* article:

311

	w_i	$1 - \alpha_i$	β_i
United States	.50	.30	.15
Japan	.25	0	0
Germany	.20	0	0
United Kingdom	.05	—	.85

The combination of the elasticity weights w_i and the deviation from purchasing power parity $1 - \alpha_i$ yields a somewhat surprisingly heavy weight on the United Kingdom because its high relative inflation rate in the 1970s kept its exchange rate closer to purchasing power parity vis-à-vis Japan and Germany than the United States. This would appear to be a feature of high-inflation countries. But the predicted relative price movement may differ significantly from the actual movement, despite a coefficient near unity, particularly when the inflation rate is high, so there still may remain significant variations in the objective despite the use of the LS basket.

Using the LS notation, predicted relative price movements would be calculated from $r\tilde{p} = \Pi\Omega^{-1}\hat{s}$ with residual errors $\hat{u}$ and $\check{r}p_h = \Gamma'\Omega^{-1}\hat{s}$ with residual errors v. The objective function (10) then turns out to have the observed values $OB = \hat{w}'\hat{u} - v$, with variance $\hat{w}'\Sigma\hat{w} + \sigma^2$ if Σ is the variance-covariance matrix of $\hat{u}$ and σ^2 the variance of v, respectively.

While this variance is certainly minimal within the class of fixed-weight currency baskets, given the numéraire, it should be noted that the choice of numéraire currency will affect the variance-covariance matrix Σ and σ^2. To give an extreme example, the Chilean peso as numéraire might receive a high weight if its value were close to purchasing power parity in a regression analysis. Choice of numéraire is, then, crucial: LS advocate a choice with inflation rate the same as the domestic rate.

This brings me to CY's chapter, which as noted previously takes minimization of the inflation rate and its variability as the objective of exchange rate policy for a "peripheral" country. Their conclusion that a small, open economy should peg to a large trading partner (a "metropole") with a similar, stable, monetary policy is very sensible and is derived from a clear, simple model. It is so clear and simple that perhaps the title of the paper ought to include the words "small and open," to emphasize that the country is assumed to produce no nontraded goods. One wonders a bit about the empirical application.

The conclusion that a trade-weighted basket will shield a peripheral country from the effects of deviations from purchasing power parity among metropoles appears to stem from a particular definition of that concept. Equation (4) defines deviations from PPP among the industrialized countries in terms of consumer price indexes. While this is an acceptable long-run definition, it must be recognized that the goods-market arbitrage which is expected to enforce it operates first and most directly in the markets for traded goods, and only secondarily and indirectly on the prices of nontraded goods. Thus, as in the cited Dornbusch reference, we may define the deviation from traded-goods PPP as

$$\zeta = \pi_{12} + p_1^T - p_2^T = \pi_{12} + p_1 - p_2 + \theta_1 - \theta_2$$

and the deviation from overall PPP as

$$\zeta + \theta_2 - \theta_1 = \pi_{12} + p_1 - p_2$$

Under the CY's assumption that the domestic price levels in the industrialized countries are determined by monetary factors [equation (5)], these deviations from overall (or consumer price) PPP would then enter into the rate of inflation for a basket peg (13) even if trade weights are chosen. When metropolitan inflation rates differ significantly, θ_1 and θ_2 can be nonzero for relatively lengthy periods of time. Thus, I would limit the applicability of their second conclusion on the basket peg to insulation from deviations from traded-goods PPP rather than overall PPP.

Let me also note that the determination of inflation rates in the metropolitan countries is likely to be a good deal more complicated than equation (5), although the quantity theory is undoubtedly a useful short-hand. The evidence is given both in Table 6-1, where one can see the imperfect correlation between inflation rates and the growth of money per unit of real GNP for the industrial countries, and in Tables 6-3 and 6-4, where it is apparent that pegs based on inflation rates and money growth rates differ significantly.

To conclude, I have found both papers to be very useful and stimulating contributions to the further development of this area of research. Each in its own way will prove useful to those seeking to define appropriate policies for countries that must cope with floating rates among their trading partners.

RESPONSE BY LESLIE LIPSCHITZ AND
V. SUNDARARAJAN TO STANLEY BLACK'S COMMENTS

The discussants' comments indicate a detailed thinking through by them that is flattering. We have managed to hold your attention; now let us see whether we can answer your criticism.

First, some general points. Nowhere do we suggest that the exchange rate, a financial variable, can be manipulated to maintain disequilibrium values for real variables. We do, however, acknowledge the possibility of deviations from equilibrium during which the exchange rate can influence real variables. We do not use exchange rate policy to maximize the ratio of export to import prices, but we solve for this ratio from a model of trade and find it to be a function of various underlying factors, such as the degree of monopoly power as well as relative prices. Insofar as the variance of the terms of trade about equilibrium (owing generally to financial shocks) is nonzero, we do employ exchange rate policy to minimize this variance.

It is important to stress that the model used and the particular results should be seen as an expository device aimed at making the general point that price information essential to the determination of exchange rate policy is usually available only after a delay, and that all information on prices, even that of a probabilistic nature, should be built into the determination of the basket weights. We are not wedded to the partial equilibrium trade model used, but, by using the same model as in the Branson and Katseli-Papaefstratiou paper, we are able to contrast the two sets of results. In this context Robert Flood's point that any regressions of the sort we suggested, in order to find the parameters of the optimal basket, would have to be in rate of change form to avoid nonstationarity is well taken. The analysis could easily be done in rates of change, though, for simplicity of exposition, we ignored problems of this sort.

Responding to Stanley Black's comments requires more detail. We agree with the point that the predicted relative price movement may differ from the actual movement so that variations in the objective may persist despite the adoption of the optimal basket. However, as long as the estimated parameters are stable, the variance of the objective variable will be minimal within the class of fixed-weight baskets. We disagree with the note of caution on the choice of numéraire. In the comment there seems to be the implication that there are two dimensions to the variance-minimization problem: the choice of the numéraire and the choice of the basket weights for a given numéraire. We can see no reason why a change in the numéraire should have any substantive effect and believe that Stanley Black's results derive from the fact that he is using a simplified formula (from the numerical example in our 1980 *IMF Staff Papers* article) which assumes a stable rp_h and thereby enables us to treat the vector Γ in the optimal weight formula as a null vector.

This requires further elaboration. The expression $OB = \hat{w}'\hat{u} - v$ derived by Stanley Black is the observed value of the target variable when the optimal basket is substituted into the original expression for OB. Assuming zero covariance between u and v, the variance of OB is given by $\hat{w}'\Sigma\hat{w} + \sigma^2$. A change in the numéraire will alter $\hat{u}$ and v and hence Σ and σ^2. There is no problem with all this.

However, the value of the target variable, OB, is invariant with respect to the choice of the numéraire unless the weights change. The elasticity weights are predetermined and the optimal basket weights should not change in response to a change in the numéraire. Suppose that $\hat{\beta}$ represents optimal basket weights and $s_h = \hat{\beta}'\hat{s}$. Now suppose that currency n is used as the numéraire instead of currency 1; we would get

$$s_h - s_n = \hat{\beta}'\hat{s} - s_n = \hat{\beta}'(\hat{s} - \hat{s}_n) \tag{1}$$

where $\hat{s}_n$ is a vector with s_n repeated n times. Note that $\hat{\beta}'\hat{s}_n = s_n$ because the elements of $\hat{\beta}$ sum to unity. Thus there is only a change in the units in which the value of the basket is computed for determining the home-currency exchange rates, and this cannot lead to a change in the optimal basket.

If the optimal weights do not change as the numéraire is changed, then the value of OB should remain unchanged—that is, although $\hat{u}$ and v change as the numéraire is changed, the sum $\hat{w}'\hat{u} - v$ remains unchanged. Its variance, too, should remain unchanged.

It is easy to see why a change in the numéraire will not affect the optimal basket weights, and hence the value or variance of OB, in a two-currency case.

Using our original notation,

$$OB = w_1 rp_1 + w_2 rp_2 + w_1 s_1 + w_2 s_2 - rp_h - \beta_1 s_1 - \beta_2 s_2 \tag{2}$$

If currency 1 is the numéraire, $rp_1 = 0$ and $s_1 = 0$, so that the expression for OB may be reduced to

$$OB = w_2 rp_2 + w_2 s_2 - rp_h - \beta_2 s_2 \qquad (3)$$

or, reverting to the symbols of the earlier part of our chapter,

$$OB = w_2(p_2 - p_1) + w_2(e_1 - e_2) - (p_h - p_1) - \beta_2(e_1 - e_2) \qquad (4)$$

In this case the optimal weights are

$$\beta_2 = w_2 \left[1 + \frac{\text{cov}(rp_2, s_2)}{\text{var}(s_2)} \right] \qquad \beta_1 = 1 - \beta_2 \qquad (5)$$

where $\text{cov}(rp_h, s_2)$ is assumed to be zero.

If currency 2 is the numéraire, $rp_2 = 0$ and $s_2 = 0$, so that the expression for OB may be reduced to

$$OB = w_1(p_1 - p_2) + w_1(e_2 - e_1) - (p_h - p_2) - \beta_1(e_2 - e_1) \qquad (6)$$

But, remembering that $w_1 = 1 - w_2$ and $\beta_1 = 1 - \beta_2$, this may be written as

$$OB = w_2(p_2 - p_1) + w_2(e_1 - e_2) - (p_h - p_1) - \beta_2(e_1 - e_2) \qquad (7)$$

Equations (4) and (7) are identical, and if we minimize the variance of OB from either expression we get the same set of optimal weights.

The numéraire should be chosen with care not because the choice influences the variance of OB, but because the choice helps to reduce the number of parameters to be estimated. If, with a particular numéraire, we get a stable rp_h, we may ignore the vector $\hat{\Gamma}$ and use the simple formula

$$\hat{\beta} = \hat{w} + \Omega^{-1} \Pi \hat{w} \qquad (8)$$

If we change the numéraire so that rp_h moves around, we can no longer ignore the vector Γ and we have to use the full formula:

$$\hat{\beta} = \hat{w} + \Omega^{-1} \Pi \hat{w} - \Omega^{-1} \Gamma \qquad (9)$$

There will, however, be no change in $\hat{\beta}$. If we continue to ignore Γ when the numéraire is changed we will get silly results, such as a peg to the peso, which might be far from optimal. In other words, Stanley Black's criticism applies to the uncritical use of the simple formula from the numerical example in our *IMF Staff Papers* article.

COMMENTS BY DON ROPER ON BENJAMIN KLEIN AND MICHAEL MELVIN: "COMPETING INTERNATIONAL MONIES AND INTERNATIONAL MONETARY ARRANGEMENTS" AND PASCAL SALIN: "LESSONS FROM THE EUROPEAN MONETARY SYSTEM"

Competitive Monies, Financial Innovations, and a Real Monetary Standard

The inflation for the last decade and a half has generated new academic research on whether the private sector, outside the control of official monetary authorities, might produce higher quality monies. Pascal Salin, for example, believes that there is considerable potential for new competitive monies to curtail inflation, and that the continued control of money by central banks does not appear to be resulting in a public good. Benjamin Klein and Michael Melvin, on the other hand, are skeptical about the potentialities of new "competitive monies" on the grounds that the production of hand-to-hand currency is a natural monopoly and that the commercial bank production of deposit monies is already competitive.

My major purpose is to evaluate these issues in light of recent financial innovations. Thus far, it would appear that the innovations are not making prices more stable; the price instability has been responsible for the innovations. At the end of my discussion, I outline a proposal for achieving price stability. I call the proposal a real standard in contrast to the gold standard in which only one commodity price is stabilized.

It is a pleasure to comment on the courageous chapter written by Klein and Melvin—"courageous" because the authors are willing to make unusually bold statements about the foundations of Western monetary arrangements. They recognize that the previous work that Lance Girton and I have done on currency substitution and monetary competition is "completely opposite the entire spirit" of their study, and they regard us and others (which must include Salin as well as

Hayek) as "utopian" in our views on these matters. Rather than seeing seigniorage as government-protected rent that is reflected in the low quality of money, they view it as "a necessary price paid by the money demander to assure quality." If you think that the U.S. inflation experience has been bad, just imagine, according to their logic, what it might have been if the Fed had not received seigniorage in excess of $10 billion in 1980.[1] Although Klein and Melvin have stimulated me to think further about the social versus private costs of producing paper and deposit monies, my view remains opposite the spirit of their work for reasons which I develop below.

On one issue I tend to agree with Klein and Melvin. They argue that concurrent circulation of multiple hand-to-hand currencies is inefficient because the transactions costs involved in quoting prices (as international airlines currently do) in multiple currencies can be significant. The need for a "uniform currency" was, after all, a powerful argument underlying the passage of the U.S. National Banking Act in 1863. And I suspect that the natural monopoly argument may be even more applicable with regard to check-clearing systems. It is probably more efficient for financial institutions to hook into the same (worldwide) system than to have duplicate wire services. But our agreement ends here.

One reason for our different *Weltanschauungen* is that I view the market as already producing important substitutes for government-controlled monies. A current substitute for hand-to-hand currency is plastic money or bank cards. It is surely the case that the demand for government paper monies has been substantially lowered (from where it would have been otherwise) as a result of bank cards which have emerged in response to high inflation rates, the market manifestation of unusually large seigniorage profits. Card users receive a positive real yield of the inflation rate on their average debit balances and they incur a negative real yield of the inflation rate on their average inventories of currency. This has given currency holders an incentive of twice the rate of inflation to substitute bank card debit balances for paper currency balances. The large differential real yield has failed, however, to totally eliminate the role of paper currency because the two media are *im*perfect substitutes.[2]

To appreciate the potentialities of alternative means of circulation produced outside the domain of central banks, it is instructive to recognize how bank cards avoid the transactions costs associated with multiple pricing. Bank cards allow for the separation of two accounting units. When one uses a money such as paper or coin, the units in which money balances are denominated must be the same as the units in which prices are quoted. With bank cards, the unit in which prices are quoted and the units in which balances are denominated can differ! With American Express or Visa cards, for example, one can make a purchase in, say, francs and be billed in dollars.

The separation between the transactions unit and the units in which balances are denominated is also possible for deposit monies. Holders of Canadian bank demand deposits can write U.S. dollar checks against their Canadian dollar accounts. This separation allows the market to avoid the transactions costs incurred when merchants have to quote multiple prices.

Klein and Melvin argue that substitution between deposit monies should *not* be expected on the basis of differential yields since banks already pay competitive rates of return or, when they are subject to interest ceilings, they pay implicit yields that are usefully assumed to be competitive. But even if the competitive model is a useful approximation to the relation among commercial banks, a large number of depositors have found commercial banks uncompetitive compared with money market funds (MMFs), the deposits of which are checkable.

MMFs may currently be the most important example of a money produced outside the banking system. The money produced by MMFs is based on the separation between the units in which checks are drawn and prices are quoted (for example, dollars) and the units in which an MMF's account liabilities are contracted, viz., shares of a fund's assets. The dollar value of MMF liabilities (the exchange rate between dollars and units of an MMF account) are determined daily by the dollar value of their assets. Hence, the exchange rate between the unit in which an MMF account is contracted and the unit of paper money is floating (though not necessarily unstable). Since different funds hold slightly different baskets of financial instruments, the exchange rate between, say, Fidelity and Dreyfus monies equals the relative values of shares of their respective portfolios. Although the wave of financial innovation may not be over, a large number of monies are already circulating with floating exchange rates in the United States in very non-utopian fashion. This is disguised by the fact that they are all keyed into a dollar-based check-clearing system.

Once we recognize the difference between the units in which deposit[3] monies are contracted and the currency units in which checks are drawn, the profoundly revolutionary possibilities of MMF-type money become obvious. If MMFs held assets that were indexed to commodity prices, their monetary liabilities would thereby be fixed in real purchasing power over those commodities.[4]

With the purchasing power rather than the dollar value of MMF money guaranteed, commercial banks would be at an even greater competitive disadvantage. To repeat an argument emphasized by Lance Girton, MMFs would presumably compete among themselves by choosing financial instruments indexed with different price indices. Households might hold MMF money contracted against the CPI and businesses might hold MMF money contracted against the PPI.

Purchasing power money is possible if indexed debt is available to back the monetary liabilities of financial institutions. For whatever reasons, financial contracts have not generally been written with escalator clauses. The short-term instruments held by MMFs may, however, provide a reasonable approximation to the "real" backing that would be provided with indexed debt. Unfortunately, we do not know whether short-term money market instruments are good hedges to inflation. If we had two kinds of short-term instruments, indexed and nonindexed, then the correlation between the two prices would indicate the degree that MMF liabilities approximate purchasing power money. Without that information, we just judge whether MMM money is a good hedge against inflation on the grounds of how well we think inflation can be predicted over the near future.

The introduction in Europe of any privately produced money, not tied to government money, could follow the example of U.S. money market funds. Apart from legal restrictions, there is no reason why checks could not be written in *any* major European currency against an account in a fund based in Europe. The name "Europa" has already been proposed by Salin and others for a constant purchasing power money. It might be difficult, as Klein and Melvin insist, to completely displace European *paper* government currencies, but an MMF-type Europa would provide an attractive alternative to commercial bank money pegged to government currency.

Salin, both here and in his more lengthy treatment of similar issues, a 1980 monograph entitled *European Monetary Unity: For Whose Benefit?*, has argued that the fixed rate regime of the EMS is not a policy for stopping European inflation. In his opinion, a fixed rate policy can only be justified if it is producing a public good. The problem is to determine what the public good might be which is being provided. The traditional answer given by proponents of fixed rates is that perfectly stable exchange rates should decrease uncertainty and facilitate international commerce. Salin believes that the provision of economic stability meets the crucial non-excludability criterion for an economic good: "it cannot be provided only to those who pay for it." But he argues that exchange rate stabilization does not necessarily promote economic stability. "If the variability of some variables is constrained by public intervention, other variables have to carry a greater part of the burden of adjustment." A particular example of his general point is the argument developed by Milton Friedman that the increase in certainty about the price of foreign exchange may increase uncertainty about the quantity of foreign exchange available at the certain price.[5]

To understand what the policy of fixed exchange rates does provide, it is important to distinguish between the question of what policy ought to be and the question of why policy is what it is. Economists have often noted that the official fixed-rates-facilitate-international-trade argument has been frequently contradicted by governmental introduction of controls when the maintenance of fixed rates has become difficult. Rather than a fixed rate being a means to an end, it would appear that it becomes an end in itself.

This apparent reversal of means and ends can be explained using the view that Salin and that Girton and I have proposed—that the fixed rate policy of the EMS is a vehicle for maintaining a cartel in the production of money.[6] Fixed rates impose similar inflation rates on the member countries. If, in addition, the structure of their domestic banking industries are not too dissimilar (for example, commercial banks offer comparable interest rates on comparable deposits), then the real yields on their monies will be comparable such that the incentives to shift between monies is minimal. Although Salin insists that fixed rates merely impose a common inflation rate rather than lowering the overall inflation rate, it is not clear that the public fully realizes this. Fixed rates are reminiscent of the gold standard and, to the extent that this illusion is operative, it enhances confidence in the monies and augments the demand for such monies. In fact, this is why I think the size of the bands in which rates are allowed to fluctuate tend to approximate the bands that existed under the gold standard—it replicates an outward manifestation of the gold standard and thereby enhances confidence in the currencies. In short, international trade may sometimes be subverted to the "goal" of fixed rates to maintain confidence in and the demand for national monies.

Central banks in the EMS earn rents or noncompetitive profits that are turned over to government treasuries and used to help finance other government services. This revenue source may be exploited during wars and other fiscal emergencies. Rather than fixed rates *being* the public good, they help secure a revenue source *for* public goods such as national defense. For over a decade, Western governments have, I think, unintentionally exploited potential seigniorage profits and this has induced the emergence of bank cards, MMFs, and academic research on alternatives to the production of government-controlled money.

What might the world be like if price inflation continues to force financial innovation and the relaxation of bank regulations? If we take our cue from bank cards and MMFs, it looks as if deposit monies can be created which will provide a reasonable real return but that monopoly paper monies will still circulate and, perhaps, continue to pay negative real returns. This means that the hallowed argument connecting Pareto efficiency and competition is less applicable to paper monies than to deposit monies.

If government paper monies cannot be driven from circulation by privately produced substitutes and if deposit monies continue to be linked to a check clearing system in which units of the paper money are used as numéraire, then it would appear that the financial innovations induced by inflation will not stop the inflation. The basic numéraire of the system could fluctuate in purchasing power even if all deposit monies were contracted in purchasing power units.

The problem with stabilizing the purchasing power of hand-to-hand currency stems from the problems that would be associated with making money convertible into a basket of goods. How can the issuer inventory and warehouse the "basket" of goods and how can money holders take delivery of such a basket? Under the gold standard, money issuers pegged their liabilities to a single commodity, gold. Richard Timberlake has pointed out the widespread use of "transportation currencies" issued by U.S. railroad and canal firms in the nineteenth century. Railroad currency, for example, was redeemable for trips between certain cities. Alfred Marshall proposed to broaden the basket to two commodities in his plan of symmettalism in order to increase the stability of the value of money. But the broader the basket, the more difficult are the inventory and delivery problems. This may be why monies have traditionally been convertible into a single commodity.

To obtain stable purchasing power and avoid the inventory and delivery problems that would exist if (paper) money were convertible into current goods, money could be convertible into *future* goods. If central banks made their liabilities convertible into indexed debt, their money would represent command over goods in the future. The result is what I call a real standard in contrast to a gold standard or any other single commodity standard.

This real standard works through the medium of indexed debt and provides future goods as the backing to government paper monies. The creditor, of course, does not take delivery in goods, but receives an amount of money equal in value to the contractual obligation of the debt.

It is important to notice that pegging the money price of indexed debt does not fix the interest rate. The instantaneous or one-period market yield of debt is

$$i = \frac{C}{Q} + \frac{d(\ln Q)}{dt}$$

where C is the money value of the interest *payment*, Q is the money price of the debt, and d(ln Q)/dt is the capital gain against money. If Q is fixed by the central bank, then the capital gain term is zero. To use this standard formula to consider the yield on indexed debt, divide C and Q by the money price of goods, P, to obtain

$$i = \frac{C}{Q} = \frac{C/P}{Q/P} = \frac{c}{q} = \left(\frac{c}{Q}\right) P$$

where C is indexed to P by the equation C = cP where c is constant, Q is fixed by the convertibility arrangement, and q = Q/P is the deflated value of the debt. The point of this formula is that the market interest rate varies inversely with q, not Q! Pegging Q does not fix i; instead, it forces i to move with the price level since c is fixed by indexation.

To determine the price-level stabilization property of pegging the money price of (presumably government) interest-bearing debt, it is useful to consider the portfolio-balance equation for two assets, (high-powered) money and (government) debt. Let us begin with an LM equation, free of money-illusion:

$$\frac{M}{P} = L(r_m, r_b, \ldots)w$$

where r_m is the real yield on money, r_b is the real yield on bonds, and w is real wealth. If real wealth is composed of money and bonds, then

$$w = \frac{M}{P} + \frac{BQ}{P}$$

where B is the number of government IOUs outstanding, each

324 THE INTERNATIONAL MONETARY SYSTEM

bearing the same real interest obligation, c. Since no explicit interest is paid on money,

$$r_\pi = -\pi$$

where π is the (anticipated) rate of inflation. The real yield on bonds is[8]

$$r_b = \frac{c}{q} + \frac{d(\ln Q)}{dt} - \pi$$

$$= \left(\frac{c}{Q}\right) P - \pi$$

since, by assumption, the money issuer is fixing Q.

If, in keeping with most macroeconomics literature, we assume that the proportion of wealth held in money depends on the *differential* real yield, then

$$L = L(r_b - r_m, \ldots) = L\left[\left(\frac{c}{Q}\right)P, \ldots = f(P)\right] \qquad f'(P) < 0$$

Thus, given the issuance of bonds, B, the public chooses how much B to convert into M at the fixed price Q on the basis of P.

Let me motivate this analysis by suggesting a scenario of price level change following a new issuance of government debt. Begin with the assumption of a static (i.e., no-growth) economy with an equilibrium price level. Now suppose that the government issues new debt, that is, B is increased. Given the initial value of P, the central bank will monetize just that amount of B such that the percentage increases in B and M are equal. This new introduction of outside wealth will put upward pressure on prices. With a higher P, the public will sell some of its M back to the central bank at the fixed price Q in order to hold more B. They will substitute M for B until portfolio balance is reattained. It is apparent that M is completely endogeneous and that the driving force behind the system is the government issuance of new interest-bearing debt.

The price stabilization feature of this plan is predicated on the fundamentally new incentives facing the government. Within traditional institutional arrangements, a government faced with a large deficit is inclined to ask the central bank to support the government securities market in order to lower the treasury's cost of borrowing.

Its cost of borrowing is lowered in two ways. First, the central bank creates more money and thereby imposes an inflation tax on money holders. Second, the inflation lowers the real burden of the government's outstanding debt. With the proposed change in the institutional arrangement, these incentives are replaced with an incentive operating in the opposite direction. Not only will an increase in government debt directly raise the real debt burden by the amount of the debt, but if the deficit leads to higher prices the real cost of new borrowing will go up proportionately. If the government wishes to reduce its borrowing costs, it must issue less debt than the growth in demand generated from real economic growth. To lower its real borrowing costs, it would have to create lower prices by lowering the rate of growth of its outstanding debt. Although I have not offered a complete model of price level determination, an approximately stable price level should follow from a stable ratio of government debt to real national income.

This result is analogous to the usual argument that inflation will result only if the rate of growth of money is greater than the rate of growth of real money demand. The suggested policy changes shift the determination of commodity prices from the demand and supply of government money to government debt-and-money and reverse the usual incentive structure which has been biased toward inflation.

NOTES

1. In my opinion, the seigniorage or the tax on cash balances is usually overemphasized relative to the transfer of resources resulting from the lowering of government's real debt due to inflation. In some preliminary work with Jeffrey Threadgold, we have tentatively estimated that the U.S. federal government acquired an average of over $10 billion (1980 prices) annually from 1967 through 1979 as the result of not having its debt indexed. By contrast, earnings of the Federal Reserve System did not reach $10 billion until 1980.

2. The partial displacement of paper currency by bank cards contradicts the view that floating rates are necessary to suspend Gresham's law—that fixed rates are a necessary condition for good money to displace bad money. This view of competing monies plus its corollary, that the operation of Gresham's law presupposes fixed rates, is true only for commodity monies or paper monies convertible into a common commodity. Since it is impossible to pay explicit interest on nondeposit money (and still have it circulate), a fixed exchange rate between two nondeposit monies implies equal real yields (viz., the common inflation rate). Thus, fixed rates have been, historically, proxies for equal real

yields. Since explicit interest can be paid on deposit monies, fixed rates between deposit monies does not preclude currency substitution induced by a differential real yield. Furthermore, if the exchange rate is fixed by direct intervention in the exchange market rather than through convertibility into a common commodity, then the Gresham's law distinction between "good" and "bad" monies is no longer relevant. We now distinguish between the quality of purely fiduciary monies on the basis of their real yields. Consequently, the higher-yielding money can drive the lower-yielding money from circulation even if their exchange rate is fixed. Cf. Dennis Flynn and Roper, "Gresham's Law and the Modern Theory of the Demand for Money." *Eastern Economic Journal* 8 (April, 1982).

3. MMFs are not considered "depository" institutions because their liabilities are not contracted in government money. But for purposes of contrast between medium of exchange such as paper, coin, and commodity monies, it is useful to classify bank deposits and MMF accounts together as "deposit" monies.

4. Earl Thompson has associated this sort of outcome with competition in monies. See "The Theory of Money and Income Consistent with Orthodox Value Theory," in *Trade, Stability, and Macroeconomics*, ed. George Horwich and Paul Samuelson (New York: Academic Press, 1974), pp. 527-51.

5. "The Case for Flexible Exchange Rates," in *Essays in Positive Economics*, ed. Milton Friedman (Chicago: University of Chicago Press, 1953).

6. "The Theory of Currency Substitution and Monetary Integration," *Economie Appliquée*, 33 (1980):137-60.

7. "The Significance of Unaccounted Monies," *Journal of Economic History* 41 (December, 1981):853-56.

8. The instantaneous yield can be found by differentiating the formula for the present value of a bond. Since the instantaneous real yield is assumed to vary over time, the relevant capitalization formula is

$$q(t) = \int c \exp \left[- \int r(s) \, ds \right] d\tau$$

where the limits of the inside integration are from t to τ and the limits of the outside integration are from t to infinity. This assumes the bond is a perpetuity to simplify the analysis. The argument in the text holds for notes or bonds, but not for bills and it is assumed that interest is paid frequently, say, daily.

ABOUT THE EDITOR AND CONTRIBUTORS

Michael B. Connolly is Professor of Economics at the University of South Carolina. He has held previous teaching positions at the University of Florida and Harvard University, and visiting positions at the Graduate Institute of International Studies, Geneva and the University of Uppsala, Sweden.

His articles have appeared in the *American Economic Review*, the *Journal of Political Economy*, the *Quarterly Journal of Economics*, and the *Journal of International Economics*.

Dr. Connolly has a B.A. degree from the University of California at Berkeley and an M.A. and Ph.D. from the University of Chicago.

Joshua Aizenman is Assistant Professor at the University of Pennsylvania, Philadelphia, Pennsylvania.

Dr. Aizenman has published in the area of International Economics. His articles have appeared in the *Journal of International Economics*.

Dr. Aizenman holds a B.A. and M.A. from the Hebrew University of Jerusalem and a Ph.D. from the University of Chicago.

John F. O. Bilson is an Associate Professor of International Economics at the Graduate School of Business, University of Chicago, and a Research Associate of the National Bureau of Economic Research,

Inc. In 1980, Dr. Bilson was the Robert Eckles Swain National Fellow at the Hoover Institution and a Visiting Associate Professor of International Economics at Stanford University. Dr. Bilson has previously held appointments at the International Monetary Fund and Northwestern University. Dr. Bilson holds B. Econ. and M. Econ. degrees from Monash University, Australia and a Ph.D. from the University of Chicago.

Michael David Bordo is a Professor of Economics at the University of South Carolina, Columbia. Until 1981 he was Associate Professor of Economics at Carleton University, Ottawa.

Dr. Bordo has published widely in the fields of monetary theory, economic history, and the history of economic thought. His articles have appeared in the *Journal of Political Economy*, *Journal of Monetary Economics*, *Journal of Money*, *Credit and Banking*, *Journal of Economic History*, *Explorations in Economic History*, *Economic Inquiry*, and *History of Political Economy*.

Dr. Bordo holds a B.A. from McGill University, an M.Sc. from the London School of Economics, and a Ph.D. from the University of Chicago.

Walter Enders is Associate Professor of Economics at Iowa State University. During the 1980–81 academic year, he was Visiting Professor at McGill University in Montreal.

Dr. Enders has published in the area of International Trade and Finance. His articles have appeared in such journals as the *Journal of Money*, *Credit, and Banking*, *American Economic Review*, *Journal of International Economics*, and *Southern Economic Journal*.

Dr. Enders holds a B.A. and M.A. from the University of Toledo and a M.Phil. and Ph.D. from Columbia University, New York.

Jacob A. Frenkel is Professor of Economics at the University of Chicago and a Research Associate at the National Bureau of Economic Research. He is an Editor of the *Journal of Political Economy* and a member of the Editorial Board of the *Journal of Monetary Economics* and *Economic Letters*.

Dr. Frenkel has published widely in the areas of International Economics and Macroeconomics. His publications include *The Monetary Approach to the Balance of Payments*, 1976 and *The Economics of Exchange Rates*, 1978 (which he edited with Harry G. Johnson).

Dr. Frenkel holds a B.A. from the Hebrew University of Jerusalem, Israel and an M.A. and Ph.D. from the University of Chicago.

Benjamin Klein is Professor of Economics at the University of California, Los Angeles, where he has been since 1968. He has held visiting positions at the National Bureau of Economic Research, the University of Chicago Law School, and the University of Washington.

Dr. Klein has published widely in the areas of monetary theory and industrial organization. His articles have appeared in the *American Economic Review*, the *Journal of Political Economy*, the *Journal of Money, Credit and Banking*, *Economic Inquiry*, and the *Journal of Law and Economics*.

Dr. Klein holds a B.A. from Brooklyn College, City University of New York and an M.A. and Ph.D. from the University of Chicago.

Harvey E. Lapan is Professor of Economics at Iowa State University. Dr. Lapan holds B.S., M.S., and Ph.D. degrees from Massachusetts Institute of Technology. Before moving to Iowa State University in 1972, he taught at Northeastern University. He spent the academic year 1976–77 as a Visiting Research Fellow at the Institute for International Economic Studies in Stockholm.

Dr. Lapan has published in the areas of Economic Theory and International Economics. His articles have appeared in the *American Economic Review*, *Journal of Economic Theory*, *Journal of International Economics*, *Econometrica*, and other leading journals.

Leslie Lipschitz is a senior economist at the International Monetary Fund.

His published work has dealt chiefly with exchange rates and financial policies. Much of it has been oriented to problems of developing countries.

Mr. Lipschitz holds an M.Sc. from the London School of Economics and Political Science.

Michael Melvin is currently an Assistant Professor of Economics at Arizona State University. Prior to receiving his Ph.D. from U.C.L.A. in 1980, Dr. Melvin was a research assistant for the National Bureau of Economic Research.

Dr. Melvin has forthcoming publications in the *American Economic Review* and in an NBER volume, *The International Transmission of Inflation*.

Robert A. Mundell is professor of economics at Columbia University. He has published widely in international monetary economics and is the author of two landmarks in economics: *International Economics* and *Monetary Theory*. He was previously Editor of the *Journal of Political Economy* while a member of the department of economics of the University of Chicago. He was a staff economist of the International Monetary Fund prior to joining the University of Chicago.

Professor Mundell has a B.A. degree from the University of British Columbia and a Ph.D. from the Massachusetts Institute of Technology.

Pascal Salin is Professor of Economics at the Universite de Poitiers and holds a Ph.D. from the Universite de Paris. He is the author of many books and articles in French and English on the problem of international monetary systems and, in particular, on the private issuance of money.

V. Sundararajan is a Senior Economist at the International Monetary Fund. He has published in the fields of econometrics, input-output economics, investment theory, and trade. He received his master's degree from the Indian Statistical Institute and his doctorate from Harvard University.

Dean Taylor is Associate Professor of Economics at State University of New York at Albany. He previously taught at the University of Florida and held visiting appointments at the University of Amsterdam and the University of California at Los Angeles.

Dr. Taylor holds a B.S. from the University of Wisconsin, an M.Sc. from the London School of Economics, and an M.B.A. and Ph.D. from the University of Chicago.

Henry C. Wallich is a Member of the Board of Governors of the Federal Reserve System. He was previously a professor at Yale University from 1951 to 1974 and was a member of the President's Council of Economic Advisers from 1959 to 1960. Dr. Wallich has a doctorate from Harvard University.

DeLisle Worrell is Director of Research at the Central Bank of Barbados. In 1979–80 he was Visiting Fellow at the Woodrow Wilson School, Princeton University.

He has acted as consultant for UNCTAD and UNDP and has been a Visitor with the Federal Reserve Board and the Federal Reserve Bank of St. Louis.

His articles have appeared in *Social and Economic Studies*. He holds the Ph.D. from McGill University.

Abdelhadi Yousef is an assistant to the Executive Director of the International Monetary Fund, Washington, D. C.

Mr. Yousef holds a B.Sc. from Kuwait University, Kuwait and a Ph.D. from the University of South Carolina, Columbia, South Carolina.

DISCUSSANTS

Stanley Black is a Professor of Economics at Vanderbilt University. He was previously Special Assistant to the Undersecretary for Economic Affairs, U.S. Department of State, 1977–78, and an associate professor of economics at Princeton University, 1966–71. Dr. Black has published his work in leading journals in the fields of macroeconomic policy and floating exchange rates. He holds a Ph.D. from Yale University and a B.A. from the University of North Carolina.

Don Roper is a Professor of Economics at the University of Utah. During 1977/78 he was a visiting fellow at the Australian National University, and from 1970 to 1975 he was a senior research economist at the Board of Governors of the Federal Reserve System. Dr. Roper has published his work on the foundations of monetary theory in leading U.S. and foreign journals. He holds a Ph.D. from the University of Chicago and a B.S. from the Texas Technological University.

Joseph Whitt, Jr. is an Assistant Professor of Economics at the University of South Carolina. Dr. Whitt's research is in the area of international economics. He holds a Ph.D. from the University of Chicago and a B.A. from Yale University.

John F. Wilson is a Senior Staff Economist at the Board of Governors of the Federal Reserve System. He was previously a Research Associate at the University of Pennsylvania, 1971–73, and a Staff Economist for the Undersecretary of Economic Affairs, U.S. Department of State, 1977–78. Dr. Wilson holds a Ph.D. from the University of Pennsylvania and a B.A. from Williams College.